Caroline Bauer and the Coburgs

VIZETELLY'S HALF-CROWN SERIES.

CAROLINE BAUER

AND THE COBURGS.

VIZETELLY'S HALF-CROWN SERIES.

PARIS HERSELF AGAIN. By GEORGE AUGUSTUS SALA. Ninth Edition. 558 pages and 350 Engravings.

> "On subjects like those in his present work, Mr. Sala is at his best."—*The Times.*
> "This book is one of the most readable that has appeared for many a day. Few Englishmen know so much of old and modern Paris as Mr. Sala."—*Truth.*

UNDER THE SUN. ESSAYS MAINLY WRITTEN IN HOT COUNTRIES. By GEORGE AUGUSTUS SALA. A New Edition. Illustrated with 12 page Engravings and an etched Portrait of the Author.

> "There are nearly four hundred pages between the covers of this volume, which means that they contain plenty of excellent reading."—*St. James's Gazette.*

DUTCH PICTURES and PICTURES DONE WITH A QUILL. By GEORGE AUGUSTUS SALA. A New Edition. Illustrated with 8 page Engravings.

> "Mr. Sala's best work has in it something of Montaigne, a great deal of Charles Lamb —made deeper and broader—and not a little of Lamb's model, the accomplished and quaint Sir Thomas Brown. These 'Dutch Pictures' and 'Pictures Done with a Quill,' display to perfection the quick eye, good taste, and ready hand of the born essayist— they are never tiresome."—*Daily Telegraph.*

HIGH LIFE IN FRANCE UNDER THE REPUBLIC. SOCIAL AND SATIRICAL SKETCHES IN PARIS AND THE PROVINCES. By E. C. GRENVILLE-MURRAY. Third Edition, with a Frontispiece.

> "A very clever and entertaining series of social and satirical sketches, almost French in their point and vivacity."—*Contemporary Review.*
> "A most amusing book, and no less instructive if read with allowances and understanding."—*World.*

PEOPLE I HAVE MET. By E. C. GRENVILLE-MURRAY. A New Edition. With 8 page Engravings from Designs by F. BARNARD.

> "Mr. Grenville-Murray's pages sparkle with cleverness and with a shrewd wit, caustic or cynical at times, but by no means excluding a due appreciation of the softer virtues of women and the sterner excellencies of men."—*Spectator.*
> "All of Mr. Grenville-Murray's portraits are clever and life-like, and some of them are not unworthy of a model who was more before the author's eyes than Addison— namely, Thackeray."—*Truth.*

A BOOK OF COURT SCANDAL.

CAROLINE BAUER AND THE COBURGS. From the German, with two carefully engraved Portraits.

> "Caroline Bauer's name became in a mysterious and almost tragic manner connected with those of two men highly esteemed and well remembered in England—Prince Leopold of Coburg, and his nephew, Prince Albert's trusty friend and adviser, Baron Stockmar."—*The Times.*

THE STORY OF THE DIAMOND NECKLACE, TOLD IN DETAIL FOR THE FIRST TIME. A New Edition. By HENRY VIZETELLY. Illustrated with an authentic representation of the Diamond Necklace, and a Portrait of the Countess De la Motte engraved on steel.

> "Had the most daring of our sensational novelists put forth the present plain unvarnished statement of facts as a work of fiction, it would have been denounced as so violating all probabilities as to be a positive insult to the common sense of the reader. Yet strange, startling, incomprehensible as is the narrative which the author has here evolved, every word of it is true."—*Notes and Queries.*

GUZMAN OF ALFARAQUE. A Spanish Novel, translated by E. LOWDELL. Illustrated with highly finished steel Engravings from Designs by STAHL.

> "The wit, vivacity and variety of this masterpiece cannot be over-estimated."— *Morning Post.*

CAROLINE BAUER
AND THE COBURGS.

CAROLINE BAUER (from a Crayon Drawing).

VIZETELLY & CO., 42, *CATHERINE STREET, STRAND.*

TRANSLATOR'S PREFACE.

THIS version of Caroline Bauer's Memoirs contains all the matter in the three volumes of the original work having relation to important personages in England, and likely to prove interesting to the English reader of the present day.

How far in its substance or details Caroline Bauer's narrative may coincide with, or deviate from, exact fact, or how far the merit of its style may be due to its German editor, it is not proposed to discuss here at any length. If the whole were a mere "literary hoax"— a stigma with which it was sought high-handedly, and surely not very advisedly, to quash its English existence, it were the most unintelligible and motiveless of hoaxes. The book is not written in a flippant spirit, but with the writer's whole mind and heart, occasionally, if not even normally, in a too vehement tone, and very possibly not always with strict judicial impartiality for the two sides of the main case it treats. The writer is naturally well-disposed to represent herself in as favourable a light as possible; but no one questions her superior ability, and unless seriously restrained by a sense of truth she would never have presented such a lame and altogether damnatory defence of herself as she does. There are numberless passages in the book which, as she well knows and painfully, sometimes involuntarily, confesses, tell badly against herself, and which, if truth had ceased to exercise an imperative, however unwelcome, sway over her, she could by an easy touch have turned more, or entirely, in her own favour.

Her essentially deprecatory apology for herself, especially when viewed in connection with her loud sense of injury, is, indeed, most trustworthy testimony to the substantial truth of her statement. She appears quite stunned or capable only of passionate complaint to God and man at the supreme disappointment in her life, but, according to her own evidence, she had logically and properly no other result to expect. The reader is at a loss whether to give way to exasperation or to smile compassionately at her interested want of logic. Whether in anger or pity he must needs tell Caroline Bauer that her misfortune was not that she was deceived by Prince Leopold or Baron Stockmar—by no means; her sole and whole misfortune was the disposition of mind, on her part, which rendered such deception possible. Leopold and Stockmar were but one among ten thousand similar accidents flying about, all ready to take advantage of such proclivity to deception. Nor, on the other hand, is it the object of the narrative to slander any person. The writer is abundantly impetuous and vehement, but withal of fair complexion, of rich, sweet blood, full of life and activity, singularly free of bile or gall, and really incapable of lasting resentment against any mortal. There is truly no morbid trait in all her book, unless it be some slight bitterness against herself, a trace of virulence on the whole pardonable—especially if it had a more decided savour of piety in it.

As one good clue to the personal character and disastrous history of Caroline Bauer, the reader is recommended more particularly to the subtle criticism which appears under the name of the first Count Bismarck (pp. 52-54), the substantial truth of which is confirmed by all the rest of the book, whole and sundry.

Caroline Bauer, as she came from the hands of nature, is an uncommonly fair, happy and attractive creature, though fate and fortune contrived sadly to disfigure the original workmanship. Yet to the very end, all through this book of hers, the reader will still recognise rich endowments of nature, nay, even good dispositions and hereditary moralities, such as may exist without the immediate support of personal character (of character *transcending* nature and fate).

As to how far, again, the literary style is ascribable to Caroline Bauer's German editor, it need only be said here that if the Caroline Bauer portrayed in these Memoirs, for the most part apparently without design, and ever so far most effectively, is the creation of her German editor, then, or so far as such is the case, must every quality, style included, of that Caroline Bauer be the paramount property of the German editor who created her; but as this is a claim he does not even distantly advance, the autographic style natural and constitutional to the Caroline Bauer of the Memoirs must be deemed essentially the rightful possession of the Caroline Bauer of history. All style, so far as it has any significance, is constitutional, and an editor has altogether perverse conceptions of fact who would " change the style " of a person if he do not at the same time commensurately change that person's identity, a transformation rather beyond the ordinarily understood limits of an editor.

The book is crowded with literary portraits more or less fully drawn, none, however, mere cut and dry characterisations, but all of them characters conceived interiorly; all in growth, in perpetually changing identity, true each through all variety of circumstance and development to his underlying individuality; and whoever would claim

that this is all or mostly fiction on the part of Caroline
Bauer must credit her with extraordinary art.

On the whole, the reader may safely accept the motto
preceding this English edition, so excellent as a piece of
literary texture, as a fair indication of the spirit and purpose
of the whole work.

The book has withal a very serious side.   It affords a
true glimpse into the theatrical world, and the world of
fashion and wealth mainly patronising it and determining
its character. Is the play-house really the arena of the
alone genuine, wholesome, and legitimate play of men who,
by the handsome discharge of worthy tasks, have honourably earned the exhilaration of mind that can look on mimic
scenes, even of pain and terror, with elevated delight; of
men who, by reason of the completeness of their nature
and the maturity of their character, can wholesomely enact
so many various parts? A player is properly a man who
is master of so many forms and experiences of life, who is
no longer, like the uninformed multitude, liable to be
victimised on those various arenas, but to whom all the
wrestle and temptation of those arenas, which is the snare
and discomfiture of the majority, is wholly comprehended
and grown to be mere "play;" whose proper function,
therefore, is to elevate the crude commonality to his altitude
by mirthfully delineating to them from his lofty standpoint
all those various forms of life which he enacts and disposes
of like a radiant god. Such is the primary, and such still
substantially, the only legitimate meaning of player; and
how far actual "players" are such, or how far they are the
outrage or negation of such, may be profitably studied in
these Memoirs.

CONTENTS.

NOTE BY THE AUTHOR.

MY career as *artiste* I have already published in my two
works, "From My Life on the Stage" and "Theatrical
Tours." In the work now before me I intend presenting
a picture of my life as woman—a life very largely taken
up with matters of the heart. It has, however, been my
misfortune never to find the right person as object of
my love, the one, only person whose love I could have
returned with my whole pure soul. Such a person it was
never my fortune to meet; and so, alas! this heart and life,
created by heaven to be happy and make others happy,
have been the scene only of the wild play of passion, or of
cold calculation, and so have gradually come to ruin!
This history, however, I elect to relate in the sad hope
that my life, with its flowers and thorns, its errors and
disenchantments, may serve as a warning to young hearts
not yet lost. And should these confessions of a lost life
serve to save but one human heart, one human life, from
perdition through personal weakness and foreign intoxica-
tions, this public offering will not be made in vain.

CAROLINE BAUER.

"Begreifen Sie nun, theurer Freund, wie das Nieder-
schreiben der Memoiren mir hier auf dem Qualberge zum
muthigen Weiterleben und Weiterkämpfen hilft? Es
erleichtert mein Gewissen, dies redliche Prüfen der Ver-
gangenheit und dies Gerechtsein-Wollen allem Erlebten
gegenüber. Mir ist es, als könne ich ruhiger sterben, wenn
ich Denken, Fühlen, Handeln von mir und der Mutter klar
vor der Welt dargelegt habe.

"KAROLINE BAUER."

"Do you understand, then, dear friend, how the penning of
these memoirs on the mountain of torment here encourages
me to continued life and struggle? It lightens my conscience thus honestly to overhaul the past and endeavour
to render just account of all I have experienced. It seems
to me as if I could die more peacefully when I have laid
before the world a clear record of all that with mother I
have thought, felt and acted.

"CAROLINE BAUER."

CAROLINE BAUER

AND THE COBURGS.

———◆———

CHAPTER I.

BIRTH, PARENTAGE, AND CHILDHOOD.

I WAS born, as testified by my certificate of baptism in the vestry book of the Protestant Church of the Holy Ghost at Heidelberg, " in the year of our Lord 1807, on the 29th March, at Heidelberg, and on the 10th April baptised Caroline Philippine Auguste Bauer; daughter of Herr Heinrich Bauer, lieutenant and adjutant in the Grand-ducal Baden regiment of light dragoons, and Christiane Stockmar, of Coburg, his spouse. Sponsors: Herr Amtmann Karl Wagner, and Caroline, his spouse; Herr Oberamtmann August Becker, of Brunswick, and Herr Major Bauer, of Cassel; and by proxy in their absence, Charlotte Stockmar, *née* Ramdor, of Coburg."

The absent sponsors above-mentioned are my uncles and aunts; Charlotte Stockmar is my maternal grand-mother.

At my cradle stood my sister Lottchen, five years old, my brother Karl, aged four years, and a second brother, Louis, two years old. Those were mournful days. My father, absent both at my birth and baptism, fell, after his promotion to a captaincy of horse, at Aspern, and died the 28th May, 1809.

I thus early became an orphan, though in the happy innocence of childhood all witless of my misfortune. There was left me, however, the best of mothers, who had but one joy in life—her children. I loved this good and beautiful mother, who now, at the death of my father counted only twenty-seven years.

I grew up in the tumult of those warlike times like a wild boy among my wild brothers. From my father, in whose veins pulsed the fiery blood of the Poniatowskis, causing my mother many an anxious tear, in spite of their cordial mutual love, I inherited—to my misfortune!—a hot, passionate heart, easily and powerfully moved. I might have been about four or five years of age when I once was about to fling myself out of the window, for being thwarted in my will, but was snatched by my mother, when already half-way over the window-sill, and well beaten for my wickedness. I cried, kissed my distressed mother, and in a few minutes was romping about with my brothers on the streets.

This light, impulsive heart—lightly excited, lightly consoled—came to be the bane of my life, so soon as the whirlwinds were let loose to play their wild game with me. A character to stand fast to its own centre in the midst of the storm was what was wanting to me.

My first taste of deep sorrow came when I was seven years old. My angelic sister, Lottchen, and my good grandmother, both died in March, 1814. The same year, in autumn, my mother removed to Carlsruhe, for the sake of giving her children a better education there. My free-and-easy-going brother, Karl, who both outwardly and inwardly was most like my father, entered the grand-ducal school for gentlemen's sons, to qualify himself for a commission in the army. My brother Louis, again, wanted to be a merchant, while I was to be made a governess. I received the best education, and took a distinguished place in the school, more particularly at the pianoforte.

If only there had been no theatre! But from the first time I saw the performances in the Grand-Ducal Court Theatre, there was no thought in me by day, no dream by night, but only—the theatre! The sum of earthly bliss for me was all on those enchanting boards! No presentiment had I then of the danger lurking on those boards for the poor, foolish heart—the danger of a whole ruined human life!

My brother Louis having been placed in an institute at
Neuchatel, in order to prepare himself for a mercantile
career, I followed him thither in 1820, that I might there
perfect myself in French; and in the spring of 1821 my
mother also took up her abode there, to be near her children. She lived in the house of the good minister's widow
at St. Blaise. In a letter from there addressed to her
cousin, Louise Becker, married to a merchant, Leopold of
Hamburg, after referring to her other children, she says:—

" Lina, too, is big and stout, and in blooming health.
Her nose, which in childhood procured her the name of
' big nose,' has happily abated its too prominent development, so that her mother herself is now entitled to call
Linchen quite a pretty, comely girl. She has studied this
year to very good purpose; speaks French fluently and
with a pleasing accent; is the first in music among
the boarders; and has, in other respects, made marked
progress. And, with it all, she is still ever the same gay,
happy soul; the same natural, good Lina of the purest
childlike sense as formerly, with nothing of constraint or
affectation in or about her. The music you gave me for
her has given her no end of pleasure. She at once played
the pieces at sight. The splendid polonaise and the Hamburg Waltz are her favourites. Here at this glorious lake
I am received with great affection, and see the best of company almost every evening. In fine weather we go into the
fairest gardens and enjoy the most charming view of the
lake and the Alps; after that comes singing and playing on
the guitar. When the weather is unfavourable we play
whist indoors, diversified by dancing to the accompaniment
of the pianoforte. Louis and Lina I have the pleasure of
seeing twice a week.
" On my speaking with Lina about her future as
governess, a tear started into her eyes at the thought of
having to renounce her idolised stage, but she soon re-
pressed those signs of grief, and, embracing and kissing
me tenderly, promised to double her diligence during the
last months, so as to approve herself useful in the world.
She is ambitious to achieve a great deal, in order to give

pleasure and be one day helpful to me and her brothers. It is a heartfelt joy to me to see such earnest goodwill, such courage and strength of renunciation in a girl of only fourteen. For what a hard struggle it is to her to give up the stage I perceive by many little signs. For example, she entreated me, bashfully, to get the opinion of Constance von Cofran and others, as to whether in the last comedy, *La Rosière*, by Madame de Genlis, she had not fairly sustained the part of the silver-haired curé. And, remarkably enough, all agree that the old French priest was quite a wonderful performance for so young a girl."

With all earnestness and zeal I thus piloted my way towards the post of governess. On returning in the autumn with my mother to Carlsruhe, I resumed my lessons on the pianoforte with music-director Marx, and no later than the following winter played Mozart's Concerto in D minor, with orchestral accompaniment, in the Carlsruhe Museum Society, and with so much success that my mother was urged on every side to have me trained for a *virtuoso* on the pianoforte. But where to find the means? My poor mother was then deeply bowed down under new cares. Her elder step-sister in Eisenach had instituted a suit against her for payment of 12,000 thalers of the paternal fortune which we had inherited from my grandmother. Supposing my mother lost the suit we would then be reduced to beggary, for the step-sister might perhaps lay a distraint on her widow's pension. In such a case I could think of no resource but to throw myself in close embrace with mother into the Rhine.

Luckily, on the 7th May, 1822, we learned that the decision had gone in our favour. While the law-suit was pending I again pressed my mother to let me become an actress. My uncle and godfather, General Bauer, in Cassel, would not, however, give his consent, and wrote—
" A Bauer on the stage! Sooner a dairymaid! Her talent in recitation will be available to her in any other calling, especially as a governess or music-teacher."

In a letter of the 2nd June, 1822, my mother wrote to her cousin in Hamburg :—

" Yesterday I received a letter from my brother John, chief-magistrate of Rodach, near Coburg. His eldest son, Christian, raised to the rank of baron by the King of Saxony, has been married to his cousin, Fanny Sommer, since last August. She is an only daughter, and at the death of her parents will come into a fortune of from 80,000 to 100,000 thalers. A short time ago he set out with Prince Leopold, who loves him as a brother, on a tour through Italy, and is now expected in Coburg on a visit. My brother has invited me and my children to come there and to Rodach. So after some years' absence I shall again see my dear beautiful home. It is of special interest to me to talk with my nephew, Christian, on the future of Louis and Lina. In his influential position he may, if so disposed, be of great use to them."

Accordingly in September, 1822, we drove to our relations in Coburg. This journey was to decide my whole life. In Coburg were spun the first light golden threads which in the changes of years imperceptibly wove themselves into a fateful net—fateful for the poor innocent bird rejoicing in its Spring.

CHAPTER II.

COBURG.

DOWN to the end of last century there lived in the agreeable little town of Coburg the well-to-do manufacturer and merchant, Ernst Friedrich Stockmar. Having often had money transactions for the Court committed to his care, he received the title of Landkammerrath. The Court was in a state of perennial financial embarrassments, although Duke Franz Josias, on the death without heirs in 1758 of Prince Henry of Schwarzburg-Sondershausen, had come in for a rich inheritance of shining gold and silver. This brilliant fortune, however, turned out a curse rather than a blessing to the Court of Coburg. They gave themselves up to too extravagant living, accustomed themselves to all manner of luxury—and at last, one evil day, found that the whole inheritance had been squandered away. To continue this life of racket, the duke, duchess, prince, and princesses, wantonly contracted debt on debt, as the Landkammerrath could tell to his own cost. Under Franz Josias' successor, Duke Ernst Friedrich and the Duchess Sophia Antoinette, the burden of debt had risen to such a height that the emperor appointed a commission in Coburg to take in hand the administration of the duchy and the liquidation of the obligations, when it was found that the total revenue of the small State amounted to 86,000 thalers a year, and the duke's debts to over a million! The whole family were now reduced to a yearly maintenance of 12,000 thalers. Referring to the ducal household in 1780, Johannes Von Müller writes: "Ernst Friedrich lived so frugally that he had no more than three courses, seldom saw much company at table, and dressed plainly." The 12,000 thalers, however, did not suffice even for this humble style, and the family took anew to borrowing on pledge and word of honour. The good loyal

Landkammerrath would see with dismay the approach of the Court-messenger to his substantial house in the market-place of Coburg, or his charming residence in the suburbs, called the "Glockenberg," carrying something wrapped-up in his hand or under his arm; an infallible sign that the ducal family were again wanting to borrow of him "on-pledge."

The faithful subject would never, however, accept a pledge, as being too disrespectful to the august personages, but always lent again and again without so much as the duke's note of hand. In return, he never received a penny of interest nor any of the hard-won money back again. His perpetual fear of ducal demands had the effect of making a hypochondriac of the old Landkammer-rath in the last years of his life. He shut himself up in the Glockenberg, inaccessible to almost all the world, only not to the ducal messengers with their silver dishes and golden ornaments.

By his first marriage, Ernst Friedrich Stockmar had a son, Johann Ernst Gotthelf, born 1760, and two daughters. Having been early left a widower the Landkammerrath paid his addresses to the fair lady-in-waiting on the Princess Caroline of Coburg, Charlotte Ramdor, daughter of the celebrated surgeon in Brunswick, who had once been called by the Empress Catherine II. to perform an operation in St. Petersburg, and received from the empress a set of brilliants as a present to his wife. This ornament passed into the hands of my mother, but in the sad French times went the way of all silver and gold and precious stones.

The Princess Caroline of Coburg, born 1755, was the daughter of Duke Ernst Friedrich, and through her Bruns-wick mother had become the rich and highly-honoured abbess of the Ladies' Convent of Gandersheim, entitling her to a seat and vote in the Rhenish Bench of Prelates, a considerable Court, with its own hereditary offices, besides a large jurisdiction to which even the Kings of Prussia and the Electors of Hanover had to resort in respect of the Dornburg domain and Elbingerode.

The lovely Charlotte Ramdor, highly cultivated, of

cheerful temper, witty and amiable, was the favourite of the princess-abbess and her circle. In company with the princess she came to the Court of Coburg. Whether from gratitude towards their unselfish deliverer from pecuniary embarrassments, or from some other cause, the Princess Caroline and the Coburg Court lent their countenance to the suit of the Landkammerrath, who, though now forty, and considerably older than the lady he courted, was yet a stately man held in universal esteem. In fine, he led home the charming but dowerless Court lady, who proved a faithful wife to him, and a good step-mother. The son was a comfort to her, but the two daughters turned out a real affliction to her. The elder of them inherited her father's gloomy disposition, and died in a lunatic asylum. The younger, hateful outwardly and inwardly, became the "bad aunt" of Eisenach, who by her unjust testamentary lawsuit cost my mother and her children so many tears.

Not till after seventeen years of wedlock had the wife of the Landkammerrath, Charlotte Stockmar, the pleasure of pressing a child of her own to her tender bosom—her sweet, gladsome little Christina, that,- like a sunbeam, would lighten up the clouded soul of her misanthropic father.

The old Landkammerrath Stockmar died in 1793, when his little Christina was only ten years old. In his picture he imposed on me, his grandchild, by his air of handsome dignity and his penetrating eyes. He had been a fellow-student with Gellert in Leipzig, and his most trusty intimate friend. On his death it was found that the debts owing to him by the ducal family had accumulated to 17,000 thalers, of which he had never received any interest, nor have my grandmother or her children ever seen a penny of this sum. The duke and court, to be sure, remained ever graciously affected towards them.

Christina Stockmar became the playmate of the young princes, Ernst, Ferdinand, and Leopold, and of the princesses, Sophia, Antoinette, Juliana, and Victoria, the sons and daughters of the Hereditary-Prince Franz, who would often come to musical performances on the Glockenberg.

and play hounds and hares with merry little Christina. On one of these occasions the Princess Antoinette tore her Sunday dress on a gooseberry bush, and was inconsolable in her dread of her severe mother, a bigoted princess of Reuss-Ebersdorf. None of the princesses had more than a single Sunday dress each. Christina Stockmar, however, quickly fetched needle and thread, and so cleverly mended the rent that Antoinette's mother never came to know anything of the great misfortune. Christina was fondest of the Princess Victoria, for her amiability and her many talents. After many years' separation, these early playmates were again to meet each other in England. Princess Victoria had become Duchess of Kent, and mother of the little Princess Victoria, now Queen of England, and Christina Stockmar, widow of Captain Bauer, and mother of Countess Caroline Montgomery, whom Prince Leopold of Coburg called his spouse —in the utmost secrecy, to be sure, so that England and the Parliament should hear nothing of it.

Of all the princes, Christina Stockmar liked the eldest, Prince Ernst, the best. He was light-hearted and, true enough, often light-minded as well, but always of a frank and happy temper; whilst the youngest brother, Prince Leopold, was of a cold, reserved, and calculating disposition, appearing almost always in a brown study.

In September, 1795, the hereditary-princess set out with her three beautiful eldest daughters for St. Petersburg, on a bridal show. The Empress Catherine, who had before summoned three princesses from Wurtemberg to Berlin, and three princesses from Darmstadt, as also two from Baden, to St. Petersburg, that her son Paul and her grandson Alexander might choose themselves consorts from among them, had now ordered up these princesses of Coburg, to make a selection out of them for her still almost boyish and always knavish grandson, Constantine. In spite of all the warnings of the sad fates which had overtaken so many German princesses in Russia, the poverty-stricken princesses of Coburg were unable to resist the golden winks of the all-powerful Czarina. And what humiliations were in store for them at St. Petersburg!

Catherine and the whole Court made sport of their modest toilet and shy demeanour. The empress sent her tailors and milliners to render the German princesses presentable at Court. And how did Constantine treat these poor beggars? Pretty much in the same style as he did the recruits given him for playthings; of whom, in putting them through their exercises, he would occasionally bash in an eye or whisk off an ear. He would have none of the princesses drawn up for his selection and inspection. They were too maidenly coy for his taste.

The empress had, therefore, to come to his help, and proceeded in an original manner. She stood at the window and looked down on the princesses as they alighted from the carriage. The first got entangled in the unwonted Court train, and fell on the ground. The second, taking warning from that catastrophe, sprawled out on all fours. The third and youngest, the pretty little Juliana, hardly fourteen, took her train up in both hands and gracefully sprang to the ground. "That's the one! She will do for our wild Constantine," said Catherine.

"Very well, then, if so it must be, I'll wed the little ape. It dances very prettily," chimed in Constantine, carelessly.

On the last day of December the hereditary-princess arrived in Coburg again with her two rejected daughters "amid great illuminations and rejoicings," as an old print has it. The marriage of the Princess Juliana in St. Petersburg, who on her changing to the Greek confession took the name of Anna Feodorovna, was celebrated with great gala at the Court of Coburg, on the 24th February, 1796. And yet it was the unhappiest day in the life of the poor victim. The brutal Constantine treated his consort like a slave. So far did he forget all good manners and decency, that in the presence of his rough officers he made demands on her, as his property, which will hardly bear being hinted at. Such a life the unhappy lady could not long endure, and returned to Coburg soon after the death of the Empress Catherine. From 1802 she lived separated from her husband. Not till 1820, when Constantine contracted a morganatic marriage with the Polish Countess

Grudzinska, after she had been raised to the rank of Princess Lowicz, was his formal divorce from Juliana effected by the Czar Alexander.

The marriage of the Princess Antoinette was to turn out fateful for her playmate, Christina Stockmar. On the evening of the 5th May, 1798, Major-General Prince Alexander of Würtemberg, arrived in Coburg as suitor, and in his suite his equerry, Heinrich Bauer, an uncommonly handsome madcap of eighteen.

The Bauer family came from Poland where they bore the name of Poniatowski, a modest branch of the princely house. In the middle of last century a Poniatowski emigrated from that country on account of his Protestant faith, and purchased himself a small estate in the neighbourhood of Cassel. Husbanding his own land he now called himself simply by the name of Bauer, and the Landgrave Friedrich VIII. gave the family a new coat-of-arms—a husbandman cracking a whip. His son became "intendant" under the Landgrave Friedrich IX., and father of three sons. The eldest entered the army and rose to be general—the same who would sooner see Lina Bauer tending cattle than on the stage. A son of his came to be general in turn, and after the French war commandant of Strassburg. As such he visited his Cousin Lina in the Bröelberg near Zürich.

The old Hessian intendant's second son, Georg, became Minister of War, but turned eccentric, and in a fit of misanthropy burned all the Polish family papers.

The third and youngest son was the wild Heinrich. In him, more than in any of the others, surged and foamed the restless Polish blood. He was handsome and exuberant of strength and spirit like Mars; proud and bold like a young lion; wanton like a wild foal; generous like a Poniatowski; easy-minded like a cornet — a spoiled favourite of gods and women!

The nasty old Landgrave Wilhelm IX. "Mushroom Jack," as he was called from the huge growth on his neck, could not, however, bear this pretty whirlwind that not seldom ventured to rebel against the despotic whims of his master. All in vain did the old intendant conjure his

son to be pliant with the landgrave, and all in vain did
the landgrave, himself, clap the defiant "Poniatowski"
(as he would ironically name the young madcap) under
confinement once and again—that only whetted our Heinrich so much the more. To avoid worse, the father sent
his unmanageable Heinrich in his sixteenth year to Brunswick to be trained as an equerry by the then famous
equestrian master, Heinersdorf. As such, he entered in his
eighteenth year the service of Duke Alexander of Wurtemberg, and soon afterwards came in his suite to Coburg.
For him, too, this visit was to turn out a suitorship. At a
ball he saw the fifteen year old Christina, and fell head
over ears in love with the bright, lovely child. The very
same evening during a graceful minuet the young equerry
made his fiery declaration of love, and took her heart by
storm. Next morning he stood before the widow of the
Landkammerrath and begged the hand of her daughter.
It cost little Christina many a battle and many tears to
gain her mother's consent. The marriage of such "children" was, of course, a matter for the future, "they
must wait some years."

In autumn the equerry again arrived in Coburg
from Vienna, bringing with him for Princess Antoinette
the marriage jewels from Prince Alexander. The latter
soon followed. The betrothal was celebrated by a *diner
en famille* on the 15th, the marriage was performed in all
quietness on the 17th, and on the 18th the event was
further signalised by a dinner in the "Riesensaal"
(giant hall), by the firing of cannon, and by a grand reception and play in the evening, followed by a supper in
the same giant hall.

The old journal we have before referred to, which
endeavours to report this event in terms equal to the
occasion, says nothing, however, of the deadly horror
pictured in the face of the angelic, beautiful young bride
scated beside her consort. Prince Alexander was shock-
ingly ugly. A huge tumour disfigured his forehead, and
there was something bestial in the expression of his face.
The poor creature suffered, besides, from—gluttony!
When the young spouse awoke in the morning after the

wedding she saw with horror how her husband, with brutish voracity, was gnawing a huge ham bone—a sight the unhappy one could never forget.

Prince Alexander suffered from another and no less hateful disease—from the meanest avarice. His equerry, Heinrich Bauer, had once saved his life by drawing him, at the risk of his own life, out of a bog, into which he had sunk up to the neck on the occasion of a hunt; but in this exploit the equerry lost his gold watch with its beautiful seals. In his first sensation of gratitude, the prince promised to repair the loss, but always forgot, though in his forward way the equerry did not forget to remind him often enough of it. When the prince would ask: "Bauer, what o'clock is it?" he would quietly put his hand to his watch pocket, and then say, as if suddenly recollecting himself, "Ah! I forgot your Highness; my watch is still sticking in the bog, and not yet——"

"Never mind, Bauer, I shall think of it, and look you out another watch."

It never went further, however. The prince paid his debt of gratitude neither to his equerry nor his equerry's family.

Nearly thirty years after that sad marriage in Coburg I was to meet Prince Alexander. In 1828 I was performing a short engagement in St. Petersburg as Royal Prussian actress. Prince Alexander had removed to St. Petersburg as brother of the Empress-mother Maria, and had been appointed Imperial Russian General-in-Chief, and Director-General of Land and Water Communications in the Russian Empire. Death had long before freed the poor Princess Antoinette from this monster. His Highness wanted to see the widow and daughter of his former equerry, Heinrich Bauer. A strange shudder crept through me when, with my mother, I entered the dismal, sepulchrally-silent palace of Prince Alexander.

What an unsympathetic personage stood over against us! A thick, bloated body, on thin legs, in silk stockings and buckled shoes; the broad, ugly, inexpressive face strongly flushed; the huge glistering tumour on the bald, flat forehead; the eyes glassy and bloodshot. Turning in his trembling hands a golden snuff-box, his Highness could hardly put the usual conventional questions to us. Only one word to my mother did not sound hollow:

" I was the unconscious cause of your marriage with Heinrich Bauer, when I fetched him with me to Coburg, and afterwards sent him thither with the marriage jewels. Bauer was a handsome, chivalrous wooer for the hand of the charming Christina Stockmar."

I could not omit reminding his Highness of the trifling adventure he had had in the bog with his equerry, and of the watch that had been lost on that occasion.

His Highness had no recollection whatever of the affair. He did not so much as engage a box for himself on my benefit night.

Indignant, I said to my mother: "How well it was of my father to leave this curmudgeon and take service with the noble Archduke Ludwig in Vienna."

On the 2nd February, 1799, Prince Alexander with his spouse and his equerry left Coburg to return to his post in the Imperial-royal army, leaving Christina Stockmar also to mourn the absence of her dear Heinrich Bauer, to whom she had been secretly betrothed. She did not, however, renounce all the pleasures of her young maiden days. She was a diligent and much-loved member of the Coburg Amateur Company, and in two old play-bills of that time, I read that Mademoiselle Stockmar took the part of *Julie von Wangen*, the lover, in the comedy of "Schachmaschine," adapted from the English.

In August, 1800, Prince Alexander, of Wurtemberg, took service in Russia, moving first to Riga, of which he had been appointed commandant. Seeing the Land-kammerräthin Stockmar would never have consented to her dear and only daughter going to the far arctic Russia, Heinrich Bauer remained provisionally in Vienna as equerry to the Archduke Ludwig.

On the 8th September, the reigning Duke Ernst Friedrich died, and was succeeded on the throne by Franz Friedrich Anton. The sons of the latter were the Hereditary-Prince Ernst and the Princes Ferdinand and Leopold.

A journal of the brave Imperial-Royal Field-Marshal Prince Friedrich Josias of Coburg, which passed into the possession of Prince Leopold, and was printed as MS. at his expense, describes the ceremony of the old duke's funeral, and how towards evening the body was placed in parade, and the whole court, all the counsellors, all strangers, officers, the town council, the clergy, the professors and students, as also the oldest citizens, had to appear at court in prescribed mourning; how the body was borne by master-tradesmen through the castle-chapel, with hearse which was drawn by six horses, &c., &c.

In January, 1801, Heinrich Bauer was again in Coburg pressing his mother-in-law about the marriage. There was no want of feasts at the time.

"On the 19th January, being the birth-day of the reigning duchess, all the young members of the family together with some ladies and cavaliers of the court, dressed as peasants, assembled at the house of the Chief-Marshal von Wangenheim, whence they marched with music to the quarters of the duchess, and announced themselves as the village community of Ketschendorf come to tender their congratulations; a diversion which falling out as a surprise passed off very happily. At noon, there was great gala, and a grand dinner to forty-one persons. In the evening there was a drawing-room at the Princess of Wurtemberg's."

The bridal pair took a lively part in the comedies. On an old playbill, kept as a relic by my mother, may be read:—

"By permission of his Highness, on Wednesday, 28th January, 1801, there was played by some theatrical amateurs—'Dus Schreibpult, oder die Gefahren der Jugend' (The Writing-Desk; or, The Dangers of Youth). A play in 4 acts, by Kotzebue. *Dramatis personæ:*—Diethelm, a young merchant, by Herr Privy Counsellor von Wangenheim; Hermann, his first clerk, by Herr Wirth, court advocate; Flink, his servant, by Herr Bauer, equerry;" &c., &c., &c. All, all, all long ago dust and ashes!

"Admission—First parterre, 48 kr. (1s. 4d.); pit, 30 kr.;

gallery, 15 kr. To be given in the Ducal Court Theatre, and to commence at 5 o'clock."

Soon after, the happy equerry led his charming young wife to Vienna—and now, after an interval of 21 years, his widow with her children returned to her native place.

Many changes had meanwhile come over the place. Princess Juliana, Grand-Duchess Anna-Feodorowna, had left her tyrannical husband, Constantine, and returned to Coburg. Princess Victoria had married the Hereditary-Prince of Leiningen, Emich Karl, and, as his widow in 1818, Edward, Duke of Kent, who, however, died in 1820, leaving behind him a tender little daughter, Victoria— "white and round, like a stuffed dove." Princess Sophia had married the Austrian cavalry captain, Count Emanuel Mensdorf.

Duke Franz had died soon after the battle of Jena, while the Hereditary-Prince Ernst stayed with the fugitive court in Konigsberg, sick of nervous fever. The French occupied Coburg, and administered the affairs of the country. Not till the 28th July, 1807, did the reigning Duke Ernst, now 23 years old, make his entry into Coburg, amid the ringing of bells, the firing of cannon, and bugling of postilions.

"The Prince of Leiningen and Prince Leopold, on horseback, rode in front of the ducal carriage, after which came the dowager-duchess with the Princess of Leiningen. The procession went to the meadow, where the duke alighted and was received by a group of girls, some sixty in number, all dressed in white, their heads decked with oak-leaves and corn-flowers in such a way as to form a V.V.E., i.e., 'Vivat Ernst.' Two of the foremost presented, on a cushion of white silk, a garland of flowers and a poem; two smaller girls, from their horns of plenty, strewed bouquets at his feet. Here the duke resolved to continue his entry on foot, while the girls followed in order."

In the new court of the young duke, who greatly fancied life and love, feast now succeeded feast, each ever more fantastic than the one preceding it, and this, too, in spite of the severe sufferings of war. One journal, for example, records a *fête* of the 29th August, 1809, in honour of the birthday of the Duchess of Wurtemberg. "In a Chinese house a company played music and presented a poem. Then appeared a village all illuminated, and a grand procession with music playing. Thirdly, a grotto, and a nymph singing an aria and presenting a poem. Fourthly, a hermitage, where the hermit sang a song to the accompaniment of a harp, and presented a poem. Finally, an obelisk, with an illuminated dancing-place under the open heavens and lovely moonshine. And so the merriment continued without pause into the morning."

CHAPTER III.

THE DUKE OF COBURG AND THE FAIR GREEK.

In October, 1807, the reigning Duke Ernst went with his youngest brother, Prince Leopold, then seventeen years of age, at Paris, to pay their homage at the feet of the all-powerful Emperor Napoleon. Here, in Paris, Duke Ernst started a love affair which was soon to attain a world-wide notoriety—though not, indeed, to the honour of the house of Coburg.

At a ball in Paris the handsome and fiery Duke Ernst saw a charming young maiden of fourteen, Pauline Adélaïde Alexandre Panam, who was descended from a Greek family settled in Montpellier, and was soon universaly known by the name of " the fair Greek." The enamoured duke proceeded to a vigorous courtship of the fair Greek, offering her his protection, his influence, and his fortune. She might consider him as a brother. Another day he proposed to her to become lady-companion to his sister, the Grand-Duchess Constantine. In fine, the fair Greek very soon succumbed to the seductive arts of the duke.

In April, 1808, the duke returned to Coburg. Mademoiselle Pauline followed her lover, who had promised that his mother would receive her into her court circle. By the duke's command she travelled in male attire.

Hardly, however, had she arrived in Coburg when the poor creature began to experience how she had been duped. To his grief the duke had to tell her that his mother would not consent to admit her into her circle because she was—French! He would, however, take care of her with all affection.

The poor French girl, still in her male dress, suffered the most dreadful *ennui* in the still town of Coburg, and all the more that her protector kept her secluded from the world, like a prisoner—an experience very much like what

I was myself to endure twenty years later in England, at the hands of the prudent brother of the circumspect duke.

At the command of her ducal lord, Pauline had soon again to quit Coburg and retire to a still more secluded dwelling in the neighbouring manor of Esslau. Here the duke introduced his mistress to his sisters, the Countess Mensdorf, and the Grand-Duchess Constantine. Prince Leopold, eighteen years old, also paid an amorous visit to his brother's mistress, by forcing his way into her bedroom at seven in the morning, while the fair lady still lay in bed.

In her "Mémoires d'une jeune Grecque," Pauline describes Prince Leopold in these words : "He was a tall young man, with a false look and a disagreeable, sentimental smile. After having in the worst possible French apologised for the way in which he had introduced himself to me, he began lamenting my fate and blaming his brother."

The duke heard of this visit, and in his jealous fury made such a scene with his fair mistress that it was a fortnight before she recovered from the effects of it.

When the lady gave her protector the hope of his soon becoming a father, he grew more tender and attentive. He even allowed her to take part in country court festivities under all sorts of disguises; now as peasant, now as lady; and was always contriving some opportunity of showing her his fondness. After one such festival at Rosenau, for example, he made her climb up a ladder to the window of her lord, under a pouring rain accompanied by thunder and lightning, and, the ladder being too short, his Highness let down a chair, on which Pauline, wet as a drowned kitten, managed to clamber up.

The unhappy Greek had to await her time of confinement in the remote Amorbach, the summer residence of Prince Leiningen, under the eyes of this brother-in-law and the duke's sister Victoria. The duchess-mother of Coburg, from the pious race of Reuss-Ebersdorff, wrote to the mistress of her eldest son the following characteristic letter in French :—

"Adieu, my poor Pauline! Cherish the pious feelings you show in your letter, and the good God who directs

our hearts will have pity on yours, which is so beautiful.
IIo will pardon you your past errors if, as a believer, you
return to tho path of virtue; it is not so difficult as one
thinks. You will soon be a mother! May this holy name,
although you owe it to an error, fill your soul! It will
save you for the future! As soon as your sister comes,
withdraw as far as possible from these parts for your
lying-in.   (Signed),
        "THE DOWAGER-DUCHESS OF SAXE-COBURG."

Pauline found herself very miserable in Amorbach,
where no one troubled himself about her, or took any care
of her. She addressed herself to Prince Leiningen, and
received tho following reply, which was little consoling:

"I know the people with whom you have to do. I
cannot enough advise you to mistrust them. For have
I not myself been the dupe of their promises? And did
they not amuse me with fair speeches before I entered
their family? And when I did enter, they did not keep
a single one of their engagements."

Pauline now found her way back to Coburg. The duke
there clapped her under lock and key! The fair one, however, was not to be taken aback, but boldly pushed into the
apartments of the dowager-duchess. A violent scene
arose between the two ladies, till the duke again made all
possible promises. The very same evening he renewed
these promises: "My mother will take on her the care of
your future, and bring up your and my child."

Next day the duchess-mother, what by wheedling and
what by threatening, induced the unfortunate Greek to
take oath that she would never become the recognised
mistress of the duke, but would rather endeavour to keep
him apart from her. Having sworn this, "My dear
Pauline, my daughter," was allowed to embrace the pious
duchess, and even to lend her a very nice *robe en cœur*, her
Highness wishing to have a dress made for herself in the
Paris fashion.

In September, 1808, Duke Ernst went to St. Petersburg for six months without taking any thought for his
victim. Pauline being thus left destitute of all means, her

sister, who had hastened to her side from Paris, applied to the dowager-duchess, who was taking the waters at Carlsbad. She received the brief, concise reply:

"I demand the most absolute secrecy regarding the relations between Pauline and my son. I am indulgent, but vengeance is in my power.

(Signed) "AUGUSTA."

Later on, the dowager-duchess sent the unfortunate woman five louis d'or, with the advice to assume the title of a married woman, and to give out that her husband had been ordered abroad!

Prince Leopold added 100 florins, but complained strongly of Pauline's want of economy; very characteristic bearing on the part of my honest, economic Prince Leopold.

On the 4th March Pauline, in need of money, linen, fuel, and even food, was delivered of a ducal son in Frankfort-on-the-Maine. The duke now sends her from Memel 1000 francs, with instructions to represent herself as the widow of a superior French officer who had been killed in Poland. She was at liberty to assume any name she pleased. The duke afterwards ordered her to call herself the widow of a Hanoverian officer.

In February, 1809, the duke returned from Russia. Pauline sends him the first tiny locks of the little Ernst August. In July the duke visits mother and son in Frankfort, and again makes the most golden promises, without, of course, keeping them.

Pauline, or, as she is now officially called, "Madame A. H. Alexandre," impelled by the courage of hunger and despair, again descends on the Court of Coburg like a bursting bomb-shell. The duke and his worthy mother are beside themselves with alarm and rage. The pious dowager-duchess, at last wheedling the poor creature, advises her: "Young and pretty as you are, you have a rich future and a great deal of pleasure in store for you. Let me have the child and—amuse yourself in Paris!"

Pauline refusing to yield, the duke and his mother send their servants to the hostelry where Madame Alexandre is staying, and have her things thrown from the window

into the street, while the landlord is commanded to give
no more food to the obstinate Frenchwoman. When,
however, the servants attempt to snatch the child from the
mother, she springs like an enraged lioness on them.
"Monsters! you venture to put hands on the son of your
duke? You must first kill me."

Abashed, the servants slink away. Pauline keeps in
Coburg. Negotiations go on back and forward for a month.
Then, by command of the duke, Major Czymbowsky lays
before the duke's cast-off mistress the following contract:—

"A yearly pension of 3000 francs will be paid Madame
A. H. Alexandre.

"Madame A. H. Alexandre will, with all speed, quit
the country of his Highness, the Duke of Saxe-Coburg,
and never return thither. Otherwise articles 1 to 5 of this
contract to be null and void.

"Executed in two copies at Coburg the 25th April, 1810.

"By command (Signed), VON CZYMBOWSKY."

Pauline repairs to Dresden with her son—of course
without receiving her 3000 francs of pension. Only
through the good endeavours of the French ambassador,
Serra, does she succeed in now and again drawing some
trifling sums from Duke Ernst. When, however, in May,
1812, his Highness went to Dresden with Prince Ferdinand
to be present at the meeting of the Emperors Alexander
and Napoleon, the enamoured duke pays his fair one a
tender visit in the Hôtel de Cologne, where Pauline lodges
with the little Ernst August, supported by the Austrian
ambassador, Esterhazy, and several French generals, as
also by the compassion of her landlord. The duke vowed
he would raise the pension to 6000 francs, but told his
victim soon after she would henceforward get only 1000
francs, though he would, *par grace et par bonté*, see that
the child he had never recognised as his son was educated.

Scared back by the tumults of war, she returns to
Frankfort. There, in December, 1813, she again en-
counters Duke Ernst, who takes command of the 5th Corps
of the German Confederation against his once idolised
Emperor Napoleon. On this occasion he gives his little

Ernst August a beating, and heaps the grossest insults on the mother, till Grand-Duke Constantine comes to the protection of the abandoned mistress and the whipped son of his brother-in-law, of whom he mockingly said: "He rules over six peasants and two village surgeons."

With hypocritical repentance and affection Duke Ernst again returns to mother and son, opens his purse and sends his treasures to Vienna under the escort of a court runner. On the way—so Pauline asserts—several attempts were made to put an end to these inconvenient witnesses of ducal lust: once by the upsetting of the carriage over a precipice, and then repeatedly by poison.

In Vienna, Pauline finds a protector—and, as was said, a lover also—in the grey-haired Prince Ligne. Prince Ligne, during the Vienna Congress, leads Duke Ernst back into the arms of "Madame Alexandre," and compels him to open his purse. All the world takes an interest in the fair Greek, of whom Prince Ligne, the great connoisseur of beauty, asserts that she is not only "one of the most beautiful women in the world," but, in respect of virtue, like an angel—"ange aussi,"—having only once in her life been led astray by a duke. Prince Metternich offers to bring up little Ernst August as his son—not, however, according to the Greek, from any kindness of heart, but only in the interests of the duke to render her harmless. He even wanted to get the encumbrance out of the way by help of the Vienna police, but her powerful friends, Prince Ligne, Prince Eugène Beauharnais, Prince Narishkin, &c., gave her money, which the father of her son again withdrew from her. An Italian, Pioni, six times attempted poisoning her. By whose commission?

By advice of Prince Ligne, the young Greek writes her "Mémoires," and after the prince's death seeks refuge with her son in France, there to publish them. To prevent this latter step, the duke makes new golden promises which are not kept.

In those days the Russian General, Von Nostitz, once adjutant to Prince Louis Ferdinand, who fell at Saalfeld, writes in his journal of the Vienna Congress:—"The Duke of Coburg is tall and stout, yet not to the particular

credit of tall men, who are often not unjustly reproached
with littleness of mind. On the whole, the Coburgs are a
well-disposed, honest family, yet mostly defective in
intellect, especially Prince Ferdinand, now Austrian
General, who has a handsome, regular face, with a thinly
contracted nose, in which intellect alone is wanting."

When already thirty-three years of age, Duke Ernst
in 1817 married the charming Princess Louise of Gotha,
heiress of the Duchy of Gotha, after the hand of the
Russian Grand-Duchess Anna-Paulowvna, which had been
promised him, was refused, in consequence of the scandal
with the "young Greek."

The old, original "Patriarch of Rodach," Superintendent
Hohnbaum, the paternal friend of the young poet Rückert,
writing in 1817 to his son in England about the lovely
princess, says:—

"Our duke has led home as his wife the Princess of
Gotha. The celebrations in Coburg and Rodach were something terrible. My old head had to produce a triumphal arch
and two poems. In Rodach the high party dined, and I
had the pleasure of sitting beside the young princess who
also remembered you. She is an extremely natural and
amiable creature. In Coburg, however, they will keep
her in the polishing mill and under the roller till she turns
out smooth and even like the rest."

What a deep and accurate glance on the part of the
old superintendent of Rodach! The sad end of this
unhappy princess testifies all too truly to the fact.

After a few months the old superintendent of Rodach
writes to his son:

"You do her wrong in remarking that the young princess's remembrance of you was likely nothing but an idle
court phrase. She told me a great deal of the intercourse
of her father with you. Altogether, it is my belief that no
idle words can ever have desecrated her lips nor any court
vice have corrupted her heart. In my eyes she is an
extraordinarily rare creature."

Poor young princess, whom a cruel fate made successor
to the fair Greek, and to so many, many others!

CHAPTER IV.

BARON VON STOCKMAR.

SUCH was the state in which my mother found her native place on revisiting it after so many years' absence, and such its state when I now drove into Coburg for the first time, little dreaming how in this town my destiny was to be determined for my whole life—now, and still more fatally seven years later.

My mother's family received us with the utmost affection. Uncle "Justizamtmann" (chief magistrate) had come with his mercurial, frolicsome, youngest daughter from Rodach to greet us. A grand, jovial, amiable uncle! His grandson, Ernst, Baron von Stockmar, at one time treasurer to Queen Victoria, and then in a similar confidential situation under the Prussian crown-princess, till a disease of the spine forced him to sad retirement, speaking in his memoirs of his father, says, concerning the Justizamtmann: "He was a lively, cheerful, humorous, kindly benevolent man, accomplished, fond of books, a scientific jurist. He owned the manor of Obersiemau on the Bavarian frontier. Once on returning from that property—so at least his children tell the story—the following conversation struck up between him and an acquaintance he met: 'Where have you been?' Stockmar—'On my estate.' 'What were you doing there?' 'I was going about nursing feelings about the property.' 'And what kind of feelings were they?' 'Vexation.'"

My eldest cousin, too, Caroline, and her husband, President Opitz, pleased me very much by their cordiality. I was, however, of course, most interested in my cousin Christian, who by his cleverness had already raised himself to be baron and confidential friend of a prince.

Cousin Christian was then—in the summer of 1822—thirty-five years old, no beauty, but of a fine, slim, superior appearance, showing somewhat Anglified manners; with eyes expressive of lively sagacity and which looked at me very penetratingly as though they would probe into my most secret thoughts. His genially pleasing and winning smile was not seldom dashed by a bitter flavour, giving decided token of ascendancy, of satire or irony. The mixture in his bearing, too, of German and English, of the citizen and the courtier grated on me. It carried the impress of his whole distinguished career.

His eldest son, Ernst, relates the following characteristic anecdote of Christian's boyhood—"Many traits have come down of the boy's merry, humorous, unswerving spirit and sanguine nature. With some astonishment the mother once heard him exclaim while he was sitting at the family table and pointing to the dishes, 'Some day I must have all this silver!'—to which the mother quietly replied, 'If you can manage so much, I've no objections.'"

In the years 1805 to 1810 Christian Stockmar studied medicine in Wurzburg, Erlangen, and Jena, and in Wurzburg struck up an intimate friendship with young Friedrich Rückert, whose father held office in the Bavarian Exchequer. Rückert describes his friend of this period as an earnest, diligent young man, of rather reserved and superior demeanour. It was a friendship which renewed itself in the evening of the life of the two men, when Stockmar lived in Coburg and Rückert close by in Neusess, and lasted to Stockmar's death.

From 1810 Stockmar acted as assistant-physician to his maternal uncle, Sommer, in Coburg. Of these days, Christian Stockmar writes:—

" In the year 1812 I became town and country physician, and as such set up a military hospital in Coburg during that great year of war. It soon became filled with French and allied, and then with Russian sick and wounded. The hospital typhus, which everywhere dogged the armies, settled on this hospital as well. Several deaths among those in immediate contact with the hospital inspired such dread in the physicians that only an old surgeon and I had the courage to perform the duties there. These on my

side I continued to render up to November, 1813, when,
after having resisted the infection over a year, I was
seized by the fever in its most dangerous form. For
three weeks I lay between death and life, but soon after
recovered so rapidly that in January, 1814, I was able, as
head physician, to accompany the ducal Saxon contingent
to the Rhine. Arrived in Mainz, I was commanded as
staff-physician of the 5th Army Corps to the hospitals
being erected under Stein's government in Mainz, Oppen-
heim, Guntersblum, and Worms. Here I stayed as one of
the directing physicians till the autumn of 1814, when I
returned to Coburg."

During these campaigns Stockmar had come into closer
relations with the young Prince Leopold, and when in
1816 the latter became the consort of Charlotte, the Princess of Wales, he called Stockmar to England as his
private physician. On the 29th March, 1816, Stockmar
landed at Dover. When Princess Charlotte died in child-
bed on the 6th November, 1817, his physician, Stockmar,
had already so much gained the confidence of the prince
that the latter, by the corpse of his spouse, weeping and
embracing him, made him promise that he would always
keep by him as his friend. Cousin Christian then ceased
to be physician, and henceforward lived with Prince
Leopold in England and on his travels in the capacity of
secretary, treasurer, court-marshal, and confidant. At the
present moment he had just returned from a tour through
Italy with the prince, who went to Vienna in the beginning
of September to meet the Emperor Alexander, while
Stockmar remained behind with his young wife in
Coburg.

Frau Fanny von Stockmar! She was always a pro-
blematic figure to me, especially as Cousin Christian's wife.
She was the only daughter of Christian Stockmar's uncle,
on the mother's side, the rich apothecary Sommer. She
was not at all pretty, and had been brought up in the style
of the lower burgess class. She was of a crabbed temper,
which grew ever bitterer and sourer with her years, till
it culminated in a mixture of gall and vinegar. It was

a loveless wedlock. Christian married the 100,000 thalers for the sake of being able to hold a perfectly independent footing in relation to Prince Leopold. He felt that his power rested on this independence. With the help of this independence Baron Christian von Stockmar was able, throughout a long and important career at the Courts of London and Brussels, to maintain his political and personal power down to the time of his death. He did not covet money for itself, but as a means to his object—his ambitious objects. Ambition and love of power were the main features in his character, the motives of his actions. He therefore married the money of his unamiable cousin, Fanny Sommer, and took her with it as an inevitable part of the bargain. But as a shrewd diplomatist he knew how to arrange matters so that his wife should not be particularly troublesome to him. He married her only on the condition that he was to live free and unencumbered in England, while she was to have the charge of the children in Coburg. Now and again he would visit his family in Coburg in summer, and bring with him, for his wife, not love but fair diamonds, presents from princely persons, whose favour the shrewd diplomatist had gained. But several years might pass, during which Stockmar saw neither wife nor children. As far as my knowledge goes, he never took his wife with him, either to England or Brussels. She sat in silent Coburg, consuming her heart with jealousy, and scraping, scraping, ever scraping the money together. With advancing years she ossified more and more into personified avarice, and by this avarice revenged herself, latterly, in a dreadful manner on her poor old dying husband for neglecting her in her youth.

Cousin Christian was then—1822—the most amiable, the most charming of cousins. He purchased from my mother her last paternal inheritance—the beautiful Glockenberg, near Coburg. He procured our Louis a situation in the mercantile house of his brother Karl Stockmar, in Augsburg, and me he made the happiest—actress! He soon gained my whole childlike confidence, and so I disburdened to my cordial cousin the weight of my surcharged, passionately theatrical heart, complaining to him how

I was to become an old, sharp-nosed, spectacled governess just because my uncle, General Bauer in Cassel, wouldn't have his name on the playbill, nor see a Bauer with the noble Poniatowski blood in her veins on the ignoble boards. I had to declaim my favourite Hebel and Schiller poems, as also his favourite ones from Rückert. He listened with his smile which grew ever more friendly, and then, in his original, humorous style, said:

"Aunt Christina! what is destined to be good vinegar sours early. Hitherto our family has not been blessed with artistic talents; it will give me pleasure to be able to call an artist cousin, and a cousin artist; but this I beg for myself, Lina, that you become a real, noble, able actress, and that at each appearance on the boards you put on new shoes and gloves. That you owe to your art and the honour of the family."

So then it was settled, in spite of my uncle the general in Cassel, that I might become an actress. In exultation I flung myself on the neck of my good, sagacious, grand cousin. In that hour there was hardly a happier creature in the world than young Lina. How beautiful yet was life! How good all men! With what golden splendour did the sun smile, with what joy did the birds sing, with what bliss did the flowers spend their bloom and perfume! The whole day I could have danced and sung: Rejoice in life! With Cousin Christian we paid a visit to the princely house. The reigning Duke Ernst received us in his charming creation, the Rosenau, with great friendliness, although he was ailing. He had shortly before, while out hunting, been gored by a wounded stag, and still carried his arm in a sling, and his head bandaged. He was a handsome, stately man. The fiery glances with which he reconnoitred me I was to understand later on.

I frisked about, in wild play, through the handsome shaded park with two brisk boys: the brown Hereditary-Prince Ernst, four years old—the now reigning duke—and the altogether lovely, blond-locked Prince Albert, whose whole figure savoured of the angelic. He was to become the consort of Queen Victoria, and father of the Prussian crown-princess.

I caught a hasty glance of the mother too of the young princes, the unhappy Duchess Louise—an exquisite, charming lady, with blond locks and blue eyes. Bitter strifes were already vexing her married life and clouding the sunny prime of her children.

The scandal with the "fair Greek" was still going on; although she had had many successors in Coburg. Madame Alexandre Panam threatened to publish her "Mémoires." To avenge herself for so many infidelities, and beguile the sense of solitude in her heart, the Duchess Louise had now, too, taken to spinning and weaving tender filaments of love outside. The sparrows on the roofs of Coburg chirped to each other of the amours of the duke and duchess.

We were received by the pious dowager-duchess coldly and loftily. I fairly shivered with cold before this strict and proudly-moral dame. On a wall of her reception-salon hung the portrait of a handsome, slim young man, with large, melancholy eyes and an earnest expression about his mouth.

He was the favourite son of this frosty princess— Prince Leopold, who was still mourning the death of his spouse, Princess Charlotte.

What a hearfelt sympathy I had with the sad, handsome prince! And was he not, too, the loving master and friend of my good, humorous cousin Christian!

And after seven years?

The most merciful gift of the good God is to hide the future from us.

CHAPTER V.

I BECOME AN ACTRESS.

WITH what joy did I return, about the end of September, 1822, from Coburg to Carlsruhe! I had got the better of all the scruples of my mother and the whole family! I was permitted to become an actress! Intoxicating thought!

In my innocence I had no suspicion of how dangerous a slope the boards form; how smooth and slippery, and how many a lightly-tripping foot had slid on it and fallen, to the ruin of the whole life!

It is the peculiar bliss of innocent childhood to pluck flowers while playing on the brink of the abyss.

And I was still, in my fifteenth year, an innocent, unsuspecting child, that looked on the tree of knowledge as only a kind of delicious apple tree, offering us rich, juicy fruit.

Ah! it was not long I was to continue so naïvely simple. In the new world of the green-room people grow worldly-wise at a dreadfully rapid pace.

With pleasure and diligence I now began to prepare myself as an actress. Day and night I had no other thought, no other aim, than how to qualify myself as soon as possible to tread the boards. I zealously pursued my dramatic studies with Professor Aloys Schreiber, while I also began the practical part of my training under the care of Mademoiselle Demmer. I committed parts to memory and played them under her direction.

Accordingly, in three months, I was able to step on the stage of the Court Theatre in Carlsruhe.

In a letter from my mother to Cousin Leopold in Hamburg, under date 23rd December, 1822, she says:—

"Lina yesterday made her *début* on the stage as *Margaret*, in Iffland's 'Hagestolzen,' and delighted all the town. Everybody here knew what a *penchant* Lina had for this profession, and the house was therefore so crammed by 5 o'clock that there was hardly a place left. She was received with much cordiality by the officers, who no doubt wanted to honour in her the daughter of a gallant comrade. This caused her a little embarrassment for a few minutes, but she soon recovered herself and played beyond all expectation—so well, so naturally and sweetly, that I was myself astonished. The loudest applause was accorded her, and at each scene they shouted out 'bravo.' This rose in the end to a perfect storm of enthusiasm, so that you would have thought the house was coming down. She was not prepared for all that, and yet returned thanks in a few words so pretty and simple that everybody was taken with them. To-day one visit succeeds the other, bringing me congratulations on such a talent, for it is maintained that she played better than Madame Händel-Schütz, who also appeared here and reaped much applause. Lina played as though she had been ten years on the stage. The players at the rehearsals were all surprised at her assurance. As anxious as I was before the event so glad am I now, for I alone know that, besides her talent and her inclination in that direction, Lina was induced to the stage by nobler motives, which are and must remain a secret to every one. The whole town wants Lina to get an engagement here, and even the princely house has expressed itself highly satisfied and desirous of keeping Lina. Grand-Duke Ludwig, with all his frivolity and love of pleasure, is kind, and will doubtless never forget that her father fell a sacrifice to the country, and that he owes us compensation for this loss. Lina waited on him in person, and begged permission to make her *début* here. He received her altogether like a father. All boxes and stalls are already taken for her second appearance, which is to come off four weeks hence, as *Elise Valberg*, in Iffland's play.

"What, however, makes me indescribably happy is the certainty that after all this wonderful intoxicating evening, Lina is still quite the same—as modest and hearty as a child, 'Do you love me, mother?' were her first words to me on our return yesterday evening from the theatre.

"Lina's teacher, also, is quite enraptured at this first great success, and says that ever since Carlsruhe had a theatre there has been no such joy and satisfaction, although the most celebrated artists and artistes have performed in it.

"Be at ease, therefore, you and my good Louise, regarding Lina's future. She will ever, and in every respect, be an honour to the family. At first there were a great number here, especially the clergy, against Lina's being an actress; now they are all unanimously of opinion that it would be a sin to stop the development of such a talent."

In another letter to my father's sister, Frau Amtmann Caroline Wagner, in Ziegenhain, near Cassel, my mother wrote :—

"It was only reluctantly I gave my consent to Lina's new theatrical career. Nor would my brother nor the rest of our relations have given their approval if they had not come to know Lina better, and grow fond of her. Her cousin Christian, in spite of his brilliant position in the world, was the first heartily to recognise Lina's decided talent, and to induce me and the family to leave the question to be decided by her first appearance. If Heinrich had lived to see yesterday evening! How proud he would have been of his Lina! She is his perfect picture, both in soul and body. Your brother will also reconcile himself with his niece being an actress, when once he has seen her on the boards. Do remind the general how often the brothers used teasingly to call you ' the *comediánte.*' Now they are punished for it, seeing a Bauer has, after all, figured on a play-bill, and will, God-willing, only do honour to her art and her family. To-day Lina romped about me and her brothers, and laughing roguishly, said, ' Did I not always tell you when my brothers called me "Big-Nose," that so, exactly so, must the nose be formed for the stage, if it is to be of any effect, and this nose will some day redound to your honour *en face* and *en profil,* and in the papers people will speak with the greatest respect of Mademoiselle "Big-Nose?"'"

I would willingly have removed to Hamburg, but Lina would not have it, as she wills *never* to marry. All her desire is to be independent, esteemed, and held in honour. She would assuredly have been Heinrich's favourite, for she is most like him of all the children. She has his fair hair, his open blue eyes, his honest heart, but also his easily moved sense. Pure is her heart, and shall remain so."

CHAPTER VI.

FIRST LOVE.

THOU good, happy mother; happy in the blindness of thy purest mother's love !

"Pure is her heart, and shall remain so !" As if thou hadst had so much in thy power ! But just as little as I didst thou know the slipperiness of the boards and what a steep incline they make downwards. Only too soon were the scales to fall from our horror-stricken eyes !

I was sixteen, pretty, sought after, lionised, the *enfant gaté* of Carlsruhe, and I was only a public player ! It was the most natural thing in the world, then, that love should soon approach me—love in all shapes, delicate and coarse, noble and base—love sweet as nectar, all bliss and paradise—love, again, that was false, a " grovelling passion," as Sophia Schröder called it—a demon that poisons and blights the heart, dragging soul and body into the mire.

And yet I had the happiness of passing through heaven before falling into purgatory with its consuming flames.

I was barely sixteen when, for the first time, I loved with the strength and ardour of a pure, young heart, as yet all undesecrated by an ignoble thought. My heart was a fair and fragrant spring-flower that opened to the first kiss of the sun, before the noxious mildew or hoar frost of night dropped into its calyx. I loved—and I was loved in return.

Among the many admirers who approached the young actress with their homages, flowers and verses, enamoured looks and gallant speeches, sighs and fopperies, there was also a young man from Hamburg, Edmund Amberg. He had come to Carlsruhe in August, and brought us greetings from Cousin Louise Leopold. He was handsome and amiable, of fine culture and tender heart—so altogether different from our gruff cavaliers of Carlsruhe. And he looked so pale and ill! It was thought his chest had suffered from too severe study, and that he had come to our milder climate for the benefit of his health. He approached me with such true cordiality. I could read in his sparkling eyes how fondly he came, and my heart rushed, to meet him at the sound of his footsteps. The word "love" never passed between us. But his flowers, his verses, every tone of his soft, melodious voice, his beaming eyes, the pressure of his hand in the club dances, all proclaimed "I love thee!" and he knew I loved him in return. I had not the power of hiding it. And why hide it? This first true love, the purest and noblest of my whole life, did make me so rich and happy, such as no later triumphs on the stage were able to.

And then came the hoar-frost in the night, which with one blast shrivelled all the blissful blossoms of my poor little heart—ah, so happy till then!

It was an evil, evil evening when my mother and I yielded to a pressing invitation to a party at my colleague, Amelia Neumann's.

Amelia Neumann, née Morstadt, was the most brilliant artiste and the most seductive beauty of our stage. In her playful coquetry she was irresistible for old and young. At Leipzig, while on a professional tour, she gathered around her a perfect love-court of minnesingers and knights-errant. In her honour her worshippers founded an "Order of Roses," and raised the object of their worship on the shield as "Queen of Roses." At Vienna the devotees of Neumann procured the gold slipper she had worn in the opera of "Cinderella," and drank out of it, each in turn, in champagne, to the health of their goddess. In Berlin even the busiest physicians were at her feet, so that she got the name of the "Medicinal Venus."

Amelia Neumann was twenty-three years old, and had shortly before become a widow. In that fatal party she was in deep but most coquettish mourning. She wore a black but very open velvet dress, which contrasted altogether seductively with the rosy flesh of her luscious figure and her rich golden locks. Madame Venus in the Hörselberg could not be more bewitching, more enchanting.

The truth of this poor Amberg, too, was to experience that evening. Madame Venus threw the net of her golden locks after him, and enticed him with the dulcet tones of her silver voice, and infused into him the fatal fire of her resplendent blue eyes, which spoke forget-me-nots, and smiled to him with her pearly teeth; and Tannhäuser was caught—lost in Venusberg.

Did she love him? No. She only grudged me this "conquest.". With genuine Carlsruhe rudeness she had said what was, of course, with all speed carried to me by sympathising colleagues: "What! This young foul-nose* will already join in the game, and even compete with me! I shall show her what she is about!" And she did show me her power. I yet see her eyes, directed away from poor Amberg, all in a flame, to smile scornfully down on me. She could yet, however, hardly feel how deeply those eyes wounded me.

I returned home from that party more dead than alive. I was like to sink fairly into despair for shame and pain. I felt years older for that evening. The secret dream of youth and innocence lay stripped of its illusion behind me. I had tasted of the tree of knowledge.

My mother took me in her arms and wept with me. More experienced, however, in the ways of the world than I she dried her tears and subjected my poor sick heart to drastic cure. She pushed on the business of my making a professional excursion, and evoked my pride as a maiden and an artiste.

We drove, then, to Mannheim. I was to appear three evenings, in no less a part than "Preziosa." I had need of all my energies to do myself credit before the art-loving public of the old theatrical town of Dalberg, Iffland, and Schiller. And I stood the test and—recovered! In contending for the laurels I came to myself again, and a due appreciation of the value of my heart. The man who would so lightly lose himself in the frivolous play of a vain coquette was not worth the tears of a true heart.

And when Edmund Amberg, soon after my return from

---

* In original, ". R - - znase," for Ranznase (rancid nose).

Mannheim, saw into the frivolous game, and wakened out of his ruinous intoxication of love; when the sparrows on the roof twittered how his fair goddess could not resist the golden lures of the lustful old Grand Duke Ludwig; and when, therefore, poor Tannhäuser, cast out of Venusberg, wanted to come penitently back to me, I had gained strength to reject his renewed advances.

My first struggle with my heart! My first conquest over my heart! But how much did it cost me?

How often have I since asked myself: Why was thy first, pure, blissful love not the last? If Edmund Amberg's heart—good and noble in spite of all its weakness—had not been so frivolously robbed from thee thy whole life would have taken a different course. Thou would'st, in-deed, not have been so "celebrated" an artiste and woman, but thou would'st have been happier and better; a good, faithful wife, a loving and beloved mother, with merry grandchildren, now in this the evening of thy life playing about thee; whereas, according to the course things have actually taken, thou must now look back, weeping, on a solitary, waste life, full of deception and guilt.

Why? ay, why?

CHAPTER VII.

COUNT FRIEDRICH WILHELM VON BISMARCK.

YES, " Love in all shapes" approached me, in spite of my tender sixteen years; claiming the old-established right of regarding a public actress as a commodity to be struck down to the highest bidder.

So was it a hundred years ago—so, fifty years ago—so, still to-day—to the shame of the commodity, but to the disgrace of the buyers as well.

In Carlsruhe of that day—1823—there resided Count Friedrich Wilhelm von Bismarck, General of the Royal Wurtemberg Cavalry and Resident Minister to the Court of Baden. He was married to the Princess Augusta of Nassau-Usingen. At once a famous hero in the wars of deliverance, a distinguished military writer, and a man of talents and many accomplishments, he was beyond question the most considerable personage in Carlsruhe, and, next to the princes of the court, the most eminent in rank. His past life, replete with incident as it was, might almost be called adventurous. The "star of Bismarck," which, later on, was to shine out with still greater brilliancy, was beaming over him.

As far back as the time of Charlemagne, the Bismarcks had emigrated from Bohemia into Brandenburg, where they built the castle and little town of Bismarck and the village of Burgstall. A branch of this knightly, and occasionally also knightly-foraying, family had transplanted itself to Westphalia, where, however, it grew ever more impoverished. Friedrich Wilhelm von Bismarck was born in Windheim, 1783. His father had fought as an officer of hussars, in the Seven Years' War, in which he was so severely wounded that he had to retire on a scanty pension. His young sons, Louis and Friedrich Wilhelm, were early sent out into the world to seek their fortunes as soldiers. Louis entered the service of the house of Nassau; Friedrich Wilhelm, when only thirteen years old, joined the army of Hanover as a cornet, but on the disbanding of this army in 1803 went over to Nassau, to be with his brother.

The very same summer Princess Augusta of Nassau, daughter of the reigning Prince Friedrich August, then twenty-five years old, took so great a pleasure, in the midst of the unrestricted intercourse of court life in the residence-town of Biebrich, in the blooming and spirited lieutenant of the guards, Friedrich Wilhelm von Bismarck, who then counted only twenty years, that, although already betrothed to Prince Ludwig Wilhelm of Hesse-Homburg, she favoured the handsome lieutenant with her love. Consuming ambition it was which had driven him out into the world to push his fortune. And his audacity was quite a match for his ambition. He did not, therefore, let this love, though properly belonging to another, pass by him unheeded. The listening boscages of the fair garden of Biebrich Castle and the hushed apartments of the princess could tell stories. It was a secret, forbidden love, like that between the Princess Amalia of Prussia and the Potsdam lieutenant of the guards, Von Trenck. Friedrich von Bismarck was, however, happier in his love and life. His love did not end in the dreadful casements of Magdeburg, nor his life under the Parisian guillotine.

All in vain did Louis von Bismarck, who knew the secret and the dangers of this love, warn his brother to fly the neighbourhood of the princess, and betake himself to England to join the German Legion which was there being formed out of the former Hanoverian corps.

Friedrich von Bismarck remained beside his lady-love. One of her letters addressed to him in the beginning of 1804 breathes the most tender and devoted passion:—"Dear, best, and only friend, I every day feel more deeply and clearly that I can never live content without thee, and yet my feeling for thee is ennobled now by a passionate exaltation which would make me willing to die for thee, and now by a tenderness which would triumph over self-love and jealousy, if I were only sure that another could make thee happier than I could."

And the nuptials of the princess and the Prince of Hesse-Homburg were to take place on the 2nd August; for to no purpose did the princess confess her love for Bismarck to her mother, and pray for the postponement, at all events, of the wedding. "Marriage among princes," she was told, "was not an affair of the heart, but a duty."

On the evening of the 1st August accordingly, when her princely intended was already in Biebrich Castle, she took leave of her beloved Fritz with passionate tears, and next day went to the altar with her unbeloved Prince of Homburg. The third day after the marriage Friedrich von Bismarck left Biebrich secretly, without taking farewell of the princess, and departed for England to join the German Legion.

Neither happiness nor blessing could follow such a marriage. A few months after the wedding the princess left her husband and returned to Biebrich. Soon after came the legal divorce.

The princess and Bismarck now set all machinery in motion with a view to their union. The mother of the princess at last gave in, but the father would hear nothing of such a "mésalliance."

After a separation of eighteen months, the lovers secretly met again in Frankfort-on-the-Maine. He then returned to England, where, in a duel, he shot his superior officer, Captain von Quernheimb, but was acquitted at the English assizes.

In the summer of 1807 Friedrich von Bismarck found his way back to Germany, and entered the Wurtemberg regiment of chevaux-légers as first lieutenant. The Duke of Nassau was at last persuaded to consent to a "secret" marriage between his daughter and her lover, which was performed in the princely palace of Frankfort by Pastor Mang, a friend of Bismarck's, in presence of the bride's mother, but not of her father.

After the honeymoon, which was passed in a garden-cottage in the suburbs of Frankfort, Bismarck returned to his Wurtemberg regiment, and the princess to the ducal court in Biebrich. After a year's absence the young couple saw each other only for a few hours secretly

in the post-house at Sinzheim, and afterwards for a fortnight
in Frankfort, a short time before Captain von Bismarck was
called to take the field under Napoleon against Austria—
at the same time with my father.

In the battle of Ridau, on the 1st May, 1809, Bismarck, who had his horse shot under him, distinguished
himself so highly by his bravery and coolness that a few
days afterwards Massena presented him to the Emperor
Napoleon in the castle at Ems, with the words, "Voilà, un
jeune officier allemand, qui donne beaucoup d'espérance."

Bismarck encountered the greatest dangers in the campaign of Napoleon against Russia. But here, too, the star
of his wonderful fortune protected him. At Borodino he
had three horses shot under him, and of his regiment of
chevaux-légers only 65 men were left. Major von Bismarck, however, came out of the engagement without a
wound, and was promoted to a lieutenant-colonelcy.

After the close of the war the King of Wurtemberg
raised Quarter-master General of Cavalry von Bismarck to
the rank of a hereditary count; and after the death of the
Prince of Nassau-Usingen, Count Bismarck led his wife,
Princess Augusta, to a home provided for him in the
Margravine Palace in Carlsruhe. In 1820 he was appointed envoy extraordinary and accredited minister to
the Grand-ducal Court of Baden.

Holding so distinguished a position, the stately man of
forty years approached the actress of sixteen with his
gallant attentions. Every time I appeared on the stage
he sat beside his ageing spouse in the margravine's box, and
devoured me with his large, round, disagreeably prominent
blue eyes. He sent me flowers, verses, sweets, and
possibly also a splendid set of jewels, of which, in the
spring of 1824, mother wrote to my aunt at Ziegenhain—
"What friends and patrons Lina has already won! Just
fancy, at Christmas last she received by post a box containing a golden comb, besides necklace and ear-rings, set
with the most beautiful amethysts, and a note in French I
herewith enclose. Who the donor is we know not. Some
guess the Grand-Duchess Stephanie of Mannheim, others
the Margravine Friedrich. In short, it is a secret."

I believe Count Friedrich Wilhelm von Bismarck sent me that present secretly, in order that his spouse, the Princess of Nassau-Usingen, might know nothing of it.

Hardly three months after I received that magnificent Christmas present, in March, 1824, there appeared in the leading Stuttgart newspaper, the *Morgenblatt*, the following from Carlsruhe :—

"During my short stay here, I must send you an account of a lovely acquisition of this stage, a real jewel such as another theatre would hardly be able to show. I mean Mademoiselle Caroline Bauer. Every theatrical representation appears like a picture in which several leading characters come to the front, engrossing among themselves most of the interest and importance of the play. The public takes part in the fate of these principal characters, betokening their interest by loud applause, by sympathy, by tears, by expressions of joy. Such interest on the part of the public is properly threefold. It has reference, in the first place, to that which the poet has put into the part; secondly, to that which mimic art is able to make of the part; and lastly, to the sympathy aroused by the representing individuality through peculiar position, personal beauty, education, descent, unsullied reputation, family relations. These make up an inseparable *ensemble*. Any talent, however eminent, loses by immorality or baseness of conduct. It is for that reason the interest in Mademoiselle Bauer is so pronounced. The interest in this blooming artiste is greatly raised by the fact that she is the daughter and sister of an officer. To this is added a stainless reputation, a rare harmony of virtue, personal charms, highly cultivated understanding, sprightliness, cheerfulness, vivacity—the credit of all which she owes to no mere report, but which she fully substantiates in her performance.

"I saw Mademoiselle Bauer in several parts, *e.g.*, as *Baroness*, in the 'Rehbock.' It was a difficult part, not, indeed, in its general representation, but in its particular shading. A married part is, in any case, difficult for a young, delicate maiden; but when the part brings the married woman into indelicate positions, where *équivoques* chasing *équivoques* hold the ear as in a state of siege, and in so unequivocal a manner that the public is kept in incessant laughter, then must the embarrassment of the young maiden who counts only sixteen summers necessarily increase the more she is involuntarily carried away by the play of her fellow-actors with which she is encompassed. This embarrassment was visibly expressed in the part of Mademoiselle Bauer, but yet her part did not only not suffer from this cause, but the interest in her individuality was enhanced by it. For this embarrassment was not due to any want of confidence, of assurance in her play; it did not at all reflect on her art, but on the maidenly shame of the sweet, tender virgin who finds herself transferred into an element of *équivoques* foreign from her nature, and which she knows not how to escape. This embarrassment, therefore, heightened her charm as being, indeed, in the given circumstances, a so far necessary accident to her performance, and not to be dispensed with, except at the expense of her maidenly delicacy. From this point of view the interest of her whole representation gained. The conflict between the part she played and her native sentiment, between her outward performance and her inward state of mind, was not to be disguised.

"This performance is the last I saw during my stay here. The first in which I saw Mademoiselle Bauer was *Gabriele*, in the 'Nachtlager von Granada.' When the fair young maiden, lamenting the loss of her beloved dove, appears with such inimitable grace, and yet so unassumingly on the scene, and when the strayed prince-regent then comes up, the public are not in the least surprised that his astonishment at finding so sweet a maiden in that wilderness should rapidly pass into soft feelings of love. This part appeared to me to be sustained with particular delicacy by the young artiste.

"It was not in my power to obtain the opportunity of making the personal acquaintance of Mademoiselle Bauer, for access to her is difficult; yet I deemed it my duty to direct attention to this rising artiste, who deserves friendly recognition."

This amiable, anonymous critic was Count Friedrich Wilhelm von Bismarck. Did he send to his princely lady the expressions of his enthusiasm for the young, pretty actress? Did any one suspect the author, to whom access to our house was not become so very difficult?

The critic's real intention was to become only too apparent shortly after that notice.

One day at noon my brother Karl, the easy-minded, hot-blooded lieutenant, came running home in high excitement, hardly able to find words for the matter which inspired his heart of twenty years with pride and transport. He could only stammer out:

"Lina, just hear the news—it's a great stroke for us all. I was riding—there meets me the count—the general —Bismarck, also on horseback—and he speaks to me—in such a friendly way—so free and easy, as though he, too, were only a simple lieutenant with twenty florins a month. And he praises my horse, and praises my riding, and invites me to ride along with him. And we ride to Baiertheim, and he says to me that he had always a great interest for me, for the sake of my deceased father, whom he had learned to know in the Austrian campaign, and whom I resembled so much—and he would see to my advancement —and whether I had any debts, and whether he could help me with his purse—perfectly free and easy, like a good comrade. But don't be thinking, Lina, that I told him—about the paltry scores against me with Fratel and Meyer-Itzig— but you don't need to know that either, and see you don't be telling mother—but a 250 florins or so would set me on my legs again. And, next, the count spoke of you, Lina, of your great talent, and your charming 'Preshiosa,' and your beauty and loveliness and virtue—and he was all in a flame —and he said that he loved you—and if it wasn't for his old wife you should be countess—and if you would only have confidence in him, and could love him, and wait patiently a year or two till his old wife was dead, he would marry you, and would give it you in writing, and make over all his fortune—and would now care for you as your tender friend—for all of us—and double my lieutenant's pay—ah, Lina, what luck!"

I cannot deny that all this flattered my vanity. But my good angel preserved me from becoming a married man's lover and living in expectation of the succession on the death of his old wife.

I have still to acknowledge that Count Bismarck remained my careful friend and protector, though he did not become my lover. Later on, when he became envoy of Wurtemberg to the Court of Berlin, he there visited us in all honour, and wrote many another kind word about the artiste Lina Bauer. To his influence, moreover, I owe it that I was able to stay in Berlin, without breaking my contract with the Carlsruhe stage, and after an interval of years return to Carlsruhe, in the way of an honourable professional visit.

Not till twenty-three years after that declaration of love on horseback did the Princess Augusta of Nassau-Usingen die, the last of her race, in July, 1846, in Wildbad, after having suffered for years from complete paralysis on one side. Two years after that event Count Bismarck retired from public life to his beautiful estate near Constance, on the Boden See, where he married the lady-companion of his late spouse. He died in Constance in 1860.

And, curiously enough, ten years afterwards I was to make, in the most friendly way, the acquaintance in Switzerland of the widowed Countess Bismarck, an amiable lady, and her sweet daughter. I could not avoid asking myself then : " Would'st thou have been happier now if thou hadst then waited, without scruple of conscience and heart, and for reward become Countess Bismarck ? "

I believe I should.

CHAPTER VIII.

LUDWIG, GRAND-DUKE OF BADEN.

ONE other temptation, in 1823, approached the sixteen-year-old actress in Carlsruhe, in the person of the old reigning Grand-Duke Ludwig. He was then sixty years old, had never been married, and was the most dissolute prince of his time. It was told quite openly in Carlsruhe that when margrave he had lived in criminal intercourse with his step-mother, Countess Hochberg, *née* Geyer von Geyersberg, the morganatic spouse of the Grand-Duke Karl Friedrich, and that the young margrave, Max von Hochberg, was at once his step-brother and his son! Nor did any one impose on himself any restraint in talking of the legion of his amours and of his avowed mistresses.

And now I was to figure as tenth in this latter series of grand-ducal beauties. Major Hennenhofer, notorious as a negotiator in transactions of this sort, who had commenced business in this line when Ludwig was margrave, and had his name linked in the Kasper-Hauser and other scandals—the same major now called as official pander on me, to make me the most brilliant offers on the part of his master.

Here, too, I was preserved by my good angel and my disgust at the old crowned debauchee, who was yet so ready with moral saws, as the annexed letter of my mother will testify. The good God, however, who is indeed so eager to rescue and support His earthly children, so long as they are willing to be rescued and supported, sent me a friendly helper in my need, who snatched me away from all these dangers and temptations of Carlsruhe.

The director of the new Königstadt Theatre of Berlin, Heinrich Bethmann, came in search of artistes to Carlsruhe as well, saw me play, and made me the most enticing offers. My Carlsruhe contract, however, ran for two years longer. My mother and I had to resolve on seeking an audience of the Grand-duke, and the dissolution of the contract.

In a letter dated April, 1824, from my mother to my aunt in Ziegenhain, she says:—

"The Grand-duke received us very graciously, but would not hear of a formal rescission of the contract, in order that Lina, in case she should find herself deceived in her expectations at Berlin, might be able to return to her old engagement in Carlsruhe, which he would then gladly improve as far as the funds of the theatre permitted. Still, he would allow Lina leave of absence for eight months to enable her to perfect herself as an artiste in the representation of leading characters, by help of the celebrated exemplars she would find in Berlin. He had no doubt, either, but Lina, even in so dangerous a place as Berlin, would continue a pattern of virtue! If she returned to Carlsruhe it would be his care to provide for her future advancement. You may imagine, dear sister, how happy we were!

"The only question now pending was whether the Berliners would be content with an eight month's leave allowed her. Lina therefore wrote to Director Bethmann, and they signified their compliance, in the hope that Lina would later on be able to extend that limit. Her leave begins here on the 1st of May, and her pay in Berlin on the 15th. And what an advance!—from 600 florins to 800 thalers.

"You will be surprised when you see Lina again. She is now taller than I, and, as every one here maintains, has a very beautiful figure. She has the ample bust of her father, yet tapering down into a slender, supple waist. In all other respects you will find Lina the same as when she was with you two years ago in Ziegenhain; good, happy, natural, indefatigably diligent, the favourite of old and young. Our quality respect her, our *bourgeoisie* are all fond of her. There is nothing stiff and affected about her. Pure is her heart, and shall remain so. She feels altogether happy in her profession, and would not change places with the richest and grandest countess. I'll tell you by word of mouth what prospects are held out to her by a count, but at the cost of her virtue. She will never marry, either, in order to be always with me as an independent and respected artiste.

"And what friends and patrons she has already acquired! Yesterday there again comes by post from Paris a box to Lina's address, containing a lot of the loveliest satin shoes and kid gloves. In this case, however, we guess the sender to be my nephew, Baron Christian Stockmar, seeing that in Coburg he was always telling Lina, 'New gloves and shoes, my little cousin, every time you appear,' to which Lina answered laughingly, 'That's all very well, if we could afford it.'

"We expect our position in Berlin will soon set us free of anxieties, for you may suppose, dear sister, that this first year of the theatre has cost us more than it has brought us in. As an officer's daughter, Lina, of course, can never appear except well-dressed, and she has now got a very fair wardrobe. The only thing she yet needs is a real Turkish shawl, and *that* my nephew will send us from England before we leave here.

"Lina is still to get lessons of the best teachers in Berlin, in science and art, particularly in music, because she has a great taste and an uncommon talent for the pianoforte and singing. She has already publicly played and sung at two concerts here with great applause.

"In January we were in Mannheim, where Lina gave three performances, and pleased the public beyond ordinary, particularly as ' Preziosa.' The grand-duchess assured us she couldn't remember ever having heard a performance so much talked of. But Lina does play the part to perfection, and as ' Preziosa ' has given here far more universal satisfaction than the celebrated and very beautiful Madame Neumann. It is quite a peculiar charm of maidenly grace and virginal innocence that Lina has shed on ' Preziosa,' and the want of which a delicate sense would miss in the case of married women playing the part. And yet with what anxiety I looked forward to Lina

making her *début* as ' Preziosa,' seeing that this part is
one of the most difficult, even for actresses of years'
standing on the stage. The celebrated Stich for whom
'Preziosa' was written shines in it, and our Neumann tours
about on it. It was, therefore, the universal opinion here
that Lina could not succeed in this part after Neumann; it
was too difficult for a beginner ! Even the players who
yet so sincerely admired Lina's ' Margaret,' shook their
heads sceptically ; and I entreated Lina for everything in
the world to wait some months yet with ' Preziosa.' But
Lina said, very determinedly : ' Mother, I *must* now at all
costs play " Preziosa," even though I were to die on the
stage for it. I asked for the part as my *début*, and I must
needs feel ashamed my whole life long if, from vanity and
presumption, I had committed myself to more than I could
perform. And how I should be ridiculed and mocked if I
were to throw off my armour before the battle has begun—I,
a brave soldier's daughter ! Courage, mother ; be you, too,
a brave soldier's wife ! I have the assured feeling in me,
the good God will stand by me and help me to conquer, as
He has indeed so wonderfully helped us in the past ! ' And
I could not resist her any longer. But I shall never forget
the anxiety with which I entered my box that evening,
and saw the theatre crammed and in the greatest commotion. Sympathy, curiosity, the malicious pleasure of seeing
a breakdown had filled the house to overflowing. I felt
very near fainting. My heart beat so dreadfully loud I
was frightened the neighbours would hear it. I could not
get rid of the anxiety that Lina would make a *fiasco* of the
piece, and would be run down for her vanity and arrogance
—she, who is modesty itself ! But everything, *everything*
went well to admiration. Lina played with an enthusiasm
and sweetness such as made me thank God with all my
heart that I had not compelled her to give up the part.
You may now judge for yourself, dear sister, how this
' Preziosa ' was extolled by the fiery Heidelberg students,
who flocked in hundreds every evening to the play. I was
often thinking the house would come down under their
tempestuous cheering. I could not, however, help laughing when between whiles I heard a young consequential

voice from the parterre: 'Why, man, my father has given her lessons, and I have danced with her; ay, danced! She dances divinely. Let me dance with her, and let who likes take all the beauty of the Heidelberg landscape to himself and welcome.' It was the son of our good Professor Aloys Schreiber, who rejoices like a child in Lina's success. If Heinrich had lived to see that day."

CHAPTER IX.

WILHELMINA MAAS.

WILHELMINA MAAS was born in Berlin in 1786, or thereabout, and while still of a very tender age took a part in the ballet, as angel and elf. And she was the most charming lovely angel and the daintiest little elf to be found on any boards in the world! But all that hopping and springing did not content her ardent spirit and ambition. She wanted to speak on the stage, for she felt she would speak well. So she came to the director, Iffland, and besought instruction and a place as actress. Iffland made the tiny thing declaim a piece before him, nodded with satisfaction, gave the little child comfits, and now and again a little theatrical instruction in his bureau. Then when Wilhelmina was sixteen years old, but still a child in appearance, Iffland sent her to the "Master," Goethe, in Weimar, who just wanted a young, pretty, talented maiden to train for the part of a lover. Goethe at once adopted her and in his "Annals" speaks of "her pretty figure, her gracefully natural manner, her fine-toned voice, her whole happy individuality."

In Berlin, a young Count Königsmarck approached her with the warmest homage, a scion of that proud Swedish family to which belonged the unhappy Count Philipp Christoph von Königsmarck, who loved the beautiful Electress Sophia Dorothea of Hanover, and who that late July evening of 1694 was murdered in the Electoral Castle, at Hanover, by the jealous Elector, afterwards George I. of Great Britain. The sister of that unhappy count was the bewitching beauty, Countess Aurora von Königsmarck, who set so many hearts in flame, and even when abbess of Quedlinburg lived and loved so wantonly—and died so wretchedly. Voltaire called her "the most celebrated woman of two centuries." Charles XII. of

Sweden, ever proof against love of woman, was so afraid
of the enchantment of Aurora's beauty that when in 1702,
on commission of her princely lover, August of Saxony,
she came to visit Charles in his camp at Courland, in order
to induce him to a favourable peace—he deemed it safer
to keep her out of his sight.

And the hot, wild blood, and the demoniac beauty of
that old Philipp Christoph, and of that Aurora von Königsmarck glowed and burned after more than a hundred
years in that descendant of the proud countly family—
to the misery of the poor, sweet artiste, Wilhelmina
Maas, and to his own misery. They were not merely
to taste "Love's glowing raptures," but also "Love's
freezing woe." Her love was bliss without rest—and
without rest is no real bliss.

Count Königsmarck was so passionately enamoured of
the charming actress that, in spite of the protest of his
family, he repeatedly offered her his hand and his name.
But Wilhelmina Maas was noble and proud enough to
desire not to thrust herself on a family that refused to
recognise the artiste as one of themselves. And she loved
Count Königsmarck too sincerely to be willing to be the
cause of an estrangement between him and the members
of his family and the associates of his position. With her
loving heart she brought him the offering of her self-
denial, and became the count's mistress, while it was still
in her power to become his consort.

The enthusiastic, art-devoted Count Königsmarck was,
however, not satisfied with the love of the sweet artiste—
nor with her triumphs as naïve youthful lover—he wanted
to have her admired by all the world as the first tragic
actress of her century. Her very successes as Maid of
Orleans, Eboli, Thekla, did not suffice his ambitious love.
She must also win triumphs as Phädra, Medea, Lady Macbeth. And his morbid ambition infected her beyond cure.
In her overweening self-esteem she ever more and more
mistook the sphere congenial with her true talent, and
passionately struggled beyond its compass. She neglected
her successful parts, and aspired towards unattainable
pieces. She studied with Königsmarck "Iphigenia," "Lady

Macbeth," and "Medea," and was bent on playing them in
Berlin, so that when Iffland refused compliance with that
demand, she scornfully gave in her resignation. The poor
infatuated Wilhelmina Maas rushed headlong to destruction.

In the autumn of 1822, Wilhelmina Maas came to
Carlsruhe. I first saw her as "Sappho," and with all the
public looked with wonder on the dainty little *tragédienne*.
Every pose, every movement in the picturesque Greek
drapery was a faithful copy of the antique—but all too
punctilious and artificial. The elocution was correct and
melodious, the voice sweetly sonorous, if not quite strong
enough for the part—but the house remained cold, for this
"Sappho" was cold. Her declamation, her action presented
nothing of the flaming and consuming passion which
arrests those within its influence, and sweeps them resistlessly along with it—passion which must proceed direct from
the heart, if people are to be affected by it. Instead, we
had here exhibited to us an altogether clever artistic performance on the part of a reflecting and experienced
actress—not the inspired, love-glowing, old Greek poetess
who, in despair, throws herself into the sea.

The divine, tragic spark was wanting, and without fire
there is no kindling flame.

Of course I had already heard of the strange relations
subsisting between the actress and the Count Königsmarck.
I looked with curiosity at him when passing him in the
street. He was called in Carlsruhe "Count Ahasuerus."
He was, too, almost a weird-like appearance to keep aloof
from in the still provincial streets of our residence-town.
A tall, slender, stooping figure, with shaggy beard, in
slovenly dress and clumsy boots, he hurried along, taking
wide steps, looking at nobody, whisking his arms generally
in the air, and murmuring indistinctly to himself. In the
museum he would sit for hours together, silent and motionless, staring at the newspaper, or over it into vacancy, with
his large wide-open eyes—till, suddenly, he would start up
and dash into the open air without a good-bye to any one.
He exchanged a word with no one in the museum, and
made no visits. He lived quiet and retired in the hotel, and

only went daily during calling time to see his lady friend.

When after my engagement I had to pay a visit to the elder members of the theatre, I at first refused calling on Mademoiselle Maas till my mother rebuked me for my heartlessness.

"Child, Mademoiselle Maas is not happy, neither as artiste, nor in her love for the count. Assuredly, this love is the greatest curse to both."

So we both visited her. My colleague received us rather reservedly and formally, but with the utmost courtesy. In her grey silken gown, and sweetly fresh white morning cap, she looked like an elegant lady of superior rank. There was no trace in her conversation of theatrical scandal, jealousy of others' parts, petty rivalry or malice towards any one.

My attention was chained to a large, lovely oil-painting hanging opposite me on the wall.

It was the "Maid of Orleans" scarcely past girlhood, leaning against an old oak. Luxuriant locks ripple over the sweet innocent child's face; the pious eyes look up with enthusiasm towards heaven, and the lovely mouth is slightly opened. Nothing could be more sweetly charming or more gladdening to the heart than this sweet "Joanna" —a chaste spring flower, hardly yet waked by the kiss of the sun!

And this blessedly sweet, blooming "Joanna" sat over against me : pale and careworn, faded and embittered ; her youthful dreams of bliss and love, of eternal sunshine and ennobling fame, all blasted—and she now an ageing, weary, weary actress.

My heart was heavy, and my eyes grew moist.

Wilhelmina read in my face what passed in my soul. With sobbing voice she said :

"I see you hardly recognise the original in this 'Joanna.' Time and the storms of life and the heart leave their ineffaceable traces behind. This picture represents the 'Maid' as a simple, innocent shepherdess, as an inspired seer, with her eyes fixed alone on that high goal set for her by God Himself. She is still the pure virgin. Her eye has not yet noticed Lionel—her heart has not yet yielded to earthly love, to the demons of infatuating, destroying passion."

I was fain to cry aloud, but my voice was stifled in my breast when I looked into the burning, restless eyes of "Ahasuerus," which almost devoured the lovely picture on the wall. In these, large, blue, still ever demoniacally beautiful, lurked an unspeakable mockery, a painful irony.

The count had entered by the open door of the adjoining room and approached on the soft carpet without being perceived.

      *   *   *   *   *   *   *

When my mother and I at the end of May, 1824, took sorrowful leave of Wilhelmina Maas, before departing for Berlin on my new engagement, she said to us with tears in her eyes:

"Greet my dear Berliners. With consuming longing I think of that golden time when I was there—the 'Joanna' you see in the picture."

In Berlin we afterwards heard that she had given up—or lost?—her position in Carlsruhe, and was wandering about in the world with Count Königsmarck, from stage to stage.

Then—about the beginning of 1829, I think it was—an "old acquaintance from Carlsruhe" desired to see us. It was Wilhelmina Maas.

How pale and mournful, and how faded and broken-down she appeared.

"I am but the shadow of the old 'Mina."

"And your friend? You are now quite alone in the world?" hesitatingly asked my mother.

"All alone! Count Königsmarck has made his peace with his family. I myself advised him to part with me and draw closer to his relations—for I felt that his love to me, which was no longer sustained by my successes on the stage, was for ever extinguished. He wanders alone restless through the world. He is now in Paris."

"But you, my poor, dear friend!—and your love so faithful, so true and self-sacrificing!"

Deeply affected we took leave of each other ! We all knew it was an eternal farewell.

How long Wilhelmina continued to live and suffer on earth I have never been able to find out. But she lived long enough, at any rate, to learn to her grief that her unhappy "Ahasuerus," Count Königsmarck, was murdered in Paris.

The report goes that Wilhelmina died some time in the 30's (1830-1840).

CHAPTER X.

FRIEDRICH WILHELM III.

IN the autumn of 1824 I accepted an engagement in the
Royal Theatre, and on the 9th November, before I had yet
appeared on the royal stage, and before King Friedrich
Wilhelm III. had yet addresséd one word to me, he was
secretly married, in the church of Charlottenburg Castle,
to the Countess Augusta Harrach.

When, next day, the secret was noised abroad in Berlin,
every one was struck with surprise and astonishment, and
thought he had a perfect right to be indignant at this
fancy "the old gentleman" had taken into his head. The
unknown "step-mother" that had presumed to take a
Louise's place became an object of hatred itself. It was
not enough to have a Catholic crown-princess, but we
must also have a "Catholic step-mother." As a matter of
course, the king and the whole court would become
Catholic, and then the country itself would naturally have
to follow suit!

The Catholic Church of St. Hedwig was broken in
upon, and when the thieves found the altar candlesticks
were only of nickel-silver they replaced them on the altar
in a few days, with a slip of paper stuck on them on which
was written: "Oh, my stars! crown-princess and Princess
Liegnitz—and yet not so much as a silver candlestick in
the Catholic Church! Rather scurvy, is it not?"

The ready, biting wit of the Berliners rang the changes
without end of the "step-mother" and the "queen-by-
night," who fell into the rank of princess by day.

Then, again, it was said that the troops, in making their
salute to the king, no longer cheered with a "Hurrah,"
but "Harrach."

Then, again, "The marriage would be taken for a fable,
if it were not impossible to find the 'moral' in it!"
etc., etc.

It was related that the princes, in particular the crown-prince, were furious on the subject of the "step-mother," and that the princesses, the king's daughters, who happened to be all present at the time, Alexandra-Charlotte of Russia, Alexandrina of Mecklenburg, and Princess Louise, who was betrothed to Prince Friedrich of the Netherlands, were in perpetual tears—nay, that Prince Karl was ordered to two days' arrest for his rudeness to the "step-mother."

My first meeting with the king took place shortly after his second marriage, at one of the so-called "Brühl Balls" in the concert-hall of the theatre. They got the name of Brühl Balls from the intendant, Count Brühl, who arranged them and issued the subscription-invitations for them. In a letter to my brother Louis I wrote:—

"I have now 'seen' the Brühl Balls, for there is little or no dancing. People converse, look about them, and take envious note of each other's toilettes. The gentlemen walk, the ladies mostly sit on the raised seats round the walls. The king promenades indefatigably through the throng, and talks affably to a great number, smiling paternally, as if glad to see his children happy. I was sitting modestly and retiredly with my mother and a family we were on friendly terms with, enjoying the sight of the brilliant maze, when all at once it was whispered to me: 'Come down, the king wants to speak to you;' and for the first time I stood before Friedrich Wilhelm the Good.

"I felt how all eyes were turned on me, to watch how I would deport myself. My eyes were dazzled; but scarcely did I meet the mild, kindly look of the king when I was at once composed. The king, in his well-known fragmentary style, which is never stuffed out with preambles or flourishes of any sort, said: 'Glad Brühl got you for my stage—often seen you in Königstadt Theatre—felt much pleasure—like a lively creature—much pleased.'

"'Your Majesty makes me happy.'

"'When appear?'

"'The beginning of January.'

"'In what pieces?'

"' " Beschämte Eifersucht;" " Jurist und Bauer." *
"' 'Good!—like comedies—wish you success.'
" The king then nodded kindly and passed on.
" Hofruth Henn offered me his arm to conduct me back
to the gallery; but I had difficulty in getting there.
Every one wanted to be introduced to me—see me—speak
to me."

At this ball Princess Liegnitz appeared for the first
time in her new dignity before the Berliners. And how
she was stared at and criticised'!

I still see her vividly in her private box, as though it
were no further back than yesterday I had actually seen
her there, in her dress of azure blue, a turban of white
crape, with marabout plumes, on her dark locks. She was
no beauty, but looked fresh and blooming.

She sat there shy and abashed, as if at a loss what to
do with herself and the public. The king appeared in the
box of his consort only for a few moments, and spoke to
her without sitting down. He, too, it appeared, felt a
little embarrassed in the new situation.

The king was pleased when the leading members of the
opera, the drama, and the ballet appeared at these Brühl
Balls, in the concert hall, and at the larger subscription
balls of the opera house, and when the dancing went on
briskly. At the masked balls the young members were
formally commanded to appear. They received the most
brilliant costumes from the theatre wardrobe.

A few young officers, who looked on at the dancing as
if bored, the king reprimanded, saying, " Why not dance?
Are you made of wood? Better, then, keep at home."

A splendid subscription ball in February, 1826, was to
be of still greater importance to me. Madame Brede,
actress to the Court of Wurtemberg, and a friend of
Rahel, a celebrated beauty, joined my mother and me. In
her charming dress of white satin, and a garland of
roses wound round her classic head, she drew all eyes on
her.

---

* " Jealousy put to Shame;" "Lawyer and Peasant."

-I wore white tulle over rose-coloured satin and ' orange blossoms, and felt, too, quite nice and blooming.

On his first round, the king approached me with his brilliant suite. At his side walked an English officer of high rank, in scarlet uniform emblazoned with gold, with a mighty aquiline nose of extraordinary curve—the Duke of Wellington, the famous hero of the War of Deliverance.

The public reverently stepped back on both sides. The king graciously nodded to me, with a smile which seemed to say, " Ay, we are all very prettily dressed ! " I also noticed that his Majesty drew the Duke of Wellington's special attention to Augusta Brede and me.

The duke looked complaisantly at us—started—observed me penetratingly—whispered a word to the king, who thereupon stood and regarded me fixedly in astonishment. And throughout the evening I could repeatedly observe that I was an object of quite peculiar attention to his Majesty and his English guest.

A young officer of the royal suite, having afterwards engaged me to dance with him, was able at last to satisfy my burning curiosity. He had quite distinctly heard the Duke of Wellington whisper to the king in French: " What an astounding likeness to our late Princess Charlotte of England, the consort of Prince Leopold of Coburg."

We shall soon see how fateful this resemblance was to prove to me.

Since ever, as royal-court actress, I belonged to the select number allowed to play at the small private weekly theatricals in the " Palais," I became repeatedly distinguished in the friendliest manner by his Majesty.

This " Palais," called the " Princesses' Palais," was connected with the king's own palace by an archway across the Oberwallstrasse, and in this " Palais," the king in his fondness for the theatre had erected a modest little amateur stage, where almost every Monday, unless the king was absent from Berlin, and even in that case should there be visitors at court the king desired specially to honour, comedies were played, music performed, or ballets danced.

Unless some inevitable hindrance came in the way the king visited a theatre regularly every evening, winter and summer. At the stroke of six the king entered his small side box, and before the door of the box had yet ceased creaking the conductor gave the signal for the opening of the overture or of some brisk air, preliminary to a comedy or farce. Even when the king, in summer, was staying in Potsdam, on the Pfaueninsel,* in Paretz or Charlottenburg, and the fairest weather invited people into the open air, his well-known and much-patched yellow caleche with the two snorting horses was sure to pull up in front of the theatre a minute before six. The king did not mind twelve or sixteen miles of dusty roads for the sake of enjoying anew, in Berlin, some comedy or farce that was often tasteless enough and which he had seen dozens of times before. During his regular sojourns, moreover, at Teplitz, the king never missed a single night in the hot, stifling, little theatre, where often a very moderately-equipped strolling troupe would play their stale old farces before him, which he would sit out till the curtain dropped for the last time—to the death almost of his suite.

Only on festive occasions, when he had distinguished visitors, did the king appear in full uniform with cocked hat in the royal central box, and in such a case generally only through the first act. He would then exchange his tight uniform for his long easy grey coat, without epaulettes and orders, with which he would retire into his comfortable corner in the little side box, where he was concealed from the eyes of the public. My august gentleman did not like being put about. From the stage, however, he was open to our observation, and in most cases he sat there apparently not much interested.

During the *entr'actes* the king frequently came by a secret door on to the stage, took notice of the new decorations, machinery, and costumes, and addressed a few friendly words to the actors. He had positively enjoined that on the stage not the least attention was to be paid him. "Everything to go on its proper course" was his

---

* Peacock's Island.

order. The curtain was not to rise a minute later on account of his presence. "In this matter the public is king!—No fuss on my account! Dreadful!"

This once nearly caused a little embarrassment. His Majesty had stayed rather long on the stage. The curtain rose—and the astonished public saw the august legs making a hasty exit.

On another occasion the king sat on a flying machine, which, at the conclusion of the ballet just ended, had brought some fairy queen or goddess to the stage; and he was having a comfortable chat with the solo-dancer Lemière, when all at once the royal seat was seen re-ascending to the theatrical sky. The manager, however, by his prompt and expert action saved his Majesty this involuntary aerial flight.

In new operas and ballets, and even in farces, the king attended the rehearsals, though given in the morning. He took a particular fancy to the melodrama, "Robinson Crusoe," which the Berliners could not endure, so that it had to be discontinued after the second representation. In reference to this affair my august gentleman at a dinner of Papa Timm's, said to me, "A pretty and brisk play. Piece much pleased me. Don't understand Berliners. Too smart public"—a very characteristic utterance on the part of the king, who did not seek in the theatre any great excitement or instruction or even artistic pleasure, but wanted to be entertained agreeably, and without any mental exertion of his own. He had, therefore, no liking for "classical pieces," and could not bear tragedies. On the other hand, he was never tired of watching the graceful steps of a Lemière, Hoguet, Galster, Gasperini, who were accordingly held in high preferment.

Above all, Mademoiselle Lemière stood high in his favour. She had come from the Paris opera in 1817, and was far from a beauty, being, indeed, lean as a skeleton; but she was graceful and elegant, lively to an excess, and, like a real Parisian, could chat away in an amusing strain without end on nothing at all, to the great entertainment of his Majesty, who had no particular talent himself for conversation, but took all the more pleasure in others talking to him. Theatrical scandal itself did not shock him, and when his entertainer would stickle at some specially piquant passage his Majesty would administer gentle encouragement.

In spite of his openly pronounced predilection for Mademoiselle Lemière, and in spite of her great influence with him, his Majesty never had any amour with the bold dame, nor with any other artiste—nay, he steered altogether shy of any impure love affair whatsoever. So at least his private chamberlain Timm maintained, adding: "His Majesty is much too bashful for such a thing, and the image of his unforgettable Louise prevents him." After the king's death Louise's likeness was found in a secret case of the order of the Black Eagle which he wore on his breast. The queen's rooms were kept exactly in the state in which they were in her life time. In her bed-room the Bible lay beside her golden dressing table.

The royal intimacies with the ladies of the theatre the Berliners were wont to call "his Majesty's patting flirtations;" for the most the king allowed himself in that way was but to pat a fair cheek, a round shoulder, or a plump arm. Whoever understood the trick of snaring pretty pats, looking tender and tickling his Majesty's ears, was sure of fine presents. I, for my part, cannot boast of any great royal presents, although the king was always very gracious to me. Once when Timm was distributing the Christmas gifts I received a beautiful set of black lace, but by mistake, seeing it had been intended for a dancer. On another occasion I got a Parisian hat, and frequently a basket of Sans-Souci fruit.

Lemière lost a great deal of her influence with the king through her altogether crazy passion for the handsome harp-player, Desargus, a countryman of hers. She married her lover in spite of the king's warnings, and had to pay dearly for her infatuation. Desargus was a gambler, and soon treated his unhappy wife so badly that a separation followed. Years afterwards I again met Madame Lemière-Desargus as a very elegant lady in Baden-Baden. During the late Franco-German war she died in poverty in Paris.

There was a great deal of jesting about these "virtuous *danseuses*," and the good Papa Timm as "head eunuch of this remarkable harem." His Majesty, however, was really in dead earnest about the virtue of his stage artistes. On a new engagement his first question was, "How is her reputation?" If the answer was not favourable, the instant rejoinder was:

"Pity for it; otherwise well pleased. But send her away; not to be used. Such a thing is infectious!"

And the king himself was very careful in protecting the character of his artistes.

At a ball in the Saxon Hall in Teplitz, the then still-reigning Duke of Brunswick danced repeatedly and passionately with a young, fair, and virtuous actress, and paid marked court to her besides.

At last the king beckoned the young maiden to him, and whispered to her:

"No more dancing with the duke. A '*mauvais sujet.*' No honourable intentions. Injures good reputation. And a good name more precious than fine gold. Follow my word, dear child!"

In other respects, too, the king showed a real paternal care for the well-being of his stage actors, and not merely of the "virtuous *danseuses.*" In these things he altogether deserved the name of "Friedrich Wilhelm the Just."

By his delicate, respectful behaviour, the king always showed that the person was of more account in his eyes than the artist! He was never too exalted nor too far removed from them when there was a question of protecting his dear comedians from the caprices and disfavour of the public or prejudiced critics, or from the arbitrariness of superiors.

And when I was myself compelled to invoke his Majesty's protection against a prince of his own house, I did not appeal in vain, and his favour continued the same.

And when through sickness or distress an artist was reduced to need assistance, the good Friedrich Wilhelm ever showed himself of open heart and open hand.

How often did the king pay Ludwig Devrient's debts, Unzelmann's, Wauer's! To provide also for the old age of these incurably improvident persons he made their contracts last for life.

And when Wauer, while unwell, was taking a part in a play in which he had to eat to excess, the king sent his adjutant to enjoin Wauer on no account to eat so much, however much the play should suffer. The king's anxiety was not to be allayed till he was assured it was not meat Wauer was swallowing, but only some quite innocent preparation.

The good king's passion for the stage was a great cause of concern among the pious, and many pamphlets appeared in the way of warning to him, such as Tholuck's " Voice Against the Theatre." All this,.however, had no effect on him. The monarch, otherwise so anxious and strictly orthodox, paid not the least attention to prayers and warnings of that kind from the hearts of his people.

Prince Wittgenstein having once in Teplitz expressed to his Majesty his weariness of a certain play of little merit, which he had heard many times before, the king replied with a smile :

" Do you think, then, that such things give me pleasure ? I go to the theatre only for the sake of being able to think there without being disturbed, and reflect on all important matters that have happened during the day. There I am not required to listen to the speeches, whereas elsewhere speeches are either directly addressed to me, or, at all events, uttered with a view to my hearing them. Here I am alone with myself."

This explanation is, no doubt, true in part, but only in part. For his solitude in the Berlin theatres was rather dearly purchased by some hours' drive from Potsdam and back, whereas in his garden at home he had no need to speak or listen to speeches unless he wanted; and one would imagine he could meditate State affairs to better purpose in the leafy calm of the Pfaueninsel or in the stillness of his study than in a noisy theatre. In my opinion, the solution of the psychological riddle is not very far to seek.

His Majesty went night after night to the theatre, driven by habit and—*ennui!*

One of my most pleasing reminiscences is that in the year 1827, in the comic opera of " Joconde," by Isouard, I was at his Majesty's special desire allowed to play and sing in the theatre of the New Palace at Potsdam, as *Edile*, along with Henrietta Sontag. The singer who had studied this part was taken ill, and the king had honoured guests he wanted to entertain with a performance of Sontag. At the moment of need no substitute could be found, for it was not to be expected of leading stars like Milder-Hauptmann, Seidler, and Schultz-Killitschgy, that any one of them would brook standing in the way of foil to Henrietta Sontag.

In the circumstances the opera manager, Karl Blum, came flying to me with the message, "You must help us out of our difficulty by singing as *Edile*. You are musical. Your *Edwin* was quite a brilliant performance"—and, thereupon, Blum opened the piano, thrust the music into my hand, and started the accompaniment.

"I—sing with Sontag before the Court!" cried I, beside myself, "my senses reel at the very thought—and, besides, study the part at a twinkling!—die sooner."

But Blum set to stroking me into compliance, by assuring me the court would be informed how I had yielded only out of complaisance, and meanwhile he was ever fingering off snatches of the sweet enticing melodies *Edile* had to sing—till I was caught, and at once fell to a death and life study of the part. The rehearsals passed well, but on the occasion of the finishing rehearsal in the New Palace I stood trembling and distressed, for the king with his suite was close by, behind the orchestra.

After the first trio, and at the end of the first act, Friedrich Wilhelm the Good suddenly appeared before me on the stage, and with genuine paternal mildness said:— "Not be anxious—I know very well—sing only from desire to oblige—very handsome—praiseworthy—will do very well—thanks! thanks!" Thereupon the affable monarch nodded in cordial friendliness and disappeared. That inspired me with fresh courage. I breathed freely, resumed my singing and playing cheerily, and did not discredit myself in the evening. Next day I received from Private Chamberlain Timm, in the name of the king, some delicious Potsdam grapes and a charming Parisian hat. This present, nearly the only one I received from the Prussian Court, made me happy on account of the billet accompanying it, "Let *Edile* remember with pleasure the sacrifice she made."

The drives to Potsdam were always one of our greatest treats. The summer festivals in the New Palace generally entertained the king pleasantly for the whole day. To the private *diners*, which Papa Timm had to prepare for us in Potsdam Castle simultaneously with the royal table, and where we were served with the same dishes, only a few select persons were invited—the dancers Lemière, Hoguet, Galster, Gasperini; and, from the opera and drama, only Henrietta Sontag and I. During dessert the king would drop in for a comfortable gossip, but without sitting. He would lean reposingly against a table or a commode, while we formed a semi-circle around his Majesty, awaiting his most august address. The king, on such occasions, liked us to answer free-and-easy and chat away without restraint.

Thus, for example, the exalted ruler, smiling, with finger in threatening attitude, said to me:

"Have a care!—ruin my lieutenants—heard a bird sing—what about the pipe?"

And I had to reply: "Yes, your Majesty, why are the lieutenants so silly? The young madcap who paid the manager ten thalers for the pipe I smoked from in the last performance of ' Nehmt ein Exempel dran ' * in the Potsdam Stadtheater is assuredly allowed too much pocket-money by his mamma. If I were his mother I would keep a tighter hold on the purse-strings. And it was not so much as a good smoking pipe—bah!"

The talk went on in this strain. Green-room tales, old and new, with and without a wrappage, came on the carpet, till it was time to dress for the theatre. The king went away. Papa Timm stuck packages of the remaining dessert into the hands of his "children," and away we hastened merrily across the wide drill-ground to the theatre.

The affable monarch, past fifty years of age, was still

---

* "Take an example by it."

ever handsome and stately of person, full of dignity and mildness.

Of the two brothers of Queen Louise, Georg, the Grand-Duke of Mecklenburg-Strelitz, was mild and kindly, while Duke Karl was the ingenious *maître de plaisir* of the court. They had always some words to say to us when we met, generally of a jocular nature.

Their sister, the still charming Piincess Frederica, Duchess of Cumberland, was a lady of whose gallantries and passions Berlin had many piquant stories to tell. We could always depend on some cheerful word of gossip from her lips.

I fairly shuddered at the lion head and suffering eyes of her consort, the Duke of Cumberland, afterwards King of Hanover, when he came up so close to my person that we almost touched noses, and with his English accent said: "Miss, charmant ausgesiihn als Bedduinin—sühr glücklicher Bedduine."*

Prince Wilhelm, the king's brother, was of handsome, chivalrous-like figure, with whom so many ladies fell in love, during the Vienna Congress, to their misfortune. He was in the habit of passing us by coldly—from a feeling of shyness, it was said.

The youngest brother, Prince Heinrich, was not so shy, and lived with his evil passions in Italy—exiled, in a manner, and almost fallen into oblivion.

The Princess Wilhelm was greatly honoured and distinguished by the king. She was long and lean. With her earnest tendencies she was no particular devotee of the play and players, but her eyes expressed great goodness of heart.

The king's sisters, Wilhelmina, Queen of Holland, and the unhappy Princess Augusta of Hesse-Cassel—who suffered so much at the hands of the Countess Reichenbach, the "dark Martha," the ruling mistress of her consort, that with her son, the electoral-prince, she retired to Bonn—these stately, kind princesses stayed occasionally on visits in Berlin and Potsdam.

---

* "You looked charming as a Bedouin girl—would I had been the Bedouin man!"

D

The Crown-Prince of Hesse, a fine, slim young gentleman, with sweet pleasing features, once invited me to pay a professional visit to Cassel. I had to answer him that General Bauer in Cassel had no wish to see his niece on the stage.

It was not long before there was talk of a passionate fancy on the part of this dainty, quiet crown-prince for the wife of Lieutenant Lehmann in Bonn, who afterwards deserted her husband to become Princess of Hanau.

The poor Princess Augusta had therefore not only to suffer the tragic fate of being carried back to Cassel by her husband who had fallen upon her by surprise in Bonn, and there endure the presence of the Countess Reichenbach, *née* Ortlepp, installed as all-powerful favourite; but was also compelled to recognise a Princess of Hanau, the divorced wife of Lieutenant Lehmann, as her morganatic daughter-in-law.

Whoever at that time, in the midst of the Berlin court festivals, looked on the Crown-Prince of Hesse, the little Prince Georg of Cumberland, and the king's sons, and observed their friendly and merry intercourse one with another—who, then, whose eye took in images of this description, would have ever ventured on prophesying that on some future day—forty years distant—these cousins then so mutually joyous would, as reigning princes, stand hostilly opposed to one another, sword in hand, and that, moreover, Crown-Prince Friedrich Wilhelm of Hesse-Cassel and King Georg of Hanover would live and die as exiles far from their overturned thrones?

In truth, there are no more moving dramas on the stage than those constructed by real life.

In these private court festivals of Friedrich Wilhelm III., were also to be seen "the king's beautiful children," as Heine rightly calls them—in truth a delightful picture. Verily, "a handsome vigorous race of princes! Not one unshapely branch on this stem!"

When, for the first time, I played in the "Palais," the Grand-Duchess Alexandra was staying on a lengthy visit at her father's court. A lady of delicate and yet royal

presence, who could be amiable to the degree of enchantment—when she liked. She asked me whether I hadn't a
mind to give them a performance in St. Petersburg? It
would be a pleasure to her to see me there.

This kind invitation I responded to in February, 1828.
The Empress Alexandra received me in St. Petersburg
with the same kindness as did the Grand-Duchess in
Berlin.

The story went that the Princess Charlotte of Prussia
had a secret early attachment to the handsome General
von Natzmer, and that she had once written a letter praying her royal father to give his consent to her marriage
with the general, but that her lady-in-waiting had prevented the letter from reaching the hands of the king.
The Princess Charlotte thus became, not the wife of General von Natzmer, but Empress of all the Russias.

The Grand-Duke Nicholas was truly the handsomest
man I ever saw. Cousin Christian Stockmar draws a very
characteristic portrait of the grand-duke, when twenty
years old he came, in 1816, on a visit to the Court of
Prince Leopold and the Princess Charlotte of England in
Claremont—a portrait which could still pass as fairly appli-
cable ten years later.

In Christian Stockmar's diary may be read under date,
November, 1816 :—

"Nicholas is an extraordinarily handsome, seductive
youth; taller than Leopold, without being thin, straight as
a pine; his face youthful like his, and regular to the
utmost degree; with a free beautiful forehead, beautifully
curved eyebrows, supremely beautiful nose, beautiful little
mouth and finely cut chin. His lips are just shaded by an
incipient moustache.

"He wears the light-horse uniform, a quite simple green
tunic with red, silver colonel's epaulettes, a small faded
star, a white sword-belt, and a steel sabre, with leather
sword-knot. In his bearing he is lively, without any trace
of embarrassment or stiffness, and yet altogether becoming.
He is full of talk, and speaks French excellently, accompanying his words with not ill-suiting gestures. If

everything he says is not exactly clever, it is at least all highly pleasing, and he seems to have a decided talent for paying court to ladies. In his speech when he wants to lay special stress on anything, he shrugs up his shoulders, and casts his eyes rather affectedly towards heaven. In everything he shows much confidence in himself, yet apparently without any pretention.

"He did not make much of the Princess (Charlotte), who seemed to pay more attention to him than he to her. He ate very moderately for his age, and drank nothing but water. When, after conversation, Countess Leven played the piano, he kissed his hand to her, a proceeding which seemed highly curious, though also decidedly pleasing, to the English ladies. Mrs. Campbell could find no end to her praises of him. 'What an amiable creature! He is devilish handsome; he will be the handsomest man in Europe!' The Russians left the house next morning. I was told that on his retiring to rest a leather sack filled with hay was brought from the stable by his people for the grand-duke, such being the material on which he always slept. Our English friends deemed this an affectation."

Cousin Christian and Prince Leopold were, however, afterwards inclined to regard this "devilish handsome man" as a complete—play-actor.

In Berlin I never saw the Grand-Duke Nicholas pay court to any lady but his consort, of whom he was passionately fond, and to her he did pay court in the most graceful manner. In St. Petersburg, however, the Emperor Nicholas extended his addresses to other beauties as well. My fair colleague, Charlotte von Hagu, was particularly distinguished by the handsomest man of all the Russias on her professional visit to St. Petersburg, and was also summoned by the Czar to Kalisch when, in 1835, he went to the Princes' Congress there.

The Hereditary Grand-Duchess Alexandrina was in reality "that shining majestic type of woman" of whom Heine enthusiastically writes:—"She resembles those chivalrous ladies reflected with so much loveliness to our imagination from the magic mirror of old fairy tales, and which leave us in doubt as to whether they are saints or amazons. I believe the sight of these pure features has made a better man of me."

It was said that a Dr. Stuhr fell so passionately in love with the beautiful Princess Alexandrina that he went crazy, followed his goddess about step by step, and in all earnest offered himself to the king in writing as his son-in-law. The king had the poor fool put into an asylum.

This "shining majestic type of woman" was specially interesting to me because of her resemblance to Queen Louise. The hereditary grand-duchess, however—whom George IV. of England, "the first gentleman of his time," courted in vain, because Friedrich Wilhelm would have no "*mauvais sujet*" for his son-in-law—was esteemed very proud. We actresses had for her no existence.

Her husband, on the other hand, the "Red Paul," was affability and good nature itself. He was no beauty and did not pass for particularly clever.

The king's youngest daughter, Princess Louise, was sweet, quiet, and lovely like a flower. In May, 1825, by command of his Majesty and through Timm's mediation, I was permitted, along with other favourites of the theatre, to witness the splendid festivities attending the marriage of the Princess Louise with her cousin, Prince Friedrich of the Netherlands. It was remarked by every one that Princess Liegnitz, though the king's consort, took no part in the bridal procession, similar to that of the royal princesses, but trotted after them with her lady-in-waiting and bearing her own train. Nor did she appear at the gala dinner.

On the departure of the newly-married couple to the Netherlands, the king gave them an agreeable surprise by hastening before them another way and anticipating their arrival in Magdeburg. His Majesty, in Magdeburg, had in turn the pleasure of a surprise—from his pet dancers who had also, unknown to him, hastened thither that the king might not there miss his favourite entertainment.

The crown-prince, a stately gentleman, well filled out, of thirty years, showed no liking for us actresses, and was incessantly indulging in sarcasms against his father's predilection for theatrical ladies. Neither he nor his brothers ever spoke to us at the festivals in the palace—the former, it was said, from disinclination, the others from prudence.

The lovely crown-princess, on the other hand, never let an opportunity slip of addressing us a friendly word. And how hearty in doing so sounded her marked Bavarian accent!

Thus she came up to us when, after his death, we played Pius Alexander Wolff's comedy, "Der Mann Von Fünzig Jahren,"* for the first time in the "Palais," and in a friendly tone addressed Amelia Wolff:

"Did it not gladden your heart to see the memory of your late husband, whom we all admired and respected, so honoured in this production of his? The piece pleased me very much. You, dear Wolff, and Ludwig Devrient played to perfection, and Mademoiselle Bauer, too, was charming!"

And when Amelia Wolff, all in tears, kissed the hand of the kind princess, the latter continued, still more feelingly:

"Seeing you conceive and practise your art as indeed a noble art, and not as a trade, it will yet prove a solace to your mourning heart."

I had thus at last the pleasure of being able to admire those wonderful, large, soul-speaking eyes in immediate presence—in truth, the most beautiful I ever gazed on. Even when a child, I had in Baden-Baden been impressed in the distance by those eyes, in much the same way as I was by lofty towers.†

"Ah, dear Lina, what grand models we have here to contemplate and study for the representation of princely personages. It is impossible to imagine action and speech more graceful, more simple—and yet withal so majestic—than we have here in our king's daughter!"

The crown-princess lived in the happiest harmonious wedlock with her dear Fritz, a wedlock of such honest

* "The Man of Fifty Years."
† "Thurmaugen"—literally, "tower-eyes."

affection as is usually to be found only in the middle classes. She was, nevertheless, often in tears, because the blessing of children she so fervently prayed for was denied her.

A charming characteristic trait was told of the crown-princess. When the Prussian crown-prince in his search of a wife came to visit her, she, then Princess Elizabeth of Bavaria, quickly pulled off the high shoe she was in the habit of wearing on one foot to neutralise a limp she otherwise showed, in order that her wooer might not be deceived in respect of this physical flaw. And he took his Eliza in spite of her slight limp—and never rued the bargain!

The Crown-Prince, Prince Wilhelm, his brother, and Prince Friedrich of the Netherlands, I had already, in July, 1819, when a girl of twelve years, seen riding past in a carriage in Carlsruhe. According to the fashion of that time they wore Scottish dust-mantles of blue and green stripes, and in their youthful bloom and spirits pleased me beyond common. In the evening they appeared at the theatre, where Calderon's "Life a Dream," was performed, and then pursued their way to Baden-Baden, where were staying the Bavarian and Swedish royal families, with plenty of daughters to show—an object which, it was said, was not outside the scope of their travels.

Even now in Berlin the handsome, chivalrous-like Prince Wilhelm was being perpetually disposed of matrimonially. One day he was engaged to a Princess of Wurtemberg, next day to the Princess Marianna of the Netherlands, or Princess Maria of Weimar; the following day to the Princess Cecilia of Sweden, with whom as a child I had once danced so gaily. No greater pleasure could Prince Wilhelm have accorded me than to lead home the sweet Cecilia. It was, however, said that Prince Wilhelm would have nothing to do with all those beautiful princesses, and would not marry at all unless he were allowed his ardently-loved Princess Eliza Radziwill—a step forbidden by unfeeling politics and sorry court etiquette.

Was it this passionate, hopeless love which at that time rendered him completely insensible to the beauties of the theatre?. Prince Wilhelm passed by us, cold as ice. And yet I once had the pleasure of speaking to the prince—behind a screen. It was in the spring of 1828, during my professional visit to St. Petersburg. Prince Wilhelm was then staying there on a visit to his sister, the Empress Alexandra. Some conjectured he was there to try and win over the empress-mother in favour of his betrothal to her grand-daughter, Princess Augusta of Weimar, who was also passing the winter with her parents in St. Petersburg. Others, again, were of opinion that his purpose by this visit was to make a last effort in behalf of his alliance with Eliza Radziwill, to which the Empress Alexandra had always been well-affected.

In any case, I arrived in St. Petersburg in March, 1828. In order to ensure my success, it was of the utmost importance that I should make my first appearance in the Winter Palace before the court. This object was, however, beset with great difficulties, as the Empress Alexandra was to leave St. Petersburg three days after my arrival, to spend the spring in the Crimea. All machinery had to be put in motion to make it possible to secure a representation at court in which I might take part. My friend Timm had furnished me with a letter of recommendation to the empress's chief chamberlain, who promised to do his best for me. I had hardly alighted from the travelling coach when, in company with the director of the German theatre, Helmersen, I hastened to the all-powerful gods of the theatre—Prince Wolkonski, Prince Cutaizow, intendant of the German theatre, and Prince Dolgorouki, intendant of the French theatre—and all promised me their furtherance of my wishes.

When, however, the attainment of my object grew ever more questionable, I was advised to seek the mediation of Prince Wilhelm with his imperial sister. I therefore again hastened to the Winter Palace, and through the prince's adjutant, who was an acquaintance of mine, begged an audience of his Highness. This was at once granted me. The prince appeared in the reception-room, and, along with myself, was not a little embarrassed. While I was preferring my request I heard steps,

advancing, and, in my confusion of mind, stepped
behind a large draught-screen. The prince follows me.
In embarrassment we stand face to face with each other,
till I find composure to stammer out my petition. The
prince promises me he will speak to the empress; and
the curious audience behind the screen ends.

Thanks to the prince's mediation, the representation at
the court was realised. I selected the comedy, "Der
Mann im Feuer," * in which shortly before I had won
a great success at Riga. In the precipitate rehearsal in
St. Petersburg, however, my spirits failed me. My colleagues had not so much as learned up the words of their
parts properly; and in their dependence on the reading
of the prompter drawled out beyond endurance a graceful
comedy all liveliness and *esprit*. Nor did the stout
phlegmatic Barlow nor the starveling Wiébe at all fit the
parts, the one of the general, the other of the fiery lover.

In rather desperate humour I finished my toilet that
evening on the pretty stage of the large, magnificent hall
—behind a screen, for dressing-rooms there were none.
I wore white satin with a blond covering, a set of pearls
and a rose in my hair. When I was done I entered the
hall to look more minutely into its decorations, with a
view to diverting my thoughts. All at once a side door
opens, and Prince Wilhelm and the Prince of Orange
stand before me with friendly greetings. With my best
curtsey—such as on one occasion acquired me celebrity
—I expressed my thanks for his Highness's kind recommendation, but also my apprehensions that I should make
a *fiasco* with my defective *ensemble*.

Thereupon the prince said with great kindness :

" Oh, she who pleased so well in Berlin will do herself
no discredit in St. Petersburg. I have already seen you
play in this piece, and admired you."

Nor on this occasion, either, did I make a fool of myself. The empress laughed heartily, and the emperor
warmly applauded me. When, after the close of the
piece, I again went behind my dressing screen, and wiped

---

* "The Man in the Fire."

off the paint, Prince Wolkonski brought me a beautiful golden fillet, with a star of brilliants—"de la part de l'impératrice.'

Afterwards, when in his father's palace at Berlin, Prince Wilhelm would greet me, in crossing my way, a radiant-smile ever passing over his handsome, manly face. He remembered, like me, the embarrassing minutes of the audience behind the screen in the Winter Palace of St. Petersburg.

When in May, next year, I quitted Berlin "to follow other stars in England," as Varnhagen has it, the royal Prussian city was busking itself to celebrate the nuptials of Prince Wilhelm with the fair Princess Augusta of Weimar.

The king's third son, Prince Karl, of whom Heine, in 1822, writes, "that handsome, youthful form, with meek features and lovely clear eyes," was not so shy as his brother Wilhelm. He was of a jolly nature, delighting in all kinds of sport with horses and dogs—and it was asserted that he was not quite so indifferent or alien to the young ballet beauties as might have been (or was intended to be) gathered from his demeanour at the dances in the "Palais."

In readiness of retort and wantonness of wit, the nimble prince was nearly a match for his brother the crown-prince. A capital anecdote is told of him.

The young Prince Karl was paying a visit to Munich and its eccentric King Ludwig I., so devoted to art, the brother-in-law of the Prussian crown-prince. King Ludwig had then the odd whim of trying everybody with conundrums. For example:

"What would you do if you were a dentist?"

The reply to this always came from the king himself, with no little complacency :—

"I should pull out the bad tooth of the time."

Again, "What would you do if you were a diver?"

Answer, "I should plunge into the sea of forgetfulness."

Prince Karl, too, now came in for this practice at the hands of the king. Luckily, however, he had got warn-

ing beforehand, and when, with a highly consequential
air, the question was addressed to him:
"What would you do if you were a dentist?" the
prince, with the utmost gravity, replied:
"Your Majesty, I should—plunge into the sea of forgetfulness."

King Ludwig I. of Bavaria never again tried his conundrums on Prince Karl of Prussia.

With the same successful presumptuousness he cut
through the Gordian knot when hindrances interposed
themselves in the way of his marriage in February, 1827,
with the beautiful and tenderly-loved Princess Maria of
Weimar. The proud mother of the princess, Grand-
Duchess Maria Paulovna, wanted to have the marriage
celebrated in Weimar. King Friedrich Wilhelm, on the
other hand, claimed this honour for Berlin, and no mortal
could see his way through the block thus brought about
by starched etiquette, till the impatient bridegroom cleared
the passage: "In Charlottenburg I was born, baptised,
and confirmed, and have ever vowed that only there should
I be married." And so there the marriage took place, but
in the greatest privacy, the proud mother of the bride
absenting herself from her eldest daughter's wedding
rather than yield precedence to the Crown-Princess of
Prussia.

The princess thus wedded to Karl of Prussia was a
charming young bride, beaming with good spirits and
happiness. At the next performance in the "Palais" she
came up to us, bringing Amelia Wolff hearty greetings
from her old master, Goethe. And many another friendly
word she had to say to us after that.

The king's youngest son, Prince Albrecht, was a long
slip of a lad, blond, and still so young that there was not
much to say about him. Shortly after my leaving Berlin
he married the sweet Princess Marianna of the Netherlands—a luckless marriage!

Princess Liegnitz, showing ever the same marble composure on her blooming countenance, was always a riddle
to me. She was never heard to laugh heartily; her eye
was never seen to flash any emotion. So she appeared at

the festivals in the "Palais," so at the king's side in the carriage, so in the box at the theatre. Was it phlegm? Was it calculated policy, or, according to another theory, the reverse? Did the princess, in her still somewhat equivocal position, feel comfortable or uncomfortable? I know not. The princess never spoke to us actresses.

Prince Friedrich, son of the late Prince Louis and Princess Frederica, Duchess of Cumberland, showed in his whole presence a touch of the ideal, of the loveable and prepossessing. His consort, the unhappy Princess of Anhalt-Bernburg, with delicate, pale face and large, melancholy eyes, already a languishing flower, seldom appeared at court. Had she any presentiment of her dreadful fate?—of the mental darkness, inherited from her mother, which was to overtake her, as it did her unhappy brother, clap her in pitiless solitude in the castle of Ellern, near Düsseldorf, and there keep her to waste away almost all the season of youth, the season which for others means the season of bliss, and bloom, and joy?

The youngest princes at the court of Friedrich Wilhelm III. were the still boyish sons of the Prince and Princess Wilhelm—Adalbert, afterwards husband of the dancer, Theresa Elsler, and Waldemar, whose slim, poetic, youthful appearance was one day to prove so dangerous to a fair daughter of Bettina's, till death snatched him so early from her arms.

Like an altogether ideal figure of romance there emerged now and again, as guest in the Court of Berlin, the Prince of Lucca, a man of bewildering beauty, with dark, burning eyes. He would be sure to disappear suddenly when the great parades began in Spring. The beautiful Italian prince was said to have an unconquerable aversion to mounting a horse and riding in the king's suite.

The young and handsome Duke Wilhelm of Brunswick was also at that time a welcome guest of his Majesty's and an intimate friend of the princes.

On the 14th of December, 1826, there fell like a thunder-clap into this joyous court life the dreadful news that the king, in descending the small iron staircase leading from the apartment of Queen Louise to his study, had slipped and broken his right leg just above the ankle.

All Berlin was plunged into the greatest agitation, and gathered in crowds in front of the palace to learn particulars. People feared the worst for him, seeing he was now fifty-seven years of age. We of the theatre hastened to Timm, whom we found crying. The doctors, however, announced that the fracture of the leg, though it would be slow in healing, was not dangerous. The Princess Liegnitz, at the request of the king, had to take her accustomed drive, and through as many streets as possible, that same day, in order to show the Berliners that they had nothing to fear.

The accident had happened on the same stairs on which the Crown-Princess Louise fell in a fright at the sight of a stranger meeting her, and frustrated her first hopes of becoming a mother.

In the palace were placed open lists, in which sympathising visitors entered their names. The king was never wearied of having the lists read out to him, with their expressions of faithful attachment, often of a genuine Berlin stamp. The king suffered most from *ennui*, being obliged to dispense with his wonted theatrical entertainments in the evening. What a joy to us it was when at length we were told that the following day there would be a performance given before his Majesty in the palace! And when the king, in a wheeled chair, appeared at our rehearsal, with all his old affability, we kissed his hands with tears of joy! And how he was cheered on his first drive out and his first visit to the theatre!

CHAPTER XI.

PRINCE DON JUAN.

WHILE I was yet on the Königstadt stage, and before my entry into the theatre of the Royal Palace, my attention had been arrested by the distinguished presence of a gentleman in general's uniform seated in the royal box; a gentleman of handsome, imposing figure, with striking and interesting features, a head of black curly hair, and eyes dark and brilliant, which pounced on me whenever I appeared on the scene, and never lifted off so long as I was there—eyes all in a glow, looking as though they wanted to devour me.

" Who is that presumptuous starer? " I asked my colleague, Fraulein Weidner.

" Ah! don't you know him? Why, it is Prince August, also called Prince Don Juan, on account of his many gallant adventures. He is the most dangerous man in Berlin. Take care, my fine little flower! "

" But he has not the least resemblance to the handsome blond princes of our king's house. He looks more like a Frenchman."

Whenever Prince August appeared at the theatre, there was ever the same bold staring on the part of his burning eyes, before which mine had instinctively to abase themselves. And the expression of his originally handsome face appeared every time more like that of a satyr, ever more repulsive.

After the first representation in the palace, he came up to us with his satyr-like smile, in the style of some pasha sure of conquest, who takes a review of his slaves to pick out the one to whom he will throw his handkerchief.

He spoke to me alone of all the artistes, and his words drove the blood burning into my face. He praised me— my fair figure, my blooming freshness, my blond hair—

just as a sportsman might his horse. His eyes burned
consumingly on me, and I could feel his hot breath. I was
hardly able to return him a few cold words. I was like to
burst into tears, and the prince passed on with a curious
smile.

. "Lina, Lina, have a care!" said Amelia Wolff to me.
"He has got you in his eye, and it is not usual for Prince
Don Juan to give up his game till once he has run it
down."

I laughed, but felt an oppression of the heart. The
dancers put their heads together, tittered, and looked
mockingly at me.

It was soon known all over Berlin that Prince August
had deemed me worthy of his attentions, and I was warned
on every hand to beware of the arch-roué. I was told
further particulars about him.

His father, Prince Ferdinand, was the youngest and least
distinguished of Frederick the Great's brothers. His
mother, Louise, daughter of the Margrave Frederick
Wilhelm of Brandenburg-Schwedt, had won a name in her
youth for her beauty and numerous gallantries—and in her
declining age for her pride. Her Italian singing-master
she had inspired with so hot a passion that he built himself
a hut on Mount Vesuvius as a remembrance of his inner
state in relation to her. Her express flame, however, was
Count Schmettau, and old Fritz (Frederick the Great) was
in the habit of calling her children " the detestable brood
of Schmettau," for whom his silly brother gathered up
treasures.

The eldest son, Friedrich, died when a blooming stripling. The second was the gifted and unhappy Prince
Louis Ferdinand, who had inherited his mother's hot blood.
The course of his unruly youth was one chain of amours
and debts. His uncle, Prince Heinrich, who died in
Rheinsberg, had made the handsome lad sole heir of his
large fortune, but the light-minded, good-natured young
prince, having been talked over by his family, renounced
his claims in favour of his father, in order to be able to
share his fortunes, later on, with his brother August. It
thus happened that when Prussia's death-daring Achilles

fell, in 1806, on the field of Saalfeld, he left behind him many weeping women and many sorrowing creditors.

Prince Ferdinand died in 1813, and the proud princess in 1820. In her testament this fine princely lady had prescribed, down to the most minute details, all the pomp and ceremony that was to attend her burial—though she failed to insert the merry torchlight dances executed by the people and soldiers on that festive occasion.

Her son, Prince August, was now the richest prince in all the Royal Prussian Court. He came in for a fortune of ten million thalers, besides the beautiful castle of Bellévue in the " Thiergarten."*

In the wars of deliverance Prince August is said to have distinguished himself by his courage and prudence. When twenty-seven years of age he fought at Jena, and in the retreat rode the noble English horse that had carried his brother Louis into death at Saalfeld, the saddle of which was still besprinkled with his brother's blood. In the marshes between Prenzlau and Pasewalk, Prince August, with his adjutant, Von Klausewitz, was taken prisoner by the French, and both were confined, first in Nancy, and then in Soissons.

In the autumn of the following year he gained his liberty, and quitted France, not, however, till he had made that fateful visit to Coppet, and the acquaintance of the lovely Madame Récamier. Klausewitz, writing from Coppet under date 16th August, 1807, says :—

" We are daily here in the society of Madame de Staël. She speaks a great deal in a very interesting way, so that one really never tires of listening to her. The flourishes about art and literature, which one may have picked up, do not, however, serve one any great length in conversation with her, as I see by a living example before me (Prince August), and so, on the whole, I judge it safer to fall back on the *rôle* of a mere listener—a *rôle* that, as I perceive, is not the worst in which a man may figure. The famous Madame Récamier is one of the company—a very common *coquette.*"

---

* Zoological Gardens.

With this "very common coquette," who, however, passed for the finest woman of her day, the ever amorous Prince August speedily struck up the tenderest *affaire de cœur*. They brought it even to the length of betrothal and exchange of rings; the fact of madame's husband being in Paris notwithstanding. Madame de Staël, in the fulness of her loving heart, blessed the union.

The fair Julia, in her perfect simplicity, then writes to her husband requesting his consent to her divorce, in order that she may contract a morganatic marriage with the handsome Prince August. Monsieur Récamier grants his spouse the desired token of his complaisance, but reminds his Julia how she was a Catholic and the prince Protestant; how the prince was not allowed to marry without the consent of the King of Prussia; and how awkward she might find her position in the proud Court of Berlin. And who, moreover, would be surety that the prince, notorious for his many amours, would keep faithful to her?

The affair, therefore, stuck for the present at the betrothal and the reciprocation of the tenderest love. Madame Récamier has often testified how the handsome Prince August of Prussia was her only passionate love. In October, 1807, after living nearly three months together in Coppet, the lovers had to part—the prince to return to the Prussian Court at Königsberg, Madame Récamier to her husband at Paris, where, however, she got herself painted in bathing costume—if costume it was—for her beloved prince, by the hand of the famous Gerard.

The prince acknowledging the picture, writes passionately from Königsberg, under date 24th April, 1808:

"How can I express the rapture that thrilled me on reading your letter and then contemplating your sweet image! Whole hours I stand before this ravishing picture, and paint me out a bliss transcending every delight imagination can conceive. What human bliss can compare with the sublime feeling of being loved by a creature like you! You know from my former letter with what impatience I await your answer, which will decide the question of my departure for Aix-la-Chapelle."

The meeting in Aix-la-Chapelle did not come off for the present, any more than it did in Carlsbad or Teplitz, whither next the love-sick prince so often and so impetuously invited his fair Julia. The prince flies to a rendezvous at Schaffhausen, but there, too, his beloved fails him, forbidden by Napoleon to leave France! Not till the victorious sojourn of the prince in Paris, in 1814 and 1815, did the lovers meet again, as, subsequently, in 1818, during the Congress of Aix-la-Chapelle, whither Julia also came at the bidding of her lover. There the prince's equipage and two mounted torch-bearers were seen standing for hours together in front of Madame Récamier's residence.

There, however, the love affair came to its end. The prince had by that time long been turning his heart to the worship of other goddesses.

That picture of the fair Julia just emerged from her bath I have seen in Berlin. The prince sent it to a public exhibition of pictures, where, as might have been expected, it rather served to draw out the stinging wit of the Berliners.

Madame Récamier drew a pension from Prince August. His portrait adorned her writing table in the Abbaye aux Bois, near Paris, till her death.

In my time among the hundred other amours of Prince August in Berlin there were two recognised sultanas. One, Mademoiselle Wichman, created by the king Countess Waldenburg, whose two daughters, the eccentric Countesses Waldenburg, had even *entrée* to the royal balls; the other, Mademoiselle Arens, a very beautiful Jewess, with splendid dark eyes and brilliant black hair, raised by the king, along with her sons, to the rank of the nobility under the name of Von Prillwitz—from a fine estate in the Neumark which the prince made over to his mistress.

It was a special wonder that the virtuous King Friedrich Wilhelm III., otherwise so strict in the matter of morals, should thus by public recognition sanction these amours of Prince August.

And now I was to be raised to the position of third recognised sultana of the prince.

After pestering me by his importunitiés at all theatrical performances in the "Palais," he came one evening on foot with his adjutant to our dwelling. What torture my mother and I had to endure that hour! What humiliation, what disgrace! And yet we dared not show our admirer, with his hankering appetite, exactly to the door—seeing he was a royal prince and cousin to his Majesty, and I a royal actress! In that hour I, indeed, felt most bitterly the degradation and danger of my situation as public actress!

When they at last went away, our honest landlord heard the prince say to his adjutant on the stairs: "And yet this young prude of a thing must be mine, though it should cost me a hundred thousand thalers!"

In what excitement—in what despair were my mother and I left!

Next morning a messenger brought us wonderful plants in pots, with large, white, splendid bell-flowers, which dispensed a peculiarly sweet narcotic perfume.

"From whom?" asked my mother of the bringer.

He showed us a card without name, with the words: "The most ardent admirer of beauty would not like to be named—but guessed!"

"Take the flowers back—we receive presents only from known friends," said my mother, and away went messenger, flowers, and perfume.

At Hofrath Henn's in Clauren, my mother and I had made the acquaintance of a highly elegant and very musical lady, who came up to us in the most ingratiating manner, and begged to be allowed to visit us. She was called "Madame Cracau," and we knew nothing more of her.

She came and overwhelmed us with her civilities. We sometimes played together à quatre mains.

One day Madame Cracau brought us a whole basketful of magnificent ornaments, asking me to choose what I like. By doing so I would give great pleasure to an admirer of high rank.

"Prince August!" I exclaimed involuntarily.

Madame Cracau smiled expressively, and gushed into praise of the handsome, chilvalrous, magnanimous prince.

" We can make no use of these trinkets, and earnestly beg of you to spare us such presents in future," said my mother, very decidedly.

After madame had tried all her arts of flattery in vain to induce us to accept them, she begged we would, at least, allow her to leave them with us in the meantime, as she had a visit she must make and could not drag the heavy basket with her.

We were good-natured and simple enough not to refuse her this request: My mother cleared a drawer in the commode, locked the basket of ornaments in it and gave Madame Cracau the key—which she took only after much resistance.

But Madame Cracau never returned.

Meanwhile letters on letters arrived, in which his Royal Highness explained his intentions in an ever more distinct and business-like manner.   He offered for my possession 100,000 thalers, and ultimately as much as 200,000, a furnished house in Berlin, and the title of baroness.   The king would give his consent, and I should live with my mother in Berlin in great honour.   My children should be recognised.

To all this my mother's sole reply was to let us alone; till, at last, she threatened to invoke the king's protection.

The epistolary love-tenders on the part of the prince then stopped; but not his underground devices to the same end.

We repeatedly wrote to Madame Cracau to take away the trinkets !   She did not answer.   One morning, coming from rehearsal in the opera house, I ran up against the elegant lady Unter den Linden.   I could not but suppose she had been waiting for me.

She met me with all her old air of friendliness, and begged to be excused for not having yet fetched away the trinkets.   She was frightened at my mother's severe looks and the bad grace in which she herself stood in my mother's regard, because of her too great complaisance towards a gentleman of exalted rank, who yet, when all was said, was uncommonly amiable.   If, however, I would

do her the great favour of going with her the two or three
steps that would bring us to her house, she would then
give me the key of the commode and beg me to send her
the things.

Madame Cracau knew how to chat away so innocently
and play the penitent so sweetly that she soon hushed all
my scruples to rest. Unreflecting as I always was, ever
yielding to the impulse of the moment, I guilelessly followed the flattering enticement of the skilled bird-catcher
into her snare. She led me to the Neue Wilhelmstrasse, and
into her very elegant ground-floor apartments, where I
again saw those exotic flowers, with the large, white,
shining cups and the narcotic odour, which had before so
offended us. She asserted they came from Bouché's
flower-garden. In vain I pressed about leaving. The
amiable lady had so many flattering things to tell me about
my last *rôle*, and so much that was interesting about her
travels, while, at the same time, she produced so many
charming engravings and nick-nacks for my entertainment, that I was fairly caught.

A carriage drove up. Madame rose, opened a grand
Vienna piano, and requested me to try a few notes on the
instrument till she had brought the key. She disappeared
into the adjoining room. I there, on the opening of the
door, caught a glimpse of a little richly-decked breakfast-
table, with champagne cups and silver ice-coolers.

With a levity of mind which is to-day inexplicable to
me, I yielded to the allurement of the grand piano, first
striking out a few chords standing, and then, carried away
by melodious fancies, I sat down, lost to every other
feeling but that of the music, when all at once I heard
the door of the side room gently open. A look that way,
and my fingers slipped with a shrill dissonance from the
keys!

Prince August entered, and approached with the smile
of a satyr sure of conquest. At the same time I heard the
door, through which I had entered the room from the passage, softly locked from without. Two steps more, and
Prince Don Juan had held me in his arms.

Though, as a rule, I am very easily intimidated, I

was at that moment surprised by a strange courage—the courage inspired by desperate fear. With a loud scream for help I sprang up, threw the heavy piano-stool at the prince's feet, rushed to the window, overturned the flowerpots as I pulled it open, and, with a cry, jumped into the street, before the disconcerted pursuer was able to catch hold of my dress.

This was all the act of a moment—thanks to the leaping exercises I had been used to when a child, and the climbing practice I had had in parts such as that of the wanton page, Paul von Husch, etc.

In the greatest excitement, without hat or shawl, I hurried, almost senseless, from the Neue Wilhelmstrasse to the Linden, through crowds of neighbours and passers-by, who assailed me with shouts and questions, till luckily I ran up against, and almost knocked over, our trusty friend Justizrath Ludolff, who was quite stupefied to find me in such a plight.

In two words I communicated to him the gist of the matter, and then for the first time the tears burst from my eyes. Ludolff called a cab to free me from the ever more importunate and inquisitive crowd. We got in, when Ludolff cried to the driver, "The king's palace," and we drove off.

On the way I had to tell my friend the story, with all the particulars. He advised me to go direct to Timm and to beg the king for an audience and for protection against Prince August. He (Ludolff) would at once lodge information at the court against the dangerous Madame Cracau.

Timm tried at first to quiet me. I should have consideration for the king, who had always been so kind to me; the whole court would be compromised by this scandal.

I was, however, beside myself, and not to be quieted, so that Timm had to go to the king and report the matter. The king, in great excitement, came into the audience chamber, and I had to repeat my story in full detail.

In the course of my narrative, the king repeatedly exclaimed:

"Infamous—horrible—*mauvais sujet*—disgrace—be

quiet, Lina—you will have compensation—let justice go its course—but I beg, spare the prince—for my sake."

I gratefully kissed the hand of Friedrich Wilhelm the Just, and hastened to my mother, who was yet all unwitting of the affair.

On calm reflection we should willingly have waived making a legal case of the scandal, if that had been still possible. The story, however, ran like fire through the whole town—with great exaggerations, of course. My call for help, and my jump from the window, had been witnessed by too many people. Ludolff had already lodged the information with the court and police, and so all my friends advised me not to stay judicial proceedings and the rehabilitation of my reputation.

The process, therefore, went its odious, exciting course. Madame Cracau was arrested. My mother and I were repeatedly heard as witnesses against her. It occasioned us no little vexation and trouble.

Cracau acquitted herself very cleverly. She sought to represent everything as a joke and an unlucky accident and to scour the prince completely white. For the rest, in anticipation of the prince's solatium, she meekly took all the blame on herself, calculating that the prince would know how to protect her.

All the same, damning revelations were brought out. Madame Cracau had in her youth been the mistress of Prince August, and became afterwards his compliant confidante. The house she lived in belonged to the prince. The two sculptors Wichmann, brothers of the Countess Waldenburg, had their studio in the house.

At our request the commode containing the trinkets was opened by a police officer, and the untouched basket of valuables handed in to the court.

Madame Cracau got off with a comparatively lenient sentence of imprisonment.

Prince August was treated to a short moral lecture from the king, after which he went on a tour of inspection as general of artillery, and at the end of it took his repose in Rheinsberg with his latest mistress, a little actress from the Königstadt Theatre.

When he returned to Berlin, the king, as Timm reported to me, said to him:

"Leave Bauer alone—decent girl—do not like it—no scandal—there has been talk enough already among the people—mischievous!"

Prince August—of whose latest *liaison* with the beautiful Ballerina Fourcisi all Berlin was soon full—left me alone henceforward of his love—but persecuted me all the more cruelly with his hate. He systematically sought to undermine my reputation as actress and as woman. He was indefatigable in spreading about evil reports of me.

When I had the misfortune to take the "false Count Samoilow" for a genuine count—a mistake which I shared with the half of Berlin—Prince Don Juan was loud in his exultation, and covered "Madame la Comtesse de Samoilow" with mockery and derision.

It was due mostly to the hatred and revenge of Prince August that I was driven from Berlin—to take shelter in a new misfortune.

This new misfortune was Prince Leopold of Coburg, whom I saw at court for the first time during a theatrical representation.

I had not yet, however, followed this new "fortune"—as people then called it, and I so fondly hoped it would prove—to England, when the worst calumnies about me were brought to the ears of Prince Leopold—from Prince August of Prussia.

CHAPTER XII.

MY happy season of youth in Berlin from 1824 to 1829 was also the richest for me in successes on the stage and in society, and in the abundance and range of the admirers of my blooming presence, its exuberant spirits and radiant art. These admirers may be grouped in three classes—social, æsthetic, and amorous.

The social life of the old Berlin of half a century ago was of the most gay and animated description. People sought and found in society compensation for the felt want of the public life of a political capital. And the little town of Berlin, as it then was—scarcely a fifth as large as the imperial capital of to-day, with its million people—imposed on this social life such an intimate and familiar character as is usually found only in a small provincial town. Everybody knew everybody, and came with everybody on every occasion to every place. And it was quite possible for such brisk social life to go on then, for society did not at that time make such pretensions as it now does. Nobody expected of another sumptuous and costly entertainment, luxurious drawing rooms, magnificent toilettes. A person might appear in the same dress at no end of parties without drawing uncomplimentary reflections on himself, and we felt ourselves supremely blessed with the light of a few sorry tallow candles that had to be incessantly trimmed by "snuffers" (a depth of sordidness hardly intelligible to the younger readers of to-day); and under this brilliant illumination we drank our cup of tea and ate our thin Berlin roll and butter from tables of birch-wood or fir, as special favourites of fortune.

One of the most hospitable, comfortable, elegant, and interesting houses was that of Justizrath Ludolff, who in winter occupied his handsome residence Unter den

Linden, and in summer his charming villa in the Thiergarten. He was a cheerful, talented and pleasure-loving
man, enthusiastic about art, artists, and—*artistes*. Indeed,
the truly amiable man ultimately fell a sad victim of the
" Sontag* contagion " then raging in Berlin.

I had hardly attained to a little celebrity in Berlin,
when Ludolff became one of my warmest admirers and
protectors—in all honour, be it understood. I was not
allowed to absent myself from any of the gay and even
brilliant festivities which this Mæcenas of exuberant parts
and vivacity arranged with artistic grace in his house, in
his garden, in some public place of entertainment, or in an
excursion to Treptow,† to the Pichelsbergen,† or to the then
celebrated Pfaueninsel,† with its wild beasts, rare flowers,
and the royal giant.

In honour of Ludolff's birth-day I once played in the
" Savoyards " along with his young nephew, Alexander
Cosmar, who afterwards acquired a name as journalist
and dramatist, and two charming Mesdemoiselles von
Winterfeld, before a brilliant company in his villa in the
Thiergarten. To crown the festival its queen, Henrietta
Sontag, emerged, as the most charming of floral fairies,
out of a gigantic flower-basket, and sang a song of homage
to our host with her sweet, bird-like voice.

In honour, again, of the adored Henrietta, Ludolff gave
a fairy ball in the winter of 1825-26, in the mirror-hall of
Fuchs's, the confectioner, Unter den Linden, then the most
brilliant place of entertainment in Berlin, designed and
decorated according to the happy plans of Schinkel. For
weeks beforehand the whole of Berlin talked of this
" event," and all the fair devotees of Terpsichore lived in
a fever of suspense till they were certain whether or not
they might count themselves among the happy few who
would receive invitations to this highly-select festival of
fairies. For, on account of the limited space, only thirty
pairs of dancers were to be invited; and it was known

---

* Sontag (Henrietta Sontag), a famous actress of that time, with
whose celebrity that of Sarah Bernhardt of the present day may
perhaps in some slight measure correspond.
† Favourite resorts of the Berliners.

that Ludolff would try by the strictest court the beauty and grace of all having any pretensions to be admitted to so exclusive a heaven. I found favour in the eyes of the court, and so became one of the elect thirty.

At length the great evening arrived. The celebrated mirror-hall—the walls, doors, and ceiling of which consisted purely of mirrors and gorgeously-gilded stucco—sparkled with hundreds of fragrant wax tapers, reflected thousand-fold on all sides. At all corners and in the window-niches were shimmering groups of flowers, and, between, dancing youth and beauty in toilettes that would fain surpass the beauty of the flowers.

How enchantingly beautiful was the sylph-like Henriettá Sontag, radiating joy; her fragrant toilette of white silk tulle, embroidered with green leaves and tendrils, over white satin, a set of emeralds and white roses in her hair.

The two lovely but poor Mesdemoiselles von Winterfeld had on charming Parisian toilettes, white crape with light blue asters, which they had received anonymously—from the generous host, Ludolff.

I wore iris gauze, with garlands of rosebuds and guelder roses, and a similar ornament in the hair.

We were, however, all outshone by the luminous Junonian beauty and magnificent toilette of the former solo-dancer, Röhnisch, whom a rich landed proprietor had decoyed from the stage. She wore *drap d'argent* adorned with pomegranate flowers, and like flowers in her light brown locks. The brilliance of her beautiful deep-blue eyes rivalled the lustre of her diamond-sparkling attire. Mademoiselle Röhnisch had been trained as a dancer along with the fair Mademoiselle Vestris, afterwards Madame Hoguet, in Paris, at the king's cost, but was soon lost to the boards. This fairy ball continued to be long talked of in Berlin, and Ludolff swam in a sea of rapture and—debts, though this latter fact was yet all unknown.

However much amiability and self-sacrifice Ludolff showed on behalf of his *protégées*, his adoration was occasionally dashed by points in his bearing not altogether enjoyable—a fact I was also to experience, along with the idolised Henrietta. He asserted for himself an unlimited guardianship over us in all matters temporal and spiritual. Nothing durst be done without his approval; no starring engagement entered into, no contract concluded, no new part studied, almost no visit paid or received until it had first obtained the blessing of our Mæcenas. And how in all such matters he could nettle and prickle his *protégée* without having himself, in his perfect feeling of patronage, any inkling of the pain he gave!

Ludolff visited us almost daily to play *à quatre mains* or talk with me. It was a relaxation to him after the rather tedious sittings at court. By a remarkable whim of chance he almost regularly found mother and me at dinner, and his remarks, uttered in all inoffensiveness and friendship, were not always an agreeable seasoning to our repast, but rather like so many grains of biting cayenne pepper strewn with all apparent or actual innocence on our entertainment.

"Do you know, poor child, that the villanous Saphir, in his to-day's *Schnellpost*,* has cut you up terribly as *Kätchen of Heilbronn?*"

"No; I read only friendly notices brought me by well-wishing friends. Saphir is, besides, known to all the world for a malicious, venal critic, whom artists serve only as a means by which he may fill his purse, or as objects for his prickly, biting wit. And it was first in the part of *Kätchen* that I was applauded by the whole house in the most friendly manner, and even called at the end. The venom of *one* spiteful quill cannot do much harm."

"And yet! and yet! The public is only too easily carried away by Saphir's dazzling wit. I felt enraged at the effrontery of this scribbling bandit. You know very well how much I take your side—I, your warmest admirer and sincerest friend. And it will annoy you, too, when you read this last libel. Here is the number of the *Schnellpost*. I bought it expressly for you."

"O, Herr Justizrath, you are *too* kind!"

"Not at all! But, *à propos*, have you noticed that your most faithful adorer on the right corner seat of

* *Express.*

the second row of the parquet, who never used to miss a
night at the theatre when you appeared, has grown un-
faithful to you?"

"Lovely Donna, let him go, he is not worthy of thy
scorn!"* But for all that, my singing and laughing did not
come quite free from my heart.

"Yes, the faithless one may now be seen every evening,
in the seat he has engaged for the season in the Königs-
stadt Theatre, worshipping the beautiful Julia Holzbecher
—or do you not think her beautiful?"

"Assuredly; she is a charming creature."

"But you are annoyed all the same—I see you are."

"No; but *you* annoy me every noon with your un-
edifying conversation. It is really a pet passion of yours."

Therewith he would dash off in high dudgeon, leaving
us in bad humour. To make matters worse, his wife
would generally come rushing to us shortly after, re-
proaching us for having embittered his precious leisure
hour following the weary court sittings.

Next day, when we were both anticipating a relief, we
would hear "kling-ling-ling," and my "warmest admirer"
would again step in with some fresh novelty to spoil both
humour and appetite. And yet if I had then had any foreboding of the sad fate which in a few years was to overtake
our talented art-enthusiast, I would have borne his often
vexatious admiration with greater complaisance.

Ludolff brought himself to ruin for the sake of art and
artistes, and especially of the adored Henrietta Sontag.
When the large fortune he inherited and increased by
the splendid practice he gained at the bar, had been all
squandered away in extravagant hospitalities and often
senseless devotion to art, and when the unhappy man at
length saw no escape from his creditors, he suddenly
vanished out of Berlin without leaving any trace of whither
he had gone. After some time a rumour got up that his
corpse had been found in the Rhine; but I have never learnt
anything for certain respecting the end of this unhappy
man, in whose house I spent so many pleasant hours.

---

* A theatrical quotation.

CHAPTER XIII.

PROFESSOR RAUPACH.

AMONG the dramatic authors of the Berlin of those days, Ernst Raupach ruled as unlimited tyrant of the stage. And how I hated the harsh, morose, ugly tyrant, who never had a good word to say to me nor a kind look to spare me, nor, apparently, in all his pieces one good part to assign me!

As if he had been snowed down from the sky, Raupach suddenly appeared in Berlin in the autumn of 1824, and his tragedies of "Die Fürsten Chewanski,"* and "Die Erdennacht,"† having already had a successful run on the Berlin stage, he at once became an object of universal attention, and all the more so when the Berliners became acquainted with him personally, with his shocking ugliness and repellent harshness.

Raupach was but forty years old when I first saw him, but had by that time already passed an eventful life. As son of a country parson, he studied theology in Halle; and when a youth of but nineteen, his character had taken its pronounced form of abruptness and bitterness for life. In acute consciousness of his personal ugliness and unloveableness, the young student writes with a touching candour to his elder brother, a teacher in St. Petersburg:—

"When my boyish days were over, if I had only found a friend and adviser in whom I could have reposed my whole confidence, I should assuredly have grown up into a sincere and active friend of my fellow-man. I had indisputably a good heart, deep and vehement feelings, ready to shed tears of compassion for every misfortune, however far removed from me, and energetic also to

---

* "The Princes Chewanski."   † "The Night of Earth."

help others, even beyond my ability. If now I had had a friend like-minded with myself, who would have cherished these feelings in me, I would gradually have outgrown all the childish element that might still cling to them, and the succeeding gravity of maturer age would have doubtless confirmed me into a genuine man. But such a friend was not given me, and I became ridiculed and mocked for these sentiments of mine. This drove me back on myself. I began to be ashamed of my humane feelings, and to despise the men who ridiculed me on account of them. I thus gradually began to deem myself better than others, and the contempt I cherished for many imperceptibly extended to still more, and at last to almost all of my own age. I took no trouble to come near them and acquire their love. I have, therefore, down to the present day, never had a true friend, nor learnt the art of gaining such. The respect of others I well know how to procure myself, but never their love. Nobody loved me, I loved nobody. Love, however, is a necessity for man. I therefore loved —myself. So, at least, I explain to myself my unlimited self-love, especially at that time."

When twenty years of age, Ernst Raupach, like his brother, went as tutor to Russia. He lived in Moscow and St. Petersburg. In his leisure he composed, in genuine youthful enthusiasm: "Die Fürsten Chewanski," "Die Matrone von Ephesus,"* "Die Erdennacht." "I compose," he wrote at that time, "because I want to enjoy my life. All enjoyment of the soul consists in the exercise of its energies. The highest exercise, and, consequently, also the highest enjoyment, is creation, the production of what has not yet been, for such is a kind of imitation of the Godhead. Of all human creations, however, those of the poet most approach the creations of eternity, for they are least subject to the limitations of the terrestrial."

As Professor in St. Petersburg University, Raupach married a beautiful, amiable governess, Cæcilia von Wildermuth, of Switzerland. After but one year of

---

* "The Matron of Ephesus."

wedded life he became a widower, and by this stroke of fate was rendered only the more bitter and misanthropic. St. Petersburg had become hateful to him. Raupach went to Italy, and there, while the Congress of Verona was sitting, wrote "Lebrecht Hirsemenzels, eines deutschen Schulmeisters, Briefe aus und über Italien," * full of wit and satire. This name of "Hirsemenzel" stuck hatefully to poor Raupach, in Immermann's "Münchhausen."

In his full consciousness of being a poet Raupach wanted to settle in Weimar, that he might there divide the empire of Parnassus with Goethe. The gray Prince of Poets received the angular, unbeautiful, unpolished Hirsemenzel Raupach, who yet defiantly flourished his poetical abilities, with an air of such inaccessible distance and cold reserve that in resentment the new claimant turned his back on the proud Ilm city of the muses. He, however, left behind him in Weimar, as the fruit of a fugitive love-affair, a little daughter, who, from the drama of her father, received and retained the nickname of "The Daughter of the Air."

In more savage humour than ever Raupach therefore came to Berlin in the fall of 1824.

He first went to the Theatre Bureau and handed the secretary, Teichmann, the MS. of a comedy, which was at once returned him, as being written in too small and illegible characters.

Discharging some spleen at the members of the Bureau, Raupach turned away scornfully, minded to quit the thankless Berlin and its theatre, likewise, for ever, when the pliant Esperstedt, guessing who the unmannerly stranger was, ran after him, and, with a thousand apologies, begged back the illegible MS. It was the comedy "Lasst die Todten ruhn," † in which I had to play the pitiful subordinate part of *Eliza*. Raupach stayed in Berlin accordingly, and soon worked himself up to the position of autocrat of the Berlin stage, tyrannising over every one: king and court, theatre intendant, managers, actors, and public.

---

* "Letters of Lebrecht Hirsemenzel, a German Schoolmaster, from and on Italy."
† "Let the Dead rest."

This unconstitutional dictatorship—such as surely no dramatist ever before wielded on the stage—Raupach gained at one stroke, by his tragedy of "Isidor and Olga," which produced such tremendous effect in March, 1825, carrying all Berlin in a storm of commotion with it, and which had to be repeated countless numbers of times. The universal interest in the piece was intensified by the report, which soon got abroad, that in "Isidor and Olga" the poet had written out a sad event which had actually occurred in Russia, and of which he himself had been witness. It was a deep cutting stroke delivered at the accursed serfdom of "Holy Russia."

And with what perfection, with what overmastering power was the tragedy played! Madame Stich appeared milder and more youthfully tender than seemed elsewhere compatible with the acrid twang of her nature. How she electrified the audience by the one passionate word to the prince, "Ich lieb' ihn ja!" (I do love him!)

Krüger rendered the prince in a flaming glow of delirious passion, magnificently voiced by his grand, sonorous tones.

Pius Alexander Wolff was a noble sympathetic *Isidor*, now moving the audience to tears, now inspiring horror and revulsion; in every case arresting, chaining, and carrying his audience resistlessly along with him. In the main scene, in his struggle with the horrors of Russian serfdom, how he convulsed the audience with insuperable dread. To the present day I still hear the poor *Ossip* (Devrient) trodden under foot, robbed of all his life's happiness, degraded to the post of a buffoon—I still hear him in this humiliation tell his tale to *Fedor*, in the manner of an embittered and maddened demon—till he comes to speak of his love for *Axinia*, and then his rich warm heart breaks out like the sun from amid the clouds, and dissolves in tearful words: "My Axinia had eyes like violets, so sweet and blue. So often as I have since seen violets I must needs weep. She died when she was to bring forth my child. Thanks to God, she took it to the grave with her. One serf less—Fedor, why dost thou not laugh at the buffoon Ossip?"

E

I, too, was carried away by " Isidor and Olga," but had
to lament that Raupach did not seem even to think of me
in the allotment of its beautiful and effective parts.

With surprising swiftness Raupach followed up "Isidor
and Olga" in the next three years by a host of tragedies
and comedies. But never was any but at best only an
insignificant *rôle* assigned to me.

Raupach was in truth strikingly ugly. A long, thin,
ungraceful figure in slovenly clothes; spider-like arms
and legs, with tremendous hands and feet. The angular
head bristled with thick, erect, unkempt hair, like a brush,
the forehead was low, the nose plump, the lips like blood
sausages, the eyes having that "false look" which makes
it impossible to tell whither they are directed.

One day I said mockingly to Madame Dötsch:

" Did you ever see an uglier man than this professor?
I once saw an idol roughly hewn out of a block of wood,
called Vitzliputzli. Whenever I see Raupach I must needs
think of Vitzliputzli."

" But still he is a learned man, and writes such beautiful
pieces, and ever mourns the death of his sweet spouse,
whom he lost after such short happiness."

" Ah, she died so soon assuredly only of Vitzliputzli!
The very thought of those long spider arms embracing,
and those sausage lips kissing, me, would be the instant
death of me, from pure horror."

" If I reported that to the professor?"

" No matter! Worse parts Vitzliputzli cannot give
me," I answered, in desperation. " And, besides, I think
of leaving a stage where the right of seniority rules as
despotically as in the army."

But how I was to be punished for my arrogance and
injustice! How terribly was Vitzliputzli to be revenged
on me!

Soon after this scene, I sat one evening, during the performance of " Rafaele," alone in the green-room, awaiting
my strangulation in the last act. I was, for other reasons
also besides those referred to, dispirited and thoughtful.

So sitting, I was roused out of my dreamy reflections
by a friendly voice:

" Why is *Ikelula* so sad ? "

I started up in fright. Raupach stood before me.

" And *you*, Herr Professor, does it please *you* to take note of my sadness, or of me at all ? " I answered, with irritation.

"Certainly. I have long been watching your painful brooding. You were wont to be so merry. And why should I—I, in particular—not take note of it ? "

" Because, altogether, I do not seem to exist for you—and your good parts," I blurted out.

"You think so ? " he said snappishly, drawing up doses of snuff vehemently all the while. " You may, for all, be mistaken. I follow your fine, gay talent with great interest."

" And let this 'fine, gay talent' play the dreariest parts, such as this miserable *Ninias*, and this insipid, sorry *Ikelula*," I said, laughing savagely.

" And yet were you not called before the curtain as *Ikelula* in the first performance ? " he said, with utmost composure.

" Only from sympathy, to be sure, because I was strangled. The public wanted to see the famous *Ikelula* once more alive. And yet you, then, Herr Professor, found fault with *Ikelula's* death-cry as not quite natural. Herr Director Weiss repeated the censure to me. As though I could know how people cried when being strangled ! I have never yet had any experience of it."

" Ay, ay, ay, my little spitfire, you are getting quite beside yourself ! " interjected the insufferable Vitzliputzli, with his rough, dry laugh.

I, however, blazed into wilder passion than ever.

" Yes, you laugh—that is quite like you—and my heart is like to break because you systematically ruin my talent and my position on the royal stage. You are unjust, Herr Professor, for you do not consider that young talents must push ahead. You are partial, for you write beautiful, graceful parts for older established actresses. Would it do any harm to Madame Stich or Madame Unzelmann if you now and again let me, too, get a thankful *rôle* by which I could test and further my talents ? Yet it gives you pleasure to present me to disadvantage before the public in the paltriest, pitiablest and most ridiculous parts! You do me wrong. But I will bear it no longer; so much I am due to myself and family. My brother Karl has, besides, again undone a horse with riding, and I am to raise another —the third this year—and my fee 1200 thalers. No, I shall beg his Majesty for my discharge, and go to St., Petersburg, where a starring engagement with a view to a permanent contract is offered me, and then I shall need to play no *Niniases* and no *Ikelulas* "—loud sobbing choked my voice.

Taking a gigantic pinch of snuff, he said with emphasis:

" Glad to see that your blithe temperament is capable also of passionate excitement, for in the three—new— beautiful parts I have assigned you——"

" What, do you presume so far as to make mock of me?" I struck in, vehemently.

" But wait a moment, will you, till-I'm done, you sputtering saltpetre!" harshly exclaimed Vitzliputzli. " Well, then, in the three—new—beautiful parts I mean to assign you—that of *Malvina* in my new play of " Vater und Tochter;"* *Countess Flora von Tourelles* in the comedy of " Ritterwort,"† and *Miss Matilda Lindsay* in my " Royalisten," ‡ some sparks of feeling and their passionate expression will serve you in good stead."

" Three beautiful—new—parts—assigned to me—really to me, you all-golden Herr Professor? How shall I thank you? O do now, over and above, prove to me that you pardon me my rudeness off-hand, by kindly going through with me the three—new—beautiful parts."

" To be sure—with all my heart. But *Ikelula* is called for on the stage!"

For certain no *Ikelula* ever died with so much pleasure as I let myself be strangled that evening.

And peace was struck between Raupach and me—for ever. We never afterwards met in the theatre or in company but he had always a kind word, an instructive hint, a good advice for the young personator of human

---

* "Father and Daughter." † "Knight's Word." ‡ "Royalists."

beings—and I had no more remembrance of Vitzliputzli and his ugliness. If anybody had said to me " Raupach is beautiful as Apollo" I believe I should have taken the observation for the most natural thing in the world.

When, then, the parts were written out, and *Malvina* and the *Countess Flora von Tourelles* were in my happy hands, Raupach came to our house to tea one evening to go through the pieces with me. I was astonished to find the professor so trimly dressed. He wore a blue dress coat with gold buttons, in the newest fashion, irreproachable gloves, punctilously-tied white cravat, stand-up collar, stiffer and higher than ever—and the bristly mop itself dressed and pomaded—all like a young lieutenant—or wooer.

At the tea table Raupach was as mild and tame and amiable as was possible for such a morose and reserved nature as his. His icy grimness thawed ever more and more.

I then recited to him my part of *Malvina* in the play of " Vater und Tochter," adapted from an English novel. When I closed the passionate concluding scene, the dramatist exclaimed : " Bravo ! Bravo ! " and in the public performance the audience confirmed this applause.

I was quite in love, too, with my part of *Flora von Tourelles* in " Ritterwort." Raupach had written the play, and particularly the dumb knight, for Pius Alexander Wolff when he was lying ill of throat-consumption and not allowed to speak, and yet longed so much to tread the boards again. His strength, however, proved unequal even for this dumb part, and the play lay unacted till after the death of the artist. On the 3rd November, 1828, it was brought on the stage for the first time—with thundering applause. The dumb knight was rendered with simplicity and dignity by Rebenstein ; the heartless coquette, who extorted the vow from the knight not to speak for so many years, was given by Madame Unzelmann. I appeared at first in charming page costume, hovering around the beloved knight as his guardian angel. The scene in which I picture to myself how the voice of the revered man would sound, if he were not dumb, was especially well received—" Like the song of the nightingale warbling sweet notes of love?—No, it would peal like the rolling thunder."

And Raupach's visits to us became more and more frequent, while he declared freely and frankly that he felt himself uncommonly happy at our friendly tea-table with mother and me; and I, too, on my side, found the odd hypochondriac, in whom a rough husk concealed a noble kernel, growing ever more amiable.

In the spring of 1829, Raupach went through the part of *Matilda Lindsay*, in his "Royalisten," with me.   In the course of this exercise, he one evening spoke sorrowfully of his sweet, saintly spouse, now resting for so many years by the distant Neva, of her naïvely blithe nature, her simplicity, her dark locks, deep-blue eyes, and sweet flower-like face.

"O, how fair and lovely must your Cæcilia have been —and how"—I stopped short in embarrassment.

With a smile, half-waggish, half-pathetic, Raupach took me up:

"And how could so dear a creature marry such an old, nasty, morose block of an idol as Vitzliputzli!   Yes, you are right!   But love is blind—and I did not make my Cæcilia unhappy!"

I sat burning with shame and penitence.   I then started up and clasped Raupach cordially in my arms, pleading with tears in my eyes:

"Let bygones be bygones.   Forgive the thoughtless word of the childish Lina and passionate *artiste*, who fancied herself kept in the background by you, and who now likes you so dearly."

I felt a cordial kiss on my forehead, and the long arms heartily embracing me, while a voice, touched with feeling, whispered in my ear:

"And you are not really dead on account of these spider arms touching you; and I may, perhaps, be allowed to—hope."

I had the greatest desire to answer, modifying the words of *Francisca* in " Minna von Barnhelm " :

" ' Herr Professor—Herr Professor—do you want no blonde Frau Professorin ? ' "

But my fate was already cast—I was already destined elsewhere.

My prudent mother interrupted this scene of confessions of the heart by a refrigerating jest.

On the 9th April, 1829, I played with delight and applause, along with Ludwig Devrient and Amelia Wolff, in the ." Royalisten." Only twice more was it vouchsafed me to play the beloved part of *Miss Matilda*. It was, altogether, my last new character but one on the Berlin stage. Then in May I followed my evil star to England.

Raupach wrote altogether 117 plays for the stage, that is 19 more than the number produced by the prolific Kotzebue.

When in the course of time murmurs began to be raised against the everlasting Raupach and his everlasting "Hohenstaufen," the author composed a drama of middle class life, "Die Geschwister,"* under the assumed name of " Leutner," to demonstrate to his enemies that he was no mere *protégé* of the court and the intendants, and was not trading on his name alone. And this he demonstrated to satisfaction, for the "Geschwister," by Leutner, had a better run than the previous pieces of Raupach.

Three years after this successful experiment, in 1840, Raupach's farce of " 1740, oder die Eroberung von Grüneberg," † was so dreadfully scraped out of the house, that the poet, in ill humour, flung away his pen for ever.

He continued in the same favour at court. Raupach was appointed to deliver lectures on history before the Prince and Princess of Prussia. At the literary tea-evenings held by King Friedrich Wilhelm IV. Raupach had his place beside Alexander von Humboldt.

Later on, in St. Petersburg, Dresden, and elsewhere, I played to advantage many a part in Raupach's pieces, as I have also, since those Berlin days, exchanged many a friendly greeting with the poet, from a distance.

With astonishment, but with no less joy, I heard, in 1848, when I was in Switzerland, that the old Raupach had, in

* " The Brothers and Sisters."
† " 1740, or the Conquest of Gruneberg."

spite of his 62 years, married my former colleague, Pauline Werner, who, during my Berlin period, used to play in children's parts, and that by this happy marriage he had taken a fresh lease of life.

Pauline Werner was a soft, fair, clever girl, but of no distinguished merit as an actress. On the other hand, she won several successes as a writer for the stage, under the letters " A. P." In Dresden, I played with pleasure in her piece, " Noch ist es Zeit." *

After this sunny, if also brief, happiness in the peaceful evening of his life, Raupach died in Berlin, in March, 1852. During the late Franco-German war I heard of his widow distinguishing herself by deeds of charity and care of the sick. How gladly I should have been in her place, free from demonish bonds !

---

* "It is yet Time."

CHAPTER XIV.

ZELTER, MENDELSSOHN, BERGER, MEYERBEER, AND MOSCHELLES.

IN the Berlin of my time there were, in particular, three houses that gave the tone in all matters of music; those of Zelter, Mendelssohn, and Beer-Meyerbeer, with all of whom I came into friendly contact.

Zelter, far advanced in his sixties, I first made the acquaintance of, at the house of his daughter, Frau Dr. Rintel, which stood opposite the Königstadt Theatre, the house in which mother and I resided in the beginning of our Berlin days. Dr. Rintel was a physician in large practice, and a son of his afterwards published a life of Zelter.

. Zelter, then of such advanced age, was a man of tall, robust, sturdy build, in whom the quondam master mason was still readily recognisable; of shrewd, doughty features with open blue eyes. A genuine Berlin original; blunt and direct of speech beyond expression; bristling with hostile points like a porcupine; hot-tempered and cantankerous; full of humours and caprices of his own; but yet, withal, in the heart of him true as steel. When in conversation about music he grew warm, and his opulent mind found free and fluent expression, it was easy to understand why Goethe delighted so much in intercourse with him, called him his friend and brother, and addressed him so many affectionate letters about yellow turnips, music, poetry, the theatre and friendship. Zelter, on his side again, never heard the name of his "sweet, divine friend" in Weimar mentioned, but his eye would lighten up in a holy glow of intense love and enthusiasm, and he would speak of Goethe as a necessity of his existence, " as indispensable to him as the light of morning."

On Sunday it was occasionally my privilege to dine at Rintel's with Zelter, and on these occasions I always sat beside him. He took pleasure in my cheerful gossip and laughter; and he who was wont to be so earnest a man; who could not bear large, noisy parties; who was long in getting over his displeasure with his daughter for having once cunningly forced him into giving a ball at his house, in order to shine in the light reflected from her father—he, the aged Zelter, would, in such a private, homely circle as that referred to, thaw into the most capital stories, to which, with his pungent humour, he knew how to impart such a racy flavour.

He would, for example, repeat with great gusto how once in 1809, on his arriving at Königsberg, where the court was exiled, and Queen Louise was absorbed, heart and soul, in Pestalozzi and the introduction of his method of education into Prussia, he received an invitation from "Kirchenrath" Busolt to dinner, and had the highest honours accorded him as "Herr Doctor," to his own infinite bewilderment, till at last the Pestalozzian company discovered, to their horror, that this guest of theirs was not the genuine "Herr Doctor Zeller," who was to reform the Prussian national schools, but—oh, heavens!—a bird of a very different feather.

Next door to Zelter lived a Mademoiselle Niqué, who sang every morning and evening with the voice of a cornet, "To see my Romeo," driving the old man to the verge of despair. Once, while suffering under the infliction of this sing-song, he sprang in a rage from his seat where he was at work, and rushed into the room of his daughters, Dorothea, Rosamund, and Louise, to whom their music-master was just giving a lesson on the pianoforte. Zelter seizes the inoffensive master by the shoulder, gives him a shaking, and shouts into his ear:

"Sir, get me a husband for Mademoiselle Niqué, or I am a gone man!"

The teacher rushed out dumbfounded, and the alarming news spread through all Berlin that Zelter had gone out of his mind.

I had the pleasure of being present at two Zelter festivals; one on the occasion of laying the foundation-stone for the new building of his beloved Academy of Singing, in the summer of 1825; the other in honour of Zelter's seventieth birthday, on the 11th December, 1828, a festival to which Goethe contributed his lengthy poem of the " Bauenden, Dichtenden, Singenden,"* as also a " Tisch-lied " (convivial song).

One musical evening I had the privilege of spending in the house of the old master, along with Ludwig Berger and Felix Mendelssohn, besides two lovely young singers, nurslings of Zelter and the Academy of Singing, is parti-cularly dear in my remembrance. Berger played with his own and Zelter's most famous pupil, Felix Mendelssohn, a Beethoven sonata, *à quatre mains*—and how! Such playing on the piano I had never heard before! Then young Felix, still almost a boy, played a fantasia on a theme on which Zelter had played some notes before him—and the stream of harmony gushed forth fresh as spring, wild and sweet as the jubilance of the lark. Zelter, with his stiff fingers, accompanied a young, beautiful, remarkably pale lady, who sang in alto his magnificent compositions to the two songs of Goethe, " Rastlose Liebe," † and " Der König im Thule," ‡ compositions which to this day still seem to me the finest ever yet given of those poems. Before she sang the last song, Zelter said to the lady, " Imagine you are sitting alone by the sea-shore, and dreaming of the King in Thule; let your voice float over the waves into remote space, in tones soft and free. The last notes must attenuate into solemn evanescence, as though sinking in the sea."

Felix Mendelssohn was two years younger than I, a youth of sixteen summers, the most attractive, the most loveable presence it is possible to conceive. With his beautiful, immaculate face, his long, dark, curly hair, his benign, intelligent brown eyes, his lovely virginal mouth, he might have served a painter as a model for Benjamin, while Zelter would have furnished an excel-lent patriarchal Jacob. The relation between teacher and pupil was also a genuinely patriarchal one. Zelter

---

* "The Builder, the Poet, the Singer."
† "Restless Love." ‡ "The King in Thule."

always addressed Felix with the intimate " Du" (thou), while the latter hung with pious reverence on the lips of his master. When at table, and seated beside me, his natural liveliness asserted itself, and we were soon in the reciprocation of the merriest jests and laughter, so that Zelter nodded to us radiantly, and in friendly words said, "The eyes and cheeks of you two happy young persons glow like carbuncles. Pity there is no dancing at old Zelter's!"

In the next following years I often danced with Felix. As a Berlin student he was an unsurpassably good dancer, an " accomplished rush of wind," as Rahel named one of his compositions.

He was only fifteen years old when he composed three operas, which were performed in the Mendelssohn house. On the completion of the comic opera in three acts, " Der Onkel aus Boston," * Zelter said to him, " Up till now thou wast my apprentice ; now hast thou approved thyself journeyman, and thy next step must be the mastership." And a master he became, if not in opera composition. The practice of this latter art was spoilt for him by the coolness with which his first opera, "Die Hochzeit des Kamacho,"† was received on its first and last public performance in the Berlin Theatre on the 29th April, 1827—an opera for which Klingemann, son of the director of the Brunswick Theatre, wrote the words—as also by the chicanery of the theatrical world which the young composer suffered from on that occasion. The music director, Spontini, treated him and his opera with a high air of pitying patronage, and, pointing to the dome of the French church in the Gens-darmenmarkt, ‡ said to him, " Mon ami, il vous faut des idées grandes—grandes comme cette coupole !" (My friend, you need to have grand ideas—grand as that dome.)

And yet when the grand ideas of the spiteful maestro, and all the sound and fury of his monstrosities of operas shall have long sunk into their everlasting oblivion, the world will still listen with delight to the warm, cordial tones of Felix Mendelssohn !

Altogether charming were the little concerts held every

* " The Uncle from Boston." † " The Wedding of Kamacho."
‡ Market of the Gensd'armes.

Sunday morning in the house of the Mendelssohns, and
at which Felix's compositions were mostly given.   The
young composer conducted a small select orchestra, his
highly gifted sister Fanny—afterwards wife of the poetical
painter Hensel—played at the pianoforte, Eduard Devrient
sang, and the *élite* of musical Berlin, with Zelter at their head,
formed the critical public.   The most celebrated *virtuosi*
and singers who came to Berlin esteemed it an honour to
make their *début* in these concerts.

In honour of the birth-day of his parents, musical or
theatrical surprises used to be prepared beforehand by Felix
and his sisters and brother, Fanny, Paul, and Rebecca.   In
a masquerade of this description, Felix, seventeen years
old, appeared in the character of a Tyrolese, and went the
round of the company with a packet of bon-bons whence
each drew sweets and verses composed by Felix himself, one
of the rhymes reflecting on the captious criticism that had
been levelled at his opera.   "In whatever strain or quality
the composer produces his work, the critic is sure to censure
it for not being produced in the opposite strain or quality,
and therefore the composer ought to compose according
to his own will and ability, heedless of criticism."

I saw Felix Mendelssohn for the last time on the 11th
March, 1829, in the Academy of Singing, when, twenty
years old, he conducted, like a young demi-god, Bach's
great passion of St. Matthew, which, after the composer's
death, no one had yet ventured on executing, not even Zelter.

Immediately afterwards he went to England as an
artist of universally recognised eminence.   When, a few
weeks later, I followed him thither, I was not allowed
there to exist for him, "for reasons of high import."
When in May, 1836, I was in Leipzig on a starring
engagement, Felix Mendelssohn, director of the celebrated
" Gewandhaus " concerts, was lingering by the Rhine and
Main, with the prospect of conducting the performance of
his " Paul " in Düsseldorf, and under the direction of
destiny which in Frankfort was to make him fall in love
with the sweet Cécile Jeanrenaud.

Thanks to the recommendation of Zelter, Ludwig
Berger, the most highly prized teacher of the piano in

Berlin, already burdened by more engagements than his weak health was adequate to, did not yet refuse to add me to the list of his pupils.

Berger, a native of Berlin, was close on fifty years of age when I made his acquaintance; he was a loveable and noble man, but a hopeless hypochondriac. With the hope of there being able to wed the sweet love of his youth, the charming singer, Wilhelmina Karges, of Frankfort-on-the-Oder, he departed in 1805, with his revered master, Clementi, to St. Petersburg, hoping to achieve an assured situation for life as pianoforte teacher by the golden banks of the Neva. There he acquired the friendship of John Field, whose merits as a player on the piano he ranked superior even to those of Hummel and Moschelles, and from whom he received instruction. With the recommendations of Clementi and Field, and by the aid of his own rare ability as a teacher, Berger, in two years after his arrival in St. Petersburg, had gathered about him such a large circle of scholars that he was able to summon his intended to his side. He set out for Courland to meet her, and there, in a despicable little hamlet, celebrated the happiest day of his life—his marriage with Wilhelmina. Ten months after that event, however, he stood, shattered for the rest of his life, at the grave of his happiness—the grave of his wife and child. His soft heart never quite recovered from this terrible blow. His health was for ever undermined. After an absence of ten years he returned to Berlin.

There he composed his finest songs, many of which are still sung at the present day, though the singers generally know little about the composer. Such are his Müller songs, which were only cast into the shade by Schubert's compositions on the same poems of Wilhelm Müller; his "In einem kühlen Grunde,"* "Als der Sandwirth von Passeier,"† "Die Letzten Zehn vom vierten Regiment,"‡ etc.

---

* "In a cold Ground."

† "When the Sandwirth of Passauer" ("Sandwirth," an old expression for a village innkeeper; "Passeier," or Passauer, a chain of mountains in the Tyrol; the song referring to Andreas Hofer, who raised an insurrection against Napoleon, in the Tyrol, in 1809).

‡ "The Last Ten of the Fourth Regiment."

In Berlin, together with the gifted Bernhard Klein, the composer of the opera "Dido," who died so young, and Ludwig Rellstab, Berger founded the "Berliner Lieder-tafel" (Berlin Choral Union), and composed for that body his most beautiful quartettes for men's voices.

The sun, however, that should have radiated warmth and strength into his life, had set for him too early, or Ludwig Berger would assuredly have grown to be one of the greatest song composers in our time. But such happiness was not allotted to him. Melancholy clouded his days and paralysed the courage and the joy that would have sustained him in productive work. He died in February, 1829, of nervous apoplexy, while standing at the piano by a pupil, marking time. His death was attended with more kindness than had been his life. His friends and grateful pupils placed over his grave the appropriate epitaph: "As artist, great; as man, noble, truthful, liberal-minded."

Next to the house of the Mendelssohns, the Beer villa in the Thiergarten gathered together under its roof all the musical celebrities of Berlin and the most famous concert and opera performers. There Hummel, Moschelles, Kalk-brenner, Spohr, Paganini played—there Henrietta Sontag, Angelica Catalani, Wilhelmina Schröder, Devrient, Nan-netta Schechner, Sabina Heinsetter sang the compositions of the son of the house, Giacomo Meyerbeer. Originally called Jacob Beer, he fell heir, while yet a boy, to the rich inheritance of Herr Meyer, and so had the name "Meyer" prefixed to his own, while, moreover, he Italianised his fore-name of Jacob into Giacomo, during his long residence in Italy.

Madame Beer sat enthroned in this rich house, exercising a perfectly royal hospitality and beneficence, so that people in Berlin came jestingly to call her the "Mother-Queen."

The most interesting to me of all the persons in this house was the young Michael Beer, the noble and amiable poet of the "Paria," a tragedy in one act, which, under the emblem of an Indian paria, attacked the "Hep! Hep!"*

---

* A "Hetzenruf," a call to summon people to the persecution of the Jews.

a call which was even then far from having sunk into dis-
use, and contended for the honour of Judaism. He was
the author, also, of the "Struensee,"* for which the poet's
brother, Meyerbeer, afterwards wrote the music. I have
acted with success in the tragedy in Dresden, when the
young poet was already long dead. Michael Beer, in the
art of poetry, meant truth and not fiction, to a degree such
as can hardly be said of any other poet. I met the family
of Meyerbeer again in Paris in the autumn of 1829, and
later still at the coronation festivities of the Emperor
Ferdinand in Prague.

Of all the *virtuosi* passing through Berlin, the dearest to
me was Ignatius Moschelles, who came to Berlin in November, 1824, and who, when only thirty years of age, by his
performances in Vienna, Paris, and London, had acquired
the world-name of the "Prince of Pianists." He gave
three brilliant concerts in Berlin, and played in several
charity concerts. In those days Zelter writes to his friend
Goethe respecting his wonderful play: "Moschelles plays,
in truth, in such a style that it is necessary to enjoy a
draught of Lethe before hearing him, so as to forget all his
predecessors. The fellow has hands which he turns like a
shirt, for he plays not at all badly with his nails."

In a charity concert held on behalf of the sufferers from
the inundations of the Rhine, I first came into personal
contact with Moschelles. Count Röder of Carlsruhe, one
of the acting committee, invited me to contribute to the
benefit of my compatriots. I wanted to give a recitation,
but, by way of fresh allurement to the Berliners, was
required to make an exhibition on the piano. My sudden
removal from the Königstadt Theatre at that time had
created some sensation, and my name stood well in the
fashionable world. My prudent mother deemed it would
be a pity to let this repute die away for want of use before
I had given my first performance on the royal stage. I
had, therefore, in company with my most zealous musical
admirer, the excellent pianoforte player, Greulich, who
visited us almost daily, to perform in public the Rondo

Struen lake.

Turc, *à quatre mains*, by Czerny—in the same concert in which Moschelles also played. The Prince of Pianists was good enough to say some kind words to me about my playing. The critique which appeared was, however, malicious enough to report : " Mademoiselle Bauer, in her charming toilet of white tulle with natural geranium blossoms, made a brilliant *appearance*."

Soon after, Moschelles paid us a visit. We were both to take part in a concert that Karl Blum was giving in Potsdam. This time, I kept to my own element and recited. In our house, however, the good Moschelles, probably from a desire to gratify my mother's proud heart, made so great a sacrifice of his skill as to play *à quatre mains* with me the overture to Don Juan, giving me, while doing so, the most valuable suggestions in his own delicate way.

When on the morning of the 15th December, Moschelles drove up in his carriage to take us to Potsdam with him, Felix Mendelssohn came running towards us, with glowing cheeks, to take once more a tender good-bye of his revered master, who in these few weeks had become at once his beloved teacher and his friend for life. The eyes of both were moist.

Half a century after this occurrence, when both friends had long been dead, it affected me strongly to read in Moschelles' diary what in these days of his first meeting with Felix he wrote about him and the house of the Mendelssohns :

" This is a family such as I have never yet known, and the fifteen year-old Felix a phenomenon such as is nowhere else to be found. What are all prodigies of children beside him ? They are prodigies of children, and that is all. This Felix Mendelssohn, on the other hand, is a mature artist, and yet only fifteen years old. We remained at our first meeting for several hours together. I had to play a great deal, where it had been my proper intention to hear and see compositions, for Felix had to show me a concerto in C minor, a double concerto, and several motets, all full of genius, and yet, at the same time, correct

and masterly. His elder sister Fanny, also of infinite
endowment, played fugues and passacailles of Bach's by
heart, with admirable precision. I think she is rightly
called ' a good musician.' Both parents give one the impression of the highest culture, for they are far from
proud of their children. They are concerned about the
future of Felix, doubting whether he has endowment
sufficient to effect something of permanent merit, something truly great, or whether, like so many talented children, he will not suddenly discredit all the fair hopes he
has raised. I could not sufficiently assure them that, convinced as I was of his one day demonstrating his mastership to the world, I felt no misgivings whatever about his
genius. Yet I found it necessary to repeat my assurance
again and again before they would believe it. Such are
not the ordinary parents of remarkable children of the
kind I meet so plentifully."

Nor during the drive to Potsdam did Moschelles ever
tire of testifying his admiration for Felix Mendelssohn.
All of a sudden, however, he was seized by the most
violent headache, and he sank back on the cushion pale
as death, with closed eyes. But he still persisted in
playing. And after my mother had applied some paint to
his face to disguise his ghastly appearance, and he had
tottered up to the piano, he did play in presence of the
king and court—like a very god.

In Potsdam we took leave of Moschelles. He set out
on a triumphal tour through the spectacular world. Only
years after, when Moschelles, out of love for his friend
Mendelssohn, had removed from London to Leipzig, was
it permitted us to celebrate our friendly meeting again in
Dresden.

CHAPTER XV.

A POLISH COUNT.

AMONG my admirers in that Berlin period was a young Polish count, one year younger than myself.

He came frequently to visit us; we sang French duets together; he sang Polish songs, and taught me the genuine "Mazurka." I did not dislike flirting with him. Mother and I looked upon him as a goodish sort of spoony youth, to whom his *chère mère* was not very liberal of pocket money, and who himself evinced an uncommon talent for economy. He never once allowed his admiration for me to betray him into the expense of a bouquet, or other such mercenary token of attention.

Monsieur le comte was proud of his ability not to understand a word of German. He hated Germany, and Russia still more, because his Poland was subject to her power. French was his only language, and he had the fantastic trick of foisting to the end of every third word he said, in a tone impossible to imitate, " Moi, mademoiselle, moi!" How many a laugh had mother and I over this famous " moi!" Between ourselves we used to call this self-complacent stripling of an admirer, "our Moi!" or "Moi-kin."

If any one had then told me, " Twenty years hence, you will know better about this, dear ' Moi '—this incessant I, and only I—and feel no more inclined to laugh at this chick of an I; this 'I' will wring many hot tears from you; this headstrong, icy-cold, selfish ' Moi ' will be your master and tyrant, and you his will-less slave "—I should never have believed it.

CHAPTER XVI.

COUNT SAMOILOW.

IN the spring of 1827, at a dancing party in the house of General Count von der Goltz, I was introduced by the still youthful son of the house to a nice, young, elegant Count Samoilow from St. Petersburg. We danced, chatted, and laughed together. The interesting stranger engaged me several times to dance with him, and paid court to me in rather a conspicuous manner. I soon came to be teased about this new ardent admirer, and the teasing was not at all displeasing to me.

· The young Count Goltz, who was greatly taken with the brilliant Russian, told me that his friend, Count Alexander Samoilow, had been politically a little compromised in the St. Petersburg "throne-revolt" following the death of the Emperor Alexander. His family, however, was held in great esteem at the Court of the Emperor Nicholas, and very rich, and he would soon receive a free pardon and be permitted to return to Russia, so soon as a little grass had grown over those youthful indiscretions of his. He was the best good-fellow in the world, and the most amiable of chums and companions.

Next day the young Count Goltz called at our house with his friend Count Samoilow. The latter visited us after that more and more frequently, giving me to understand, in an unambiguous manner, that he was deeply in love with me. We met each other, moreover, in the best social circles. All the world was bewitched by the handsome, rich, high-bred Russian. My friends congratulated me on my brilliant conquest. My admirers, and, above all, our Polish " Moi," fell into jealousy of Count Samoilow. My enemies envied me my golden adorer and his fine-sounding title.

And I? I felt the friendliest interest in this fine

admirer, who lived in such elegant style in Berlin, who showed an imposing equipage and retinue of servants, and spoke so prettily of his large estates in Russia. I was not particularly deep in love with Count Samoilow; but I did not reject his addresses. I thought it would be very nice to be raised, as Madame la Comtesse de Samoilow, completely above such temporal cares as used to plague me when my salary would not meet my expenses. My prudent mother, besides, considered this match a first-rate provision for me.

And now Count Samoilow formally proposed for my hand. He showed us a letter from Justizrath Bauer (remarkable enough!), from St. Petersburg, giving an account of his great fortune. He would settle on me, as his wife, 6000 thalers yearly, by way of pin-money, and if I wanted I might still keep to the stage.

When my mother interposed that there could be no question of a public betrothal till his parents had signified their consent, the count after some time brought a letter from his father, in which the latter not only pronounced his warmest blessing on the union, but intimated the intention of the parents to shortly visit Berlin, and the prospect they had of soon obtaining the complete pardon of Alexander, at the hands of the Czar Nicholas.

Meanwhile, my mother had prudently instituted enquiries regarding her future son-in-law, and all she learnt was of the most favourable complexion. Thus, at a party she asked the Privy Councillor Dr. von Gräfe whether he knew the Count Samoilow, and he answered hurriedly, " Yes, to be sure, a very good, rich St. Petersburg family." Then the conversation was unfortunately broken off by other guests.

We also heard that Count Samoilow was on terms of intimacy with the Russian Embassy, and we ourselves, in the course of a promenade Unter den Linden, saw my betrothed salute the Russian Ambassador Alopeus in a courteous and cordial manner, and the latter return the salute in a friendly way.

I thus became the much envied *fiancée* of Count Alexander Samoilow. He made me a present of a few pretty, but not at all expensive, trinkets.

But this golden fortune was not to last long.

One day the young Count von der Goltz rushed in the greatest excitement into our room and plumped out all at once the dreadful news:

"Count Samoilow is a swindler. He is just being taken to prison. He is no count, and his name is not Alexander Samoilow. He has swindled the Russian Embassy of large sums—cheated a rich St. Petersburg tobacco merchant, in this town, of a thousand thalers—falsified all his papers—what a misfortune for you!"

Yes, what a misfortune for the poor mother and for me! We stood there thunderstruck and dumbfounded, capable of no word and no thought. Was it possible, then? We sank into each other's arms and gave vent to our despair in bitter tears.

Soon our most approved friends came to visit us—Justizrath Ludolff, Hofrath Henn, Private Chamberlain Timm, &c.—to testify their sympathy, and assist us by word and act. Timm at once came on a commission from the king, to console me and offer me leave of absence, if it would be painful for me to appear publicly at the next performance.

My friends, however, counselled me not to yield to the storm, but to put on a bold face and defy it, so as not to give my ill-wishers and enviers the gratification of seeing me shattered by the blow. And I had the strength to appear the very next evening as *Fridolin* in Holbein's " Gang nach dem Eisenhammer."* My friends prepared me a friendly reception, and I played with as little embarrassment as though I had never seen Count Samoilow. That, of course, was only possible in virtue of the fact that my heart had never been a party in the whole affair.

In the *entr'acte* the king appeared on the stage, and said to me in a paternal tone : " Poor child—don't be sad —unfortunate—very unfortunate—*mauvais sujet!*—let him go—the right one will come."

Berlin showed me its sympathy by—a superabundance of invitations! Every one wanted to cheer and divert me,

---

* " Walk to the Iron-hammer."

and show that I had lost nothing in its eyes by this experience. For my consolation I was told that Hofräthin Henrietta Herz, the celebrated beauty, and one of the most honoured ladies in Berlin, had in her youth undergone a similar experience. A Portuguese Jew had paid his addresses to her, allured her with the tale of his immense treasures, black servants, and parrots that were on the road for him, and then, by way of finish, bolted with her father's silver snuff-box.

My ill-wishers, however, enjoyed their triumph—Mademoiselle Stich and her most intimate followers, and, above all, Prince August. I received infamous anonymous letters, which all sang the same tune, that the chaste princess of the theatre had prudishly rejected a Prussian prince in order to fling herself into the arms of a Russian valet.

During the trial at the criminal court the unhappy Samoilow behaved very well towards us. No word tending to compromise me escaped his lips. He craved my pardon; his passionate love for me had caused him to involve me also in the deception.

It is my opinion to this day that it was not for money that the unhappy man was bent on swindling us. He knew very well we were poor; and it would have been easy for him to have fooled the richest maidens in Berlin.

Mother and I had to suffer a great deal that was disagreeable in this affair. We had to give evidence on oath, and deliver up the small presents I had received; but I was spared the pain of being brought as a witness face to face with the unfortunate man. He was soon conducted to Spandau, and I never saw him again.

As soon as I found out his deception, my sympathy with him was extinguished. He ceased to exist for me, and I continued to play on the stage with zeal and pleasure, till in a short time my old cheerfulness all came back to me. I even so far got the mastery of my feelings that next winter I played a part in Wolff's new farce, "The Valet," to show that I was myself able to laugh at the sad farce that had occurred in my own life.

The piece was first played in the "Palais," before the king

and court, as were almost all-lively novelties. The handsome Duke of Lucca was present. "The Valet" had a very great success. Amelia Wolff played the rich Jewish widow, *Madame Hirsch*, with delightful humour and the most perfect accent. I still hear her sing, in an ecstacy of love:

> "Dich in meinem arm zù schliessen,
> Himmel, welch' ein augenblick!"*

I played the chambermaid, *Albertina*, merrily and saucily, without betraying the least indication that this valet story had any interest for me in particular. At the conclusion of the farce, stepping to the middle of the stage, I had to say: "A valet! Dear me! dear me! if I had only known!" Here Prince August laughed loud and spitefully. The king, however, shouted "Bravo!" and clapped his hands conspicuously.

"The Valet" was given for the first time in the theatre on the 5th March, 1828. Curiosity, sympathy, and spiteful gratification had filled the house. My friends were prepared for a little theatrical disturbance. The piece, however, passed off merrily. Only a few rich Jews were offended at this *Madame Hirsch*, and gave no more invitations to Wolff and his wife to their parties. Many of my friends were displeased at the "Tartuffe Wolff" for writing "The Valet," and at me for playing in it. With the levity of youth, I made light of it then, and can hardly now understand my want of tact. It was all possible, only because "Count Samoilow" had become a matter of complete indifference to me.

I played four times in public in Berlin in "The Valet." Then, in February, 1828, I set out on my theatrical tour for St. Petersburg.

During my so successful performances in Riga, I was again reminded of Count Samoilow. Two years earlier he had made his *début* there as political refugee, had commenced a love intrigue with a beautiful maiden of high position, got betrothed to her, and then, when his

---

* "To clasp thee in my circling arms,
   Oh, heavens! what a bliss were that!"

swindleries came to light, had to decamp. The unhappy girl died of grief.

In St. Petersburg, a pale lady of gentle appearance and in deep mourning called on us. When she saw me she burst into tears, and begged my forgiveness that her unhappy only son Alexander had done us so great wrong. His father, Organist Grimm, had died from sorrow over his prodigal son.

I tried to console the mother.

When for a long time after I heard no more of "Samoilow," I was disposed to believe that the whole foolish affair was forgotten, as I myself had almost forgotten it. The name "Samoilow," however, wove itself as a dark thread through my life. When with affectionate ardour I hastened to meet Prince Leopold of Coburg, I had hardly set foot on English soil when the first malicious word that greeted my ear was "Samoilow." The prince had received anonymous letters from Berlin which, proceeding, as they assuredly did, from accomplices of Prince August, painted the whole affair to him in a light reflecting the most unfavourably on me. I was represented as not merely the *fiancée*, but the mistress also of the Russian valet.

Years afterwards, in the late autumn of 1834, when I was fulfilling a starring engagement in Berlin, I again got some trace of Samoilow-Grimm. He wrote to me from the House of Correction in Spandau, and in the most affecting manner begged my pardon for the deception he had practised on me. I never answered him.

The last I heard of Samoilow was that he died in prison at Munich.

But how often is his name still sounded menacingly or even accusingly in my ears.

And yet, I believe, I was unfortunate in this affair, and not culpable.

*   *   *   *   *   *

In proof of the unvarnished truth of the above report, I here insert the documental account of the affair of Samoilow, by Karl Rogan, clerk to the criminal court. In his history of the Berlin " Hausvoigtei" (head-quarters of the police), speaking of " Count Samailoff " (as he writes the name, differently from my spelling), he states, *literatim:*

" Of all adventurers who have ever played a part in the Prussian capital, Alexander Samailoff takes indisputably the first place.   However many adventurers may have appeared on this scene, none before him or after him has been able, like him, to introduce himself, under the guise of a gentleman of rank, into the highest circles ; by the display of intellectual parts and dazzling wit rapidly pre-possess himself in the favour of old and young, of gentle-men and ladies, deceive the most wary and sceptical people, and lead a life of the highest worldly splendour at the cost of others.

" In truth, however, he possessed those physical and mental qualities requisite to the playing of such a part in the world.   In the best years of his life, in full strength, of athletic form, with the head of an Apollo, he· was altogether a man of imposing figure.

" With these personal advantages, which, moreover, in no respect lacked anything of the nobility of stamp im-pressed on the gentleman of highest quality, Samailoff united the noblest manners.   His every movement be-tokened the ease and elegance which distinguish the gentleman and testify to that finish of person which is the result of life-long familiarity with the *salons* of the fashion-able world.   From the high-breeding of his carriage one would have taken him, not for a Russian by birth, but for a polished Frenchman.

" It was in the spring of 1827 when Samailoff came to Berlin, and by the luxurious life he led, by his gentlemanly manners, by the interest in his favour he contrived to create in every one who came within the spell of his presence, he soon attracted universal attention. · Samailoff understood to a high degree the art of easily forming acquaintances, and succeeded in this all·the more readily that people met him half way.

" Invitations poured in on the handsome and gallant Russian from all sides, and he soon became a favoured guest in the *haute volée* of the capital,

" Samailoff appeared in the character of a Russian count. He described his father as occupying a high office of State in St. Petersburg, and spoke of himself as *attaché* to the Russian Embassy at a German court. No one ventured for one moment to call his statements in question, for everything about him spoke in his favour—his person, his brilliant qualities, his apparent wealth, his costly equipage and retinue of servants.

" Of all his acquaintanceships there was one in particular which he much cultivated. In the theatre he had made the acquaintance of the talented Caroline Bauer, the crowning figure among the disciples of Thalia at the Berlin Court Theatre. Her achievements there had captivated him, for in fact, too, they were of the highest order, and the charming Caroline, with dazzling gifts of nature, was the favourite of all the public.

" Samailoff sought and found access to the all-bewitching artiste. In the nearer intercourse thus effected she made an even greater impression upon him, and, carried away by her amiability, he confessed his love and admiration for her, and how he could not live without her.

" Caroline, who on the stage had always been counterfeiting the exclusive part of lover, felt, on her side too, towards Samailoff the reality of love, and responded to the declaration of his sentiments by a confession of her feelings for him. Samailoff was happy.

" Caroline's mother, to obviate any prejudice falling on the good reputation of her daughter, desired the public betrothal of the happy pair. He therefore concluded a contract of betrothal with the fair actress, engaging to pay a considerable sum by way of indemnity if, by reason of his father's refusing his consent, he should be unable to keep his word.

" All the world envied the beautiful Caroline her conquest of the rich young count, and in the higher circles, where, perhaps, another connection for Samailoff had been thought of, people sneered haughtily at the *mésalliance*

" This relation of betrothal had lasted only a few days when Count Samailoff's visits to the house of the fair Caroline were discontinued. The distress of the bride on this account was only too soon heightened by the pain of recognising how grievously she had been mystified, when the secret veil which had hitherto cloaked the actual circumstances of the distinguished Russian was suddenly torn off.

"Alexander Samailoff, whose proceedings and manner of life the Berlin police had long been watching, was at length unmasked.

"We find him as forger and impostor in the Hausvogtei. He was neither count nor son of high Russian State official, but—a servant who had left Russia in the retinue of his master, who was travelling abroad, and had been dismissed for misbehaviour. As fortune-hunter he had then wandered about in the world, and so had come to Berlin to play the part of a count. His great talent as an adventurer enabled him readily to find credit among people who advanced him large sums of money on forged bills, by which he was enabled to support the part he had assumed. With what ability he played his part we have already seen.

"On being put in prison, Samailoff, with great insolence, continued to arrogate to himself the title of count, nor would he abate any of his high pretensions till at last evidence of the most overwhelming weight was produced, establishing the fact that he was nothing but an impostor of humble origin.

"The news of the actual circumstances of the handsome Russian, who had so consummately imposed on the highest classes of Berlin, spread through the whole town like wildfire, and for weeks nothing was talked of but the bold impostor.

"The greatest mortification, of course, fell to the lot of the talented artiste whom Samailoff is said to have sincerely loved.

"The bold adventurer was condemned to six years' penal servitude. Shortly after his liberation, he emerged in another part of Germany to play the same game over again."

CHAPTER XVII.

HENRIETTA SONTAG.

OF Henrietta Sontag Goethe sings:—

> " Ging zum Pindus, Dich zu schildern ;
> Doch geschah's zu meiner Qual :
> Unter neun Geschwisterbildern
> Wogte zweifelnd Wahlum Wahl.
> Phœbus mahnt mich ab vom Streben ;
> Sie gehört zu unserm Reich ;
> Mag sie sich hieher begeben,
> Findet wohl sich der Vergleich." *

"Saddle me the hippogriff once more, ye muses, that I may ride into the old Sontag times!"—so might I sing, slightly parodying old Wieland.

Who is able to dream himself back with me into those old times of half a century ago, now all hushed into everlasting silence—those times when all Berlin was but one charmed organ of sensation for an all-captivating illusion to play on—when, to the touches of this sweet illusion, all Berlin responded in rapturous and ever more rapturous shouts of jubilation : " Henrietta Sontag!—Sontag!—Sontag!—the unique, the incomparable, the heavenly!"

Such sweet illusion will now be intelligible to but a few contemporaries, round whose wan lips will play a melancholy smile, while a tear will also moisten their sunken eyes, as they recall the old charm. Posterity will make mock of it, and pityingly shake their heads at their grandfathers and grandmothers for this Sontag frenzy.

And yet were they fair and radiant, those old Sontag times, now passed into the inane ; fair and radiant, like

---

* " Went to Pindus to describe thee, to my torment, as I found ; for I kept going round among all the nine Muses, and could never settle which you were most like. Phœbus bids me give up the attempt : ' She belonged to his realm. Let her come hither, and it would be seen she was among her peers.' "

the sunny spring, with its fragrant blossom-fluśh and its sweet songs of birds!—fair as the bright season of youth!

Spring, too, it was, in fact, when, like an epidemic intoxication, the sweet illusion—the Sontag infection, as it was called—came over Berlin on a night in May, and unrestrainedly seized possession of ears, eyes, hearts, brains, tongues, hands, and pens, and ever more dangerously, ever more beyond power of rescue!

The young Königstadt Theatre, when it yet counted its existence only by months, lay seriously ill—of deficit! The seven directors—six financial officials, and a lawyer—looked despairingly. in their distress for some saviour, masculine or feminine.

Who was the first to speak the hopeful words?—"Only a *prima-donna* can save us—only Henrietta Sontag in Vienna!"

History has forgotten to mention the name of the author of that happy suggestion. Perhaps it was my art-devoted admirer, Justizrath Ludolff!

Ludolff was with his young friend, Ludwig Rellstab, on business in Vienna in May, 1824, when both for the first time heard and saw Henrietta Sontag.

Speaking of this event, Rellstab says: "However charming was her mastery over the technics of music, and however powerful the impression of her graceful exterior, I did not then anticipate the. success she was afterwards to achieve."

Only two masters had then recognised the high value of the young artiste: Karl Maria von Weber, who in 1823 wrote the "Euryanthe" for her, and Beethoven, who, at his great concert in May, 1824, committed to her and Caroline Ungher the solos of his Mass, and in his disorderly bachelor hall treated both the fair singers to roast from the restaurant and sweet wine. The wine, however, agreed so ill with the young, frolicsome maidens that Henrietta had to excuse herself from appearing at the opera next day. About this dinner at Beethoven's Frau Ungher-Sabatier writes, half a century afterwards, not without emotion:

"I 'still see the plain room of the house in the Land-strasse, where a string answered the purpose of a bell-pull.

In the middle of the room stood a large table, on which were served roast beef and the *famous* sweet wine. I see the second adjoining room filled to the ceiling with orchestra music. In the midst of it stood the piano, which Field, if I mistake not, had sent Beethoven from London. Jetty Sontag and I entered the room with the feeling of entering a church, and we endeavoured—alas! in vain—to sing before our beloved master. I remember my arrogant remark that he did not understand how to write singing music, because a note in my part of the symphony was above the reach of my voice; to which he answered: 'Only learn, and the note will come.' From that day forward this saying of Beethoven's spurred me to diligence."

Of "Jetty Sontag" Beethoven said: "She is diligent, to be sure, but without much schooling."

Weber set as high value on Sontag's "Euryanthe" as on Schröder-Devrient's performance of the same piece. Although in their conception and presentation of the part the performances of the two were as widely-removed as possible, he could not yet venture to say which was the better of the two. If Schröder-Devrient's "Euryanthe" bore the palm for its energy, majesty, and passion, yet was Sontag's rendering, on the other hand, inexpressibly graceful, cordial, delightful to soul and sense.

With an enthusiastic impression of the fair Henrietta in his heart, Justizrath Ludolff returned to Berlin, and was never tired of singing her praises. And when he ascertained that the young singer, on the breaking up of the opera, was going to quit Vienna, a mandatory was expedited to her from the Königstadt Theatre, invested with full power to engage the sweet nightingale for Berlin, if only he could succeed in winning her. Yet he had to return without success. Mamma Sontag* was an uncommonly politic dame, and understood the art of whetting the appetite for her dainty fare. She produced her first at a number of Austrian theatres, and then proceeded with her on a starring engagement to Leipzig.

---

* Henrietta's mother.

At the first news of the intelligence, a number of directors of the Königstadt Theatre hastened thither with special post horses to hear the wonderful bird sing, and, if possible, entrap it. These were Justizrath Kunowsky, Martin Ebert, the rich Herz Beer and his wife Amelia, parents of Meyerbeer, and the secretary to the theatre, Karl von Holtei. When, on their arrival in Leipzig, they found other fowlers already in waiting, and among them a deputy of the Berlin Court Opera, they hastily yoked their horses again, and drove a day's journey to meet the *Prima Donna* coming from Prague.

Such affecting zeal—and a salary of 7000 thalers for one season—was more than Mamma Sontag and Henrietta could withstand. They signed the contract with the Königstadt Theatre, on the condition, however, that, whether for better or worse, it should take Mamma Francisca and Sister Nina Sontag into the bargain.

And so, then, came the sweet nightingale to Berlin, where she conquered by her appearance before ever she had yet sung one note in public. The Sontag fever now ran in hot combustion through the whole body of the town. The Kaiserstrasse, in which the "heavenly maiden" dwelt, did not empty the whole day long of equipages, horsemen, and foot passenges, all bent on visiting, seeing or being seen by the idolised one.

When, however, on the 3rd August, the birthday of Friedrich Wilhelm III., she for the first time stepped before the Berlin stage lights as *Isabella* in Rossini's "Italienerin in Algier," then was the whole of Berlin but one house of joyously infatuated devotees, all drunk with the most blissful enthusiastic intoxication.

How in those days the Berlin worship of the divine Henrietta vented itself in million-fold pious utterances of the name — the sacred name " Henrietta " — now in soft aspiration; now in jubilation; now in ecstatic frenzy; now in groanings that cannot be uttered! "Henrietta" was a watchword; "Sontag" a spell to conjure with. Where two or three met together in the street, there was the name " Henrietta Sontag," the conductor of common inspiration. In all assemblies, whether

in beer or wine houses, hers was the name that called them
together. The fish and vegetable huckstresses in the Gen-
darmenmarkt, almost forgetful of their carps and onions,
thought devoutly on the "Italienerin in Algier." The
cabbies in their box-seats spelt out with rapture the endless hymns to the "divine Jetty" printed in the newspapers. The laurel trees were soon stripped of their
foliage, and bouquets mounted in price, for laurels
and bouquets drifted every evening only to the
feet of the divinely intoxicating "Italienerin." At the
booking-office of the Königstadt Theatre people had to
fight for tickets, and in the press of the evening many
was the dress-coat tail, the lady's shoe, the false tress, that
was torn and lost. Whoever had not seen the "Italienerin" was still in heathen darkness, was an ill-starred
straggler, whom the enlightened world looked down on
askance with a compassionate smile.

The royal opera and theatre showed a dismal void so soon
as Henrietta Sontag appeared in the Königstadt. Even
the faithfullest of our old and young theatre guard, who
came to our house from habit, from a spirit of contradiction, or because no ticket was to be had "on the other
side of the Spree"—these, too, looked at us players and
singers with compassion, and let their thoughts wander to
the Königstadt.

And how many indiscreet words were told us to our
face! Once, when an enthusiast would never have done
chanting to the charming singer, Caroline Seidler Wranitzky, the triumphs of her rival and the flowers which
every evening were showered on her at the Königstadt
stage, the young lady at last stopped him short in irrita-
tion and said: "It is no concern of mine, let them stifle
her with flowers!"

A lady who had never shown me any great good-will,
said to me in a tone of mortifying sympathy: "Don't be
vexed at people yet speaking only of Sontag, and still
finding her the only beautiful, the only lovely person. This
star, too, will set, and then those now in the shade will
come to the foreground."

One of my old admirers was ever dinning into me:

F

"Don't give yourself any trouble on the stage. It is all of no use. To-day, in Berlin, there is but one *artiste* who awakens interest and gains applause. It is foolish to contend with Henrietta Sontag for the palm."

Is it any wonder I was irritated at the new phœnix I had not yet seen? It is not given to every one to answer, as did Mademoiselle Milder-Hauptmann, when some one inconsiderately asked her whether she thought Nanetta Schechner the finest *Emmeline* of our time? "Since," she proudly replied, "I have seen Mademoiselle Milder-Hauptmann as *Emmeline*, I do not presume to give an opinion on other *Emmelines*."

In this far from agreeable mood I was found one day by my esteemed pianoforte teacher, Ludwig Berger. He looked excited and disconcerted. My first question was, of course, "Now, what say you to Sontag?"

Then he pettishly broke out: "No, I will endure this mania no longer. Here in your house, at least, I thought to find rest from the everlasting Sontag—Sontag—Sontag —and now you, too, start on her before I have taken off my hat. I came to excuse myself from giving the pianoforte lessons for four weeks. I must away from here for some time, to breathe another air; the Sontag epidemic of this place is killing me."

"Have you, then, seen the phœnix and heard its voice?"

"No, nor will I have anything to do with the prodigy. I have already more than enough of the everlasting Sontag! Sontag! Wherever I appear—in the street, in society, in the wine-house—I am at once pestered with, 'The queen of all nightingales, is she not? An incarnate angel! Have you heard, then, how in Stralau yesterday she ate fried eels and potatoes with their jackets on, and drank white beer over and above? If it only agrees with her! The heavenly maiden!' If I but stick my head out of doors, every snob's apprentice roars, every sempstress chirps, into my ears the same sing-song of the 'Italienerin:'

"'Ich rufe Dich, Geliebte,
Mit meiner Liebe Tonen,'*

---

* "I call thee, beloved, with the tones of my love."

meaning by that the divine Sontag. If I take a paper in my
hands, I read at once Sontag—Sontag—Sontag! I read only
when and whither she took a drive—in what company she
was—what she said and sang, what she ate and drank. And
what trite witticisms about Sontag (Sunday) and the Jäger
(hunter) of a tenorist, and the Wächter (watcher) of a
bass singer you are made to hear. 'Der Wächter der
Sontag Jägerei' (the watcher of the Sunday hunting) is one
of the least insufferable. To-day the most recent Sontag
pun, which was flung a dozen times into my face on my
way thither, runs: 'Why does Sontag mostly sing *mezza*
(*half*) *voce?* At the wish of the directors, because it is
necessary to hear her at least twice in the same part, in
order *wholly* to hear this part.' No, I can no longer stand
this craziness. Perhaps in four weeks Berlin will have
sobered down a little, and remember that it has a Milder,
a Schulz, and a Seidler as God-favoured songstresses. I
am going to Frankfurt-on-the-Oder."

So excited and bitter I never before saw my friend,
who, on the contrary, was wont to be so mild and fair in
his treatment of others. A good idea then came into my
head, and I said:

"Revered master, I, too, have not yet heard Sontag.
What say you to us two, before you set out for Frankfurt-
on-the-Oder, hearing together the 'Italienerin in Algier?'
We shall then ourselves form an opinion about this new
goddess of the Berliners. Perhaps we shall thereby find
to our composure that the momentary rapture has been
provoked only by the charm of novelty, which after a
time must wear away. Should we ourselves, however,
fall under the spell!"

"Never in time!" said Berger. He did, however, drive
with mother and me next evening to the Königstadt Theatre.
We made but slow progress, for the whole length of
the long, narrow Königstrasse was choked full of carriages
and foot-passengers, all steering for the one "Italienerin."

At last we did get seated at our costly places. The
elegant public was in a pleasurable excitement. A humming and singing of "Sontag, Sontag," quivered through
the densely-filled house. Friends and acquaintances pressed

up to Berger, and congratulated us on the opportunity we would soon have of seeing and hearing the goddess! Justizrath Ludolff would not leave off pressing on me his large Paris opera-glass, that I might be able to enjoy and admire his favourite. He nearly turned somersaults in his rapture.

During the overture, conducted with great animation by the youthful, little, curly-headed Stegmeyer, the expectant hum and bustle went on unchecked. "She" was not yet on the stage—she for whose sake alone the whole company was there assembled.

At last there stepped on the boards—a delicate little lady, giving an impression of youthful grace, in a sky-blue dress, and a little white hat trimmed with a feather. Her fine, maidenly, forget-me-not face, all fresh and blooming, and full of grace, was set off with blonde locks, bright blue eyes, and a charming little girlish mouth, which, when opening to a sweet, blithe smile, displayed the most beautiful pearly teeth. The whole figure, both still and in motion, was a charming picture of happy youth, of the graceful play of maidenly nature—pretty, however, rather than beautiful.

With what jubilance was she received, and how she was overwhelmed with flowers and garlands! When she bowed her thanks for these expressions of regard, her child-like face beamed with such pure and perfect bliss that one could not help spontaneously rejoicing with her in her triumphs, and heartily according her them.

And, next, she opened her little bud of a mouth just as a bird of the woods might its little bill—so naturally, so without a trace of embarrassment or self-consciousness; and the sweetest, clearest bird-notes warbled through the house.

The voice was neither full nor strong, but clear as a bell, liquid as water, bright as silver, particularly in the middle tones—of easy mobility, of distinct articulation in every tone, and of a molten quality that was irresistible. And how sweetly she trilled, like the clear jubilance of the lark! Then she shone out brilliantly in the most difficult passages and "roulades" by her peculiarly high falsetto—as precise as an exquisite "flute-clock." Her *mezza* and *sotto voce* were beyond comparison—beyond possibility. And then all flowed with such spontaneous ease, with such perfect want of exertion, from the dainty little mouth, which I never once saw disfigured (such as I saw afterwards, in quite a shocking manner, in the singing of Catalani), that the listener yielded himself up to the enjoyment without the least qualification of any kind.

With a charming petulance the "Italienerin" played and sang the provoking duet with the delightful Taddäo—Spitzeder, whose *vis comica* Sontag herself was unable to resist.

In the second act she appeared in magnificent Turkish dress. At the close of her song, "O my Lindoro," at the words "Dear Turk, dear Turk," she transported the house by her wonderfully pure and exquisite staccato, so that the cheering would never come to an end.

I, too, was taken captive, and joined with all my heart in the universal applause, even if I felt that the frenzy of intoxication was carrying people beyond just limits.

The scepticism of my friend Berger thawed more and more. Most he had to say was in the way of praise, yet he had also somewhat to censure in her too frequent *mezza voce*, her occasionally rather conspicuous *coloratur*, her deficiency in intellect and warmth of the heart. His summing up, however, was in the friendly words, "Henrietta Sontag is not the greatest singer I ever heard, but one of the most loveable!" And he did not fly from her and the Sontag contagion to Frankfurt-on-the-Oder. Yet Ludwig Berger held stoutly to the opinion in which I then concurred, as I must still do at the present day, that the wild Sontag enthusiasm was an exaggeration and a morbid symptom of the times.

Ludwig Robert called Sontag's singing "flute-lispings and nightingale warblings."

The "Italienerin in Algier" had to be given forty-two times by Sontag in the Königstadt Theatre. Altogether in the two years, from the 3rd August, 1825, to the end of September, 1827, she appeared no less than 211 times in seventeen different parts in this theatre, during which the enthusiasm of the Berliners knew no reaction. I, too,

have heard her several times on this stage, as *Bertha* in
" Schnee," as *Angelina* in Rossini's " Cinderella," as *Sophia*
in " Sargines," as *Anna* in the " Weisse Dame," and as
Matilda in " Corvadino," and I liked her ever more and
more, not only as a singer, but also, as a loveable, happy-
tempered, and, in spite of all the infatuating homage paid to
her, modest young maiden—for such I found her to be when
I became acquainted with her in society. There she was
blithe without any embarrassment, and often forward like
a child. And what an amiable and pleasant colleague was
this celebrity when later on we appeared together in public
concerts in the court representations, and I had even to
sing the " Edile" while Sontag played " Hannchen " in the
old opera of " Joconde," by Isouard.

There was no trace of jealousy between us; we moved
in the same circles, danced at the same balls, and, in
particular, experienced unforgettable fair hours together
in the hospitable house of Justizrath Ludolff in the Thiergarten. There Sontag lived throughout one summer, and
put up with a small spare room, feeling so much at home,
as she did, in the amiable and art-loving family. -

There, too, land excursions were arranged, long drives
taken, charades performed, *tableaux vivants* represented,
dances got up, in all which Henrietta proved the most
enterprising and forward of us all. She was a daring
rider, and liked even to stalk through the garden on high
stilts, proud of her feat in this department.

My mother once said to her, " But, my dear, if you
were to slip and hurt yourself ? "

" God forbid ! Frau Rittmeisterin," she laughingly exclaimed, and for a few seconds stood on one stilt, enjoying
our looks of astonishment like a child.

One mild evening we were sitting in front of the house,
chatting confidentially to each other, when Henrietta
suddenly slipped off unperceived, and after a little time
she opened the window above us and sang out, in flute-like
tones, an aria from the " Barbier of Sèville." All at once
she stopped short, and, imitating Mademoiselle Stich as *Julia*
to the point of deception, she declaimed, with sweetest
voice:

" O Romeo! Romeo! wherefore art thou, Romeo?
  Deny thy father and refuse thy name;
  Or, if thou wilt not, be but sworn my love,
  And I'll no longer be a Capulet.
            Romeo, doff thy name,
  And for thy name, which is no part of thee,
  Take all myself."

I, imitating Wolff as *Romeo*, at once struck in—

  "I take thee at thy word:
  Call me but love, and I'll be new baptized—
  Henceforth I never will be Romeo."

And so, to Ludolff's delight, we played the scene in the Berlin Thiergarten as though the sky of Italy overarched us.

This was Sontag's most joyous innocent season, as she afterwards assured me. A Christmas Eve we both spent at Ludolff's will continue unforgettable to her as to myself.

On the Christmas Eve referred to we and some other intimate friends were present at the distribution of the Christmas gifts. Little presents lay hidden under flowers, which were sought and found amid no little laughing and merriment. While the pretty rarities were being admired there came sounding to our ears from the adjoining salon:

"Kemmt a Vögli gefloge, setzt si nieder auf mei Fuss."*

"Ah, the Tyrolese!" we shouted, in joyous surprise, and listened to the lovely song.

Our kind host had sent for the brothers and sister Rainer from Fügen, in Zillerthall—at that time great favourites in Berlin, having often sung in the opera-house and at court—though it must have cost him a great outlay of money, seeing the most considerable families in Berlin were ambitious to engage them for their parties. They were three brothers and a sister, who sang popular songs with truly magnificent voices. After they had sung "Steh nur auf, steh nur auf, Schöner Schweizerbu,"† Sontag took the Tyrolese girl to the piano to hear to what giddy height her voice might reach. They tried it together, Sontag lightly touching the piano, tone for tone, and singing

---

* "A Bird comes flying and lights on my foot."
† "Do get up, do get up, my lovely Swiss lad."

along with the girl. But soon she laughingly called out, " I can no further." Then, at the request of the Tyrólese, she sat down to the piano to sing something. She selected Mozart's divine, " Ihr, die ihr Triebe des Herzens kennt."* We thanked her in transports. With great composure, and nodding with their heads the while, the Tyrolese said in their dialect, " Du singscht recht arti."† We roared with laughter at such praise, and Henrietta, too, seemed highly amused at being able to " shing nish."

The Tyrolese had then to exhibit their country dance— their real simple country dance. The eldest danced with his sister, the two others sang the melody to the dance. It was not long till we were all tripping it, O how happy!

Ludolff wanted to let his idol enjoy another triumph, and challenged the Tyroler to say which of the ladies had the prettiest foot.

We did not resist this joke, in order not to spoil the pleasure of the amiable Justizrath, but formed in a circle round our judge, each of us showing the tip of her foot; Henrietta, her tiny Cinderella foot very gracefully beside mine.

The Tyroler took up his task with the utmost gravity, contemplating both persons and foot-tips with attention, and with all the composure in the world. And at last, O horror, he awarded the palm—to me!

The Justizrath called out embarrassed, " You have surely made a mistake. Here, here" (pointing to Sontag), " is the lady with the smallest foot."

The Herr Tyroler was, however, not to be diverted from his choice, and answered with perfect equanimity, " Ja, de do ischt de klaanschte, und hat de klaanschte Fuss! De do aber" (pointing to me) " ischt gross und hat doch de klaane Fuss. Also hat de do den Priss!"‡

It is scarcely possible to describe the merriment which followed this Judgment of Solomon. Only the Justizrath

---

* "You who know the heart's impulses."
† "Thou shinghest quite nish."
‡ "Yea, she there isht the shartest, and has the shartest foot. But she there" (pointing to Caroline Bauer) "isht big, and has yet the shart foot. So she there hash the prish."

and I did not join in. We were both stunned, a circumstance which seemed only to heighten Sontag's mirth, who, in the midst of her laughter, kept repeating: "I don't at all take it amiss, dear, ha, ha, ha! I *am* the shortest—ha, ha!—and the poor Justizrath cannot come to himself again on account of 'she there!'"

On saying "Good night," Sontag assured me: "I never had such a happy time of it." At the same moment she invited the Tyrolese to come next morning to her house in the Alexander Square, opposite the theatre, where she lived with her mother and her sister Nina, and where she gave a splendid lunch to the happy singers of nature.

The king, too, was much interested in the Tyrolese, and had them to sing in the Palais. He only regretted that the words of the songs were so little intelligible, and, therefore, ordered the leader of the singers to write down a few verses in plain German, with a view to getting them printed for the benefit of the court.

When, however, the Tyroler, with all the complaisance in the world, wrote down "in German"—

> "Ein hübsche warme Kuhd
> Ist Sommer und Winter guet;
> Im Winter gibt's a Schlafmutz
> Im Sommer gibt's a Huet."

Then the king said: "Better, after all, not have them printed."

The Tyrolese then went to England, where, too, they sang before the Duchess of Kent and at the most fashionable parties.

To her mother and her young sister Nina, one of the very dearest of girls, Henrietta Sontag was the most loving and self-sacrificing daughter and sister.

The mother was a clever woman, and an actress in routine parts. During Henrietta's starring engagement in Leipzig, in May, 1825, she appeared successfully on the stage, so excellently managed by Hofrath Küster, as *Maria Stuart*, *Baroness Waldhull*, and *Elizabeth* in the "Drei Wahrzeichen,"* without, however, carrying the public

---

* "Three Tokens."

away with her. I have seen her play several times in the Königstadt Theatre cleverly and intelligently ; but I still missed in her play the animating pulse of the heart. On account of her short-sightedness, which reached to quite a distressing defect, she had, moreover, got into the habit of blinking with her eyes in a manner unpleasing to observe; and poor Nina did the same.

When Mamma Sontag grew more intimate with us she liked to relate stories of her past life, in which she would bring up many affairs of the heart with astonishing candour.

When no more than fifteen years old, Francisca Marklof had married, at Aix-la-Chapelle, the actor, Franz Anton Sontag, member of a strolling company. He was very popular as " buffo." Francisca played the parts of merry lovers, and sang with agreeable voice in vaudevilles and little operas. In the winter of 1805-6 both played in Coblenz. There, on the 3rd January, 1806, at six in the morning, Frau Francisca was delivered of a little daughter, whom a neighbour, Mademoiselle Gertrudis Lof, held at the christening, when she received the name of Gertrudis Walpurgis Sontag, as it stands in the registrar's records in Coblenz.

This Gertrudis Walpurgis Sontag was destined to become our nightingale of world celebrity, after having assumed, from some whim or other, the forename of Henrietta, or " Jetty."

" The words, in truth, I hear; but my faith in them is defective. I have reason rather to believe that Henrietta was born a few years earlier, and that the politic mother, to make a prodigy of her child, took two or three years from her age, foisting on her as her baptismal certificate that of her younger sister, Gertrudis Walpurgis, who died early." Thus Eduard Genast says, in his " Diary of an Old Player," following the account of a friend of the family of Sontag, who knew the two daughters, Henrietta and Nanni (later Nina), and who reported that Henrietta was born in 1804. And Karl von Holtei, who, in the days of the Sontag fever in Berlin, was a passionate enthusiast of the fair Henrietta Sontag, and on the most intimate terms with her, gives 1803 as the year of her birth.

Be that as it may, when she was yet but seven years old, " Jettchen " sang and played with applause the "Lilli" in " Donauweibchen"* Soon after, her father died, having had the misfortune to break his leg on the stage. Frau Francisca then got an engagement in the Court Theatre of Darmstadt, which, however, was not of long duration. She committed her two daughters, Henrietta and Nina, to the care of her mother in Mainz, and set out into the world in search of a new engagement. Iffland was so well satisfied with her performance in Berlin, that he was on the point of engaging Francisca Sontag when he died. Ultimately Francisca found an engagement under Liebich's management in Prague.

Thither Henrietta and Nina followed their mother from Frankfort-on-the-Maine, travelling quite alone with the mail-coach from stage to stage, handed by one conductor over to another. A sorry mode of travelling ! How often must Henrietta have recalled this journey to her mind, when subsequently making her triumphal processions through the world with all the luxury of a princess !

In Prague the little Henrietta made her *début* with two arias in Wranitzky's " Oberon" so happily that Director Liebich had her trained for a singer in the Conservatorium, more particularly by the excellent singing mistress, Madame Ezegka. In May, 1818, she sang with applause the *Benjamin* in Mehul's " Joseph in Egypt." Two years later she celebrated her first great triumph as *Princess* in " Johanna von Paris." All the world was taken with her silvery voice and her charming little person.

Most taken of all, however, was the handsome Lieutenant Wilhelm Marsano, known as "the irresistible" by all the ladies of Prague, and author of many pretty theatrical pieces. He was Jettchen's first beloved admirer till, in 1820, she went for four years to Vienna as German and Italian *Prima Donna*. There Lieutenant Wilhelm Marsano had to evacuate his place in the favour of the singer to Cavalier Count Eduard Klam-Gallas. In Berlin Karl von Holtei, and then the English Ambassador, Lord

---

* "The Little Wife of the Danube."

Clanwilliam, succeeded in turn to the post of most passionate adorer of the fair Henrietta. The latter, in particular, was long distinguished as the most favoured of her lovers, till at length the noble lord was ousted from that eminence of fortune to make room for the handsome and talented violinist of the theatre orchestra.

Henrietta Sontag was not free from coquetry and a weakness for multitudinous adoration. But who would have been disposed to take any exception to her on that account? It gave her evidently a childlike pleasure to see ever more and more new worshippers sprawling around her. As Goethe said of " Lili's Park," there was no menagerie could show a greater variety of animals than she kept under her thrall.

In this motley menagerie of hers there did not fail, either, a King Lion; for such sovereign game, too, had not been proof against Henrietta's siren song and charming little person, which, both on the stage and in society, she well understood how to set off to the best advantage, arrayed with all her alluring play of eye, her "childlike" prattle, and her exquisite coquetry. Yet however much he, too, had been affected, our royal lion, from a native shyness of his own, had not yet his courage stimulated to the point of claiming the lion's share in her favour.

Nor was Mamma Sontag herself yet disposed to renounce the sweet game of love; with her, however, love became a blind and dangerous passion. She had at that time a *liaison* known to all the town with the excellent actor Wegener of the Königstadt. Even marriage was talked of. Then the lover died. He was the father of Karl Sontag, the present popular *bon vivant* of the stage. Of his Francisca's twelve children it was but few that poor Franz Anton Sontag lived to see.

How different was the young Nina Sontag from both mother and sister! I think she never had and never wished to have an admirer. While quite a young girl she was already of an earnest and reserved character, old beyond her years. We called her by the name only of "little granny." She played small parts, but without any pleasure or indeed any special talent, merely to please her

mother and sister. To them she was devoted with a truly
unselfish love. Certainly never did the most intoxicating
triumphs of Henrietta cause her to sigh or reflect how
she was not beautiful and talented and celebrated like her
sister. She only rejoiced with an inward joy at the splendid
successes of Henrietta. She was a soul the most faithful
and the most free from all envy, and as a Catholic was
even then given up to an enthusiastic piety wh ch made
her feel painful remorse of conscience at her godless,
worldly life. When once asked what was her highest wish,
she gently answered with downcast eyes, " Rest and peace
—apart from the world ! " This wish of hers was later on
fulfilled.

I have a vivid remembrance of a conversation between
Mamma Sontag and her two daughters, which is very
characteristic. Henrietta had once gently expressed a
wish to visit the Pfaueninsel, near Potsdam, very celebrated at that time for its splendid flowers and wild
animals, and the favourite residence of her royal patron.
The matador of all Sontag admirers, Justizrath Ludolff, at
once, therefore, arranged a grand excursion by land and
water. My mother and I were also invited to the party.
We started by carriage in the prime of a glorious summer
morning. At the Glincke Bridge we entered gondolas, all
decked in festive bunting and garlands. In the midst of
singing we landed on the fair island. The morning passed
away in country pastimes and in walks. On a wide lawn
a number of games were played. Henrietta was the
gayest and the nimblest in running and springing, to
the delight of her guard, old and young ; but likewise to
their secret anxiety, fearing, as they did, that their sweet
nightingale might heat herself overmuch, and so catch
cold and hoarseness. But she made mock of all these
apprehensions with her clear-ringing laugh, " Nay, it will
do Jetty no harm ; and I do feel so happy ! "

At the splendid dinner to which we were treated under
the old lime trees, and by the foaming champagne, the
conversation naturally came round to the subject of sweet
love, and so to kisses in general, and hand kisses in particular.

Mamma Sontag said decidedly—"I never kissed a man's hand, even though I were madly in love with him; and never, never shall I stoop so low."

"But why not, then, mother?" gaily struck in Henrietta. "The hand of a loved and esteemed husband I should willingly kiss, without feeling that I had done anything amiss."

The whole guard, young and old, clapped their hands and cried out enthusiastically, "Bravo! bravo! Heavenly word! Sweet angel!" and demanded of every lady at the table to give her opinion in turn on the subject of kissing.

Nina Sontag said, in quite a grandmotherly tone—"I have no opinion about kissing, as I have never yet thought about it. Yet I believe, for certain, I shall never kiss either a man's mouth or hand, just as little as he will mine; for I shall never marry."

We all laughed at this odd answer of the sixteen-year-old maiden, and the earnest way in which she said it. And yet it was the truth Nina spoke.

When it came to my turn I said boldly, "If I had to marry a man twenty years older than myself, because he had made great sacrifices for my sake, or that of my family, I should willingly kiss his hand from gratitude, and perhaps his hand still more than his mouth. A young husband, however, would have to kiss my hand."

The whole Sontag guard, of course, cried out, "The divine Henrietta has hit the bull's-eye."

Henrietta's love for her younger sister Nina was truly touching. It was a love so blind that *la diva* on every occasion loudly asserted that Nina's voice and talent for singing were much more considerable than her own outfit in that respect. "Nina will soon cast me into obscurity on the stage by her beauty, singing, playing, and fame!" And whoever ventured on taking the least exception to that assertion was sure to be sharply corrected by Henrietta for his want of judgment.

Altogether, Henrietta evinced on every occasion an extraordinary fund of good nature and kindness of heart. I once saw her come fagged and weary from the rehearsal in the Königstadt Theatre. Excitedly she said to Justiz-rath Kunowsky—

"I cannot appear to-morrow as 'Weisse Dame.'* Altogether, I cannot sing so often. You over-estimate my strength. I shall get ill. Please countermand the 'Weisse Dame' for to-morrow."

When, however, Kunowsky explained the great losses the management would suffer by such a step, seeing that all the tickets were already sold for the next day, then did the charming White Lady of Avenel *not* fail to make her appearance on the morrow.

Only once did Henrietta baulk the treasury of the Königstadt Theatre, in order to do a good turn to a friend!

On this matter Moschelles, under date 21st Nov., 1826, writes in his diary:

"Concert-day. Fräulein Sontag being prevented from assisting us directly, because the management of the Königstadt Theatre refused their permission to her singing outside their theatre, assisted us indirectly by reporting herself hoarse. Instead, therefore, of appearing at the Königstadt, she came with my wife to our concert. When I thanked the celebrated singer for this kindness, she answered with the sweet smile peculiar to her—'But, dear Moschelles, should not an old Viennese friend be able to frustrate the cabals of a theatre director? 'S Jettel ist immer noch 's Jettel.'" †

Henrietta's behaviour to an old rival, that had formerly caused her much grief of heart, was truly magnanimous.

Once, Unter der Linden, she heard a little ragged girl sing in genuine Viennese Bäuerle's popular song, "'S gibt nur a Kaiserstadt, 's gibt nur a Wien,"‡ a song which Holtei's "Wiener in Berlin"§ had rendered popular in Berlin. Henrietta handed a copper to the little singer, and asked her kindly how she was situated, who were her parents, and how she had come to Berlin.

---

* "The White Lady."
† Viennese for "Jettel (little Jetty) is still the same Jettel."
‡ "There's only *a* Kaiserstadt; there's only *a* Vien."
§ "Viennese in Berlin."

The child then sadly answered, "I was born in Vienna. My mother is very poor and blind. She was once a great, splendid singer; her name is Amelia Steininger."

Amelia Steininger! With what a start did Henrietta Sontag hear the name! Amelia Steininger, the Vienna *Prima Donna*, had from the first day the young Henrietta Sontag arrived in Vienna from Prague, never ceased persecuting her with envy and malice, with intrigues and cabals, till at last she hounded her charming and amiable colleague (Henrietta) out of the capital altogether; and now was this old enemy become a blind beggar! But it was not triumph that Henrietta now felt! With a tear in her eye, she sought out her old colleague, to whom she did not drop a single syllable respecting the old Vienna times, but magnanimously made provision for the poor blind woman to the day of her death and for the education of her daughter.

After so much light, I may well be allowed to point to a few shades.

Besides her nicely calculated coquetry, I know of only one weakness to lay to the door of Henrietta Sontag. She had a strange passion, which, even at that time, had become conspicuous, and which, later on, was to cost the Countess Rossi many sorrowful hours, which was even perhaps in part the cause that her Excellency the Ambassadress had to return to singing for a living—the passion for gambling. In the most animated company, and at the gayest ball, Henrietta could yet retire with the gallant Russian ambassador, Alopeus, to an adjoining room, sit down at the gambling table, and hour after hour, with feverish haste, and with perhaps twenty packs of cards, play the then favourite game of Rabus.

But that, too, the Sontag enthusiasts found to be intellectual, transporting, heavenly; and all the other Sontag epithets then in use.

Under this cast of the constellations, there fell suddenly in March, 1826, out of the blue heaven, like an icy hailshower into fever-hot Sontag Berlin, a pamphlet of eleven sheets, bearing the title, "Henrietta, the fair Songtress:

A Tale of our Time. By Freimund Zuschauer.* Leipzig :
F. L. Herbig. 1826."

Then rose a cry and lamentation, as if the world were
coming to an end. The Sontag guard, old and young,
went raging through the town, and snorting out vengeance
sought where to lay hands on the scandalous pamphleteer.
The fair Henrietta, all in tears, wringing her hands, ran to
the "Palais" to beseech her august patron for protection and
satisfaction. The good king at once had the book con-
fiscated and contrabanded throughout the whole of Prussia.
The more rabid of the Sontag enthusiasts hastened with
extra post to Leipzig, and there bought up the remnant of
the accursed pamphlet, which they delivered religiously
over to the flames.

"Henrietta, the Fair Songstress" is, in consequence,
become a great literary rarity. The few copies that had
yet escaped the fire went clandestinely from hand to hand
to be devoured in secret. For weeks nothing was spoken
of in Berlin but the "high treason."

To-day all this is hardly comprehensible, and we smile
at the inoffensiveness of the pamphlet. We are accustomed to more pungent peppering in our comic papers and
polemic *brochures*. Nay, our modern singers would only
be delighted if a *litterateur* would write for them eleven
sheets of such notices as fell to the lot of the fair Henrietta.
Freimund Zuschauer has nothing but kind and good, if
not always delicate, words for the celebrated singer, and
his wit and banter are directed only to the army of
admirers who, in truth, fifty years ago laboured under no
mild form of Sontag infatuation. But even such wit and
banter as there is sounds to-day altogether harmless.

Let the reader judge for himself. I still find among my
papers a copy of the "Fair Henrietta," which had escaped
the universal *auto-da-fé*. I quote the most characteristic
passages; and first, the exordium *litteratim*, with some
elucidations of my own in brackets.

"The opera [in the Königstadt Theatre] was at an end ;
yet the storm of applause accorded to the young singer,

---

* "Free-speaking Spectator."

Henrietta, who had just appeared for the first time as a member of the theatre, seemed as though it would never come to an end. The reverberating thunder of a thousand clapping hands broke forth ever anew, while the brief intervals were filled up by the thousand-fold exclamation of the name of the fair lady. At last the curtain rose again, and the blissful vision was displayed in all the grace with which it had been thrilling the public the whole evening through. Compared with the hurricane that now burst forth, the previous storm seemed like a calm. Every man went into a transcendency in shrieking his rapture. The young singer alone was at a loss for expression, and had to retire with mute bows; but the joy which sparkled in her eyes told the tale of her feelings. Still more in-dubitable, if possible, was the expression of the eyes of the gentlemen, both old and young, during the play; there was not one of them from whose eyes the God of Love did not look out roguishly. The old Field-Marshal Von Rauwitsch [General Von Brauchitsch, commandant of Berlin], on whose head, grown grey in campaigns, hardly any hair was left—even he, in his advanced age, seemed as though he had been hit by an arrow against which he had, perhaps, presumed to believe himself too securely armoured. For not only had he plated his breast with hard iron against Amor's shafts, but had even sheathed his face to the very nose with a purple-like covering of reddish metal, fashioned, probably, by help of Bacchus rather than of Vulcan. His eyes themselves the same god had helped to glass over. Amor, however, defying all this accoutre-ment, had managed to pierce through, for the adjutant heard the marshal say, on leaving his box: ' I'd give up the flavour of Pontac for three days to buy a kiss of this d——d fine girl!' And a vow of more awful import it was not possible for him to have vowed. A similar ex-perience befel Major Kegelino [Zechelin] also, who, though almost a perfect fixture in his casino, was yet for once induced to drop his hand in the game and to dream away his time in the opera. For it was hardly possible he had heard anything, so much had he been blinded, and even stunned, by the charms of the young singer.   On getting into his carriage he called to the coachman: 'To the Königstadt Theatre!' whence he had just come out.

"Still greater was the experience of two royal counsellors, Hemmstoff [Hermstorff] and Wicke [Wilke], friends intimately allied, by their common sense of art and their common habit of attending the theatre and clapping applause—still greater, I say, was their impression of the wonder of nature. Wicke let his enthusiastic eyes linger on the fallen curtain, and then said: 'Friend, what is life without the sunshine of love? Oh, how well now do I understand the tender, sagacious poet!' 'True, very true,' replied Hemmstoff, seeking in vain to put his hand through the hair which the scythe of time had already shorn off; 'true, very true, are the words of the poet. But, dear me, I feel confoundedly hungry! Let us eat something in the restaurant below!'

"There are assembled the whole Sontag guard, old and young, round oysters and champagne, singing the praises of the fair Henrietta. . . . Wicke melts into elegaics. 'Oh, the sweet, inexpressibly sweet, lovely, charming, richly-gifted songstress! She looks smilingly at us and we weep, now with rapture, now with pain!'

"In the salon of the singer we recognise her private guard; among them the churlish Lord Monday [Clanwilliam, English Ambassador in Berlin], and the elegant Count Regenbogen. Above every one else, however, the singer favours a young unknown musician, Werner [orchestra violinist]."

The author, in closing his book, expresses the hope that nobody would be offended at his innocent sport.

But what universal rage! And when the guilt was at last brought home to Rellstab, all his friends broke with him, and he was condemned to three months' incarceration in Spandau in the summer of 1828.

With time, however, "Henrietta, the fair singer," overcame the criticism of Rellstab, too, who in the *Vossiche Zeitung* became her warmest admirer.

After this scandal, Lord Clanwilliam disappeared for some time from Berlin, but soon returned, to throw him-

self, with all his former fervour, at the feet of the goddess.
He gave a splendid supper to her and Catalini, and the
talk ran that Henrietta would shortly be Lady Clanwilliam.

At last came a day of deepest mourning for the whole
of Berlin. On the 29th May, 1826, Henrietta Sontag, in
the part of *Cinderella*, took leave of Königstadt. Although
a leave of but a few months, it was still a bitter parting.
If the Sontag guard, old and young, had before been in a
fever of delight, they were now in a paroxysm of woe.

How many dozens of times was Henrietta called that
evening before the curtain, to hear the sighs and sobbings
of her devotees! . . . The parting singer was herself
touched to tears, and sobbed out: "I do not deserve so
much love and kindness!"

At the door of the theatre she found the whole of the
large Alexander Platz densely packed with a humming,
surging multitude—the thousands who had been unable to
find a place in the theatre. They received her with thundering cheers.

Although it was but a hundred steps to the "Kaiser
von Russland" Hôtel, on the opposite side of the Alexander
Platz, where she lived, yet was she prudent enough to
have her celebrated red carriage in waiting, to avoid being
stifled by love and admiration. The whole way thither
was strewn with flowers. The red Sontag carriage was
known to every one in Berlin. So soon as it was any-
where visible, gentlemen and ladies, masters and scholars,
servants and cooks, all hastened thither to form for it a
passage of honour, and, if possible, catch a sight of the
illustrious one. And what inquiry was being constantly
made after the red carriage, after the days and hours when
Henrietta would not be using it. Every one wanted to
revel on the cushions or luxuriate blissfully in the red
corner consecrated by the person of Henrietta. To be able
to meet all demands, Herr Gentz got a second red carriage
built. Berlin, however, soon got wind of the deception,
and the red carriage let out by Herr Gentz was sure to be
suspiciously inspected by a public that would not tolerate
imposition.

In the red carriage, then, on that sad evening of May,

1826, amid thousand-voiced "vivats," Henrietta Sontag made her slow, triumphant progress to her hotel, preceded in front by a music band, and attended on every side by her guard, old and young, her escort of honour, all laden with flowers. These last were permitted to accompany their goddess into her festively-illuminated, flower-decked apartments, to spend the last evening in her sweet society. Outside in the square the excited multitude kept swaying hither and thither till late into the night, listening to the torchlight serenades of several military bands, and never weary of shouting "Vivat! vivat!" till the lovely one would show herself on the balcony, with one or another of her elect guard, and wave thanks with her handkerchief. Thereupon would swell up the thousand-voiced call: "Return! return!" And to this she would joyfully nod her head

Next morning the faithful guard gave the parting singer a festive escort in carriages to Potsdam, and assisted at a brilliant concert in the town theatre there, with which Henrietta took leave of the Court. All tickets for this concert had, of course, been long before bought up by the Berliners; and the king, too, drove thither expressly to be present at the parting entertainment. He appeared on the stage to bid his dear nightingale a hearty farewell, and wish her good fortune on her way to and in Paris. On this occasion the monarch expressed himself as follows: "Yesterday evening greatly *fêted*—the good Berliners made a great noise in the theatre, and also under your window—could hardly fall asleep—must have grown troublesome to you in the end—to me, at least, such an affair insufferable—don't like it."

Henrietta, with her most charming smile and most radiant look and most child-like tone, answered; "Ah, your Majesty, such things are nothing new to you; but when a poor singer experiences the like, for the first time, she must needs feel heartily glad."

And the king went away more charmed than ever.

Henrietta drove off to Paris under the protection of her theatre mother and companion, the Baroness of Montenglaut who had formerly played the *rôle* of reciter and authoress.

When the news came from -Paris, "We have won a brilliant victory, Henrietta has taken Paris by storm," the jubilation and triumph knew no end. The first news of the victory of Waterloo could not have been hailed with more enthusiasm in Berlin.

Report of victory followed close on report of victory. Cherubini, Rossini, Boildieu, Paer, and Auber marched at Henrietta's triumphal car.

When Henrietta returned to Germany at the end of summer she had become a world celebrity. Her journey was a triumphal progress. In remembrance of the old time when she lived in Mainz with her grandmother, as the child of a poor strolling player, and thence set out alone with her little sister Nina on the pitiful long drive to Prague, she sang German again on reaching the Main and then flew to Weimar to greet Goethe with a song. And Goethe sang to her in return in the bright verses quoted in part at the beginning of this chapter.

Goethe writes to Zelter, under date, 9th Nov., 1826 :—

" That Mademoiselle Sontag has given us a passing call, showering on us the tones of her melodious voice, marks an epoch, at all events. Every one says, of course, the like would require to be often heard and the greater number of us would fain be seated to-day again in the Königstadt Theatre. And I, too, am of the number. For in truth she would need to be first taken up and comprehended as an individual, recognised in relation to her times, become a person whom one has grown intimate with and accustomed to, before she can be lovingly enjoyed. As it was, the specimen of her talent which took us unprepared has more confused than delighted me. The good that merely flits by us without return leaves rather an impression of loss, and makes one sensible of what he has not."

The pet child, Sontag, was received in triumph by her all-enthusiastic guard, old and young, who had gone out in carriages and on horseback to attend her to Berlin, where she was féted, and on her first re-appearance in the Königstadt Theatre on the 11th September, 1829, hailed with jubilation, poems, and flowers. O Profanity! however, there mingled a few shrill whistling sounds with these cheers of welcome, because it was known that Henrietta had accepted a three years' engagement at the Italian Opera in Paris, and because she had returned to Berlin a few days over the expiry of the leave of absence allowed her.

Now arose a dreadful uproar in the house, as though it would fall in pieces. Between the applauders and whistlers there broke out a furious combat with fisticuffs. All in vain did the horrified king, who had hastened his journey home from Teplitz in order to be present at the honoured appearance of his favourite, send his adjutant twice to still the scuffle. The police had at last to imprison the ringleaders among the catcall criers; the whole performance was a scene of storm and agitation.

Then again, however, the Sontag fever began to re-assert its former virulence, or if possible it reached a height greater that it had ever before known. At the Court, too, Henrietta had every distinction paid her. Not at the Court Concerts alone did the king see and speak to her, but also at the little confidential dinners given by Timm, and even in the palace of the Princess Liegnitz.

When, in the summer of 1827, Sontag's favourite parrot flew away from her, the king sent her another by Prince Wittgenstein, with these words of pleasantry: "His Majesty has looked out for the most beautiful and the wisest parrot, even at the risk of exciting the jealousy of the Princess Liegnitz."

The Sontag fever continued to rage wilder than ever, though Ludwig Rellstab, in particular, by his criticisms in the *Vossische Zeitung*, endeavoured to abate its pitch to the best of his power.

The "Jubilee of Song" in 1827, with the splendid performances of Angelica Catalani and Nanetta Schechner, which Rellstab accounted much higher than those of Sontag, furnished him with the desired opportunity. Thus, for example, he writes in reference to Catalani and her rendering of the celebrated but difficult variations of Rode, written originally for the violin, and which Mara was the first to venture on singing:—

" Mademoiselle Sontag has by these performances acquired a great name in public. On making a comparison our judgment is to the following effect. As far as easy manipulation of voice is concerned, Mademoiselle Sontag's voice gives her in truth an advantage in a few small respects of precision, but in the delivery of the melody, and in a fluency mounting to audacity, Madame Catalani decidedly bears away the prize. Account must also be taken of the loveable manner in which the latter singer wholly surrenders herself without the least misgiving, as if under an instinct of pure innocence, to every performance, however widely different one from the other, so that even such species of song as would in general not commend themselves to a higher taste acquire from her rendering an air of naturalness, conferring on them a positive title to existence, while with other singers they rarely attain to more than the lot of being merely tolerated. The relation, therefore, between the two singers might be expressed as that of a miniature copy to an original picture in its natural dimensions."

Still more dangerous for the worship of Henrietta was the starring engagement of Nanneta Schechner, who, by the power of her wonderful tones, warm from the heart, carried away with her, especially as *Fidelio*, many even of the rabid Sontag devotees. Rellstab called her talent " a gift of heaven such as is dispensed hardly twice in one century. Whatever is in the power of a voice of splendour and glorious opulence—whatever is in the power of a deep soul uttering itself in song and noble play—was here accomplished. As far as effect goes Nannetta Schechner remains the grandest artiste of my recollection. Her soul in song warmed one like a very sun."

Four weeks after the last appearance of Schechner in the Royal Opera House, on the 16th September, 1827, Henrietta Sontag, finding the Königstadt Theatre too limited for her sphere of action, entered for the first time the arena of her rival's triumphs, and gave a series of performances as *Donna Anna* in "Don Juan," *Agathe* in "Freischütz," *Myrrha* in " Opferfest," &c., &c.; appearing in all fifteen times, for which she received the then unheard-of honorarium of 11,000 thalers—thanks to the word of a royal patron.

Under date the 27th October, Zelter writes to his friend Goethe :—

" Mademoiselle Sontag I have now twice gladly seen in the Royal Theatre, as *Myrrha* in " Opferfest," and as *Susanna* in Mozart's " Figaro." If there is no single special quality in her I have to bring out prominently, yet was her whole performance on the boards a joyful experience. Her pretty person appearing among three or four others, and amid so much that she was not accustomed to, in so large a theatre, she yet understands how to present to happy advantage; and with its perfect vocalisation and articulation, her voice, even among much stronger voices, beams down on one like a peculiarly clear star. Her face, too, keeps parallel, so to say, with her melody, as do also her arms and hands ; and all this play never repeats itself ; we get the same over again, which is, nevertheless, not the same, but something quite new. A duet was called for, *da capo ;* the two singers came back as they had gone away. Henrietta had stood before on the right side and now she stood on the left, and the whole duet seemed like another piece."

On the streets of Berlin, however, you could hear the melody :—

> " Schechner is dodt, Schechner is dodt,
> Sontag schwimmt in Kanten.
> Woher hat sie die, woher hat sie die?
> Vom Englischen Gesandten !" *

Meanwhile Henrietta, by august command, was engaged with the title of " Kammersängerin " for the royal opera, under the most flattering conditions :—

---

* May be roughly Englished—
> "Schechner is dead, Schechner is dead,
> Sontag prinks in galon d'or.
> Who gave her it, who gave her it ?
> The English g'llant, th' ambassador!"

6000 thalers salary; 2500 thalers life-pension; six months' leave of absence; a yearly benefit in the opera-house, without deduction of the costs; to sing twice a-week; on the occasion of performances in Potsdam, a royal equipage, with four horses, and rooms in the hôtel there; in each of the royal theatres two free first places daily at her disposal; she to have the election in what Spontini operas she will sing.

Even the further condition Henrietta annexed to the above was complied with, namely, that her mother should at the same time be engaged for five years at an annual salary of 1900 thalers (according to another account, 2500 thalers) and a life-pension of 600 thalers (according to other accounts, 1000 thalers), and her sister Nina be like-wise engaged.

Henrietta's engagement, however, did not come into force, because she was tied down by previous obliga-tions to Paris and London, and then left the stage as Countess Rossi.

On the 5th November Henrietta sang for her benefit *Amenaide* in " Tancred."   On this occasion the king gave her a present of 400 Friedrichs-d'or and two golden sal-vers, with personal ornaments. The Princess Liegnitz sent her a golden chain, and at the close of her last singing at court the Princess of Prussia kissed her tenderly in presence of all the people. The charming witch had be-witched all the world.

Shortly before her departure she received in addition from the king, who was the most bewitched of them all, an autograph farewell note, and a letter of recommenda-tion to the Queen of the Netherlands, a sister to his Majesty.

On her new triumphal journey to Paris, Henrietta again sang in Goethe's house in Weimar on the 11th of Novem-ber, 1827, and then publicly in his native town of Frank-furt, where the half-deaf Börne, usually so morose and pessimistic, was inspired to write his celebrated Sontag apotheosis. And he had previously been exasperated at her and the whole of the Sontag mania! He writes:—

" I had the most furious things in my mind I intended '

printing; but since I have heard and seen the Enchantress
herself, she has enchanted me like the others. How I
should like to praise this Enchantress!—but where to
find the words? A prize of a hundred ducats might be
offered to whoever would discover an adjective not before
employed in admiring application to Sontag, and no one
would win the prize. She has been called the nameless,
the heavenly, the highly extolled, the incomparable, the
highly revered, the heavenly virgin, the pearl of great
price, the virginal songstress, the dear Henrietta, the sweet
maid, the angelic girl, the heroine of song, the divine
child, the treasure of song, the German maiden, the pearl
of the German opera! I say yea to all these epithets, and
with all my heart. Henrietta might say 'veni, viderunt,
vici.' The landlord of the hôtel in which Fräulein Sontag
was entertained for a fortnight refused all payment from his
guest, and so ennobled and rejuvenated his old 'Roman
Emperor' of an establishment into a Prytaneum, whither
all Germans having any regard for the fatherland must
pilgrimage.

"Madame Catalani is said to have criticised Henrietta
Sontag in the following terms—'Elle est unique dans
son genre, mais son genre est petit!' Who, however, has
heard her as *Desdemona* in Rossini's 'Othello,' will find this
criticism very unjust. In hearing her you forgot entirely
the insipid text of Rossini's 'Othello,' and saw and heard
Shakespeare's *Desdemona*. She is just as admirable in
simple song that addresses the heart as in ornamental song
that only makes a flourish to the ears. Old men were
to be seen weeping under her influence, an effect which no
mere artifice, however incomparable and unheard-of, has
it in its power to produce. Her soft tones, her wonderful
intricacies, trills, cadences, etc., resembled the graceful
naïve ornamentations on a Gothic building, which serve to
temper the earnest severity of lofty arches and pillars, and
to conciliate the joy of heaven with the joy of earth, not
to compromise and degrade that severity. The enthusiasm
Henrietta Sontag kindled by her *Desdemona* was no
transient flare, but rather like an inextinguishable Greek
flame."

I will not speak of the new triumphs which awaited *la diva* at Paris in the great opera and in society. Here she made the acquaintance of the Sardinian Ambassador at the Hague, Count Rossi, who, in the most extravagant manner, laid his homage at her feet. Thus once after the opera the count awaited her with his carriage, himself dressed in a coachman's livery, opened the door of the carriage for her, and drove her home. Such reverence was more than Henrietta could resist. Count Rossi became the most favoured of her Parisian guard.

In the spring of 1828, Henrietta Sontag arose for the first time as a sun on England's fog; radiant, to the obscuration of all other suns; worshipped as is the luminary of the world by the sun worshippers. And not merely as a singer was she received, but in the usually so rigidly-exclusive English society, which in its *salon* concerts dared to draw a fine line of demarcation separating itself from its paid singers, even from a Pasta, a Malibran, a Schröder-Devrient—in such society Henrietta Sontag took quite a unique place. The French Ambassador, Prince Polignac, introduced her to the Duke of Devonshire, who gave her a brilliant ball in her honour. An eye-witness reports the matter to Goethe:—"Fräulein Sontag danced with peculiar grace. The world of fashion pressed round her to catch but a few words from her. This is an unprecedented distinction in London."

Nay, more than that, the Duke of Devonshire, who, in one of his musical soirees, once tapped the celebrated French singer, Lafont, on the shoulder in the middle of an aria, saying, "C'est assez, mon cher!" and Prince Pückler-Muskau, who was then making a tour of England—both almost simultaneously placed their hearts, with their dukedoms and principalities, at the feet of the worshipped singer, who, however, refused them. She felt herself committed to Count Rossi.

In Moschelles' London diary we find the following respecting this visit of Sontag to England:—

" From the 3rd April, the day of her arrival in England, she was made to enjoy no end of all that was beautiful

and kind. The charming young maiden, apart altogether
from her talent, was a most delightful and amiable creature.
In her going out and coming in she was free from all
assumption and affection. Indeed, when she is seated
at our family table we entirely forget that London is waiting with the most eager expectation on her *début*. To-day,
in the great rehearsal of 'Barbiere,' she charmed every one
with her *Rosina*. When she showed herself on the balcony,
people clapped hands to the lovely vision; when she
stepped on to the stage with her 'una voce poco fà," her
voice and song enchanted every one. Not one shade fell
on one of her London representations. The press in the
pit of the opera (where a ticket costs but half-a-guinea)
was so great that gentlemen on getting to their seats
found themselves without their coat tails, and ladies without their head-dresses. I cannot say which of her representations I deemed the most successful, for her song is
always enchanting, and although I note the absence of the
greatest dramatic effects I am yet too much taken by the
naturalness and loveliness of her play and presence to miss
anything. Even when she is singing her variations on the
'Schweizerbue' it never occurs to me to ask, 'What can
she mean by this gurgling sound?' for all she does is perfect of *its own* kind.

"At the large dinner given in her honour by Prince
Esterhazy, at which were present Prince and Princess
Polignac, Baron Bülow, Count Redern, Marquis of Hertford, Lord and Lady Ellenborough, Mademoiselle Sontag
sang enchantingly in the evening. The Duke of Devonshire's asking her shortly afterwards to his ball, and dancing with her, made a great sensation. The charming young
maiden wore on this evening a very transparent white
dress of crape, to which a trimming of genuine gold braid-
ing lent a classic appearance. Her graceful figure was
still further set off by rich gold ornaments in her hair and
round her finely modelled neck, and her arms and hands,
which are of a perfect beauty.

"19th July. We had once the happiness of seeing our
lovely, honoured countrywoman in a larger circle with us;
she was all that is typified by the words 'enchantment'

and 'loveableness' in every respect, both in her person and in her song. Sir Walter Scott, on a short visit to London, had called on us; he was charmed to meet Sontag, and she, who was just going to appear in ' Donne del lago,' considered it fortunate to become acquainted with the youthfully venerable sage. He was all ear and eye when she asked him about her costume as a Highland maid. 'He described to her every fold of the plaid with the precision peculiar to him. Altogether, ' Jettl' had two old worshippers among us, the second being Clementi, no less delighted than Scott. He acted fantastically like a fresh youth. It was a sight to see how the two venerable sages, Scott and Clementi, made merry with each other, shook hands with each other, and, in spite of their competitive courtship and admiration of Sontag, kept clear of all mutual jealousy."

On the 24th July "the Star of the Season" returned to Paris.

Thence suddenly resounded as far as Berlin the dreadful intelligence, that " our Henrietta, having accidentally in her *salon* trodden on a cherry stone, slipped and hurt her knee dangerously. She is not allowed to tread any stage, or visit any company. O the misfortune! O the poor angel!"

In feverish excitement the Sontag guard, old and young, ran about, inconsolable and distracted, through Berlin; and wherever two met together the first question was: "How is it? No good news yet arrived from Paris? No more word of our dear suffering one? Oh, oh, oh!"

In these circumstances Justizrath Ludolff, without long consideration, ordered post horses, and, leaving his cases and clients in the lurch, drove day and night to Paris to inquire after the welfare of the unique. He found Henrietta on a sofa, more blooming than ever, surrounded by sympathising friends and adorers. There was no danger whatever to be apprehended, she was only not yet allowed to get up. Count Rossi devoted his most tender care to her. The nasty cherry-stone!

Ludolff, nevertheless, returned from his pious visit to the

sick remarkably disconcerted. He had heard something whispered in Paris, which was soon also excitedly muttered in Berlin : " The faithless Henrietta has contracted a secret marriage with the Sardinian Ambassador at the Hague. She will, however, for some time yet still keep to the stage and retain her maiden name, for Count Rossi has no fortune, and his relations, as also the King of Sardinia, are against this union with a singer ! "

In the late autumn of 1829 I again met Henrietta Sontag and Count Rossi in Paris.

In the spring of 1830 Henrietta Sontag appeared at her last harvest-reaping in Germany, before the people of Berlin once more. She was to tread the stage no further, as being unsuitable to her Excellency the Countess Rossi. And now everybody in Berlin—in Germany—in the whole world, was long since aware that Mademoiselle Sontag existed only for newspaper advertisements and concert programmes. All the greater was the general eagerness to see how her Excellency would comport herself as the singer Mademoiselle Henrietta Sontag. The throng of people to her concerts was greater than ever, if possible.

At the wish of the king, and the stormy prayers of her adorers, Countess Rossi was induced, by way of exception, to appear sixteen times as Mademoiselle Sontag on the stage of the Opera House. First as *Desdemona*, on which Rellstab's criticism in the *Vossische Zeitung* is now all praise and admiration—" grace," " dignity," and all what not.

Zelter also admires her in this part; her beautiful dumb play, her natural, voluble way of singing, and the manner in which the identity of *Desdemona* is ever preserved, though there is always some variety every successive time she appears. The following is his report to Goethe :—

" If her voice is not the most beautiful I have known, it is yet pure, without heart, without phlegm, and therefore so pliant to her nature and will as ever to do just what is proper. Nor is her mouth the loveliest, yet is it no tongue you hear; she speaks so clearly with her lips that no words are needed. To sum up : Everything about her, from head to foot, her dress itself, is all song."

Zelter's only regret is, "that a swarm of old, grey, shallow fellows are perpetually buzzing praises and making presents to her."

And now arrived the evening of mourning, the evening of the 22nd May, 1830, when Henrietta Sontag took a final farewell of the German stage, as Rossini's *Semiramis*. When the curtain fell the public were desirous of testifying once more the enthusiasm her talent had kindled. The curtain rose again. "She stood before us" (I quote from Rellstab's report in the *Vossische Zeitung*), "a shower of flowers and poems rained down on her. Only after a long pause did she say a few words of thanks, from which we were fain to infer that it was not perhaps the last time the artiste would appear before us," &c., &c.

The king again sent the lovely player 400 Friedrichs-d'or as the price of his ticket.

Eighteen years later on, Rellstab, referring to his last Sontag criticism, added that after that performance she made one more triumphal tour through the world, but only as concert-singer, retiring then for ever from the world of art to a new sphere of life.

Two years subsequent to the date of this statement Rellstab was to see the Countess Rossi return again to the stage as Madame Sontag.

Not till after mademoiselle's great concert tour in 1830, which brought her in enormous sums—as much as 13,202 marks, for example, of net profit for three evenings in Hamburg alone—did Count Rossi, the Sardinian Ambassador at the Hague, make public his marriage with Henrietta, who had been previously ennobled by the good King Friedrich Wilhelm III. To both, however, it seemed desirable to quit the Hague shortly after that event, and Count Rossi, therefore, got himself transplanted to Frankfort-on-the-Maine, as Ambassador to the German Confederation. Here the Countess Rossi became the centre of society, charming all the world by her beauty, grace, amiability, and cheerfulness, as well as by her song and kindness of heart. She readily took part even in the most *dilettante* of *dilettante* concerts.

At charity concerts, too, held in St. Catherine's Church,

the Countess Rossi sang repeatedly, and, when once it came to her ears, that a poor invalid had longingly expressed the wish to hear Sontag once more before he died, Henrietta appeared in the most cordial way in the sick man's little room, and gladdened the sufferer by her song.

Shortly afterwards, Count Rossi, at the desire of the Emperor Nicholas, who was a great admirer of "Madame la Comtesse de Rossi-gnol," removed as ambassador to St. Petersburg, where Henrietta was enrolled among the most distinguished stars of the Court. She moved in the most intimate intercourse with the Imperial family, and sang almost every evening with the young grand-duchess duets and songs, such as the czar so greatly loved. Nay, the rigid and abrupt Autocrat of all the Russias was occasionally so softened and mildly attuned by these heavenly tones as to sing pious church trios with his lovely favourite daughter Alexandra, doomed so soon to wither away, and the Countess Rossi. At the wish of the czar Madame Rossignol also appeared a few times before the Court as *Somnambulist* and as *Lucia*. When King Karl Albert of Sardinia heard of it he deemed these reminiscences of the former public theatrical doings of his Lady Excellency very unbecoming, and in the most decided manner prohibited Count Rossi from allowing this half-public theatrical playing on the part of his spouse. Thereupon followed a sharp diplomatic exchange of notes between the Courts of St. Petersburg and Turin, in which the Czar Nicholas emphatically insisted that all the Lady Excellency had been doing at his Court and at his wish could by no means be described as "unbecoming." Not, however, till the Autocrat of all the Russias threatened to break off all relations with Turin, if the theatrical dispositions of the Lady Excellency were in any way thwarted, did the little King of Sardinia give way. He did not, however, forget this diplomatic discomfiture Countess Rossi had occasioned him.

The ambassador's lady even sang publicly before the St. Petersburgers—at a concert of Madame Ezegka, her beloved teacher at the Conservatory of Prague. The grateful heart of Henrietta summoned in 1840 this excellent teacher of singing from Vienna to St. Petersburg, and pro-

G

cured her a distinguished position at the new Theatrical School, as also many private lessons in the richest houses. Madame Ezegka became also the singing mistress of the Grand-Duchess Olga, the present Queen of Würtemberg, and of the Grand-Duchess Alexandra, as well as the two daughters of the Grand-Duke Michael. She, who, as singing mistress at the Leipzig Theatre, under the management of Hofrath Küstner, had a salary of 600 thalers, now received in St. Petersburg a yearly income of 20,000 rubles. And the concert which Countess Rossi got up for her motherly friend in grateful remembrance of her youthful years at Prague, brought Madame Ezegka a net profit of 14,000 rubles. And with it all, too, her Lady Excellency would on no account ever be anything else to her old teacher but the reverential "Jettel" of the olden time, nor would allow Ezegka to address her otherwise. than by the homely "Jettel" and "Du" (Thou).

The day after this one public appearance of Henrietta in St. Petersburg, an old Armenian, an enthusiast for music, came to her with the complaint that he had made the far journey from Charkow to the city of the czar to hear her sing, but had come too late to get a ticket. He was yet unwilling now to go away back again without having at least seen the lovely, wondrous nightingale.

Instantly the countess stepped to the piano, and sang to the old enthusiast *Desdemona's* " Song of the Willow," moving him to sweet tears, and herself moved to glad tears that she was yet able to produce such an effect.

In these days of renewed triumphs, the thought is said to have first emerged in the mind of Countess Rossi to return as Henrietta Sontag to the public opera and there achieve fresh laurels.

I know from her mother, who was then living with her youngest son, Karl, in Dresden, and with whom I was on friendly terms, that throughout this period Henrietta provided both for her mother and brother in the most affectionate manner. As to poor Nina, she had retired to a convent.

All in vain had the prudent and resolute mother tried her utmost to secure for her Nina the place of triumph on

the stage and in the favour of the public which had been
vacated by Henrietta. What a sad failure this proved to
be in Berlin, when she played in the "Weisse Dame," we
have already seen. Three years later she suffered a still
more crushing defeat in London, as Mozart's *Zerline.* It
was only for the sake of her mother that the poor victim
submitted to those new and joyless experiments. Her
quiet, unselfish heart longed for nothing more from life
than simply rest and peace. So she said to me when, in
the summer of 1840, I saw her for the last time in Dresden;
and, in saying so, a deep religious enthusiasm lighted up
her sad, world-weary eyes. Soon afterwards she entered
as a novice the convent of the Carmelites at Prague. The
nuns there wear day and night a coarse hair-cloth next
their skin, and sleep in coffins on straw. They are allowed
only fish and pulse for food, and even of this miserable
fare there is sometimes nothing to be had, in which ex-
tremity the starving creatures ring the bell of distress, by
way of appeal to the charity of pious hearts. Their special
saint is Maria Electa, whose incorruptible body has been
preserved for centuries in the convent, and, by a curious
contrivance, which the nuns call a miracle, is seen to move
hands and arms.

Poor Nina's delicate body was not long able to stand
these mortifications. The prioress herself got her transferred to a milder order, and Nina Sontag became a nun in
the convent of Marienthal, near Görlitz—following the
example of our beautiful and talented colleague of the
Königstadt Theatre, Maria Herold, who since 1833 had
been living as a nun in the convent of St. Mariastern,
near Bautzen, in Saxon Lausatia.

In the spring of 1838 I met the Countess Rossi at
Dresden, during the representation of the "Huguenots,"
in the Dresden Theatre, and four years later I again met
her, with her mother, for the last time in Dresden.
She was amiable and cordially affectionate, as in the
old collegiate time, and would not for a moment suffer
the countess and her Excellency to come between us.
She remembered with peculiar tenderness the happy times
we spent together in Berlin, when we played and sang and

danced together—and especially.that gay Christmas evening
in Ludolff's house, that had since come to such tragic grief.
She, too, had no knowledge where and how our unhappy
friend had ended, but reproached herself that in her
youthful inconsiderateness she had accepted so many
sacrifices from him, little imagining that she likewise was
thereby hastening his ruin.

Then we spoke of St. Petersburg, where I also had
lived three years. In the midst of Henrietta's joyous talk
I could, however, catch a tone of sadness.

Her mother soon after confided to me that Count Rossi
was no longer able to support his position as ambassador
in the costly city. He had no private means, and all that
Henrietta had accumulated by her singing was meanwhile
entirely spent. The count was therefore thinking of his
transference as ambassador to the cheaper town of Berlin;
but even there his ambassadorial salary would not suffice
to keep up their station. The countess was therefore
earnestly meditating a return to her artistic career. Count
Rossi had already taken initiatory steps in the matter at
the Court of Turin.

King Karl Albert, however, roundly refused to allow
the wife of his ambassador to sing for money. He gave
him, nevertheless, the advice, in confidence, that he might
separate from his wife under the cloak of conjugal
discords, and then nobody could prevent her appearing on
the stage as Henrietta Sontag.. Later on, when the
golden goal was attained, they might again make up a
reconciliation before the world.

Count Rossi and Henrietta, however, loved each other
too dearly to avail themselves of such an unworthy
expedient. They endeavoured to keep their expenses in
Berlin within the limit of the ambassador's salary. How
Countess Rossi here again became the bewitching favourite
of the new Court of Friedrich Wilhelm IV., and of
fashionable society, just as Henrietta Sontag had before
been the *enfant gaté* of the old Court of Friedrich Wilhelm
III., and of the whole town, is a matter of general knowledge. With what mixed feelings must the Countess
Rossi have again trodden those salons of the court in

which Henrietta Sontag had charmed the *elite* of society. In my mind I yet see her before me; the lovely tender girl, in white silk dress, blue asters in her fair locks, radiant joy in her forget-me-not features, such as after a theatrical musical entertainment in the Palais she stood beside me at the entrance to the ball salon, and we whispered our remarks to each other respecting the high personages dancing before us.

That even then, however, when I met Henrietta for the last time in Dresden, the possibility of her return to the stage was a matter of public conjecture appears from the following extract I take from a print of the year 1842:

"Whether the rumours afloat in 1841, that on account of the ruined state of her pecuniary affairs she intended returning to the stage, had any foundation in fact, or whether, as is said, her journey to Vienna in the beginning of 1842, had any connections with that matter, must appear in the near future. It would in any case be a pity if the figure of wondrous beauty, which at the zenith of its brilliancy voluntarily withdrew from the wondering world, should now in its declination have to appear again in public with abated force."

These rumours in the next following years came ever up again to the surface. Thus, we read in a Frankfort paper in the beginning of July, 1849:

"The *Independence* quotes from the *Observateur*, a paper usually well instructed in musical affairs, the remark that the news of the Countess Rossi going to London to fulfil an opera engagement there was without any true basis. The countess was, on the contrary, going with her husband, who had retired from the service of the Piedmontese Government, to settle permanently in Brussels! The paper congratulates the *Haute Volée* there on its new acquisition, as the lady's eminent talent had suffered nothing from time. We give our readers this report, for which the *Independence* itself does not stand surety, along with another notice to the effect that the Countess Rossi, a

few days before her departure from Berlin, called at the
establishment of Herrn Gerson there, and invested several
hundred thalers in light coloured silk stuffs, all of which
she carefully scrutinised in respect of their light effects in
the Moorish room of that firm. Whether all this scrutiny
respected Brussels society or the London proscenium, time
will determine."

And time did determine it in the very next days—in
favour of England.
The revolution year of 1848 had shattered, with others,
the throne of Karl Albert of Sardinia, and the war with
Austria had exhausted the finances of the country. Count
Rossi had every reason to be apprehensive about his
ambassadorship. His spouse thought more seriously than
ever of singing into existence, by the stage, a new golden
future for herself, her husband, and, above all, her beloved
four children. Through her devoted friend, Lord Westmoreland, English Ambassador at Berlin, she caused some
preliminary inquiries to be softly made in London as to
how Mr. Lumley, director of Her Majesty's Theatre,
would receive the suggestion. Mr. Lumley, in his turn,
with equal wariness, set inquiries afloat in Berlin regarding
the Countess Rossi, her voice and appearance, and was
charmed to learn that, notwithstanding the twenty years
which had elapsed since her appearance on the London
stage, the countess had in all that time grown—O wonder!
—only a few years older than was the enchanting Henrietta Sontag they had known before that interval—in voice
and figure! And then, by way of compensation for the
additional few years, she had acquired a novel charm for
both old and young England—for a veritable ambassadress
London had never yet seen on the stage !
So then were opened the most cautious, strictly private
negotiations, between director and singer, first through
the mediation of Lord Westmoreland, and then through
that of the pianist, Thalberg, who was performing in concerts in Berlin in the spring of 1849.
The beginning of April, 1849, Thalberg writes to
Lumley :

"Nothing positive is yet decided, but we may hope for a speedy success. The prospect of having to return to the stage appears to cause the countess the deepest affliction; she burst into tears at the bare thought of it. 'Economy,' however, is the watchword in Piedmont, by reason of the millions that have to be paid to Austria. Twelve ambassadors have already been recalled, and her husband may be the next. Or he may be reduced to a *chargé d'affaires* at half the salary. In these circumstances the countess feels how there can be no escape for her from the sacrifice. In a week in all likelihood her fate will be decided, and she will then at once write to you in London. I told her how important it would be to have the news already announced in England; but she declared that for the present these negotiations must be kept in strictest secrecy."

Soon after Countess Rossi herself writes to Lumley, who had already made her an offer of £6000 for her appearance for one season:

"When Herr Thalberg was here everything seemed to point to my being able to accept your offer. Political events seem since, however, to have strengthened the position of Piedmont, and you will understand how, at such a moment, I am not at liberty to form a resolution which nothing short of absolute necessity would justify."

Then in another letter, of the 4th of May, to Lumley:

"Decisive steps have meanwhile been taken in Turin, and by the 15th of this month at latest we must receive a categorical answer. If this should turn out in favour of your project, I should be in London by the 25th May. I am very sensible how extremely disagreeable and perplexing is your position, and would be happy indeed if it were in my power to put an end to this miserable uncertainty. On the other hand, you will no doubt see what are our difficulties, and with what delicacy we have to act! So soon as I am again Mademoiselle Sontag, your interest shall also be wholly mine; yea with all my heart, and with all my soul!"

It was not, however, till June that Count Rossi definitively lost his post as ambassador to the Court at Berlin; thereupon Henrietta immediately signed a contract for two seasons in Her Majesty's Theatre under the most favourable conditions. In spite, however, of her financial difficulties she would have shrunk from this step if she had not been assured by her old patron the Grand-Duke George of Mecklenburg-Strelitz, and by Lord Westmoreland, that Mademoiselle Henrietta Sontag would exist only for the English Opera, and that her Excellency the Countess Rossi would, without prejudice, take the place due to her in the fashionable English drawing-rooms.

And so, on the 7th July, 1849—while the German, French, and Belgian newspapers were still disputing whether Countess Rossi's purchase of light coloured silks in Gerson's meant Brussels society or the London proscenium —Henrietta Sontag stood on the stage of Her Majesty's Theatre in London, as Donizetti's *Linda di Chamouni!* received with a storm of applause by the crowded house.

What feelings must have agitated her heart in that trying moment! The thought of the past, and how, fully twenty years earlier, she had sung before that public " for the last time "—and how different all then was from now! the thought of her mother in Dresden, and " little Granny " in the convent, and the anxiety of both for her at that moment; the thought of her husband and her four children, and how all their future depended on this hour; the thought how she, now a married woman in her forties, with four children, was facing her admirers of twenty years ago: all these thoughts must have been anxiously agitating her heart, when she sent forth the first tone!

But when this first tone resounded through the breathless house—then, O wonder! those twenty years, which are wont to wither so many roses and lilies of beauty, to dim so many a bright eye, mar so many a graceful figure, and tarnish so many a silver voice—they were all as if revoked! and *Henrietta Sontag* again stood before the people of London in all the enchantment of the lovely beauty and grace of her prime, and her bright silver voice jubilated and trilled just as pure, as ear-captivating and heart-bewitching as in those old days of the year 1829. The wonder was beyond comprehension, but it was also beyond contention.

In the theatre Henrietta Sontag was now, evening after evening, overwhelmed anew with rapturous applause, and again as Lady Rossi idolised in fashionable society.

After *Linda* she sang *Rosina* in " Barbier," *Amina* in the " Somnambulist," *Desdemona* in " Othello," *Susanna* in " Figaro," and she needed not to shun comparison with the young Swedish nightingale, Jenny Lind, who had shortly before enchanted all England. But she now ventured on no *Donna Anna*—on no *Lucretia Borgia!* Henrietta Sontag always understood herself and her voice so well as never to sing a part in which she might fail, or which might be dangerous to her voice. She, therefore, never appeared in an opera by Spontini or Meyerbeer. *Lucretia Borgia* she afterwards sang *once*, but then laid it aside, as no more favourable for her—till she made her swan-song in Mexico.

Lady Rossi celebrated hardly fewer triumphs than did Henrietta Sontag. She shone, danced, and sang in the drawing-rooms of the Duchess of Cambridge, the Duchesses of Cleveland and Rutland, the Russian Ambassadress, Baroness Brunow, &c., and the most magnificent country seats in England and Scotland received the Count and Countess Rossi as dear and highly honoured guests.

At the end of the year 1849, Mademoiselle Sontag made a grand concert tour through England and Scotland with the artistes Thalberg, Calzolari, Lablache, and Piatti. On the route from Glasgow to Aberdeen the railway train was buried deep in snow—and the delicate lady had to toil on foot through the dreadful snow-storm. Count Rossi wrote on the subject to Mr. Lumley:

" If, amid these trials, in the middle of the night, and in the deepest darkness, when the snow lay six feet deep, and the storm threw us down on leaving our carriages, Madame de Rossi had evinced less courage and energy, we should all have been found dead next morning, frozen in the *coupés*. At night every trace of the railway carriages had

disappeared under the snow. Had we had but one hundred steps more to wander in search of a roof, we should
all have sunk down dead on the way. When we reached
the house Lablache and my servant fell down unconscious.
This dreadful incident has most deeply shattered Madame
de Rossi. She had to let the clothes on her person dry in
front of the fire. You may imagine how greatly her voice
has suffered by it, and how impossible it is for her now to
sing in concerts."

To recruit themselves Count and Countess Rossi accepted the invitations of the Dukes of Cleveland and
Rutland to Belvoir Castle and Raby Castle.

In her second Italian Opera season of 1850, Sontag
delighted the public in several new parts, as *Zerlina* in
" Don Juan," as *Miranda* in Halevy's " Tempesta," in the
" Puritans," in the " Daughter of the Regiment," and in
" Semiramis." The last part, which she chose for her
benefit, pleased least, and she set it aside as no more
suitable.

In November, 1850, Henrietta again appeared for the
first time before a Paris public as *Somnambula*. Gustav zu
Putlitz, who was just then in Paris, but in consequence of
the Prussian mobilisation had to leave next day, writes in
his " Theatrical Reminiscences :"

"The event was looked forward to with unusual excitement, and vehement were the *pros* and *cons* in regard to the
venture, notwithstanding the fact that Countess Rossi had
already proved in London the still-standing validity of her
title as first singer of the world in her own line. This
very proof, given abroad, it was which awoke the distrust
of the Parisians. It was impossible for the people of Paris
to get up enthusiasm on foreign credit—nay, properly
speaking, no celebrity existed at all till it had first received
the world-stamp of Parisian recognition. We Germans,
who had often had to break lances on behalf of our
countrywoman, were all naturally eager to be present at
her first performance. It was, however, impossible to get
a ticket for the opening evening of the Italian season, and

we had to content ourselves with the following nights. It being, however, the evening before my departure from Paris, every prospect of a seat for me was cut off, and so perhaps for all my life I was not to see, nor hear, nor experience the enchantment of this wonder of my childhood."

Through the friendly offices, however, of the band leader, Karl Eckert, who was now, at the special desire of the Countess Rossi, installed in the Italian Opera of Paris, Gustav zu Putlitz managed to get a ticket for "Somnambula" at the last hour, and so was able to report:

"The celebrated singer appeared, but was received by no sign of applause, such as her name itself justified. Those most favourably disposed towards her demanded of her to conquer a Parisian reputation by her own intrinsic power. We, friends of the singer, sat in anxious excitement. But after the very first appearance, after the first tones of her voice, the whisper ran along the rows, 'Is this really Henrietta Sontag, the mother of grown-up children, the singer who twenty years ago delighted us at the zenith of her reputation?' In point of fact, notwithstanding a certain fulness of figure, Sontag seemed so young in her appearance and in the grace of her movements, and so fresh in the ring of her voice, that the hastily struck-up story of its being not the mother but the daughter Rossi who was thus reviving the fame of Henrietta Sontag rather acquired an air of probability. Anon, however, the singer displayed her incomparable art in song, which made light of all difficulty, and so not only dissipated that foolish fiction, but utterly levelled the prejudice raised against her, and sportively, smilingly, *commanded* the applause that had been withheld from her; applause which burst forth powerfully after the first finale, and kept on mounting ever higher, on to the conclusion of the opera. Therewith was the fate of the Italian season decided, and Henrietta Sontag adopted into all the splendour of artistic reputation in Paris.

"Throughout all the many changes in the life of this wonderful woman, from the penury of her early, humble connection with the theatre, on through all the tumult of artistic triumphs, and all the brilliancy of social rank, we observe one unbroken chain of homage paid, not alone to her talent but also to her personal grace and amiability, to the heart that was not more inspired artistically than it was humanly and privately good.

"And yet, notwithstanding the feverish sympathy with which I accompanied the success of that evening, this *Somnambulist* was not yet able to efface the impression left on me for ever by another personator of the part, namely, Jenny Lind. If in the art of song, in purity of Italian style, or even, almost, in beauty of voice, the latter fell short of Sontag, she yet towered above her by her peculiar, original conception of the part, to which a molten quality of voice, indescribably affecting, lent an irresistible and undying charm.

"A year later I saw Sontag in London as *Daughter of the Regiment*, a part she sang and personated with all the wantonness of a girl of fourteen. A year after that again, I saw her, for the last time, in Hamburg, as *Susanna* in Mozart's "Figaro," in the full maturity of her art, both in song and personation, presenting the highest excellence that was ever offered me from the stage. If a finished Italian *artiste* might attain to the measure of her *Somnambula*, and a French coquette to that of her *Daughter of the Regiment*, yet was Henrietta Sontag's German rendering of the German master's *Susanna* unsurpassably perfect; perfect in song, perfect in play.

"In Hamburg, also, the *artiste* had to conquer her success. People felt misgivings about paying such abnormal prices for hearing a singer who was turned of forty. Moreover, the Hamburg stage had just at that time a singer in Sontag's line, who was justly held in high estimation, but whom no inconsiderable part of the theatre *habitués* unjustifiably deemed unsurpassable. This party took Sontag's successes for a depreciation of and insult to their native favourite, and sounds were heard of a demonstration to be got up the first evening at which the two singers would appear together. The whole public got ear of it, and with friendly intentions, though with little tact, anonymous letters were sent to the Countess Rossi, informing her of the matter, and warning her on no account to sing in 'Figaro,' as her Hamburg rival should appear as *Page* in that piece. Henrietta Sontag quietly put the letters aside, and appeared as *Susanna* on the stage. And now she so encircled the *Page* with her play and song, and so attached him to her own part, that it became impossible to bestow the least applause on the cherubim that would not have gone to the credit of *Susanna*. It need hardly be said that the applause was rapturous all through, but it continued steady in favour of *Susanna* alone, and never did any artistic achievement better deserve it."

During the great London Exhibition of 1851, Henrietta Sontag was again the worshipped "star of the season." She then for the first time sang the "Sontag Polka" composed for her, which has since become an English popular song.

In December of the same year she visted her native town of Coblenz, *fêted* like a queen. She sang at a concert for the benefit of the poor. Hoffmann von Fallersleben, who then lived close by, dedicated a poem to her, sung after the concert by a male choir under her window in the "Trier Court," beginning

> " Sei gegrüsst mit Sang und Schall !
> Königin im Reich des Klanges !
> Meisterin des deutschen Sanges !
> Fruhling wird es uberall
> Wo Du Singst, O Nachtigall !" *

Next day, after she had sung two songs for the benefit of the Little Children's School, Hoffmann von Fallersleben in another poem wished her still a "long, long" life of song; but this, alas! was not to be granted her. Next summer, while taking the waters in Ems, Henrietta felt her health so much affected that she was looked for in vain in England.

---

* Roughly Englished :—
> "Let song and shout ring out to thee !
> Thou queen of all the realm of sound,
> And most of all on German ground !
> The song of Spring we ever hail,
> When hearing thee, O nightingale !"

Once more, however, this tenderest of mothers gathered all her strength together to reap one other golden harvest for her children. She went in the spring of 1853 to America, accompanied by the leader of the band, Karl Eckert. In the midst of her triumphal progress, and of the richest harvest, she fell a victim herself to the inexorable Reaper. She died of cholera at Mexico on the 17th June, 1854. Her last words to Germany ran: "The applause here is perfectly tropical."

Her last longings were for her husband, her children, her country. What a sad, lonely death, after so rich and brilliant a life!

She had formerly expressed a wish to repose one day in the convent in which her sister Nina was nun under the name of "Juliana."

This wish was fulfilled. Her coffin arrived by ship at Dresden. The poor mother, bereft of all her daughters, could utter but one word in a torrent of tears—"The Lord gave! the Lord hath taken away! blessed be the name of the Lord!"

The young Counts Rossi bore their mother's coffin to the vault of the convent of St. Marienthal, with the inscription:

"To the best mother; the tenderest daughter; the most faithful wife; the noblest friend; and the greatest singer."

Ten years later Count Rossi died, and in April, 1865, died Frau Francisca Sontag.

For more than two decades the poor lonely nun, Nina-Juliana, worshipped, and wept, and sang hymns at the coffin of her beloved sister.

Nina Sontag died at the end of 1879.

CHAPTER XVIII.

PRINCE LEOPOLD.

("Le Marquis peu-à-peu," "Monsieur tout doucement!"—
King George IV. on Prince Leopold.)

IN what jubilant spirits did I return home, the beginning of September, 1828, from the rehearsal of Töpfer's comedy, "Der beste Ton," calling out joyously to my mother:

"To-day I bring you a nice bit of news! Just think, mother, your playmate, Prince Leopold of Coburg, has arrived at Potsdam on a visit to the king, and I am to play for three evenings before him on the little stage in the new 'Palais.' Perhaps cousin Christian Stockmar is in the suite of the prince, and he will then be able to see what in the six years since we were in Coburg, and I had to declaim before him, and he allowed me to become an actress—what, in that time, has come of cousin Lina and the little comedian. I hope I shall come out of it with credit! And will the prince, think you, be as pretty yet as he was on the picture we saw of him in Ketschendorf at the house of the proud dowager-duchess? Handsome and melancholy, like the Prince of Homburg. . . . . . How old may the prince now be?"

"He was nearly five years younger than I," said mother. "He must count thirty-eight. As a boy he was beautiful like a picture, slender and supple, with dark curls, and large, still, listening eyes, looking always as if they were in a brown study. In spite of his saucy pranks I liked his merry brother Ernst, the now reigning duke, much better than the reserved, close, moping Leopold. It would be a pleasure, after so many years, to see my young playmate. If he should visit the Berlin Theatre likewise you must look me out a good place, not in the actors' box, but in the dress circle opposite the royal box.

Yet it does seem strange that cousin Christian hasn't given us a hint of this visit to Potsdam. Can it perhaps be that Baron Stockmar, as king's guest, may not be exactly wanting to know his cousin actress and the theatre mamma of an aunt?"

"No, mother; to be sure, no. That's not like cousin Christian. Maybe he is not in the prince's suite in Potsdam. Well, I'll find out to-morrow, by Papa Timm. But what most bothers me is, that I am first to appear before the prince, and so perhaps before cousin Christian as well, as a Hottentot, in that stupid piece the king is so fond of, where I'll have to sing and dance like a Hottentot—and in that horrid red faded frock, too, that was made eight years ago for Johanna Eunicke, and now, to save expense, has been lengthened a hand-breadth by a red border, that shows as plain as a pike-staff, so to make up for my being taller than her. Whatever must Prince Leopold and his Stocky think when they see me jumping about, like a half-boiled lobster, in the style of a Hottentot! My only consolation is, that next evening I can try my best, as charming *Leopoldine von Strehlen*, in the 'Besten Ton,' to wipe away the impression of the silly Hottentot. For a third part I play in Potsdam the *Fanny* in 'Launen des Zufalls.' * I must, before the day is out, pack up my things, seeing Jäger is to take me off to-morrow morning at seven o'clock in the green theatre coach. But I bring home for the three days twelve thalers cash as extra allowance. With that we will take a little indulgence to ourselves, and you buy yourself a new velvet hat for the autumn. Amalia Wolff, Ludwig Devrient, and Rebenstein go with me in the same green carriage. I lodge with Amalia Wolff in the house of the Castellan of the Potsdam town theatre. I shall for certain be invited with the dancers to dinner at Timm's, and so will bring you a big packet of sweets."

So I innocently chattered to my good mother; and so, all unwittingly, I drove next morning to meet my fate.

I learned of the private chamberlain during the *dîner*

---

* "Whims of Chance."

that cousin Christian was not in the prince's suite. Nor did he know whether he was staying in London or Coburg, but promised to find it out through the prince's adjutant. At the dessert the king appeared as usual for his quarter-of-an-hour's chat, and said, in a friendly way, to me:

"Delighted with Hottentot—singing and dancing charming—merry piece selected to cheer sad and silent guest—already asked for you—Cousin Baron Stockmar—unfortunately not come—in Coburg—prince will report your play to him—so mind your p's and q's—be very merry—keep Devrient up to the mark."

While the orchestra, previous to the beginning of the "Hottentot," was playing a gay overture, I peered inquisitively through the peep-hole of the curtain, and saw, scarcely five steps in front of the stage, beside the king a slender, tall gentleman, in red English uniform glittering with gold, of pale, noble face, with short, black, smooth-lying hair, and great, dark, melancholy eyes. The face was interesting more than beautiful, and looked considerably older than I had anticipated. In the whole impressive appearance I was soon struck by a morbid expression of lassitude bordering on exhaustion—lassitude in the lax features, lassitude in the gait, lassitude in the slow speech, lassitude in the feeble glance of the eyes.

"This, then, is cousin Christian's apple of the eye, his friend rather than his master," thought I to myself. "How sad he looks! Is it because he is still so deeply mourning the early death of his consort, the Princess Charlotte? It must surely be fine to be loved so intensely—particularly while one is yet alive! The poor, sad prince! Well, the Hottentot must do her best to cheer him up!"

And I did my best. I repeated the words of the king to Ludwig Devrient, and we arranged all sorts of new Hottentot surprises. Meister Ludwig gave quite a delicious presentation of the strutting braggadocio of an old bachelor who pretends he has been in all countries of the world, and is able to speak all languages of the earth.

I first appeared as *Countess Florentine* in the elegant travelling dress of light blue silk, singing:

" Der Männer Herzen zu bestricken
    Gab uns Natur die grazie und Verstand.".*

I had the satisfaction to observe that Prince Leopold
had already his eye-glass steadily directed on me, and
that his whole expression had changed into one of lively
excitement—all eye and all ear.

Countess Florentine loves her cousin, who, however, has
the hobby of doating on no beauties but those of foreign
lands he has never seen. To convert him, my old confidant, Ludwig Devrient, bethinks him of an expedient. I
appear in the second scene, before my beloved cousin, as
a real Hottentot, in short, red frock, with tiger's skin,
coral trinkets, piebald feathers on my head, and sing with
Meister Ludwig a Hottentot duet, to the melody of the
duet in the " Magic Flute " between *Papageno* and *Papagena.*

Devrient began in hoarse, croaking voice, with unheard-
of humour:—

"Ritsch li clum ru britosh brätch tschum tschi."

I answered in similar dialect; then with all the strength
of our lungs we sang out :—

"Birn squam litch zu natch qual brum schwa."

Devrient was inexhaustible in his most horrible Hotten-
totish, and I tried to keep pace with him. The king with
his court laughed till their sides shook, and I could even
catch the weary, melancholy prince now and again faintly
tittering.

Next came my wild Hottentot solo-dance, which I had
studied under the direction of the little ballet-master,
Lauchery—and Prince Leopold's glass was again in brisk
movement following my extravagant gambols.

My *Leopoldine von Strehlen* and my *Fanny* on the
second and third evenings likewise rejoiced in the same
interest at the eyes of the prince. Under it all I could not
help thinking: " Can it be that, like the Duke of Wellington at the Brühl ball, he also finds some remarkable
resemblance between me and his deceased Charlotte? It
is odd, however, that during the pauses he has not once

* " To ensnare the hearts of men
  Nature gave us grace and wit."

come to the stage to convey me a kind word from cousin Christian. What will the prince later on tell the baron of me?"

I heard from Papa Timm that the prince lived very quietly at Court, and was often engaged in earnest political conversation with the king, who had decorated him with the order of the Black Eagle. The Greeks wanted to make him their sovereign, but he had many opponents to contend with.

Delighted beyond measure with my twelve thalers extra allowance, with plenty of news, and a large packet of royal sweets, I returned home late at night after the third representation. No sooner, however, did I see mother than I noticed something was wrong. She looked unusually depressed, and I soon learned the cause.

Brother Karl had written that he was again owing near a thousand florins, "debts of honour"—although no farther back than the past summer we had already made the greatest sacrifices for him. If we did not this once more, and for the last time, come to his help, he would have to quit the service and emigrate to America.

Here was a sad entertainment following the merry Potsdam excursion. How paltry now appeared the twelve shining thalers, which but a few minutes before I had counted out so proudly on the table! I burst out, sobbing with indignation and anxiety:

"My unhappy brother will be the ruin of us yet. Even in St. Petersburg his extravagances and everlasting debts would track us out and plunder us to the last farthing. What's the use of fighting and struggling? No, let him go to America! I can do no more for him."

Next morning, however, pity got the better of us, and we resolved once again to help my careless brother for the last time.

While we sat so sorrowfully planning how we were to raise the money—what trinkets we might sell and pawn—a Herr Hühnlein was announced to us. A little, stout, very fresh and brisk-looking gentleman, elegantly dressed and frizzled, stood before us, representing himself as Chamberlain to Prince Leopold of Coburg.

"Ah! no doubt you bring us news of Baron Stockmar!" said mother. "I hear he is staying in Coburg with his family?"

"And the baron will stay many months this time in Coburg, for the prince will set off in a fortnight for Italy to pass the whole winter there. But—" and here the stout Hühnlein put on an air betokening the importance of the message—"I come, not exactly with any charge from the baron, but to say that his Highness Prince Leopold requests the pleasure of paying his respects to the Frau Rittmeisterin and her daughter to-morrow morning at twelve—the day after he proceeds to Coburg. I am glad of it, for I, too, am a native of Coburg."

Of course mother promised to be the whole day at the disposal of his Highness.

"How nice of Prince Leopold to call on us!" I cried, delighted. "No doubt he brings us greetings from cousin Christian, and wants to see again little Christina Stockmar. I am all curiosity to see this interesting prince with the melancholy eyes face to face in the room with me. I wonder what he will say to my Hottentot and *Leopoldine von Strehlen!* I hope he will report to my good cousin that I am a genuine *artiste*, and do him no dishonour!"

Then we set busily to work to deck our modest little drawing-room with fresh flowers for the reception of the prince and to take counsel about our own toilet. I was in quite a peculiar state of excitement, without ever once dreaming, however, that the hour of my destiny was approaching.

Next morning we got up quite a pretty, though simple, toilet. My beautiful, stately-mother, in black silk and light sweet cap, looked very much the lady, while I in my light-blue dress, with tulle trimming, felt fresh and blooming. Towards twelve o'clock a common hired equipage drove up in front of our door, 48 Mohrenstrasse. It is characteristic of the ever-cautious prince that in making this visit to an actress he had avoided using the Court equipage which was at his disposal.

I slipped into the adjoining room, the door of which stood open, for my mother thought it better etiquette that

I should not appear before his Highness till he desired to see me.

I heard Figaro Hühnlein announce his Highness with all due formalities, and next a slow, heavy step, followed by a voice of pleasing tone, which said slowly and consideringly:

"I am glad, after so many years, to be able to salute again my nice early playmate, blithe little Christina Stockmar. I bring the warmest greetings from your nephew Christian, who is become my dear and trusty friend, to you and your daughter, whom I had the opportunity of seeing and admiring as an *artiste*. I heartily congratulate little Christina Stockmar on being the mother of so charming a daughter and so excellent and universally popular an *artiste*."

"Did Lina by her appearance, remind your Highness of her poor departed father, whose very image she is, and with whom you liked so well to ride and fence at the time when he was courting me?"

"To be sure, I was struck by her great likeness to the good merry equerry, Heinrich Bauer, who, unhappily, was to die so young, but yet more by her quite astounding resemblance to my dear departed—my consort, Princess Charlotte. I am glad to be able to convey to you and my good Stocky the words of his Majesty the King, which were: 'Caroline Bauer is not only an ornament of our stage, but she and her worthy mother are universally respected and beloved for their blameless private life.' Frau Rittmeisterin, may I not pay my compliments to your daughter on her charming and graceful play?"

"Lina will feel herself highly honoured. Lina, you are wanted!"

And so in I stepped without embarrassment and made my prettiest curtsey.

The prince rose and stared at me for a few seconds, speechless, and as if struck by surprise. He confessed to me afterwards that I seemed to him like the Goddess of Youth and Spring, so blooming and radiant, so blithe and sunny. What on the stage he had taken for red and white paint was put to shame by the natural freshness of my cheeks.

And, in truth, I felt myself getting hot and strangely embarrassed under the long and searching glance of the prince. I felt a very unusual oppression of the heart, and my voice, wont to be so bright and fond of chatting, became paralysed. The consciousness of the fact only increased my confusion, so that at first I could take little part in the conversation about Berlin, Coburg, my St. Petersburg journey, &c.; and the prince, who sat beside my mother on the sofa opposite me, taking long and frequent observation of me through his opera-glass, though the interval between us was so short, affected me to quite a distressing degree.

The nearer impression I had now got of the prince was by no means so favourable as was the impression under the illumination of the theatre, when he wore his red English uniform. His present dress was an unusually long black surtout, tightly buttoned from top to bottom. The short and painfully smooth-lying black hair, glistening with pomatum, showed itself in daylight as a—consummate periwig. Then the pale, wan complexion of the face, the weary, weary expression, the flaccid, slouching gait, the slow, considering, bated breath speech, it all conveyed the impression rather of a musty, bookish fogey and an old bachelor in his fifties than a prince in the life and spirits of thirty-eight. Only the fine, sweetly smiling mouth, and the great dark melancholy eyes had something in them uncommonly attractive and captivating.

What had made the once so brilliantly handsome and vivacious prince, who carried victory in his mien, and who had taken by storm the heart of the heiress to the throne of England—what had now made him so old and spent before his time? what could it be that had brought him to such a melancholy wreck? Was it the undying grief at so early loss of married happiness, and the hope of a throne to boot? Or was it heavy suffering that had so early spoiled the blossom and sapped the courage of youth? Or—?

I was at that time still innocent enough to take the prince for a sorely tried son of man, and to have the most heartfelt sympathy with him.

After an hour of rather tedious conversation, sustained

mostly by my mother, the prince suddenly said, with a
forced laugh and an embarrassed voice:

"*A propos!* Friend Stockmar further gave me the commission to examine his cousin—by herself. May I do so,
Frau Rittmeisterin?"

Mother looked up quite disconcerted, but still tried to
pass off the thing as a jest, getting up, however, at the
same time:

"Freely, your Highness. Lina will in duty and conscience answer the *fatherly* examiner and the kind master
of her cousin Christian Stockmar—for that she is able to
do. My daughter has nothing to conceal." Therewith
mother, casting an encouraging look at me, went into the
adjoining room, the door of which stood open.

For some time we sat in mute silence opposite each
other. My cheeks and temples burned, and my heart beat
audibly. I cast down my eyes and folded my hands, the
blood in which burned to the finger ends. What could
the prince be wanting to ask of me which mother was not
to hear? Was it really some charge from cousin Christian
he had to deliver me? Had my vexatious experiences
with Prince August and the unhappy Samoilow-Grimm
penetrated to my cousin's ears? or had the king gossiped
them to the prince? And why was he not speaking out at
once? Had he such difficulty in finding the first word?
At last I put an end to this painful suspense, and, with all
the air of cheerfulness I could muster, said:

"Your Highness, I am ready for confession. I promise
you to answer frankly and truthfully whatever questions
you put to me; for you will ask nothing but what is
proper for me to answer." The thought that mother was
hearing everything gave me courage.

And so there opened the memorable dialogue which was
to be decisive for my whole existence, which was to force
me into paths that are not clear, and render me unhappy all
my days. And yet, for all that, I said not one word in
that hour it is my duty to repent this day. Once for all,
it was my *fate;* I was *doomed* to be unhappy. Up till then
I was pure and good. This dialogue conducted me into
mazes, split me into disunion with myself, delivered me

over to perplexing situations which, with my facile, impulsive, vacillating character, I was not strong enough to unravel. I had to begin playing a part in earnest when I left off playing in the playhouse, and that is not straightforwardness and simple truth, no, but can only be baneful both to the character and the heart.

I still remember every word of that dialogue between the prince and myself as though it had all passed between us yesterday and not half-a-century ago. For how often have I since been under the necessity of referring to the words of plain truth I used on that occasion, when afterwards the prince received anonymous letters reflecting on me and even my maidenly honour. Nothing did I keep back, but answered to all I was asked with all openness and honour. This simple truth on my part on this occasion came often afterwards to be the bright shield I could indignantly oppose to the paltry-hearted petty prince and his devoted Baron Stockmar, when they accused me of having cunningly contrived the whole plot, and thrown out my dangerous nets after the unsuspecting golden prince.

But my heart, stung by a sense of unworthy treatment, is hurrying away with my pen; I must try to keep it tight in hand.

At last the prince began—at first in his old, slow, considering, pedantic style of speech, but gradually quickening into some liveliness and warmth.

" May I assure Stockmar that you have not regretted becoming actress ? "

" Never, your Highness, have I regretted it, and I hope never to regret it. To-day I doat still more, if possible, on my profession than I did at the beginning of my career. Whether I have the true qualifications for the profession of an actress your Highness will answer from your own immediate observation. My professional tour to Russia has turned out successful beyond expectation. In Königsberg, in Riga, in Mitau, in St. Petersburg I was everywhere overwhelmed with applause and kindness; and soon I shall go to St. Petersburg on a splendid engagement which will give me an assured future."

"What prospects are held out to you for this—future?"

"In St. Petersburg, with the help of some extra performances, I shall earn yearly well on for 5000 thalers, and after completing a twelve years' engagement I become entitled, as Russian Court actress, to a life pension of 1000 thalers yearly, which I am at liberty to spend where I like."

"And if you became unwell?"

"Your Highness, that is in God's hands."

After a long pause, the prince resumed, not without a faltering in his voice, and with visible excitement:

"I was thinking, in fact, of another future. Should *you*, too, never have thought of it? Strange it were if, with your prepossessing appearance, your heart or your hand should not yet have been sought."

"Oh, *sought*—yes, the one or the other or both together —often. But no happy star shone on the seeking."

"And there has never been any romance of the heart?"

"O yes, many even—many—and, more than that, scandalous ones and of great magnitude."

The prince started up off the sofa as if stung by a viper, and stood before me with increasing pallor.

"Your Highness, I beg to be allowed to say it all out. You must now learn everything about it, for I have a feeling that you, and probably my cousin Stockmar as well, have heard something of the double misfortune that, without any guilt of mine—indeed, without any guilt of mine, your Highness—has befallen me in Berlin these last years. Many an honourable offer of marriage has been made me to my gratification, but the rich suitors were not loveable, and when I marry it must be a *rich* man, seeing I am the support of my mother. Many a dishonourable tender, on the other hand, has aroused my indignation, and the thousands of such which have been laid at my feet I have scornfully spurned from me. Lina Bauer does not sell herself—not even to an honourable man, if she does not love him. And then came a handsome young suitor, to all appearance a gentleman of rank and fortune, who loved me passionately, and who was not displeasing in my eyes; I became betrothed to him, and three days afterwards found he was a villain who had shamefully deceived me. That,

your Highness, is one of the misfortunes I had to go through
that I was speaking of. The other, came from Prince
August, who wanted to seduce, and now seeks to ruin me.
O your Highness, I beg of you most fervently to ask his
Majesty whether I have said one word to you that is not
true."

The prince, in visible agitation, went several times up
and down the room, and then stopped before me, who had
also risen and was leaning against the arm-chair all in a
tremble, and his wonderful eyes looked fixedly into mine,
and I could feel his warm breath as he whispered to me:

"I know you are telling the truth, even if his Majesty
had not already confirmed it to me, when he related the
misfortune of that betrothal. As to Prince August I know
him—I know the world. And your heart was never
fettered?"

"Never."

"Your heart is to-day still quite free?"

"Quite free."

The prince seized my two hands, and drawing me close
to him, breathed into my ear:

"And if a poor, weary, weary, sorely-tried man, who
is envied by the world for his high birth and his earthly
possessions, but who yet often feels very unhappy and
lonely—if he were to appear before you and say: 'Come
with me into my golden solitude! I will love you and
honour you as my dear wife, and guard you from every
new misfortune of your heart! You shall be lifted above
all earthly cares, and your family will also be provided for!
But you, on your side, must also be able to renounce—renounce the brilliancy and fame of the stage, renounce the
homage and the noisy pleasure of the world. You must
devote yourself wholly and alone to this man, in faithful
love and trustful, happy domesticity—wholly and alone!'
If this question were put to you, what answer would your
heart give?"

I was all in a palpitation, and the tears burst from my
eyes—for was not this poor, weary, sorely-tried man standing there before me? Greatly moved, I could hardly fetch
out the words:

"If I were to follow this man into his solitude, I must needs love him above all measure!"

"And would you—with time—be able to love me so as to sacrifice the stage and the world for me?"

"I don't know, your Highness; but I think I might try—and then I would tell you the whole truth." I felt dizzy with agitation, and had to lean on the chair to keep from falling.

I felt a light kiss on my forehead, then the prince went to my mother in the adjoining room and I heard him say:

"Dear friend, you have also heard everything, and there is but little I have to add. For years now I have been longing to meet with a faithful lady friend who would fill up the blank in my home, a lady with an unselfish heart I could lovingly confide in. Many brilliant beauties I have seen willing to throw themselves into my arms, but from heartless calculation only to profit by me. All the long years since the death of my consort, I have been living alone. Now I believe I have found in your daughter the sympathetic creature I seek. At the very first glance my heart inclined to her, because she looks so wondrously like my departed Charlotte. What kind of position I could offer your daughter at my side, I cannot yet say. But that it would be an entirely honourable one, resting on a moral footing, and that it is with the purest sentiments I here stand before you, of all this I believe I can give you no better proof than that I commit all further considerations, and all externals respecting your and Lina's future, entirely into the pure hands and the true heart of Christian Stockmar. I hasten to Coburg to-morrow, and will at once lay a full confession before your nephew and my confidential adviser. He will counsel for you, as also for me, what is right and good, as no other can. He has not only the interest of his friend to consult, but the true welfare also of his niece and his family, and the spotless honour of his name. I would therefore beg you, while I am still there—that is, within a fortnight from now—to come with Lina on a visit to your nephew in Coburg. I trust that all matters will there arrange themselves to mutual satisfaction, and a friendly alliance be formed for life. The

hearty inclination to Lina I felt at the first sight I had of
her has to-day grown into passionate love. Let me depart
from here with a lively hope of an early happy meeting
again in our old native place!"

That was the longest speech I ever heard from the lips
of our usually so silent prince. For once—perhaps the
only time in his life—he followed the impulse of his
momentarily flaring, but habitually cold, heart; not weighing and ruminating like a pedant every word he said as
is the wont of "Marquis peu-à-peu" and "Monsieur tout
doucement," as his father-in-law, King George IV., called
him.

We must have formed a curious group when the prince,
holding my dumbfoundered mother's hand, stepped up to
me, scarcely breathing, and gently drew me to him, with
his beautiful mournful eyes turned beseechingly on me;
I, again, usually so resolute, so full of prompt life and
spirits, now all in tears, in a burning heat, in a ruffle of
intimidation, and quite at a loss what to make of my feelings, except that I was agreeably solaced and flattered by
this princely declaration of love; my mother, moreover,
abashed and discomposed.

Such is the picture which still ever stands before my
mind's eye.

"What am I allowed to hope?" said the prince.

Then with difficulty, and struggling to be composed, but
yet with the dignity that was proper to her, my mother said:

"Your Highness, you have so surprised us that it is
quite impossible for us to give you an answer to-day
to this question affecting our whole life. Lina must
first try her heart; and you, too, your Royal Highness,
must try yours, as to whether this sudden flame of passion
will not as suddenly expire. Yet so much I think I may
promise you even now, that we will gladly come on a
visit to our native place, if Baron Stockmar sends us a
friendly invitation on the impulse of his own heart, and if
Lina here is allowed away long enough for this short
journey—a point which seems to me very questionable
after the long leave given her for the St. Petersburg
engagement."

"Oh, at worst, ask his Majesty personally for leave, on the ground that you have family affairs about which you want to consult with Baron Stockmar. With special post-horses, six days should suffice for the journey. I shall count the hours till your arrival. But I beg of you observe the strictest secrecy about my visit of to-day, and the motive of your journey to Coburg. By one inconsiderate word everything might be wrecked. My public and private life is just now very closely watched. I have many friends—but also many enemies. And, now, heartily, good-bye; and think of me, if possible, in love! And so I wish an auspicious meeting again in Coburg."

And away went the prince, leaving mother and me almost stupefied. It had all fallen on us by surprise, like a confused dream, causing us now joy and now anxiety. In deep emotion I clasped my agitated mother in my arms and sobbed out:

"Mother, what is to come of this—a supreme bliss or another bitter deception? Shall we go to Coburg, and so take the second fateful step on this new way? or at once write to the prince, declining? Who is to counsel us at this turning of the ways, seeing the prince has expressly forbidden us to take any one into our confidence?"

With remarkable firmness my mother replied:

"Here there are but two counsellors on earth—Cousin Christian and your own heart, Lina. Christian Stockmar, since his father's death, is the head of the family, and out-and-out a man of honour. Besides, there is nobody knows Prince Leopold, and all the circumstances to be taken into account, like him who for years long has been managing the prince's affairs, and enjoys his unlimited confidence. For the present, therefore, let us wait and see whether Christian invites us to this fateful meeting with the prince at Coburg. That he will only do if such a step appears to him of good augury, both for his beloved master and for us, his nearest relations; and such, moreover, as he can answer for to his own conscience. The next thing will be for your own heart to counsel and direct you, and that is a matter in which even I would not venture to advise you either for or against. Do you think you can

love the prince, and in the desired for retirement devote
your life to him—in all honour, of course?".

"I don't know, mother," I exclaimed, half weeping,
half-laughing. "He is so much older than I, and there is
nothing at all of the ardent lover in him. On the stage he
would assuredly be whistled out in playing such a part.
He gave me the impression rather of a good papa, a
blinkard stuffed with musty erudition, a professor that
fancies life still throbs in his—set routine of studies. And
did you notice the periwig? Bah! And the dreary surtout
flopping about his spindle-like shanks as if it were a dress-
ing-gown? And so tightly buttoned up as if his Highness
were afraid of catching cold in this sunny weather! And
yet, for all, the prince touched and fascinated me by his
beautiful, melancholy eyes! He must have passionately
loved the Princess Charlotte, and be deeply missing her—and
feel so unhappy in his solitariness. I think it very fine,
and likely to make one happy, to try and revive the waste
happiness of a noble man But why has not the prince
long ago chosen a consort of his own rank?—the prince,
who, in his earlier youthful beauty, would assuredly have
had his choice among the most lovely princesses of all the
reigning houses?"

"There you are in error, Lina. Six years ago Christian
enlightened me on this point in Coburg. Prince Leopold
was quite poor to start with, like all Coburg princes. . It
is only to his being husband of the late Princess-Royal
that he owes his position and his income in England. He
would lose both if he married another princess. And for
this and other reasons you will be able to be only his
morganatic spouse. And did you notice how the prince
intentionally laid repeated stress on the 'quiet life' that
awaited you, and how you would require the strength of
renunciation, to devote yourself wholly to him, far from
the tumult of the world? Will you, who have been
celebrated on the stage and spoiled by society, be able to
bear such a still life?"

This put things in a new light, and for the first time
the words fell bodefully on my heart. I almost wished
the invitation to Coburg would not arrive, and that I might

view the whole affair with its solicitations as a day-dream. Only the anxiety about brother Karl's new debts awoke, between whiles, the longing for a still life, free of cares as of storms.

But now, on the fifth day after the prince's departure, there reached us a short, friendly letter from cousin Christian, inviting us to come as soon as possible for a few days to Coburg. All the rest he would tell us by word of mouth!

Not a syllable about the prince nor the object of this journey. Not a word by way of encouragement or warning. The shrewd, diplomatic cousin all over, who never shows his cards to any one! It naturally disquieted us only all the more, to learn nothing whatever as to what cousin thought of the prince's plans and hopes. To quiet my mother, however, I said, with all the gaiety possible, "It is God's wish we should meet Prince Leopold! Else cousin Christian hadn't summoned us. I will now try the last touchstone of fate, and learn whether I am to be allowed away for this journey."

Count Redern, the intendant, however, roundly refused me the six days I asked for, because I had only been six weeks back from my six months' leave of absence in Russia, and had yet in autumn to play a principal part in Raupach's "Ritterwort,"* for which I had the necessary rehearsals to go through.

In painful suspense I hastened with cousin Christian's letter to Papa Timm, and he actually procured me, at the hands of his Majesty, a "six days' leave of absence to go to Coburg on pressing family affairs." Early the very next day, accordingly, mother and I were seated in our Russian travelling coach, a bugle-sounding postilion on the box seat, and with agitated hearts away we sped into the sunny September morning—away over smiling landscapes —away to the kindly natal Coburg—away to our new golden fortune.

Yes, and the farther we drove, the merrier and hopefuller grew our hearts. Didn't my first excursion to Coburg, just six years ago, bring me much good fortune

---

* "Knight's word."

and happiness? Then had cousin Christian spoken the decisive auspicious word, " I shall be delighted to be able to name an *artiste* cousin, and a cousin *artiste*," and so; to the gratification of my most burning desire, I had become actress, and had seldom found occasion to regret it. Accordingly, mother and I resolved, with the completest confidence, to let my shrewd and noble cousin speak the decisive word regarding my future this time as well, and, that resolution taken, our hearts became light and gay. A sweet satisfaction, moreover, it was to my feelings, after six years' most persevering struggle and endeavour, to appear again among my dear relations in my mother's native place as a recognised *artiste*—to find myself again on the same ground where, as a maiden of fifteen, little Lina had so zealously studied to make her small theatrical talents shine, in order to be allowed to tread the longed-for boards. And how much we had to speak of on the way! How much had changed in that time—about us, within us, and with our relations!

In the village of Eishausen, we no longer found the friendly parson Kuhner; he had been resting for a year already in the churchyard. In Rodach we found much altered. Uncle " Justizamtmann" had died three years before of the shock caused by a dreadful conflagration of the little town, and his widow, with her daughter, cousin Rieckchen, had removed to Coburg.

On the second day after our departure from Berlin we arrived late in the afternoon at the still town of Coburg, and got out at the only good inn the little residence town then boasted, and in which cousin Christian had taken rooms for us. The attentive landlord informed us that at the desire of Baron Stockmar he would at once inform him of our arrival, and that the baron would yet come that day to welcome us. We could perceive with satisfaction that the " Herr Baron" was a very important personage in the eyes of our landlord.

We had scarcely changed our toilet after the long fatiguing ride, when we heard hasty footsteps approaching, and cousin Christian stood before us, heartily embracing mother and me, while in his brisk, lively style, he said:

mostly took the side of the poor, lovely duchess. Matters came, in the summer of 1824, to an open revolt on the part of the people in favour of the ill-used wife. The people stormed the ducal residence, the soldiery publicly espoused the cause of the duchess. The favourite of the duke, Herr von Schimbowsky, had his windows smashed in and his garden laid waste; Duke Ernst fled to Vienna and laid his complaints before the " Bundestag."* This body appointed a royal Saxon Commission to investigate the cause of the revolt in Coburg and re-establish peace.

The duchess demanded a divorce, a demand which was refused her for political reasons, as Coburg was desirous not to forfeit the inheritance of the Duchy of Gotha, of which the Duchess Louise was the last princely hereditary claimant. The unhappy lady then tried by her own com-promising life to force the duke to a divorce. Of these things the Coburg Count Korneillan relates:—" The duchess has assuredly been playing wild pranks with lovers, nor has she tried to hide them. She asserts a defiant freedom in her manners, saying and doing with innocently-saucy frankness what others conceal; and with it all she is loveable to a seductive degree."

Not until 1826, after she had been living for two years at St. Wendel on the Rhine, under the name of Countess of Pólzig (or, as others say, Belzig), separated from her consort and her two sons, did the duchess obtain her formal divorce from the duke. She then married the Coburg Lieutenant, Alexander von Hanstein, raised to the rank of Count of Pölzig by the Duke of Altenburg (according to others, Hildburghausen!), and lived with him in happy wedlock by the Rhine or at Paris. In this latter place I again met this remarkable lady, who died there in 1831, without having ever again seen her two sons, Ernst and Albert. Even in death, however, she continued to assert her wayward humour. She had settled on her husband, Count of Pölzig, a considerable annuity, on the condition that he was *never* to separate himself from her corpse! If he were to spend but one

---

* Diet of the Confederation.

night in a house which did not harbour at the same time her own remains, he forfeited his annuity.

For years the unhappy count dragged everywhere about with him in the world the embalmed corpse of his spouse, till one morning he discovered to his horror that the precious coffin had vanished without any trace. As his annuity, however, still continued to be paid, and he found another life-companion in Fräulein von Karlowitz, he consoled himself about the loss.

The family of Coburg-Gotha had put a period to the incessant journalistic news of the " travelling corpse."

*   *   *   *   *   *

The morning after that merry, popular festival at Rosenau, which closed with a brilliant display of fireworks, Christian Stockmar took us up in his carriage for a fateful drive to the estate of Füllbach. Cousin did the driving himself again, to prevent any gossipy coachman catching a syllable of news not intended for him, and he was in his gayest spirits, drizzling out the pungent humour peculiar to himself. Only when the pleasant Füllbach came in view did he, all at once, become grave. Pointing to a modest house, almost hidden among old trees, he said: "Perhaps there your future is to be decided for life! May it be so shaped that we may all one day look back on this country-house and this hour without regret! Once more, however, I conjure you, Lina, do not let yourself be persuaded, at this early stage of the business, into giving a binding promise. Reserve for yourself the completest liberty till the spring, till the return of the prince from Italy, leaving him the same liberty. Perhaps he will bring a crown home with him, and in that case you go to St. Petersburg as Russian Court actress with the consciousness of having gained in the free King of Greece a helpful friend for life. I heartily wish, both for you and the prince, that this may prove the happy solution of the brief romance of love; and in that case none of you would have any reproach to make, one against the other."

Yes, why did not this happy solution set me free before I had tied myself?

For half-a-century now I have been brooding com-

mostly took the side of the poor, lovely duchess. Matters came, in the summer of 1824, to an open revolt on the part of the people in favour of the ill-used wife. The people stormed the ducal residence, the soldiery publicly espoused the cause of the duchess. The favourite of the duke, Herr von Schimbowsky, had his windows smashed in and his garden laid waste; Duke Ernst fled to Vienna and laid his complaints before the " Bundestag."* This body appointed a royal Saxon Commission to investigate the cause of the revolt in Coburg and re-establish peace.

The duchess demanded a divorce, a demand which was refused her for political reasons, as Coburg was desirous not to forfeit the inheritance of the Duchy of Gotha, of which the Duchess Louise was the last princely hereditary claimant. The unhappy lady then tried by her own compromising life to force the duke to a divorce. Of these things the Coburg Count Korneillan relates:—" The duchess has assuredly been playing wild pranks with lovers, nor has she tried to hide them. She asserts a defiant freedom in her manners, saying and doing with innocently-saucy frankness what others conceal; and with it all she is loveable to a seductive degree."

Not until 1826, after she had been living for two years at St. Wendel on the Rhine, under the name of Countess of Pölzig (or, as others say, Belzig), separated from her consort and her two sons, did the duchess obtain her formal divorce from the duke. She then married the Coburg Lieutenant, Alexander von Hanstein, raised to the rank of Count of Pölzig by the Duke of Altenburg (according to others, Hildburghausen!), and lived with him in happy wedlock by the Rhine or at Paris. In this latter place I again met this remarkable lady, who died there in 1831, without having ever again seen her two sons, Ernst and Albert. Even in death, however, she continued to assert her wayward humour. She had settled on her husband, Count of Pölzig, a considerable annuity, on the condition that he was *never* to separate himself from her corpse! If he were to spend but one

* Diet of the Confederation.

night in a house which did not harbour at the same time
her own remains, he forfeited his annuity.

For years the unhappy count dragged everywhere
about with him in the world the embalmed corpse of his
spouse, till one morning he discovered to his horror that
the precious coffin had vanished without any trace. As
his annuity, however, still continued to be paid, and he
found another life-companion in Fräulein von Karlowitz,
he consoled himself about the loss.

The family of Coburg-Gotha had put a period to the
incessant journalistic news of the "travelling corpse."

*   *   *   *   *   *

The morning after that merry, popular festival at
Rosenau, which closed with a brilliant display of fireworks, Christian Stockmar took us up in his carriage for
a fateful drive to the estate of Füllbach. Cousin did the
driving himself again, to prevent any gossipy coachman
catching a syllable of news not intended for him, and he
was in his gayest spirits, drizzling out the pungent humour
peculiar to himself. Only when the pleasant Fullbach
came in view did he, all at once, become grave. Pointing
to a modest house, almost hidden among old trees, he
said: "Perhaps there your future is to be decided for
life! May it be so shaped that we may all one day look
back on this country-house and this hour without regret!
Once more, however, I conjure you, Lina, do not let
yourself be persuaded, at this early stage of the business,
into giving a binding promise. Reserve for yourself the
completest liberty till the spring, till the return of the
prince from Italy, leaving him the same liberty. Perhaps
he will bring a crown home with him, and in that case
you go to St. Petersburg as Russian Court actress with
the consciousness of having gained in the free King of
Greece a helpful friend for life. I heartily wish, both for
you and the prince, that this may prove the happy solution
of the brief romance of love; and in that case none of you
would have any reproach to make, one against the other."

Yes, why did not this happy solution set me free before I had tied myself?-

For half-a-century now I have been brooding com-

plainingly over this " Why ? " " Why ? " Shall I one
day receive a proper answer to it above the stars?

* * * * *

We drove through the park to the pleasant; modest
country house. Every thing was still as in an en-
-chanted garden. Not a mortal was to be seen, not a voice
to be heard. Only a few silver pheasants strutted slowly
over the turf ; on the roof sat two white doves, with
black heads glistening in the sunshine, billing and cooing.

When the carriage drew up in front of the garden
salon, the little stout factotum, Hühnlein, in white cook's
apron, hastened to relieve cousin of the charge of the
horses and carriage. He wheezed from zeal of service,
and his good-natured full-moon face glowed like a peony,
while a bright, knowing smirk lighted up his fat mouth.
Figaro was wholly in his element—groom, cook, butler,
chamberlain, confidant, all in one—so that no outsider
might get an inkling into the secret.

In the open door of the garden salon stood the tall
figure of the prince, set off to advantage in the sunny air.
He received me in a friendly—nay, hearty—manner. He
appeared younger and fresher in my eyes than on the
occasion of my first interview with him in Berlin, while
his manner, too, was less embarrassed and constrained.
He took my two hands in his, and looking deeply into my
eyes, said: " I thank you for coming. It is a good sign,
and I am allowed to hope! "

This kindly reception restored me, too, to my cheerful
freedom ; and soon I sat at the prince's side at breakfast,
almost forgetting that my neighbour was his Highness.
Meister Hühnlein smartly served quite a stately *déjeuner
à la fourchette*, and was most assiduous in pouring out the
pearl-clear, golden Bordeaux into our glasses, and drawing
bottles of excellent foaming champagne. We dined
luxuriously *à quatre*, and as much at our ease as though
we had dined in the same style ever so often before.
We were happy human children, knowing no guile and no
distrust. Cousin Christian brimmed over with wit and
sparkling spirits. The prince thawed ever more and more,
gave me some tender squeezes of the hand under the

table, and clinked glasses with mother and me, saying,
"Here's to our soon meeting again more joyously in England!" to which my glass and heart echoed in hopeful
response.

After coffee-drinking, the prince jestingly conducted
me into the adjoining room. The door was left open, and
I could hear Christian and mother chatting away to each
other. That relieved me of embarrassment, and inspired
confidence.

The prince clasped me tenderly in his arms and kissed
me on the brow and lips, saying heartily :

"I may hope, then, that your heart is favourably disposed towards me, and, with time, will learn to like a
little a man who has been hard tried and is so much older
than yourself. More I cannot to-day ask for. I must,
however, already tell you that since I first saw you, you
have been growing dearer and dearer to me every hour,
and that I hope to find again at your side my lost happiness
—rest—peace. One thing only I beg of you to tell me
frankly and freely : Is there any man you like better than
me—whom it would be hard for you to give up for me ? "

With all my heart I was able to answer :

"No, your Highness, there is no man whom I love
better than you, and my heart feels more and more drawn
to you ! "

"I thank you. That perfectly satisfies me for to-day.
The good Stocky demands for his cousin and me a longer
period of probation—on to the time when I return from
Italy. I am agreed to that. We shall in the meantime
write to each other, and so come to know each other
better. Your cousin has also openly set forth my situation
to you. Will the quiet life of love offered to you not
make you shudder? Will you not regret sacrificing a
brilliant life as *artiste* to a poor solitary man ? "

"I hope not—so long as I enjoy your love and confidence. And my mother must not leave me?"

"No, she will remain your faithful friend, and always
be with you, when my position compels me to leave you
alone. I shall be thankful to your mother for that kindness."

of the citizen and the courtier in his whole bearing. Most of all, however, his singular talent for dictatorial command had asserted itself into greater emphasis and distinctness.

This last feature I was made to feel more particularly next morning, when cousin again appeared in the hotel—to a conference! There he was quite the *charge d'affaires* of Prince Leopold of Coburg, weighing the pros and cons with diplomatic acuteness and coolness, and with a perfectly professional plainness, setting forth all the circumstances of the case in their native nakedness, to the consternation of poor mother and me. He mercilessly lopped away all the poetic blossoms my heart had brought with me to Coburg to adorn my august admirer, and left the poor bare stalk alone standing—business! And he would tolerate no opposition.

Reclining in his sofa corner, and with his eyes steadily directed on me, Baron Christian Stockmar, "mon fidèle soutien et ami," as Prince Leopold liked to call him, began in a clear voice:

"That my master longs for the happiness of a quiet domestic love I perfectly understand and heartily approve. The stupid love affairs his Highness has been amusing himself with, to beguile the everlasting *ennui*, are the ruin of soul and body. Now and again, indeed, it seemed as if a more earnest relationship would form itself. Beautiful ladies of rank threw their nets out after the prince, who, in truth, at an earlier period was of seductive personal attractions—partly from a relish of romantic game of that kind, as in the case of the love-mad Lady Ellenborough, who has since been consoling herself, in defect of him, with the Austrian attaché to the embassy, Prince Felix Schwarzenberg; partly from calculation, as in the case of the Countess Fiquelmont of Vienna. When, however, these ladies heard of the quiet life in store for them, a life to be devoted entirely and alone to the prince, far from all the gay bustle of society, as if cut off from the world, and that their appanage, too, was to be a very modest one —then they usually shrank back with a shudder, or the prince gave them the slip himself, when he came to understand how he was to serve only as the subject of an arrant money exploitation. Prince Leopold is not rich. All he has is but a yearly pittance of £50,000, which he draws from England as husband of the late Princess-Royal; and what, by dint of great economy, he may have saved out of it in the course of years. Yes, the prince is very economical. Great treasures are not to be looked for with him.

"After so many disillusions of the heart, the prince now appears, for the first time, to be really in earnest, and to have fallen as passionately in love with Lina as—is possible to his no small phlegm. And *that* I understand perfectly, for Lina is not only a beautiful maiden in the freshest bloom of youth, but is also a loveable creature. That the prince entertains honourable intentions, and wants to form only an out-and-out honourable alliance, is a matter of course, for otherwise he had not committed the business into my hands, nor given me *carte blanche*. He knows I will stand no nonsense in the matter of honour, and that Lina's mother is a born Stockmar. The prince, therefore, at the outset, puts you under my protection, and voluntarily commits to me the surveillance of his own actions.

"The marriage, accordingly, would be of a morganatic kind, and Lina would receive the title of an earl's lady —to be sure, in greatest privacy. For if both were to be noised abroad, then might the prince's enemies raise a din about the affair in the English newspapers, and even in Parliament itself, and in that way Prince Leopold might jeopardise his yearly allowance and his position in England.

"Moreover, the prince has had the crown of Greece in prospect these three years, and at this moment negotiations are being resumed on this point. With such object in view my master will pass the winter in Italy, to be nearer to Greece. Should he then eventually be made King of Greece, it would be impossible for him to take a morganatic spouse with him to Athens. Politics would demand of him to lead home a legitimate consort to Greece. In such an emergency the secret bond which can alone unite Lina with the prince would have to be as secretly untied as it was—perhaps—tied. Be it observed, then: only before God and your nearest relations would you

bear the character of prince's spouse, while before the world, if it should perhaps be able to follow up your lost track, you would appear in a less—pure light. I deem it my duty to let you know the worst, and to make you acquainted with all the possible dangers before you.

" If any children should come of this alliance—a contingency which, speaking frankly, I should not much welcome, as it would only complicate matters the more— these children would receive the title of their mother and be provided for in a decent manner, just as provision would be made for you, Caroline, if, sooner or later, circumstances should cause a dissolution of the bond.

" You would have an income settled on you for life, which would suffice to keep you, but no more. Christian Stockmar's cousin would in such a case have to show herself still less mercenary than would a stranger. If you will devote yourself to the prince out of love, you do it at your own risk, mind you. This one concern is quite enough for me, that I know the prince is in good hands, and that I have saved him from falling into the worst. And so, no selfishness whatever, Lina; or else your cousin Christian would be the first to turn against you.

" One other point for consideration is, ' Will the prince's sudden-kindled love stand the test?' Judging by my knowledge of him, I hardly think so. The hearts of these high personages are cut out of a material all their own. And what, then, if this flicker of passion were quenched with the bridal night! You would only be the unhappier.

" My urgent and honourable advice, therefore, in the interest both of my master and of you, my dear relatives, is, let nothing be done precipitately. Commit yourselves to nothing before you have carefully tried your hearts and reins. The prince, too, must search his own mind. He leaves here in a few days for Naples. Perhaps the question of the Greek throne will there be decided, a matter which would assuredly have an important bearing on this affair of the heart.

" And, now, give me an honest answer, Caroline. Will you, unconditionally and on all points, trust my faithful counsel and commit yourself to my experienced guidance?

or, allured by this sudden conquest of yours over the prince, will you give ear to his passionate prayers (for he will speak to you to-morrow alone), and go your own self-willed way into golden happiness—or, it may be, run blind to destruction? I expect a decided yes or no!"

And, weeping loudly, I said, " Yes! yes! cousin, I follow blindly your counsel and your guidance!"

In great agitation, my mother cried, "O God! between what precipices are we here fallen. My heart says to me, 'Lina, keep free! Remain *artiste!* We are not equal to these dangers!'"

Would that we had followed this warning voice of the faithfullest mother's heart!

　　*　　　*　　　*　　　*　　　*　　　*

I was to see the prince in the afternoon. In his honour a kind of popular festival was being celebrated at the Rosenau,* the magnificent summer residence of the reigning duke, and cousin Christian wanted to take us to it. I hardly remember to have ever dressed myself for any festival in a more anxious frame of mind. Cousin's matter-of-fact explanations were hard to digest. How much uncertainty, how many painful misgivings, weighed on my mind! And that which perhaps fatefully beckoned to me in the remote distance, was it the longed-for gratification of the heart young fancy had been dreaming of?

"O mother, what new perplexities, and struggles, and tumults of the heart are in store for us. The life of man on earth is no trifling matter," cried I, in distress. "The worst, however, is that I never yet know whether I can love the prince to such degree as would be required if I am to renounce the stage and the world for his sake! What would most urge me to a quiet life free of cares is the never-ending anxiety about brother Karl's incessant new demands!"

Mother tried to bring about my composure by telling me that according to cousin Christian's estimate we had a full half year yet to think over the matter, and that as late as spring I would still be free to give a decided no. And

---

* Meaning "Meadow of Roses."

Might there yet be some one among the public who had a presentiment of the fact of the cause of my going?

In the newspaper stood a poem, signed " Wilhelm Scheerer," addressed to " Dem. Karoline Bauer," in which, after praising her art, he urges her to make her life equally praiseworthy, and in the higher social circles to walk warily amid the dangers besetting innocence and virtue.

I then accepted the verses only in the way of friendly homage; to-day I fancy I can hear a tone of mild warning in them.

Poets are also prophets !

On the 12th May, mother and I were invited to a farewell dinner at friend Timm's. We were the only guests. At the dessert the king appeared to bid me farewell and wish me happiness on my new course of life..

I could hardly utter one word of thanks, for emotion. Weeping, I kissed the good paternal hand that had shown me so much favour—for the last time !

Then the king, himself visibly moved, laid his hand on my head and said, mildly:

- "Prince Leopold is to be envied; may he make you, too, happy. Farewell ! Keep us Berliners in your friendly remembrance, and write to Timm how you get on."

Oh, why in that minute did I not throw myself at the feet of the noble monarch, as my heart commanded? Why did I not embrace his knees, pleading: " Your Majesty, be pleased to grant me a ten years' contract and an increase of salary, for otherwise mother and I cannot make ends meet ! Be pleased to grant me a small pension for the evening of my days, and I shall joyously remain here and renounce the golden allurements of England and my St. Petersburg engagement—and all my life long I shall thank you, and will live and die for the Berlin stage ! "

Yes, why in this last decisive minute had I not the courage to make this petition? Why did I let the minute slip away unused? And then all was too late !

When honest Timm visited me years after in Dresden, and I disburdened to him my whole heart, he said to me, much affected : " Yes, had you but then opened your mouth. The king was always generously inclined to you,

and would have granted your request. He, too, was unwilling you should leave "

At length all preparations for departure were made,
which was a doubly difficult task, seeing that every thing
had to be done in the most painful secrecy. Our landlord
had no suspicion of anything but that I was going on professional tours, and would—perhaps not return. The
rent of our apartments was paid up to the end of another
half year. We, therefore, left all our furniture standing,
and gave to the entirely trustworthy landlord the keys,
with the full commission to sell everything if we did not
return before the expiration of our lease.

The indispensable farewell visits were paid, at which I
became alternately red and pale, and could hardly repress
the impulse to blurt out everything. I might here date
the beginning of my equivocal attitude in life. I felt I
had already lost the simplicity of truth, and was standing
in an ambiguous light in relation to my best and truest
friends. My conversation was no longer unreflecting
spontaneity, but painful pretext. I was sensible that my
friends read in my every word, " This is no word you
are saying, but only the disguise of a word ! Instead of
speaking yourself to us, you are only wrapping yourself
from us ! Have we deserved this of you?" I could see
in my friends that, calling to remembrance my autumn
journey to Coburg and the rumours about it, they were,
perhaps, conjecturing the very truth of the matter, and
only out of discretion refrained from embarrassing me
with inquisitive questions. And yet, withal, it was not
in my power to speak out sincerely as my heart prompted
me. I *had* to be mute—or rather I had to appear a disguised person, irresponsive to kind people—for such were
my orders from London. Yes, I had fallen from the path
of simplicity into crooked courses !

Mother and I did not breathe freely again till on the
14th May we had Berlin behind us, and were rolling along
the highway to Potsdam. And yet in Potsdam a new
heart-affecting leave-taking awaited me.

The good king wanted to see me once more on the
stage—for the last time ! And so then in the evening I

Might there yet be some one among the public who had a presentiment of the fact of the cause of my going?

In the newspaper stood a poem, signed " Wilhelm Scheerer," addressed to " Dem. Karoline Bauer," in which, after praising her art, he urges her to make her life equally praiseworthy, and in the higher social circles to walk warily amid the dangers besetting innocence and virtue.

I then accepted the verses only in the way of friendly homage; to-day I fancy I can hear a tone of mild warning in them.

. Poets are also prophets!

On the 12th May, mother and I were invited to a fare-well dinner at friend Timm's. We were the only guests. At the dessert the king appeared to bid me farewell and wish me happiness on my new course of life.

- I could hardly utter one word of thanks, for emotion. Weeping, I kissed the good paternal hand that had shown me so much favour—for the last time!

Then the king, himself visibly moved, laid his hand on my head and said, mildly:

"Prince Leopold is to be envied; may he make you, too, happy. Farewell! Keep us Berliners in your friendly remembrance, and write to Timm how you get on."

Oh, why in that minute did I not throw myself at the feet of the noble monarch, as my heart commanded? Why did I not embrace his knees, pleading: " Your Majesty, be pleased to grant me a ten years' contract and an in-crease of salary, for otherwise mother and I cannot make ends meet! Be pleased to grant me a small pension for the evening of my days, and I shall joyously remain here and renounce the golden allurements of England and my St. Petersburg engagement—and all my life long I shall thank you, and will live and die for the Berlin stage!"

Yes, why in this last decisive minute had I not the courage to make this petition? Why did I let the minute slip away unused? And then all was too late!

When honest Timm visited me years after in Dresden, and I disburdened to him my whole heart, he said to me, much affected: " Yes, had you but then opened your mouth. The king was always generously inclined to you,

and would have granted your request. He, too, was unwilling you should leave "

At length all preparations for departure were made,
which was a doubly difficult task, seeing that every thing
had to be done in the most painful secrecy. Our landlord
had no suspicion of anything but that I was going on professional tours, and would—perhaps not return. The
rent of our apartments was paid up to the end of another
half year. We, therefore, left all our furniture standing,
and gave to the entirely trustworthy landlord the keys,
with the full commission to sell everything if we did not
return before the expiration of our lease.

The indispensable farewell visits were paid, at which I
became alternately red and pale, and could hardly repress
the impulse to blurt out everything. I might here date
the beginning of my equivocal attitude in life. I felt I
had already lost the simplicity of truth, and was standing
in an ambiguous light in relation to my best and truest
friends. My conversation was no longer unreflecting
spontaneity, but painful pretext. I was sensible that my
friends read in my every word, "This is no word you
are saying, but only the disguise of a word! Instead of
speaking yourself to us, you are only wrapping yourself
from us! Have we deserved this of you?" I could see
in my friends that, calling to remembrance my autumn
journey to Coburg and the rumours about it, they were,
perhaps, conjecturing the very truth of the matter, and
only out of discretion refrained from embarrassing me
with inquisitive questions. And yet, withal, it was not
in my power to speak out sincerely as my heart prompted
me. I *had* to be mute—or rather I had to appear a disguised person, irresponsive to kind people—for such were
my orders from London. Yes, I had fallen from the path
of simplicity into crooked courses!

Mother and I did not breathe freely again till on the
14th May we had Berlin behind us, and were rolling along
the highway to Potsdam. And yet in Potsdam a new
heart-affecting leave-taking awaited me.

The good king wanted to see me once more on the
stage—for the last time! And so then in the evening I

played in the little town theatre of Potsdam my dear, cheerful *Leopoldine von Strehlen* in Töpfer's comedy, " Der beste Ton," a part his Majesty himself had chosen for me. I still see Friedrich Wilhelm III. sitting in his little box, and, on my being called before the curtain for the last time, join with hand and mouth in the loud applause, and kindly nod to me—for the last time ! And then this curtain, too, fell before me—for the last time !

In the dressing-room the old female attendant, Wallburg, known to the reader of my Potsdam " Theatrical Tours," wept with me, without making any complaint or putting any questions to me. I clasped her in my arms and kissed her old wrinkled cheeks, and put a ring on her finger and sobbed out, " For a keepsake, Wallburg ! Perhaps we shall never see each other again. I am going to enter on a new life. Tongues will soon be busy about me. Don't think any harm of me ? "

The faithful soul kissed me again. She did not ask me anything, but wept.

And then we drove into the mild, sweet breath of the May night—away towards the ardently-longed-for bliss ! Bliss ?

CHAPTER XX.

TO ENGLAND.

IT was also in the month of May, just five years earlier, when mother and I drove from Carlsruhe to Berlin to seek our fortune there! Had we found it?

And now, in May likewise, we quitted Berlin and drove through sunny, blooming landscapes, southwards again— out into the wide, wide world—on devious secret ways, in chase of real fortune—shall we be able to catch it this time and hold it fast—for the whole of our earthly life?

This query engaged our minds the whole journey, and through all its strange windings.

From Berlin, by way of Frankfort-on-the-Maine, to Brussels, Calais, Dover, London! This round-about way Prince Leopold and his Baron Stockmar had prescribed for us, in order to put the world on a wrong-scent. People were to believe we were driving to our old home in Carls- ruhe. To prevent our route being betrayed, we were to take neither manservant nor lady's maid. Only my little dog Lisinka was allowed us as travelling companion. She could surely gossip nothing!

At that time mother and I were still so firmly persuaded of my shrewd cousin Christian's infallibility. But we highly admired these diplomatic measures to conceal our track. To-day, I cannot but smile at my shrewd cousin's naïveté and our own piously blind faith—but it is no sunny smile!

As though so popular and celebrated an actress could disappear tracelessly from Berlin, simply to suit the crotchet of a high gentleman in England!

And the nice diplomatic plan was a total failure. We had hardly left Berlin when there appeared in the columns of the *Spener's Gazette* :—

played in the little town theatre of Potsdam my dear, cheerful *Leopoldine von Strehlen* in Töpfer's comedy, "Der beste Ton," a part his Majesty himself had chosen for me. I still see Friedrich Wilhelm III. sitting in his little box, and, on my being called before the curtain for the last time, join with hand and mouth in the loud applause, and kindly nod to me—for the last time! And then this curtain, too, fell before me—for the last time!

In the dressing-room the old female attendant, Wallburg, known to the reader of my Potsdam "Theatrical Tours," wept with me, without making any complaint or putting any questions to me. I clasped her in my arms and kissed her old wrinkled cheeks, and put a ring on her finger and sobbed out, "For a keepsake, Wallburg! Perhaps we shall never see each other again. I am going to enter on a new life. Tongues will soon be busy about me. Don't think any harm of me?"

The faithful soul kissed me again. She did not ask me anything, but wept.

And then we drove into the mild, sweet breath of the May night—away towards the ardently-longed-for bliss!

Bliss?

CHAPTER XX.

TO ENGLAND.

IT was also in the month of May, just five years earlier, when mother and I drove from Carlsruhe to Berlin to seek our fortune there! Had we found it?

And now, in May likewise, we quitted Berlin and drove through sunny, blooming landscapes, southwards again— out into the wide, wide world—on devious secret ways, in chase of real fortune—shall we be able to catch it this time and hold it fast—for the whole of our earthly life?

This query engaged our minds the whole journey, and through all its strange windings.

From Berlin, by way of Frankfort-on-the-Maine, to Brussels, Calais, Dover, London! This round-about way Prince Leopold and his Baron Stockmar had prescribed for us, in order to put the world on a wrong scent. People were to believe we were driving to our old home in Carlsruhe. To prevent our route being betrayed, we were to take neither manservant nor lady's maid. Only my little dog Lisinka was allowed us as travelling companion. She could surely gossip nothing!

At that time mother and I were still so firmly persuaded of my shrewd cousin Christian's infallibility. But we highly admired these diplomatic measures to conceal our track. To-day, I cannot but smile at my shrewd cousin's naïveté and our own piously blind faith—but it is no sunny smile!

As though so popular and celebrated an actress could disappear tracelessly from Berlin, simply to suit the crotchet of a high gentleman in England!

And the nice diplomatic plan was a total failure. We had hardly left Berlin when there appeared in the columns of the *Spener's Gazette* :—

Selle die liebt!"* "What an enviable lot beckons to thee at the side of this noble and tender prince! Free from all the cares of life and all the cabals and intrigues of the stage!" And I prayed fervently to God to preserve to me this dear man's affections!

From cousin Christian, too, I received friendly letters. All his misgivings seemed to be overcome—all down to this one, that I would not be able to stand the quiet life offered me in an English country seat! Every now and again, however, he gave voice to his gladness at knowing his master in such good and unselfish hands, as also to his hope that not only the prince's, but his own life as well, would be rendered so much the more comfortable and enjoyable by our presence in England.

I therefore honestly endeavoured in my replies to dispel the one last misgiving expressed in cousin's letters. And I succeeded in doing so only too well.

Then—in January, 1829—sly thrusts and inuendoes of all kinds began to come prickling into my ears in familiar social circles as also in intercourse with my colleagues behind the scenes. People reflected on my sudden autumn journey to Coburg, and enquired how I had enjoyed it. Some tickled me about the handsome, rich Prince Leopold; others teased me about the amorous reigning duke. Under all this I must have appeared very much discomposed and disconcerted, till at last Amelia Wolff fairly gave me the outs and ins of the matter.

The good creature first warily sounded me. "Ducky, is it true what people are saying—that you are going to leave the stage soon and come into a great fortune?"

"What is it people are saying?" I stammered out.

"That a gentleman of high rank is in love with you, and wants to marry you morganatically. The only thing they are a little in doubt about is whether it is the Duke or the Prince of Coburg."

"And that they call a 'great fortune!'" I replied, confusedly. "Why, I feel so happy as actress."

---

* "Happy alone is the soul that loves."—*From Goethe's "Egmont."*

"Nonsense, ducky, as though one were to be always twenty and always pretty! And haven't you already had some memorable experiences on the stage? Have you not to fight tooth and claw with Stich about every new part, like dogs about a bone? And doesn't little, insignificant Leonhardt herself snatch many a nice, youthful part from you, because she is Prince Karl's *protegée*. Wasn't the pretty goose of a Mademoiselle Ku—— last year allowed to, play the part of *Preciosa* here because she was the favourite of the old Grand-Duke of Baden, and he gave her a letter of recommendation to Prince Wittgenstein? And may not any chance booby of a critic, who wants to bless you with his love, tear you all to rags in his paper with impunity if you screw wry faces to his flattering proffers? And what is it awaits you in St. Petersburg? Do not all the high divinities of the theatre there, up to the Czar himself, as I have been told, look on all that is young and pretty on the stage as property at their free disposal, to begin with? And woe, woe to you when you get old on the stage, and find you have yet to play for your daily bread! There is nothing sadder than a "comic" old woman, with an anxious heart, and half her teeth out of her head. I was once playing the *Iphigenia* and the *Leonore* in "Tasso" before Goethe; and now I am playing the *Kiekebusch* and the *Madame Hersch*,* with the Toorkish* shawl, and yet there are plenty of colleagues who would like well enough to supplant me, even in these poor parts that serve only to keep my soul and body together. That is the future awaiting you on the stage— if you will not renounce this 'high bliss' of the boards. But I notice it by you, ducky, something or other has spun itself for you in Coburg, which you dare not speak of. May it be something good for you—a true happiness! But beware, my pretty little flower, of the fate of the 'fair Greek!'"

Quite nonplussed I returned to mother and told her all that had been said to me. How was our Coburg secret betrayed? We had gossiped it to no one. And now I

---

* Jew part, and therefore written in the Jewish dialect.

Selle die liebt!"*   "What an enviable lot beckons to thee
at the side of this noble and tender prince! Free from all
the cares of life and all the cabals and intrigues of the
stage!" And I prayed fervently to God to preserve to
me this dear man's affections!

From cousin Christian, too, I received friendly letters.
All his misgivings seemed to be overcome—all down to
this one, that I would not be able to stand the quiet life
offered me in an English country seat! Every now and
again, however, he gave voice to his gladness at knowing
his master in such good and unselfish hands, as also to his
hope that not only the prince's, but his own life as well,
would be rendered so much the more comfortable and enjoyable by our presence in England.

I therefore honestly endeavoured in my replies to dispel
the one last misgiving expressed in cousin's letters. And
I succeeded in doing so only too well.

Then—in January, 1829—sly thrusts and inuendoes of
all kinds began to come prickling into my ears in familiar
social circles as also in intercourse with my colleagues
behind the scenes. People reflected on my sudden
autumn journey to Coburg, and enquired how I had enjoyed it. Some tickled me about the handsome, rich
Prince Leopold; others teased me about the amorous
reigning duke. Under all this I must have appeared
very much discomposed and disconcerted, till at last
Amelia Wolff fairly gave me the outs and ins of the
matter.

The good creature first warily sounded me. "Ducky,
is it true what people are saying—that you are going to
leave the stage soon and come into a great fortune?"

"What is it people are saying?" I stammered out.

"That a gentleman of high rank is in love with you,
and wants to marry you morganatically. The only thing
they are a little in doubt about is whether it is the Duke
or the Prince of Coburg."

"And that they call a 'great fortune!'" I replied,
confusedly. "Why, I feel so happy as actress."

---

* "Happy alone is the soul that loves."—*From Goethe's "Egmont."*

"Nonsense, ducky, as though one were to be always twenty and always pretty! And haven't you already had some memorable experiences on the stage? Have you not to fight tooth and claw with Stich about every new part, like dogs about a bone? And doesn't little, insignificant Leonhardt herself snatch many a nice, youthful part from you, because she is Prince Karl's *protegée*. Wasn't the pretty goose of a Mademoiselle Ku—— last year allowed to play the part of *Preciosa* here because she was the favourite of the old Grand-Duke of Baden, and he gave her a letter of recommendation to Prince Wittgenstein? And may not any chance booby of a critic, who wants to bless you with his love, tear you all to rags in his paper with impunity if you screw wry faces to his flattering proffers? And what is it awaits you in St. Petersburg? Do not all the high divinities of the theatre there, up to the Czar himself, as I have been told, look on all that is young and pretty on the stage as property at their free disposal, to begin with? And woe, woe to you when you get old on the stage, and find you have yet to play for your daily bread! There is nothing sadder than a "comic" old woman, with an anxious heart, and half her teeth out of her head. I was once playing the *Iphigenia* and the *Leonore* in "Tasso" before Goethe; and now I am playing the *Kiekebusch* and the *Madame Hersch*,* with the Toorkish* shawl, and yet there are plenty of colleagues who would like well enough to supplant me, even in these poor parts that serve only to keep my soul and body together. That is the future awaiting you on the stage—if you will not renounce this 'high bliss' of the boards. But I notice it by you, ducky, something or other has spun itself for you in Coburg, which you dare not speak of. May it be something good for you—a true happiness! But beware, my pretty little flower, of the fate of the 'fair Greek!'"

Quite nonplussed I returned to mother and told her all that had been said to me. How was our Coburg secret betrayed? We had gossiped it to no one. And now I

---

* Jew part, and therefore written in the Jewish dialect.

was brought into suspicious conjunction with the licentious duke! Had a letter gone amissing or been opened in the post-office? Now and again whispers oozed out of the "black post cabinet," in which any letters provoking curiosity were read.

Mother and I deemed it our duty to acquaint cousin Christian without delay of the Berlin rumours, and to ask his instructions in the matter. By return of post came the short order: All exchange of letters between us must be at once broken off till further directions. To all insinuations we were to oppose the most decisive or even bluntest denial of everything.

And so for full four months I no longer received the least sign of their existence, either from cousin Christian in Coburg or Prince Leopold in Naples. A time of the most tormenting uncertainty—mother and I hanging constantly on the rack of painful suspense.

We daily asked ourselves: What will come of it? Has the prince already forgotten you? Does the prince think only of the Greek throne—a question turning up now and again in the papers? Does he gladly sacrifice the longed-for happiness of a quiet life for the splendour of a throne? Was it all a happy dream?

And in an ever more romantic and amiable light did the prince appeal to my fancy, the more remote was the horizon whence his image hovered to me. His beautiful melancholy eyes would not out of my head. In those days of suspense and anxiety, days in which I longed for the still joys of the heart, and looked out morning and evening for a token of affection—in such days I actually fell in love with this idol of my dreams. Descried through the lengthening interval of time, this idol grew ever brighter to my longing eyes. I verily believe that if any one had ventured to make mock of the prince's wig, I would have sworn that this wig was the true halo for the poor, much-tried martyr of his heart!

Under such experience weeks upon weeks passed away in tormenting uncertainty. In Berlin the inuendoes ultimately went to rest for want of handles to take hold of. Some believed the rumour was without foundation, others that the bond which had at first been schemed or formed had long ago been dissolved.

The extent, however, to which the obscure rumour had then spread was not brought home to me till forty years later, when I came across a passage in the journals of Varnhagen. In February, 1829, Varnhagen was staying at Cassel, in the execution of a commission from Friedrich Wilhelm III., which had for its object to heal, if possible, the conjugal breach between the elector and electress on account of his mistress, the Countess Reichenbach, *née* Ortlepp. Under date Cassel, 5th February, 1829, may be read in Varnhagen's journals:

"The elector insists on his relationship to the Countess of Reichenbach being regarded and treated as a palpably unique one, having nothing in common with other *liaisons*, and as, therefore, completely legitimate; while, on the other hand, it is altogether shocking to his moral feelings that the Grand-Duke of Darmstadt should have the actress Mademoiselle Peche for his mistress and the Duke of Coburg should be seeking to lead astray the actress Caroline Bauer."

How could that rumour have reached the elector's ears in Cassel? Did, perhaps, Herr von Varnhagen himself carry it with him from Berlin? And the one small fact to which the whole affair was to be referred was my hasty excursion to Coburg and the exchange of a few letters with cousin Christian and Prince Leopold! Did people take these two gentlemen for the reigning duke's panders?

From January on to the end of April I received not a line from either Prince Leopold or Christian Stockmar. I did not so much as know whether the one was still staying in Italy and the other in Coburg.

After that I was coming home from the rehearsal one noon when I saw a young gentleman standing at the bell of our corridor. We enter the house at the same time. He inquires for my mother, and represents himself as a clerk of the banking house of Lewald, charged to pay, on the order of Baron Stockmar in London, twelve hundred thalers to the Frau Rittmeisterin and hand over a letter!

And with every question we put about the steam-packet and the passengers, the faces of Monsieur Mesiève and his satellites smirked ever more suspicion and ambiguity of expression. It was no use for me to try and look disembarrassed and cheerful at the *table d'hôte.* I did not succeed in that piece of comedy, not having the boards nor the light heart needed for an *artiste.*

At last, on the third day, as we were sitting in depressed spirits at breakfast, the waiter announced "Monsieur Unlein," and the little, stout, comfortable man stood before us, his whole rosy face radiant as ever. In vain, however, I inquired after a letter of apology or welcome from the prince or Baron Stockmar.

And what was the cause of his coming so late?

His Highness was ill of megrim, and couldn't spare his usual personal attendants.

This answer did' not much allay my misgivings. In spite of all, however, the beaming good-humour and unfailing cheery gossip of Figaro-Hühnlein, who accompanied us on an interesting walk by the seashore, availed to relieve us of some of the load on our hearts. He told us of the charming cottage Baron Stockmar had rented and furnished for us in the beautiful, fashionable Regent's Park.

"In the neighbourhood, then, of the prince's residence, Marlborough House?" I struck in.

"Well—not—exactly," drawled out Hühnlein, but soon put our minds to rest again by saying that "no place even in London could be considered distant when you had fast horses!"

Next morning at six we went aboard the steamer with our travelling marshal. Only too soon, however, we were joined by another passenger—the horrid sea-sickness. Mother and I suffered cruelly, and did not think to reach the promised land of Old England alive. Even Lisinka rolled about like a drunkard, and kept up a moaning equal to our own.

At last Hühnlein brought us the consoling news of "land!" and conducted us on deck. There, then, lay the coast of England before us! But we had no feeling for

I

its picturesque beauties, nor any question even as to the future hidden for us behind that coast. Our one thought was, quickly to bed—and sleep! sleep!

When in our English hotel we had thoroughly slept off our sea-sickness, and had next morning refreshed ourselves with a genuine English breakfast, the bright May-morning and the new world of Old England smiled on us with returning suggestions of radiant promise. Then the charming drive from Dover to London in an easy, elegant, open carriage, drawn by beautiful, spirited horses, through the exuberant, lovely land! It was like a continuous pleasure-drive through a gigantic park. On both sides of the fine, broad highway alternated trim villages with tasteful gardens, flourishing groups of trees, luscious shrubberies, and fresh-green, flower-besprinkled meadows. And all the luxuriant, smiling landscape was animate with cheerful, comfortable-looking, tidily-dressed country-people and happy, ruddy children at play. The round, sleek, pacific cows, the well-nourished, richly-fleeced flocks of sheep, the broods of piebald fowls strutting and cackling in the farmyards, called forth more than one exclamation of delight from a heart so fond of animals as mine.

The postilions, in their smart, becoming dress, looked as spruce as may be seen at home on the stage alone. And what perfect drivers are they! To guide the elegantly-harnessed horses by a briefest word seemed mere pastime to them; only now and again did the dainty whips crack lustily in the air without touching the horses. The changing of the horses executed itself in a twinkling, and we spanked along more like flying than rolling. My heart thumped forward ever fuller and fuller of hope towards our new future.

"Doubtless the prince is longingly awaiting us in the new home!" I sang out merrily to mother. "What a joyous meeting 'twill be after so much suspense and anxiety. Cousin Christian, as I hope, will have come with him, and we shall then sup again à quatre with the most perfect enjoyment, as we breakfasted in Füllbach on that occasion."

Mother endeavoured to join in blithely with me, but her

words had not the ring of the heart in them which mine had.
The nearer we came to London the more earnest and silent
she grew. Her thoughts were all absorbed in care about
me, whereas in my easy-mindedness I let mine expatiate
without a shadow of misgiving over all the novelties that
met my eyes, and over all that Meister Hühnlein explained
in his good humoured way.

The suburbs of London, which we first came upon, with
their high, grey, monotonous houses and factories and
smoky sky made a gloomy impression on me.

Suddenly I shouted out in surprise, "Ah! Prince
Leopold!"

It was only, however, a gigantic portrait of the prince
looking down on us, in red uniform and in brilliant oil
colours, from the gable of a house. And the further we
went the more frequently did we meet these portraits,
alternating with the pictures of the blond Princess Charlotte. Beneath them were inscriptions in enormous
characters unintelligible to me, as I did not know English.

Hühnlein, with a consequential air, explained that
"these pictures date from the time of the arrival of the
prince in England and his marriage with the Princess
Charlotte, both being the most popular people in the whole
of Great Britain. So speculative tradesmen and shop-
keepers availed themselves of these popular pictures as
alluring signs for their business. Here a corset-maker
and soap-dealer trumpet their incomparable wares under
the sign of the Princess Charlotte; there a blacking manufacturer and a wig-maker proclaim their inventions under
the portrait of the prince."

"Did his Highness, then, when bridegroom, already
wear a wig?" involuntarily escaped my lips.

"Ah, no!" said Hühnlein, in a manner betokening
fidelity of heart to the prince. "That has only come about
gradually. And, in truth, his Highness does not need even
yet to wear a wig, if it were not he is so afraid of cold."

What put it into my head, just on the very entry into
my new home, to think of the nasty black wig of my
heart's elect? It has such a depressing effect on the
flame of love, like some foul medicine.

It was getting dusk when we shot out of the windings of uniform, dingy streets into Regent's Park. I inquisitively reconnoitered the cottages already in part lighted up, and noticed villas and proud edifices on the magnificent terraces, half-hidden under grand old trees and blooming boscages. In the ponds on the wide lawns the first emerging stars were mirroring themselves. From blossoming shrubberies poured out the liquid strains of nightingales.

"O how beautiful, how passing beautiful!" I shouted. "This reminds one vividly of the Berlin Thiergarten, so that we shall have no difficulty in soon feeling ourselves at home here."

"God grant it!" said mother.

At last we drew up in front of an iron railing, and saw through the trees a charming little villa, brightly lighted up. A woman, in a large white hood with fluttering ribbons, came bustling forward to meet us, and saluted us in very fluent German—in name of Baron Stockmar!

"And the baron?" I asked in a tension of excitement, while we got out of the carriage.

"Regrets exceedingly at being prevented to-night from personally saluting the ladies."

"And—is—nobody—else—here—to receive us?"

My heart beat audibly, and I could hardly draw breath.

"O, yes! there is the gardener here, who has charge of the house, goes the errands, and helps me in the house and kitchen. But he does not understand a word of German, Master James," said the woman, with great volubility. "My name is Fanny, and up till now I was housekeeper in Claremont House, and enjoy the full confidence of the baron. I have therefore been set as housekeeper here in the meantime, and am entirely at the service of the ladies."

I felt no liking for this loquacious woman. Master James was a big, heavy-looking man, something like an automaton in his bearing and movements. With great gravity he came stepping towards us, carrying a lantern in his hand; with great gravity he assisted in taking the luggage from the carriage, and pushed the carriage into the coach-house.

"But a letter has been left for us?" I asked, with all the composure my utmost effort at self-control allowed me, of Frau Fanny, who led us into the sweet house, mantled all over with blossoming creepers, and very attentively helped us off with our travelling cloaks.

But not so much as a note of welcome was there for us, either from the prince or Christian!

When we were alone, I threw myself like an anguished child on my faithful mother's breast, and sobbed, "O, mother, what a sad beginning of our new—happiness! To be welcomed to a strange house by strange servants! Had we but dreamt of it in Berlin, we shouldn't have been here. For five months now I have not had a single letter, not a sign of love from the prince, who yet declared to me his love, and looked to me for the happiness of a loving home. Mother, how shall this end?"

Mother sought to console me, but in her saddened eye I could see how much she had need herself of consolation. She said: "Lina, to-morrow we shall assuredly see and speak to the prince, and everything will be cleared up to our satisfaction, else——"

Here the curtseying and perpetually-smiling Fanny announced that tea was served, and that Hühnlein desired to know whether the ladies had any orders for him. He had now to return to Marlborough House.

While Fanny ran to call Hühnlein to us, mother whispered to me, "Composure, Lina—self-command before the servants at least. The comedy, I see, is not yet over. As unembarrassed and cheerful as possible."

So we kindly thanked the good Hühnlein for his services as travelling marshal, and charged him to convey our friendliest greetings to the baron.

Frau Fanny, who was unwilling to deprive us of her gossipy company even while we were at tea, was dismissed with dignity by my mother, as we had no further need of her services. A cold "Good-night" stopped all reply on her part.

And so mother and I sat down opposite each other at the tea-table, which was brilliantly illuminated and richly served with all kinds of delicacies—in our new home—at the beginning of our new life—feeling very much as if we were in a dream. For agitation we couldn't taste a bit of anything; hardly drink a cup of tea.

Nor would chat itself go forward with us. Our hearts were too burdened with vexation and anxiety. We felt entirely forsaken and isolated.

We then betook ourselves to the beautiful bedrooms provided with genuine English comfort, with soft carpets and magnificent stately beds.

But since ever I left the Swiss boarding-house I had always shared my bedroom with my mother. And this first anxious night in London, was I-to sleep alone? I therefore crept into my mother's spacious bed. We embraced each other fervently, and prayed together :

" Unsern Eingung segne Gott,
Unsern Ausgang gleichermassen,"*

an old prayer I had been in the habit of repeating with the other children at the opening of school every morning.

" Our out-going in like measure! " This word gave us wonderful consolation. We were by no manner of means bound to this house and these new relations. We might again to-morrow morning return to Germany, to our old home.

Such was our journey after happiness!

---

* " Our in-coming may God bless,
Our out-going in like measure."

CHAPTER XXI.

O BUT HE WAS A BRISK YOUNG LAD.

A LAUGHING May morning awoke us in our new home, embowered in the freshest green and in the fragrant blossom flush of Regent's Park.

"Home!" did I say? Can "home" be so solitary as mother and I now felt at our outset on this new and brilliant world of London, and this new life sacred to the joys of the heart.

And yet, in spite of all crosses, there was much that was beautiful and interesting calling on us to look and admire. Our cottage was bright and charming, like a casket of jewels, and solidly comfortable and enjoyable as any English house might be. In the beautiful garden-salon, the wide-folding doors of which opened on a terrace wreathed in climbing roses and gay with brilliant flowers, stood a splendid Clementi grand piano, the full, song-like tone of which at once captivated me. A white marble fire-place promised the enjoyment of genial warmth in the cool mornings and evenings. My boudoir looked like a downy nest, draped all round with pink silk; the spacious airy sleeping-room, overshadowed by a stately plane-tree, was decorated white and green; the dining room was wain-scotted and furnished with bright polished oak, and its mantelpiece adorned with antique porcelain. Nor was a billiard room wanting, though its brown gold-printed leather papering suggested its occasional use as a smoking room. The bath room was perfectly enchanting, lined as it was with white blue-veined porcelain. My mother's rooms, and two attractive rooms for guests, were a stair above mine.

In addition, there was a large, well-kept, and richly-adorned park-like garden, expanding in fresh green velvet-soft lawns, blazing with beds of pranking tulips, hyacinths,

ranunculi, rhododendrons, peonies, and other flowers, fes-
tooned with groups of lilac, laburnum, and roses. Large
beds of strawberries alluringly offered their first ripe fruit
to the taste. An ornamental aviary contained below
cackling silver-white fowls; above, cooing doves and a
motley throng of twittering birds. A perfect paradise to
my animal-loving heart!

But how still it was all around this retired section of
Regent's Park! A few similar gardens and villas were,
indeed, to be seen, but only at rare intervals a solitary foot
passenger or a silent park labourer. All was slumber-
ously still, as in Dornröschen's garden of enchantment!

"What a charming golden cage have cousin Christian
and the prince sought out for us," I said, with a faint
attempt at jesting

"Yes, we are now entirely in their power—at their
mercy, or want of mercy," returned mother, in a similar
tone. Our laughing and jesting were getting rather
rusty.

After breakfast we unpacked and made our toilet for
the reception of the prince. I adorned myself with a
steel-grey silk dress, with lace trimmings and lace sleeves,
with corals round the neck and arms. My mother finished
me off with a freshly-opened white rose stuck into my
blond locks, and then surveyed me with no little complacency, imagining that such a rosy little daughter was
good enough to take even the coldest lover by storm.

But now began the torturing hours of waiting, rising
into ever more painful restlessness—hours to which even
a course of months could not accustom me. Now I
traversed the garden with Lisinka, fed the fowls, pigeons,
and singing birds, plucked flowers for a nosegay, tasted
the first ripe strawberries, and again and again looked
from the garden-gate up the road leading, as Fanny told
us, to Marlborough House. Now I would dawdle indoors to
see mother busy arranging our things, and hear the sorry
consolation from her: "Only patience, Lina, the prince
must soon come and welcome us, or, at any rate, cousin
Christian."

At last, at one o'clock, a slender horseman came riding

slowly through the park, seemingly absorbed in deep thought. He looked pale and fagged, and a shadow rested on his forehead and his shrewd eyes. It was cousin Christian. It cost him an effort to give mother and me a friendly and cheerful welcome, which, when all was done, had no free and cordial ring in it. It was clear there was something on cousin's mind oppressing him, which he tried to hide from us. He gave the curtseying Fanny and the automatically stolid James, who was leading his horse slowly up and down, some commands in English and then followed us into the garden salon.

"And the prince?" I exclaimed, with an anguished heart.

"He sends you his hearty greetings and bids you welcome to England by me. He is a slave to the proprieties, and was unable to greet you yesterday evening, having been invited to dinner by his sister, the Duchess of Kent—you know her, Aunt Christina, as Princess Victoria of Coburg."

"But we ought in any case to have received a welcome in writing in Calais and here," I struck out in a burst of temper, "if he really loves me—and unless I had believed in his love I would certainly not be here now. Cousin, in Calais before Hühnlein's arrival, and still more here yesterday evening, in the company of this spying Fanny, who is always smiling so craftily and confidentially, we thought we were going to die of solitude; and this morning as well, before you came, we felt as if entirely abandoned in a foreign country. Cousin, I wish mother and I were sitting quietly and peacefully in Berlin."

"I'd like it, too, Caroline," blurted out cousin, and then gave his speech a new turn. "And so Fanny and her inquisitive familiarity are not to your taste? Am not greatly surprised. But she can keep counsel and is faithfully devoted to the prince and me, has been many years in our service, and is out-and-out trustworthy. And for these—particular relationships—I need above everything a counsel-keeping person, as this section of affairs touches no less than the prince's maintenance and future!"

"It has to do with *my* maintenance and future as well,

cousin!" I exclaimed, nearly beside myself. "What is the matter? Does the prince not love me any more? What is the meaning of his delay—of his not coming? And what's the meaning of your cold reserved tone likewise? How different it all sounds now from what we heard in Coburg! How is it about the Greek throne? Why have you never written more to me about it? Do I stand in your way? Mother, let us start on our way back again this very day yet."

"Miss Gunpowder flares off into more questions in one whiff than ten wise men are able to answer!" rejoined cousin with a dry laugh. "And as to the prince's not coming and not writing, you mustn't forget that Prince Leopold is, and is bound to be, very circumspect. Just think what a scandal it would make in the papers if a reporter were to scent out that Prince Leopold of Coburg, who, as widower of the Princess-Royal, draws an English pension of £50,000, had made the beautiful Berlin actress, Caroline Bauer, come to England in order to marry her morganatically! And then, over and above, she is a cousin of the prince's confidential friend, Baron Stockmar, who hopes by this tie to bind the prince hand and foot to himself! If the papers hostile to us get a hold of this handle, then it would be all over with me, too, in England. Nay, the throne of Greece itself, which is still in the air, would be irrecoverably lost if it were known that the candidate for the Greek throne had played such a foolish game as fall in love with a pretty actress, and promise her marriage. Don't forget, then, children—business first and then love! It won't at all do for you to be looking at these new relationships like sentimental Germans, but like thoroughly practical mortals. Trust implicitly in my honour, and look the future straight in the face. Well, I hope I've expressed myself with tolerable clearness, Christina, and you, Caroline? Don't, now, look at me like a pair of gawkies, or as if the wind had been knocked out of you; but answer free off-hand!"

"Tolerably clear, dear Christian," said my mother, with trembling voice, "but, unfortunately, too late. If in Coburg you had spoken to us so clearly, we should not

be sitting here now with sad and anxious hearts. I fear
Lina and I are not equal to the situation here. But—
dear me! what is the matter with you, Christian? Are
you unwell? You look pale as death. Your hands are
trembling, and cold perspiration is on your brow. Lina,
quickly—a glass of water and eau-de-cologne!"

"Oh, it is already passing away," said cousin faintly,
with a melancholy smile. "It is nothing but my old
nervous state, which get worse with excitement. Only
feel my pulse, how restless and irregular it beats. I'll die
for certain one day of apoplexy, if I don't go off first with
dyspepsia. Then I'm threatened with incurable blindness
to the bargain. Ay, I've got a fairish load, for my own
part, to carry. But good-bye, for the present; I've got a
ride still to take through the Park before dinner, to try
and quiet my nerves. I didn't wish to make you uneasy,
but I had to prepare you for the present relations and for
the prince, whom you will certainly find changed. Let us
hope, however, for the best! I shall be here to-morrow
at two, and dine with you. Then we will chat with lighter
spirits than to-day."

In visibly milder temper cousin rode off, leaving us in
deepest depression.

"Mother, what say you to Christian—to his behaviour
and speech?" I asked, breaking the painful pause.

"The poor man is certainly very unwell, and his nervous
state causes me serious uneasiness," said my mother
evasively. "But now let us eat some dinner and appear
as cheerful as possible before the spying Fanny, and then
the prince will come and everything will be cleared up and
settled—for a near and prosperous bond—or for our
immediate departure. Up till now we have not the least
reproach to make ourselves, and that consciousness will
give us strength to go through the worst!"

Touched and encouraged, I embraced my noble mother.

Dinner, however, was a mere form and a pain we imposed upon ourselves before the spying servant. She had
to remove the dishes almost untasted.

And again began the torment of waiting—waiting.
The old-fashioned corridor clock struck four—struck five

—six—and no prince visible!. Restless—getting ever more excited—or even indignant, I went out into the garden and then back into the house, carrying with me the constant sting of an inward suggestion, which gnawed away at my heart like a worm: "This delay tells of no warm, happy love-longing."

Mother grew paler and paler, and found ever fewer words with which to compose my impatience and agitation.

At length, towards seven o'clock, an elegant tilbury rolled through the park, and stopped before the terrace. Muffled up like an Arctic explorer or a light-shunning high-wayman, my knight alighted, consideringly, from his carriage, and softly approached the glass door of the salon. I heard the heavy, slow footsteps, one by one, on the creaking ground. My heart beat loud and high as if it would burst. In my nervous agitation I plucked to pieces the rose my mother had with such fond hopefulness inserted in my hair in the morning, and which the long, long weary day had withered. Softly the glass door opened—then three slow, heavy footsteps, and the tall form of the prince stood before me, while trembling and deprived of all composure I leant against the chimney awaiting in silence the prince's address.

The prince, too, kept silent, nor did he strefch out any arm to embrace me, nor any hand to shake with mine. The prince's eyes surveyed me consideringly, then slowly there came from his lips :

"O, how the spring sun has burnt your cheeks!"

Every word shot freezingly through me like ice. Sobbing loudly, I wanted to run away, but the prince held me fast, and said, in an almost ghastly tone, "What's the matter? What's the meaning of tears?"

"Your Highness asks!" I burst out in extreme irrita-tion; "I hasten hither in my devoted love, risking my future as an artist, and even my maidenly repute—and you, your Highness, have no better word of welcome for me than a criticism about my sunburnt complexion. I shall leave England to-morrow again. Nobody yet knows I was here—nor why!"

"Nobody—perhaps there is though," said the prince,

with a peculiar emphasis, again looking me sharp in the face. He then, however, drew me more tenderly to him, kissed me and stroked my hair, as though I were a pouting, petted child, and whispered into my ear, "Not so touchy, missy; it was not so unkindly meant. Be good again, and look at me nicely as once, in Coburg."

I hid my face on the prince's breast and wept gently. He chucked me by the chin. I again felt the spell of those beautiful, melancholy eyes, and I could not help laughing involuntarily. A kiss sealed the reconciliation.

The prince then kindly asked after mother. She stepped out of the adjoining room. "Ah, you have been witness to the first curtain-lecture I have received!" said his Highness, trying to pass off his embarrassment by a joke.

"The delay of meeting you has excited Lina," said mother, soothingly. "She is always the same artistic creature—always fire and flame—and was very much spoiled in Berlin."

So the first storm passed away happily, to outward appearance at least. In my heart, however, I could not, the whole evening through, get over a certain misgiving. In spite of all the exchange of friendly words I still felt an estranging something or other had stepped between the prince and me. He often looked long and searchingly at me, as though he wanted to read into my soul. Suddenly he asked me:

"And you have left no sweetheart in Berlin?"

"No, your Highness," I said, piqued; "no sweetheart, else I were not here. But very dear friends I have, alas! been obliged to leave behind."

"And what address have you given for letter-writing and inquisitive friends?"

"Mother's address: Frau Rittmeisterin Bauer, *poste restante*, Frankfort-on-the-Maine. There a true and worthy friend of our family—Captain Hilpert, the Baden *chargé d'affaires*, who served under my departed father, and is faithfully devoted to mother—will receive the letters and send them to cousin's address at Marlborough House. Thither, also, will my brothers, Karl and Louis, and my former guardian, Hofgerichtsadvocat Bayer in Rastatt, address their letters."

"H'm! good! h'm! And has the private chamberlain, Timm, also received the same address of Marlborough House?" the prince further asked.

"No, your Highness, seeing Timm has already long known your and cousin's address. Besides, this faithful patron of mine will, of course, expect to receive news of mother and me, not only for himself but for his Majesty, who takes a sincere interest in my fortunes."

The prince stopped short, and then said drawlingly: "And what will you write to Timm and his Majesty?"

"I shall wait till I can announce to them the day of our departure for Hamburg, where a starring engagement is offered me, before I enter on my St. Petersburg engagement. For every hour I feel the more that I should perish in this cool atmosphere. O, would I had never come here!" Bursting into tears I plunged out into the garden, where all lay buried in the darkness of night.

The prince did *not* follow me, and immediately after I heard his carriage roll off. He had said to mother, " The spitfire will soon come to herself again. To-morrow, at four, I shall return, if not prevented."

"Mother," I cried, quite beside myself, "What is the meaning of all this? This strange conduct on the part of Christian and my royal wooer? All these captious questions, and whether I have left no sweetheart in Berlin? Has any one slandered us to the prince? But why, then, have they made us come, and wiled us out of our peace and quietness? I must have certainty, or these tormenting doubts will be the very death of me. O, why is it I have to suffer such heartrending experiences?"

"Christian must give us explanation—advice and assistance!" said mother, in her own decided way. "We have committed ourselves in fullest confidence to his guidance, and he cannot now leave us in the lurch. Write at once, and tell him what weighs on our minds since the prince's visit. We expect some explanation and assistance from him, or——"

"We shall set off to-morrow," I shouted, in the midst

of my tears. "What a happy time it will be when we again turn our back on England!"

And with trembling heart and hasting pen I wrote cousin everything—everything,—winding up my complaining and accusing letter with the words: "Hasten to us; help! save us; or you will no longer find us here!"

This letter I made James take the same evening to Marlborough House, with the order to give the letter only into the hands of Baron Stockmar, and wait an answer.

With feverish impatience we waited for the return of the messenger. At eleven o'clock James stood, with all gravity, before us, with the answer by word of mouth: "All right, the baron will come to-morrow morning at eleven." The inquisitive, smiling Fanny had, of course, to act as interpreter.

The second night in my new home, which had flatteringly promised me a new happiness of love, I had again to seek the protection of my mother's heart. We vowed to one another we would meet the threatening storms strongly, proudly, and composedly; and would sooner leave at once than expose ourselves to new humiliations and unmerited distrust. Why had the prince and Christian not hinted one word about the promised marriage? Our departure seemed to us ever less and less a misfortune.

At last kind slumber released us from all our doubts and anxious surmisings.

Next morning at eleven cousin Christian came to us after a hasty ride. He looked hot and excited, and flung himself exhausted into the corner of the sofa. In a fever of attention I watched cousin's lips and eyes.

"Now, what are we to think?" said mother, much moved. "Christian, you owe it to us to tell us the whole truth. What is the meaning of the prince's strange questions? And your want of cordiality? We have been slandered. So much is clear to me. But by whom? Has the dowager-duchess, who is evilly disposed to us, tried to draw away her son from us?"

"No, not the dowager-duchess has shot the poisoned arrow, but an anonymous writer from Berlin," blurted out Christian. "The letter arrived before you to the prince's precise address. The writer must be familiar with you, and looks as if he were deep in the secret of your relations to Prince Leopold. He speaks of the prince's visit to you in Berlin, and of the meeting in Coburg. He warns my master of your dangerous nets, which you had in vain thrown out to catch the rich Prince August of Prussia, and calls mother and daughter a couple of intriguers of the worst-kind, who would do anything for money. He makes use of the lowest terms to express the nature of Lina's love affair with the Russian valet, to whom she denied no favour, supposing him to be the rich Count Samoilow. He gives it to be understood that the St. Petersburg tour was only a cloak to hide a secret *accouchement*, and that after her return Lina took up very intimately with a rich banker, besides having had a number of golden lovers in St. Petersburg. What have you to say to that?"

As if paralysed by a stroke of lightning, mother and I sat, pale and motionless, over against our accuser and judge. We did not so much as shed a tear.

"Well," proceeded Christian, mercilessly, "do I get no answer?"

Then my mother gathered the remains of her strength together and said, with dignity:

"To such an accusation from my brother's son, repeated into our very face, we have but one answer—immediate departure. *Poor*, of course, as we came!"

"But, Aunt Christina, who would set fire to the barn to get rid of the rats? I am not your accuser, but your zealous defender against the anonymous Berliner, if you will only give me the means of defence. Who can the writer be? Who is your bitterest enemy in Berlin?"

"Prince August!" called out mother and I in one breath. And then mother related plainly and truly all the scandalous manœuvres of the profligate prince to entrap me, and, when he failed, to wreak his revenge on me.

And the more mother proceeded in her account, the clearer grew my cousin's face. He vivaciously exclaimed: "Why, it's the very thing I was thinking—that the

letter came from some discarded admirer. My august
master will stare when I tell him of the princely anonymous. Well, I shall set him to rights, and I hope the
whole hateful intermezzo will yet bear good fruit for you!"

"I have no more hope," I said, weariedly. " Let us
go off, cousin. How can any happiness follow the bond
that was to be tied where there is no mutual confidence?"

Christian went up and down two or three times hastily
through the room in deep meditation. Then he stopped
before us and said, earnestly:

"Perhaps I shall myself some time advise you to make
a hasty departure—perhaps even soon—but not to-day
yet. Such a precipitate flight were not becoming either
your or my dignity. For the present you will stay here
as *my* guests till I have got the prince to declare whether
and when he intends making you his morganatic spouse,
according to all forms of honour and morals, so far as circumstances permit. But let us allow the prince a few
weeks' time to make it up quietly with himself. That his
heart is still susceptible of any deep burning love is rather
more than I am disposed to give him credit for. The fact
is, my master is long ago perfectly *blasé*, having squandered away in delusive, transient attachments all the
'poetry of love' all the 'blossoms of the heart,' till now
all that is left is *ennui* and egoistic pedantry. I had hopes,
Lina, you might succeed in forcing up some fresh sprigs,
for the prince still loves you as passionately as his phlegm
will enable him. No precipitation, therefore, but patient
waiting. And whether you start to-morrow or years later
is all one; your future is guaranteed. The capital the
prince settled on you as far back as in Coburg is in my hands.
The interest will suffice for modest wants. Besides, you
have still a few months to the good before you need to
finally break with your St. Petersburg contract. Children!
into what foolish labyrinths of the heart has a dry old stick
of a married man like me fallen, all through my good
nature! And now to dinner—for with all this talk I am
getting hungry."

After dinner, I opened the piano to play and sing to my
cousin his favourite old German songs. I was just singing

with all my heart—to Reichardt's heart-born air, " Freudevoll und leidvoll " *—when a carriage rolled up.

"The prince!" I shouted, turning pale. "Cousin,
stay here, my heart is too oppressed!"

"Ah! Stocky, you here yet?" said the prince, on
entering. He then saluted mother and me with visible
embarrassment.

"Gracious master, I waited for you here to make you
a few communications."

"Good! Good! You will excuse us, ladies," and the
prince was about to go with Stocky into the adjoining
room when mother and I whipped out before they had
time to do so through the verandah into the garden.

After a quarter of an hour, cousin came down the
terrace in gayer spirits to bid us adieu. Before mounting
his horse he whispered to us:

"The prince has got his lesson and is now all humble-
ness. Now, Lina, it lies with you to be wise as the serpent and meek and amiable as the dove! Everything
remains, then, according to our agreement"—and he was
off like a stripling.

When we returned to the salon, I found the prince
standing at the piano and looking through my music. In
a friendly voice, he said:

"Ah, you play very difficult pieces, I see! I am glad
of it, for I am passionately fond of music, though, unfortunately, I do not myself play. If, however, you would
not mind accompanying me to a song? I find here a few
songs in the ' Urania ' I know."

Without any more ado I sat down to the piano. The
prince opened " Urania." I played, and he sang with a
very soft but agreeable voice:

"Im Windsgerausch, in stiller Nacht,
Geht dort ein Wandersmann." †

Then followed Weber's charming song:

"Horch, leise, horch, geliebte," ‡

---

* From Goethe's *Egmont*, " Joyful and Sorrowful," &c.
† " In rustling storm, in the still night,
There goes a wandering man."
‡ " List, softly, list, my love."

and so on we played and sang, on and on, as though it
had just been for this object we came to England, and we
had no other concern in the world with each other. At
last Fanny announced: "The horses are put to, as your
Highness ordered."

"Already five o'clock?" said the prince in surprise.
"The hour has passed away very quickly and agreeably
with this musical performance. To-morrow at four I shall
come again, and bring with me a selection from 'Semiramis' and 'Othello,' arranged for the piano, when we
will sing Italian duets. The Italians do compose much
more agreeably for singing than the Germans. I should
like, too, to hear Missy's celebrated reading powers. I
have just got some new books: 'Les memoires du Duc de
St. Simon,' the fantastic novel 'Picciola,' and 'The Pearls,'
by Henrietta Hanke. That will give us enjoyable hours,
while I drizzle through the reading."

"Drizzle?" I said to myself in amazement, what can
that mean? I was very soon to learn its meaning to my
horror.

Mother ventured to ask aloud: "What, then, was
really the matter with Baron Stockmar, whose nervous
affection made her anxious?"

"Ah, it is of no consequence!" was the smiling reply.
"Poor Stocky is only an arrant hypochondriac and croaker,
like all whose digestion is out of order. And so, till
to-morrow at four, adieu!"

And away was the odd wooer.

Mother and I looked at him, as he went off, quite taken
aback; and I, seized with a fit of laughing and crying,
had to bury my head in the cushions that the spying Fanny
might not hear anything.

"How the sun has burnt your cheeks!" This ominous
word would never away out of my mind. The whole aridity
of the prince's heart was typified by it. I was to experience
still more hopeless symptoms of that underlying state.

CHAPTER XXII.

COUNTESS MONTGOMERY.

I COULD not but smile bitterly, and then weep bitterly, when, forty years after the event, I read in Varnhagen's "Tagebuch," under date 11th June, 1829:

"Mademoiselle Bauer has quitted the stage to follow other happy stars in England."

"Other happy stars!" I never experienced sadder June days than those of the hapless year for me of 1829, under the foggy sky of England. My happy star seemed to have set for ever, and with it the golden sun of my young, hopeful, love-longing life!

For what life was mine in the charming villa of Regent's Park? That of a poor, petted, daintily-fed bird in a golden cage!

In loving confidence I had followed the decoy of Prince Leopold of Coburg, and under the guarantee of his confidential friend and my cousin, Baron Christian von Stockmar, I had quitted my beloved Berlin stage and committed myself with mother to a mysterious journey to England. I was entitled to expect in the prince a loving *fiancé*, who would be eager to tie the knot that would bind us in one, if not before men—seeing my prince and cousin Christian had more dread of men than God—yet at least before God, before my relations, and to the satisfaction of my own conscience.

And what did I find? The prince a suspicious, pedantic, buttoned-up "wooer," such as I have described in these first two days of my London existence; and cousin Christian nervous, out of humour, dissatisfied with himself, with the prince, with me because we had done this "foolish stroke" of love, and he, the shrewd diplomatist, had connived at it.

The prince continued, all the month of June through, the same singular " wooer" he displayed himself to be in the last days of May. Daily he came in his carriage *on a visit* of an hour or two, in stiff, starched state, thickly encased in wrappings and formalities, and wearisome beyond endurance. The music lesson then commenced: singing from the "Arion" or Italian duets. I played the piano with indefatigable industry and read aloud Henrietta Hanke's grandmotherly "Pearls," while Prince Leopold of Coburg, the princely widower of the heiress to the throne of England, field-marshal of Great Britain, and candidate to the Greek throne, sat with all the diligence and earnestness in the world—drizzling!

Of all the many incomprehensible points in my princely wooer, this one of "drizzling" was the most incomprehensible. And how detestable to me was this drizzling! I no sooner saw the prince alight from his carriage, followed by the groom with the horrid drizzling-box, than I felt seized with a spasm of yawning. And at this very day, after more than a generation, in writing down the hateful word an irresistible, distressing yawn grips hold of my heart and forces itself mercilessly up into my mouth!

But I am forgetting that my dear readers, children of another time, have, for their own happiness, no idea of what this dreadful drizzling is.

It was an invention of Paris, or rather of the Versailles Court, in the time of Louis XVI. and the unhappy Queen Marie Antoinette—ten years before the people, provoked into inhuman fury, struck off their crowns and then their heads.

The foremost ladies of the Court had no scruples about asking the gentlemen of their acquaintance for cast-off gold and silver epaulettes, hilt bands, galloons and tassels, with which, according to the fashion of that time, all clothes were then copiously trimmed. These ornamental appendages the ladies would then take with them into company, and there pick out the gold and silver threads to sell them afterwards. If an admirer of those days wanted to ingratiate himself particularly into the favour of his sweetheart he presented her, not, as in these days, flowers, perfumes, jewels, &c.—no, but, according to the magnitude of his love and his purse, some dozens of golden tassels or such like, and the lady would, in the next company she visited, proudly pick out the valuable threads entwined in the sweet presents of her noble adorer. From the word "parfiler" (to pick out threads), these thread-picking ladies came to be called "parfileuses," and the whole business itself "parfilage."

These "parfileuses" took with them into parties, and even to Court, gigantic picking bags to receive the presents of their cavaliers, and that beauty was proudest who could drag home with her the best-filled bag. A successful "parfileuse" might in this way clear over a hundred louis d'or a-year.

All the customary New-Year presents in Paris from gentlemen to ladies were made in "parfilage," and a cavalier no longer betted with his fair one so many louis d'or, but so many gold tassels for picking. Thus the Countess Genlis won from the Duke de Coigny twenty-four golden tassels, each of the value of twelve francs, because she had betted she would mount the steps of an aqueduct, and she won her bet. She then in the evening distributed these tassels among all the ladies in the drawing room, without reserving a single gold thread for herself, because she hated the unbecoming habit of "parfilage." In her "anti-philosophical" novel, "Adèle et Théodore, ou lettres sur l'éducation," which appeared in Paris in 1782, she attacked this shameless custom. Thus, drawing from a scene in real life, where the Duke de Chartres in Rainci was the victim, she makes her hero, the Knight of Herbain, relate: "One day we were assembled in the reception room, before setting out for a walk, when all at once Madame de R. observed that the golden fringes of my dress would do uncommonly well for picking. So saying, by way of merry frolic, she whisks off one of my fringes. Instantly I am begirt by ten ladies who, with a charming grace and diligence, proceed to strip me, tearing away my dress and packing all my fringes and galloons into their work-bags."

This open declaration of war against "parfilage" on the part of Madame de Genlis set all zealous "parfileuses" in hostility against the authoress. Nevertheless, the "parfilage" succumbed, and this affected, "virtuous" authoress, who was then much read, but is now deservedly long forgotten, says, with an air of proud consciousness : "My exposure of picking in 'Adèle et Théodore' gave the deathblow to this disgraceful custom, and no one has ever since seen in company any lady asking any gentleman for any picking material."

If "parfilage" was thus ostracised from the society of France as early as 1782, it was smuggled into England ten years later by the fashionable, hungry lady emigrants who fled from the bloody revolution. It came to be called " to drizzle," and that this habit of picking gold and silver threads continued in England throughout a generation later I was to learn to my horror by the drizzling of my admirer, Prince Leopold.

It thus happened that in the fairest days of June we sat for hours—death-weary hours to me—at the round sofa-table in our charming garden salon. The prince, an inch over six feet tall, sat bent in the most solemn earnestness over his elegant tortoise-shell drizzling-box, and thoughtfully picking thread after thread out of old foul silver galloons, a task apparently of no less moment than that of unravelling the threads of fate; I reading page after page of the " Pearls"—anything but precious pearls I thought them— of the good Henrietta Hanke, wife of the Silesian pastor, till an inexorable fit of yawning would come over me, and I was fain to rush to the piano and play any favourite piece that occurred to me, an exercise in which I was free to yawn to my heart's content, and not compelled to see my strange "wooer" drizzling with the monotonous regularity of an automation or picking machine, or hear the regular, drowsy " zrr, zrr ! "

Poor mother could never long support this original drizzling courtship. She grew visibly pale in her arm-chair, availed herself ever more and more of her smelling bottle, took to rubbing her eyes and temples with eau-de-cologne, then played with Lisinka—and yet had ever at last to bolt into the garden to prevent herself yawning into the prince's face. We never failed, either, to drink extra strong coffee beforehand, in order to fortify ourselves in view of these princely love-makings.

My august " wóoer " did not seem to have the slightest inkling into our torments. He drizzled on indefatigably, and at leaving was always proud to show me how much he had drizzled; and in -fact, during the year in which we were in England, his Highness drizzled out a stately silver soup-tureen, which, on the 24th May, 1830, Prince Leopold solemnly presented to his young niece, the Princess Victoria of Kent, on her eleventh anniversary in Kensington.

Doubtless Queen Victoria of England still piously preserves the drizzled-out soup-tureen as a love-gift from her revered uncle, little dreaming, I daresay, of how many painful hours this silver vessel cost me.

" I cannot stand it, Cousin Christian; I shall die of this ghastly wooing and of *ennui* in this golden cage. Never does the prince speak to me of his love, never of the hour that is to tie the bond of love more tightly and more lastingly! Never does he take a walk with me through the garden, for fear that passers-by might recognise him in the company of a young lady. I can stand it no longer— the everlasting, prosing Henrietta Hanke and the mechanical playing on the piano, while my inamorato drizzles—drizzles —and ever drizzles."

" Ay, the drizzling is dreadful, sure enough," replied cousin Christian rather dejectedly; " in that point I join with you, from my own experience; but for some time yet it must be borne in patience. Now we have said A we must not shrink like cowards from the B. Even the Y and Z are not to be beyond our courage. Let us consider the month of June as a time of probation for you, Caroline— and for the prince. Therefore, without making any bones of it, go on receiving his Weariness for an hour's visit, with the reading and piano playing—and the drizzling into the bargain. I am still ever in hopes that the June sun shall -melt the ice, and that the prince himself will speak to you of his love and his desire to tie a closer and more decorous bond with you—to call you wholly his own—as far as circumstances allow. If by the end of the month *he* does not speak out frankly to you, then will I speak very plainly

and firmly to him, so that he must come to a decision—
either marriage or your immediate departure. Leave all
the rest with good conscience to me. As yet I have
always managed to dispose the prince as it seemed good
to me. Assuredly, if I had foreseen all the difficulties
which oppose us step by step—if I had conjectured that
our Monsieur peu-à-peu and Marquis tout doucement would
evince so little strength of love for you too, I had certainly
not have allowed the foolish business to go so far. I
ought to have opposed more vigorously your visit to a
love rendezvous in Coburg, and never once yielded to your
journey to England. But I was thinking too much of the
prince's interest, and still credited him with the possession
of so much heart as to be able to begin a new life of love
at the side of your fresh youthfulness. Also for your
mother and you, I was hoping to be able to establish a
snug and independent home, free from all the intrigues and
mazes of a stage life, the perils of which even you have
already come to know sufficiently well."

"Which, however," I struck in, "are easier borne and
overcome than this drear monotony, this comfortless and
profitless life in a cage, this perpetual observance of the
humours of a suspicious master, this painful weighing of
every word before it is uttered, and this—this childish,
pedantic drizzling—by way of captivating his heart's elect."

After a pause of cloudy reflection, cousin Christian
reached me his hand and said:

"I will endeavour, Caroline, to the best of my power
to make amends for the wrong I have done you in bringing you here; at least, you shall not die of weariness in
this solitude. The drizzling I shall, to be sure, be unable
to spare you. In that matter, my power over the prince,
so dreaded by the English, is of no avail; and so, patience
till the first of July.

*   *   *   *   *   *

Cousin Christian kept his word, and did his best to
cheer and divert us. He called on us every morning in
the course of his regular ride, and had almost always a
little surprise for us; a pretty gift, an interesting novelty,

a scandal from the "high life" of London, or a merry anecdote for our entertainment *in petto*.

A veritable holiday it always was for us when cousin came to take us out for a drive. We first skirted through the fine magnificent Park, in a green corner of which was our cage. The Park was then the most spacious and handsome in London, and the favourite promenade of the fashionable world. It extended over no less than 450 acres—quite the range of a small German barony. It had formerly been called Marylebone Park, but was now named after the prince-regent, who had done so much for its adornment. The grand terraces, crowned with palatial houses, begirding the Park, were in part named from the Royal family, such as York, Clarence, Sussex, Cumberland, and Cambridge Terrace. Now and again, emerging from amid the copse, charming villas or cottages were seen, blessed, it seemed to me, with a remarkable abundance of children. These frisked about with their pretty ponies and goat-carriages all round the fresh green lawn, while the fuller-grown quality, in their most elegant equipage, drove or rode in the alleys surrounding the Park or round "the ring."

In the Regent's Park we visited the Coliseum with its imposing panorama of London, and the Diorama with the colossal magic pictures by Bouton and Daguerre. Our favourite resort, however, and one which proved an ever-renewed delight to my animal-loving heart, was the magnificent Zoological Gardens, occupying a crescent-shaped section of the Park. And yet I could hardly ever see these fine grounds with their troops of bears, apes, lamas, kangaroos, and strange birds, but I was overtaken with a home-sick longing for the modest little menagerie on the Pfaueninsel at Potsdam, kept by the good king for his Berlin lovers of nature. For, was it possible that I could ever again be so happy as I once used to be there, among my many Berlin friends, and in the company of Henrietta Sontag? "Ja, wie anders, Gretchen, war's dir, damals!" *

---

* "Ay, how different was it, then, with you, Gretchen!"— Gretchen's reflection after her fall—in Goethe's "Faust."

Cousin Christian took us also to the Grand Opera to hear Madame Lalande sing in the "Pirates," and to Eskeles* to see the battle of Waterloo, represented by hundreds of men and horses, and by such a crackle of guns and such a cloud of gunpowder smoke, as were altogether unbearable. The horses, however, were uncommonly beautiful, and the clever wee ponies particularly delighted me.

When cousin was prevented, Figaro Hühnlein, the prince's brisk, stout valet, had to accompany us to the sights and entertainments of London. We thus had the opportunity of seeing in his company, in the Haymarket Theatre, the then rather faded but still noted and, in a yet greater degree, on account of the largeness of her heart, notorious Madame Vestris sing, play, and dance in the popular "Beggar's Opera" with enchanting grace and gaiety. A few small songs, in particular, she rendered with inimitable—coquetry. She was the English Dejazet—in her male representations and in her eventful, variegated love-affairs, of which, during the pauses, Meister Hühnlein, with his comfortable, knowing, satyr-like smile, had some sufficiently scandalous stories to relate. All the moneyed youth and greyheads of London lay at the feet of the seductive siren, who turned a deaf ear to no petitioner so long as he knelt with full hands; and many a one, it was said, did not recover his feet again till his hands were empty. All the treasures of gold, however, thus presented to the goddess disappeared just as fast again in luxury and extravagance.

One little anecdote of Vestris, whispered into our ears by Figaro, has stayed in my memory, and, seeing it is in some measure relatable—a quality which can hardly be asserted of the others—I may as well give it.

Madame Vestris, like Dejazet, was proudest of the lower half of her beauty, and by no means disinclined to exhibit it in tights. One of her admirers became so enamoured of this part as to entreat her to let him have it cast in stucco. The goddess smiled gracious consent, and

---

* Astley's ?

stood as model to a distinguished London sculptor. Soon the lover had the happiness of carrying the cast home with him.

O horror! however, in a few days he saw a perambulating dealer pass his window bawling out, "Busts! busts! the beautiful, the world-famous stucco legs, modelled from nature, of the celebrated Madame Vestris."

How could this have happened? The fair lady had ordered other copies to be taken, which she gave away as particularly tender love-gifts to the most elect of her admirers; and the caster, availing himself of the opportunity, had thrown off a few dozens on his own account, for which he found rapid enough sale in those days in London.

The celebrated Charles Kemble I also saw as the recognised English master in his walk of comedy; but, on the whole, the London stage had few attractions for me. I never saw so much mannerism as then prevailed in London. What unnatural straddling, what intolerable accentuating, drawling, hissing, distorting of every tone. I saw a *Macbeth* that appeared to be nothing but a wire-pulled figure, and it was with the utmost satisfaction I beheld a *Desdemona* strangled by her husband, as she deserved to be. Her piping and squeaking provoked me to such a degree that I would fain have strangled her myself.

I felt interested in Charles Matthews, who was able by himself to entertain a thousand-headed audience the whole evening through. He played little farces for one actor, mostly parts in which disguises form an element, parts "written on his body," all with astonishing nimbleness as respects both change of dress and mask, and with ever new striking characteristics.

In the Italian opera, Henrietta Sontag and Maria Malibran sang—but I was not permitted to hear them. How easily I might have been recognised there! And it was the will of the prince and cousin Christian that I should die to the world, and live only as—a caged bird!

Friend Ignaz Moschelles was also staying in London, giving lessons and concerts. Felix Mendelssohn, too, conducted his overture to the "Summer Night's Dream," and the very first evening became the favourite of the English. And I, who had sung and danced so joyously in Berlin with Henrietta Sontag, and had played *à quatre mains* with Moschelles and Mendelssohn—I dared not hasten to them, shake hands with them, tell them how deeply unhappy I felt since I had forsaken art and the dear, hearty German players! Had I not, both by word of mouth and writing, engaged to live in the deepest retirement, wholly devoted to the man who had pledged me his love in return? But had I not some right to expect that this man would also on his side live a little for me? And all he did was to send me his valet to show me the sights of London.

Under such sad experiences the usually so blissful days of June dragged along heavily and bodefully. From Marlborough House, the residence of Prince Leopold in St. James's Park, no cheerful ray of sunshine would visit us. The prince still acted as though his only purpose in summoning me to England was that I might read to him the Mother Goody novels of Henrietta Hanke and play the piano while he solemnly drizzled.

Cousin Christian, too, grew ever more peevish and hypochondriac. His complaints had a wide enough range : Indigestion, bad eyes, sleeplessness, the bad air in Marlborough House, and the pedantic prince who was neglecting him.

Mother was of opinion that cousin should try the air of Regent's Park, and use our spare room to sleep in. I offered to lull him asleep by soft playing on the piano and the singing of his favourite songs.

The experiment was made, but did not succeed. The hypochondria would not yield to Regent's Park, nor would sleep be enticed by it. I had hardly begun, late in the evening in the salon, "Freudevoll und leidvoll," when an impatient knocking from upstairs caused me to hush into silence again. Cousin asserted that my piano playing only scared sleep all the more from him, and he returned to his residence in Marlborough House.

We sank into ever deeper sadness of spirits, and

felt ourselves ever more and more forsaken in wide, foreign, dreary London. With ever more passionate longing I pined for the joyous artistic life in Berlin I had so giddily tossed up. My thoughts were ever brooding there by the stage. Of a forenoon I would say to mother: "I should now be going to the rehearsal, or perhaps sitting with Amalia Wolff, Madame Unzelmann, and Ludwig Devrient in that dear, green, lumber-box of a coach, and trundling off gaily to Potsdam to play comedy before the good king in the new Palais. What will be the piece to-day, I wonder? And what will they be saying of me—the deserter? Can they be believing that I am making professional tours? Mother, I wish we were again in Berlin, in our modest little apartments in Mohrenstrasse, No. 48, and were eating for our dinner to-day an omelette, with bacon and a salad. Five o'clock?—they are now in the dressing-room doing their toilets. Ah! would the old wardrobe wife, Wallburg, but dress me once more, and, in tearful remembrance of the departed Mannheim dramatist, I could, on Iffland's anniversary, once more eat cheesecakes, and drink punch on the back of it, brought from the theatre confectionery, and—breathe the air of the footlights! It were nothing short of rapture to play, sing, and dance even the silly Hottentot—ay, in that scandalous, patched, red merino frock itself." And I burst into hysterical sobbing.

Mother sought to console me by saying: "Only a few days' more patience, and then the probation-time set by Christian for us is at an end, and we learn the decision, whether you are to stay here as countess or return to the stage as Lina Bauer."

Yes, the matter did come to a decision, but in such a shocking manner that this very minute while I am writing down the fact, the cold perspiration bedews my forehead in recollecting the scene.

It was on the 29th June, 1829, when cousin Christian came riding to us exceptionally early in the morning in great excitement, and no sooner entered than he threw down a packet of letters on the table, sputtering out in his lively style:

"Letters from Berlin for you, just forwarded to my address from Rittmeister Hilpert in Frankfort. I have opened and read them all to see whether you had not written imprudently to your friends. That does not appear to be the case; nevertheless, bad rumours are afloat about you and your puzzling silence. It is known that you are in London—but as what? It is believed Lina is become the prince's mistress. Timm and the king are themselves concerned, and want news. A fine story!"

"For God's sake, Christian, what then is to be done?" exclaimed mother, growing pale.

"That is my death-sentence, cousin," I sobbed in despair.

"Be quiet, children! The game is not yet up. I shall this day force the prince to come to a declaration, whether he loves you, Lina, and is minded to give you, morally and legally, an assured place at his side, as his companion for life. If not, then will I to-morrow myself conduct you back to Germany, and I should like to see who dares as much as look askance, in my presence, at the aunt and cousin of Baron Christian Stockmar."

In the greatest excitement Stockmar rode off, leaving us in deepest distress, not only for ourselves, but also for cousin, who, with his pride of independence and of honour, could not but feel it a humiliation to have to go and address such a question to the prince: "Your Highness, do you love my cousin? Will you restore to her before God the honour which the backbiting world has already robbed her of?" And, supposing the matter led to a rupture with the prince, then would cousin be made to feel it in a pecuniary sense as well, and his avaricious wife would forgive neither him nor us.

Not till a later period did it become clear to me that Stockmar's great excitement in that crisis had a deeper cause than appeared, and was, indeed, grounded in his heart and conscience. By those Berlin letters and rumours the fact was for the first time pressed home on him what a serious responsibility he had taken upon himself — a responsibility in relation both to the prince, his beloved master and friend, and to us, his defenceless relations—

when, on one side, he allowed the prince, in a sudden
flare of passion, to stretch out a hankering hand towards
me; and, on the other side, permitted me, a creature of
young exuberant life, to be sacrificed to an egoistic pedant,
the mere wreck of a man, and to carry throughout my
whole life the shadow of an ambiguous repute in the eyes
of a defamatory world.

It has long since become indisputably clear to me, clear
as sunlight, that it was Christian Stockmar's real and
bounden duty to stand up with his whole authority and
most decisively forbid every attempt on the part of the
prince to approach me, as well as all trustful response on our
part to a step of that kind, such as was implied in our
coming to Coburg and London.

But Christian Stockmar loved his master, whom he
ruled by his intellectual superiority, more than me and
mother. He would fain grant the prince the happiness of
a beloved companion for life, who would neither fleece nor
compromise him, as he had been fleeced and compromised
in so many of his "foolish love-affairs" of earlier date—
and so I was diplomatically sacrificed.

*   *   *   *   *   *

How great a moral force Stockmar exercised over the
prince came out distinctly after he laid the ultimatum before him : "Your Highness, if you love my cousin
honourably, then join hands with her for a life engagement;
otherwise we depart!"

Next day the prince came to us like a transformed
man. *Monsieur tout doucement* had awakened from his
lethargy, his frigid cunctation, his diplomatic circumspection.
The *Marquis peu-à-peu* made briskly for his goal, like a
young enamoured wooer. In noble and winning words,
such as he had used in Berlin and afterwards in Coburg,
he spoke of his love for me, and of his heart's desire to
gain for life, and unite to himself in holy bonds, a creature
who had taken his affections captive. He forgot his
pedantry and even his drizzling for that day. He again
grew eloquent and amiable—and I was happy in again finding him amiable. I was all too ready to fancy I loved him.

On the 2nd July, 1829, in our little house in Regent's Park, a sort of ceremony of marriage was accordingly enacted—but how sorry and drear! My heart to this day feels anguished and my pen now trembles in my hand when I think of it. What pitiable conceptions the prince and Stockmar had of marriage and household life!

No priest laid his hand to invoke a blessing on my head. No bridal garland adorned my hair. Christian Stockmar had drawn up the marriage-contract. He, his brother Karl, who had the care of the prince's money-affairs, and was afterwards charged with many a confidential diplomatic mission as well, and another witness, whom to this day yet I am not at liberty to name, signed the marriage-contract. In it I received the title of Countess Montgomery, and had a modest allowance settled on me. Mother clasped me with tears of joy to her heart.

And a few weeks of happiness began for me and also for the prince. Alas! they were not to extend beyond the honeymoon!

The prince was as if metamorphosed. His eyes, wont to be so melancholy, became lighted up, his whole carriage seemed to grow fresher, more animated, more joyous. He chatted heartily, free, off-hand. All pedantry was thrust aside—the Hauke and drizzling-box along with it. We sang duets together and played at billiards. We even took a walk in the twilight through the garden and counted the shooting stars, glad children that we were.

I am inclined to believe that these brief weeks of July dated the last expiring flush of romance in the life of the prince. It was the last youthful flicker of his burnt-out heart before it finally crumbled for ever into cold ashes.

And I was happy in the childish confidence of being loved. I felt my cheeks glow, my eyes sparkle, my heart throb higher! It was to be ever so!

A visit from my brother Louis added to my happiness. He came to London on commercial business, and I was proud of my handsome, clever brother. The prince and cousin Christian gave him a friendly welcome, and were glad to see us going to the theatre together and visiting together all the sights of London and its environs. How

K

altogether different now appeared Old England's sky from what it looked in the blissful month of May and the rosy month of June! My good brother rejoiced in my fortune. He saw that my secret relation to the prince rested on a moral basis, and that I was fully justified, from a moral point of view, in regarding myself as the prince's life-companion, and not as his mistress; and he was glad also to see mother and me for ever delivered from the intrigues and meshes of a theatrical life and from all pecuniary cares.

In company with cousin Christian we made an excursion to Claremont House, the prince's charming country-seat, where, years before, he had enjoyed a short interval of happiness with the Princess Charlotte, and where, on the same day, he had lost both wife and child.

We were in the happiest holiday humour. The weather was delicious. The park of Claremont was redolent of blooming roses, lilies, honeysuckle.

When, however, we visited the drear and solitary villa in the neighbourhood of Claremont House which I was afterwards to occupy, our spirits underwent a remarkable depression. My heart, that was joyfully anticipating the future, became all at once sensible of a weight like that of a nightmare. Mother heaved a faint sigh, which she then tried to cover by a cough. Christian Stockmar let his eye go round us searchingly, as if he divined what was in our thoughts. Finally brother Louis gave vent to our forebodings in the words:

"In this dismal solitude Lina will be sure to turn into a mope! This overgrown wilderness of a park, these high firs closely shutting in the house so that not a ray of light can pierce through, so that it is completely lost to sight from the highway, so that looking out from the window you cannot see a single mortal passing! And in every room the clammy air of a dungeon! All round the silence of death! Not so much as the bark of a dog! Nay, you won't stand it! A retired, still life, that is all right enough, I allow, in the circumstances—but all here looks more like a prison! The very thought of life in such a grave of a place stifles me!"

"Because there is nobody now occupying it, and there

is none of the comfort to be found in inhabited houses!"
hastily interrupted my cousin. "Let a cheerful fire be
blazing in this marble chimney, and the tea-urn singing
away on this table; let two wives be here managing and
looking after everything; and then, Lina, I warrant you
things will have a very different look."

"And as mistress of this villa my first order will be:
'Clear me away, at least, these firs from the window!'" I
struck in with all the liveliness I could muster. "Then I
shall be able to see from the window when you, dear
cousin, and the prince come riding in from Claremont
House. And the prince has also promised me a riding-
horse. It will be uncommonly nice for us to be able to
ride out together on horseback."

A wry face from cousin was all the answer he gave me.

&ast;		&ast;		&ast;		&ast;		&ast;

Before my brother Louis returned to Paris it was fixed
that mother and I should follow him thither at the end of
July, while the prince went to take the waters at Carlsbad,
and cousin Christian returned to his family in Coburg. As
Countess Montgomery, I was to stay with mother in one
of the first hotels in Paris, and under my brother's protection and guidance enjoy all the splendours of Paris—all,
however, under the strict injunction that I was carefully
to keep out of the way of all Berlin friends who might
chance to meet me in Paris, and to form no new acquaintances on the Seine. The prince and Christian promised to
visit us in Paris.

The parting dinner with the prince and Stockmar came
off in Regent's Park in the gayest mood. We clinked
glasses together in foaming champagne, wishing a happy
re-union in Paris. Next morning, at the end of July, we
set out, attended by our travelling marshal, Hühnlein, for
Dover, whence we made the happiest passage across the
Channel to Calais, and thence proceeded to Paris.

My heart was all bliss and sunshine while I sped through
fair France by the same route over which Yorick, with his
great sentimental heart, had once travelled before me.

I had as yet no presentiment that the short honeymoon
of wedded bliss had set—for ever!

CHAPTER XXIII.

IN PARIS.

On the 30th July, 1829, mother and I, with brother Louis, who had come a stage on the way to meet us, drove under the most glorious weather into the gay and marvellous city of Paris. On the first floor of a magnificent hotel in the Rue de Rivoli, opposite the Tuileries, my good brother had taken an elegant suite of apartments for *Madame la Comtesse de Montgomery et Mère*, and everything was in the most perfect order for our reception.

With a veritable thirst to find myself among happy people I plunged into the new, brilliant, pleasure-living life of Paris—like a bird escaped from its cage—jubilantly rejoining the free singers of the gay, green wood.

Of course the first thing I took up was the play-bill, for in the London theatres I had almost panted in vain for a genuine fresh comedy and the genuine intoxicating air of the footlights. And was I not now in the city of the far-famed *Théatre Français*, on which the whole of France plumed itself so much?

* * * * * *

The great pleasure which the theatrical evenings in Paris yielded me was by no means without its dash of pain. My heart was nearly consumed in me for the longing that I had for the joyful theatrical life I had so lightly whistled away. Whenever on the stage I saw a part played which I had myself formerly played with pleasure and applause, I was like to cry with the pain of home-sickness. When according to my sense a young actress played apathetically or wrong, I could hardly check myself from springing on the stage and calling to her—"Mademoiselle, I'll show you how we play this part in Germany—simply, naturally, and feelingly. This mincing and mumming is all an impertinence."

But—Madame la Comtesse de Montgomery was tied with golden chains to her box in the proscenium.

One morning I was passing by the Théatre des nouveautés. The players stood chatting and laughing away merrily at the entrance; among them Bouffé and Madame Albert, who was dividing delicious peaches among her colleagues. What a chaffing and jesting over the dainties! Then the stage manager called "Messieurs et mesdames, la repetition doit commener," and in they danced gaily. What a desire I had to accompany them on to the stage, to go through the rehearsal with my new stage-mates, to breathe the air of the boards, and to forget how the life of the Countess Montgomery was far from an enviable one.

The mysterious ambiguity of my position in life also forced itself more clearly and painfully on my mind in Paris. In spite of the strict injunctions of cousin Christian and the prince, it was impossible wholly to avoid meeting old Berlin acquaintances and friends. Thus, one evening in the *Théatre Français* Count Arnim-Boitzenburg stepped into our box to pay us a friendly greeting. The next day he called on us in the hotel. In the Odéon we met the young Count Golz—the same who had shown me so much sympathy in the Samoilow affair. Also Kommerzienrath Wilkes, one of the leaders of the old Berlin theatre-guard; and Dr. Ebeling, with his family, met and visited us—and in their looks I read sympathising queries which their lips durst not utter from delicacy: "How is it with the Countess Montgomery? What right has she to this title? What was the price she paid for it? Is she the lawful spouse of Prince Leopold? Is the Countess Montgomery happier than was Caroline Bauer, whom we once liked so much for her pleasant art, her youthful spirits, and her stainless morals? Does she not regret giving up her freedom as an *artiste*, and all the pride of her theatrical successes, for these secret golden fetters? Why did she not accompany Prince Leopold to Carlsbad if she is his lawful consort?"

And I dared not answer one of these unuttered questions. I dared not harmlessly and open-heartedly chat away *à la Caroline Bauer* with these amiable people, as in my heart I would have liked so much to do. I dared not say: "Out of vanity, and laziness, and thirst of gain, I gave up my activity as an *artiste*, which made me so happy, and have a thousand times bitterly repented it. Give me your advice and assistance how to get free again, to become an *artiste* again, the old happy Lina Bauer again."

I durst not by one word, by one look, betray anything of all that. Throughout the conversation, mother and I had painfully to calculate every glance, every smile, every word—had to be always weighing in all we spoke how to say nothing in many words; so that the visits, which in other circumstances would have been such a pleasure, were now a real torment to us. To put an end to them, we gave orders to the servant who attended on us to deny us to all visitors.

When I wrote to cousin Christian, complaining of this new affliction, and begging him to allow us the liberty of telling friends, at least, what was indispensably necessary for the honour of my good name, I was taken smartly to task. He wrote me from Coburg, briefly and to the point: "Sentimentality I have no patience with. You promised me moral strength for your new and unique position. Show it now as Countess Montgomery by a proud, assured attitude, and by breaking completely with your past. Caroline Bauer no longer exists!"

Cousin pointed out to us at the same time that unforeseen events rendered it necessary that we should prolong our stay in Paris to an indefinite time, and that it would therefore be desirable for us to reduce the expenses of our residence there considerably.

I was indignant, and mother deeply dejected. We at once gave up the hired equipage, removed from the first to the third floor of the hotel, and restricted our style of living in every way to the narrowest limits. We also visited the theatre seldomer, and contented ourselves with more modest places when we did go; so that when of an evening my brother Louis was prevented visiting us in the hotel we sat in our confined room of the third floor with a very acute feeling of loneliness and abandonment in the great metropolis of the world.

Another event came to increase our feeling of dejection and dispiritment. Brother Karl, whose levity of mind and never-ending demands for money had been, indeed, the main incentive to drive us from Berlin and the stage life into these new unhappy relations, appealed with new claims to our purse. The young, blooming, and ever light-minded officer—for whom we had, by the hands of Christian Stockmar, only three months before, cleared a debt of 2700 florins—had become ensnared by a spinster no longer in her prime, Leopoldine von Hinkeldey, sister of Major-Baron von Hinkeldey, tutor to the present Grand-Duke of Baden. In order to be able to marry her he now asked of me, in so many words, to become security for 16,000 florins, and to pay the interest of that amount, as also of my mother to renounce for the future her Baden pension of 600 florins in his favour.

We were at our wits' end. Whence were we to draw the 16,000 florins? It was quite impossible to ask such a sum either of the prince or Baron Christian.

Mother, in these circumstances, coming to a resolution, took a seat in the narrow, joggling mail coach, and, driving day and night to Mannheim, set clearly before my brother Karl, Baron Hinkeldey, and his sister Leopoldine, that it was altogether impossible for us to undertake what was proposed to us, seeing that to ask the money from the extremely economical prince would be to invoke our own ruin.

Mother's strenuous opposition to the marriage, and her solemn assertion that, instead of giving her consent to it, her curse would rest on it, availed to obtain a promise from Karl, Leopoldine, and Major von Hinkeldey, that there would be no more talk of marriage, for the present at any rate. Mother returned in composed spirits to me in Paris. But how soon, and in how much more threatening a manner, was this pistol to be again presented to our breasts!

During a walk in the Tuileries Gardens, we met Henrietta Sontag, with a bevy of admirers fluttering around her. We passed each other with a friendly nod. I saw Henrietta take an observant look of me and smile. I heard afterwards that she had written to her friends in Berlin that Prince Leopold might look forward to the joys of paternity.

From this word, occasioned by the padded-out style of dress then in vogue, there successively originated, to float in the current of the times and of busy tongues, one, two, three young immortal Counts Montgomery, and in respect of whom I barbarously outraged all the duties of a mother when I afterwards returned to the stage. *Les effets and et les causes!* Small causes and great effects !

Of the ultra-theatrical sights in Paris which we visited under the chaperonage of my brother Louis, the cell of the unhappy Marie Antoinette in the " Conciergerie " had such an effect on me that I nearly fainted. The most drastic contrasts seized hold of my mind. The moist, clammy atmosphere of a burial vault entered my lungs and stifled all my senses. We were shown the thin chip of wood which the poorest of all queens had used for a needle to patch together in her sore need her tattered duds; her chair, her table with the wretchedest crockery, and on the wall, beside it, the splendid new Gobelin tapestry representing Marie Antoinette in purple velvet, in all the glory of her beauty and regal magnificence, holding the little dauphin by the hand.

The same unearthly horror crept over me in the burial vaults of the Panthéon and in the royal sepulchre of St. Denis, in the vestibule of which there always lies the last deceased king in a coffin of State draped in black velvet, besprinkled with silver lilies (and tears), keeping watch till he is released by the corpse of his successor. A ghastly ceremony, similar to that also observed in the case of the Roman Popes.

In the chapel of the Tuileries I saw, during the celebration of mass, the venerable King Charles X. in the circle of his family, and at his feet " the hope of France," the poor little Duke de Bordeaux (who was not yet born when a foul murderer's hand cut off his father the Duke de Berri), to whom all France was now looking as her future King Henri V.

The serious, bigoted dauphin looked very much like a simpleton, and the poor dauphiness, the daughter of Marie Antoinette, as if dust had gathered on her lips and heart since, for the last time, she embraced father, mother, and brother in the "Conciergerie." The axe of the guillotine had for ever bereft her of all capacity of smile and joy in life, and her only love also, which was bestowed on the Archduke Karl, the hero of Aspern, she had been obliged to carry to the grave in its first blossom. For long now her mortified heart no more loved any one on earth; all her love was given to heaven and the souls of the blessed there, while she knew that she, too, was loved by no one here below. Poor dauphiness! Not even the Countess Montgomery would have changed places with you!

I was most interested in the Duchess de Berri, although she was far from being a beauty. The gallant Parisians then called her "la jolie laide," and never tired of telling the most amusing tales of the "jolie laide."

The duchess was but thirty-one years old when I first saw her in the *Théatre de Madame*, which was under her patronage and called by her name, and observed how with her dainty little hands, and with the vivacity peculiar to her, she always gave the signal for applause.

To confess the truth, I thought the Dowager-Duchess de Berri really ugly, at first sight at any rate. Her eye had a look close akin to squinting. Her complexion was yellowish-sallow, her under lip thick and strongly prominent, and her neck frightfully skinny.

This skinny neck served to strike out a witticism, which was going the round of Paris during our visit, from the "jolie laide," who was uncommonly ingenious and ready at repartee.

The duchess, despite her ugliness, deemed herself irresistible. On one occasion, the striking skinniness of her neck was, however, made unusually patent to her so as to raise an uneasy feeling in her mind, but anon she consoled herself, and, drawing her hand caressingly over its scraggy surface, she exclaimed: "Pah! Madame de Sevigné

dirait aussi de Moi: Rien—le plus joli rien, qu 'on peut
voir!"—as Madame de Sevigné had said of the graceful
but extremely meagre dancer.

The "jolie laide's" strong point of beauty was her
charming little foot, which was called the loveliest foot in
France, or, simply, in Paris, "Le pied de Madame!"

Madame understood, too, how to set her daintiest
Cinderella feet in the most advantageous light. She in-
vented the short dresses, which allow not only the foot
but even somewhat more than the ankle to display their
form, and no one knew how to make use of this hazardous
fashion so gracefully as did madame. Her shoes and
reticular silk stockings were, moreover, perfect marvels of
fineness and prettiness. When madame walked—or
rather glided elf-like—along the terrace of the Tuileries
Gardens, the other promenaders formed longs rows on
each side, to behold and admire "le pied de madame!"
Such a pretty little foot almost covered all the shortcomings
of the rest of the person. I have myself more than once
stood in the Tuileries Gardens and gazed at this wondrous
production of nature and art.

"Le pied de madame" was the title or catch-word of a
delicious little story, which then passed in Paris from
mouth to mouth.

Madame, who—not unjustifiably, it must be allowed—
bore the reputation of being a little eccentric, had wagered
with her royal father-in-law that in some disguise or other
she would be able to ride in a public omnibus without
being recognised.

She selected the short Indian dress and the white
lace cap of the Parisian *grisette*, and in this disguise, with
the usual large bandbox in her arm, attended by her valet,
likewise disguised, she appeared at the Place de la Con-
corde awaiting the 'bus. The 'bus stops, the conductor
lets down the little iron steps and says, in the ordinary
indifferent tone, "Entrez, mademoiselle," without taking
any more notice of the far from beautiful *grisette*. Then,
however, his wandering eye was arrested at seeing light
on the first step the prettiest foot in creation, in pink silk
stocking and in the daintiest black velvet shoe with choice

cross bands, and at once he enthusiastically exclaims: "Ah-h! Le pied de madame!" tearing his bonnet off his head, and bowing in deepest reverence to the dainty-footed *grisette*.

The Duchess de Berri had lost her wager before she entered an omnibus. She, of course, dispensed with her ride, but was in no little measure proud of the conquest her foot had won over a plain omnibus conductor.

It was related, too, with mysterious smiles, in Paris, how "le pied de madame" had been seen more than once dancing at the masked balls of the Grand Opera. It was even asserted that "le pied de madame" had been noticed on steep, dark stairs leading to an attic in the "Quartier Latin," to keep a tender rendezvous, the first filaments of which had been spun at those masked balls. It was maintained that madame was not only the large-hearted protectress of the *Theatre de Madame* in general, but likewise of many a young handsome actor in particular. All kinds of piquant tales were told of the brilliant, frolicking life in the Pavillon Marsan of the Tuileries, and in the pleasure Chateau Marsan, the residences of madame, as also of her stay in Dieppe during the bathing season, where "le pied de madame" was never weary and never worsted in the boldest swimming feats. Madame was a passionate, bold rider to the bargain.

It was whispered, moreover, that "le pied de madame" had the slight weakness of disporting on too large a footing, and was consequently unable to clear its way out of the entanglement of debts.

All these eccentricities, however, were readily pardoned to the Dowager-Duchess de Berri in consideration of her great goodness of heart, her gracefulness, and her conversational *esprit*. Although a Neapolitan princess, she was yet the very type of a Frenchwoman, with genuine Parisian *chic*, and was altogether the most popular figure at the Court of Charles X.

The feeling at that time against the bigoted Court was like the sultry temperature preceding a storm. Brother Louis repeated to me the saying, that "the Bourbons have learnt nothing and forgotten nothing in their exile." Prince

Polignac and the hated Jesuits ruled France. They were
on the eve of a new revolution. "Paris s'ennuie! Ça
ira mal!"

And things *went* a bad course—and more rapidly than
was expected. How much had changed when, a few
years later, I again saw this royal Bourbon family! Once
more it was a chapel in which the Bourbons devoutly
attended mass. But not the chapel of the Tuileries. That
was for ever closed against the expelled Bourbons. It
was the chapel of the Hradschin, at Prague, in which the
banished King Charles X. had found a refuge with his
family. How weary and apathetic he looked, the hoary
king of seventy-eight, king without a crown, the glittering
prayer-book in his trembling hands, the mechanical movement of the lips in prayer! A sad image of the ruin of
earthly greatness and grandeur!

The Duke and Duchess d'Angoulême likewise sat in
the chapel of the Hradschin. The dauphin appeared still
more will-less, still more of a simpleton; the dauphiness
still more morose and fanatic in her devotions.

And how pale looked the young Duke de Bordeaux, in
spite of his youthful fifteen years! He hardly ventured
to look up from his prayer-book, aware, as he was, that
the severe eyes of his aunt d'Angoulême and his Jesuit
tutors were upon him. He knew that it was his duty, as
future King Henri V. of France, to be just as pious as the
Jesuits demanded of him. But now and again I caught
him slipping a stealthy glance of his beautiful young blue
eyes over the prayer-book through the chapel, as if in
quest of a little youth and sunshine that were not common
visitors in the Hradschin. And when these eyes of fifteen
encountered mine, they smiled altogether peculiarly, and
stole back to me again and again. Even the strict aunt
d'Angoulême and the ossified Jesuit fathers cannot quite
stamp out the yearning and dreaming of a youthful heart
of fifteen.

But where, then, was the Dowager-Duchess de Berri,
mother of the future King Henri V. of France?

The banished King Charles X. and the banished Duchess
d'Angoulême had banished madame from their Court,

because she had followed the dictates of her heart more than those of high politics, and as wife and future royal mother of France had outrageously compromised the Bourbons.

When, after the July revolution, the outcast royal family, destitute alike of spirit, counsel, and action, sought an asylum at first in England and then in Prague, madame was "the only man left among the Bourbons"—as King Louis Philippe, with a mixture of dread and admiration, used to say—who did not give up the Bourbon throne for lost, but struggled and suffered for it.

In April, 1832, the Duchess de Berri, with a few faithful followers, crossed in a ship to France and traversed the faithful Vendée in the disguise of a simple peasant, everywhere courageously displaying the white lilies of the royal banner for Henri V. Notwithstanding her disguise, she was often in danger of being captured by Louis Philippe's agents. "Le pied de madame" betrayed its owner on more than one occasion. With admirable courage and great endurance madame bore through all the dangers, fatigues, and privations of these adventurous enterprises till in Nantes she fell a prey to the basest venal treachery of a Cologne Jew, of the name of Deutz. Pretending to be passionately devoted to the Bourbons, he had contrived to ingratiate himself into the confidence of the duchess, and then betrayed her place of refuge in Nantes to the mercenaries of Louis Philippe for 30,000 francs. For sixteen long hours the duchess lay concealed in a narrow opening behind the hot chimney plate, while the agents were searching all through the house; and not till after her clothes had several times caught fire, and she was nearly stifled to death with the smoke, did the high-spirited woman, who had risked everything for her son, "the honour of France," surrender herself.

It soon came out, however, why King Louis Philippe had staked so much Judas money and employed so many treacherous arts to entrap his dear cousin within the walls of the fortification of Blaye. The imprisoned duchess found herself under the necessity of confessing to the jailor that less than a year before she had been secretly married to the Italian Marchese Lucchesi-Palli, and was near her *accouchement.*

King Louis Philippe triumphed, and at once gave orders to set the lady Marchesa Lucchesi-Palli at liberty, and put no hindrance in the way of her leaving France. He was sensible that madame had for ever lost the spell of her influence as royal mother, and that in spite of all her energy and self-sacrificing spirit it was no longer in her power to work any mischief to his throne.

And he had calculated aright. Even the most faithful Legitimists in France forsook the Marchesa Lucchesi-Palli, and the Bourbons on the Hradschin in Prague cut all connection with her. She was not even allowed to embrace her young son, King Henri, for whom she had ventured and sacrificed so much. She was dead for all Bourbon politics.

The thought has often forced itself on me : What if the Duchess de Berri had at that time bridled her hot heart, would not, perhaps, the white lilies at this day still be floating over the Tuileries, and this proud Bourbon royal castle still be standing in all its old magnificence, instead of now exhibiting black ruins, a spectacle of the rage of the Paris commune? Whether, in that case, Henri V. might not now have been sitting on the throne of France, instead of pining in exile, as Count de Chambord, in his melancholy castle of Frohsdorf in Austria ?

Seldom, surely, has a love-hot heart had to pay more dearly for a weak hour than had the Duchess de Berri !

In Gratz I met this character of a lady for the last time, when, in 1837, I was there in fulfilment of a professional engagement. From the stage, where I was performing the part of *Marie* in the "Three Epochs," I saw the duchess sitting with her husband in a box. At the close of the representation, she came gliding along the corridor to meet me, leaning on the arm of the Marchese Lucchesi-Palli, whom she had got raised to the rank of Duke della Gracia by the hands of one of her Italian royal cousins. She addressed me in a friendly tone in French, and remarked how much my playing had reminded her of Mars in the "Three Epochs" in the *Théatre Français.*

When, in reply, I mentioned that, in 1829, I had actually had the happiness of often seeing and studying Mademoiselle Mars in the *Théatre Français*, she said to me, with a sigh: "Ah! what fine times those were—those of 1829!"

The "jolie laide" had in the interval grown much uglier, and had also broadened considerably. Withal, however, La Fontaine's saying was still verified in her: "La grâce est plus belle encore que la beauté!" Her step was still ever light and graceful—and—under—the —short—dress—there still stole in and out with unreduced charm—*le pied de madame!*

The Duke della Gracia looked handsome and stately, and considerably younger than his consort—but seemingly a man of no extraordinary wits.

I was told that the passionate wife suffered greatly from jealousy, that she kept watch over her husband day and night, and raised no end of din about his ears so often as she caught him in devious paths.

When, a short time before, the duchess had suspected her husband of exchanging love-glances and secret signs with the young and pretty daughter of a burgess living opposite her palace, she flew, in the first spurt of her resentment, into the house in question and soundly boxed the ears of the young beauty right and left; and in broken German threatened her with further measures if she (the duchess) should ever notice anything of the kind again. It was even asserted that, occasionally, after scenes of that description, the cheeks of the Duke della Gracia himself were found to be suggestively red.

The ducal palace in Gratz looked very dull and unenjoyable. Friends invited me to look through it. The interior, too, of this great house seemed to me to bear out all the promise of its exterior. It appeared to be furnished like the house of a *parvenu* who stuffs his rooms in an ostentatious and tasteless fashion. Precious art treasures, from the vanished brilliant Paris days, were grouped incongruously with new furniture. The most conspicuous object was a golden temple once presented to the duchess by the city of Paris on the occasion of the birth of her son, Duke Henri de Bordeaux. In one room the duke's dressing gown and the duchess's morning cap lay peacefully together on the sofa. In the nursery there was no want of noise and merriment. There I saw four ducal scions astir—one son and three little daughters.

Later on, when not occupying her palace in Venice, the duchess lived almost exclusively in her castle of Brunnsee,* in Southern Styria. After the death of her royal father-in-law, Charles X., she became reconciled with her son, the Count de Chambord, whose saint's day, the day of St. Henri, she always celebrated with great pomp in Brunnsee; and on that occasion the Duke della Gracia raised his glass and bowed in silence before the Duke de Chambord, an act followed by all the guests, and signifying as much as, " Vive le roi ! "

A great deal of trouble was reserved for the declining days of the duchess. Her old Parisian habit of living on a large footing, notwithstanding the wondrously small foot on which she stood, and her truly princely munificence, deranged her financial affairs to such a degree that Count de Chambord had to run to the succour of his mother and save her from the worst extremities. Count de Chambord also took over Brunnsee, but committed it to the duchess as her residence for life. This calamity shattered Duke della Gracia so sorely that he died in 1864. The duchess, too, from that time was a broken-down woman. She suffered from increasing deafness and blindness, and died the Saturday following Good Friday in 1870. She did not live to see the overthrow of the hated Napoleon and Henri V.'s new hopes of the throne.

In the salons of the Legitimist Duke de Larochefoucauld-Doudeauville in Paris, there is still exhibited to this day at solemn assemblies of the partizans of the "king," Henri V., a rare sacred relic—a wondrously small satin shoe, of faded white, stained by a few drops of blood. It is the shoe which was worn by " le pied de madame " on the evening of the 14th February, 1820, in the opera, when her husband was stabbed by the dagger of Louvel. The heart's blood

---

* Spring Lake.

of the Duc de Berri, heir to the throne of France, moistened this shoe, when the duchess bore Henri V. under her heart.

*   *   *   *   *   *

In the end of October, 1829, Christian Stockmar arrived at Paris, and took up his residence in our hotel. He was in very bad humour, and dissatisfied with all the world, and most with Prince Leopold, who was unable to come to any resolution in the affair of the Greek throne—the genuine Marquis peu-à-peu that he was.

To all questions I put the only answer I got was always the same: "Patience! patience! Things must soon determine themselves, probably sooner than the time for your re-crossing the Channel. Perhaps, Caroline, the upshot will be your longed-for freedom, a consummation I would indulge you with all my heart."

In a strangely mixed mood of mind I looked forward to the arrival of the prince. However much I longed for my golden freedom, it was yet painful to me to reflect on the bright hopes with which I had journeyed to England, and on my brief dream of "the heart" being in a few weeks perhaps for ever extinguished.

Cousin Christian visited with us Versailles, St. Cloud, St. Germain, and the beautiful woods and lakes of Montmorency, as also theatres and concerts. I had still, however, but little enjoyment of all my Parisian life. My heart was too distressed regarding the approaching result.

In the middle of November the prince arrived in Paris, but took apartments in another hotel, and daily, between three and four, came to pay us a rather frosty visit, with the ominous—drizzling box. He looked unwell, and complained constantly of his health, a subject which engaged his thoughts apparently more than I did. Carlsbad, he said, had not agreed with him. He was still more taciturn than ordinarily, and drizzled away mechanically, lost in thought, while I read aloud just as mechanically. Of cordiality, let alone tenderness, such as he had shown in the short honeymoon of Regent's Park, and which had inspired some hope in me, not a trace was any longer perceptible. We vegetated away in Paris beside each other just as joyously as we had done in our first London experience.

Yet the prince would not set me free, either, though I begged it of him with tears. He sought rather to divert me from such a thought by holding out the hope of a home-like life in Claremont during the winter.

The prince also paid visits to the Tuileries, though they seemed to give him little entertainment. It was not till afterwards I learned that these visits were for the purpose of sounding how a suit on the part of Prince Leopold for the hand of the Dowager-Duchess de Berri might take in the Tuileries, supposing the Greek throne were secured to the prince.

The answer was brief, and diplomatic: "The Greek throne safe, then the Duchess de Berri; no throne, no Berri."

How much this diplomatic game of marriage must necessarily arouse my indignation when I heard of it no person of any heart, or possessing even the least spark of human feeling, need be told. There is nothing in the world more galling to a woman than the sense of having been the mere playball to the humours of a man who holds himself unspeakably raised above her—a toy to be flung into the gutter so soon as a glittering crown offers! What to me was the most indigestible part of it all was the apparent good conscience with which the prince sat drizzling opposite to me, a fresh young creature, his legitimate spouse in the eyes of God, all the while he was hatching these new schemes of marriage. His Highness was a deep calculator, and was minded not to pitch away the pretty toy till he had first made sure of the royal crown and royal daughter.

As is known, Prince Leopold, once he had got the king's crown on his head, no more thought of the Duchess de Berri as his queen—seeing that with all the Bourbons she had been driven out of the Tuileries and France. She was no longer the sort of queen to his taste. Ay, ever and everywhere, Monsieur tout doucement!

In the beginning of December the prince and Baron Stockmar went to England. We had to stay in Paris till we received orders to follow them.

As brother Louis had also left Paris on business, and we were thus deprived of our faithful daily companion and guide to all the different sights, we sat right lonely in our cramped little rooms and looked out mournfully into the dingy, rainy December weather which put a stop even on our walking.

A sadder Christmas I never experienced than that one of Paris. The day after Christmas we returned, by high command, to England, the anxious question ever in our minds, "What awaits us there?"

CHAPTER XXIV.

THE BLISSFUL RETIREMENT.

THE sad Christmas in Paris was succeeded by a still sadder New-Year's Eve and New-Year's morning in England.

On the New-Year's Eve of 1829, mother and I, accompanied by the good and heartily-devoted Figaro-Hühnlein, reached the lonely, desolate, and mournful villa near Claremont House, fourteen English miles from London, which was to be our home for the present, and were again received by strangers. Prince Leopold stayed in London; cousin Christian, ailing and hypocondriacal, had his quarters in Claremont House. Fanny made us her impertinent curtsies, and was very officious in doing the honours of the melancholy house, smiling to us in a manner full of intelligence. I am afraid I hated this presuming person at that time—a little.

It is now four-and-forty long eventful years since I spent that mournful New-Year's Eve with mother, and yet every particular about it still stands out distinctly and vividly to the eye of my remembrance, so that I could paint it. The bitter, as well as the sweet, leaves its ineffaceable impressions on us.

'Tis a ghastly, large, naked drawing room, with brown-grown carpets and faded curtains and old-fashioned, stiff, unaccommodating chairs, and a sofa of the same characteristics covered with hard white-scoured leather. In the gigantic fire-place burn mighty logs of wood, without, however, warming the uncomfortable room. In front of the fire sit mother and I on the hard, stiff, leather chairs, at a small table richly served with cakes and sweet wine and punch, and so celebrate Sylvester—thinking longingly of Sylvester in the far, beloved Germany.

With what joyfulness had we sat just a year before in

the house of Justizrath Ludolff, in Berlin, celebrating
Sylvester! I played the red-rose fairy of the New-Year
in a Sylvester comedy, distributing roses among the guests
all round, the leaves of which, in pretty rhymes, promised
to each the fulfilment of his dearest wishes.

Poor, vain rose fairy! What has the New-Year
brought to yourself? Thorns upon thorns!

And what will the approaching year of 1830 bring us?
We did not venture on any answer to that question.
But our tears flowed, and in our hearts all was dark and
dreary, like the frigid night outside. We felt solitary and
forsaken, more than we had ever done. We cowered at
the thought of the New-Year, or even of the new day, with
the same unvaried sameness extending itself into the same
endless sameness, to the torpor of soul and body. For
what was the task of my English life? The daily renewed
and daily fruitless experiment of serving as a pretty play-
thing to divert the ennui of a blasé, egoistic, soulless
prince.

I am now a grey old woman, nearing my grave, and in
my life have had much sorrow to experience, and trials of
the most painful kind to go through, and painful trials are
still my daily portion—and yet, when I compare a Sylvester
evening on my lonely snowed-up Swiss mountain with that
old New-Year's Eve in England, a feeling of almost youthful energy and hopefulness throbs through my old heart.
I no longer vegetate—I live—I have things to provide,
work to perform, purposes to serve—and that does not
pass into the inane, but is all sure of its due effect.

In my Swiss mountain house it is also still and lonely in
winter, and but seldom does any visitor knock at my door.
But I look out from my window on lively villages by the
Zürichsee, and see busy men and happy school children
passing; and in the evening pleasantly illuminated windows, even though in the distance, behind which I am at
liberty to think nice thoughts of comfortable family life.

How different in a lonely English villa, which is not
enlivened by merry children nor happy parents, and that
stands sunk in a park over-grown with evergreen firs, all
slumbrous like Dornröschen's magic castle! Hardly even

the watch-dog ventured now and again to bark subduedly through the deadly-still, desolate Sylvester evening.

In a bed of vast dimensions, mother and I sought in sleep to forget our joyless solitude. I pretended to sleep, in order to pacify my mother. But I still long heard her sighing and weeping and praying: "Merciful God and Father, do not forsake us. Lead us the right way out of this labyrinth, or strengthen us to bear!"

Poor, poor mother! With her shrewd, experienced eye she had long penetrated the prince's character, and recognised him as a heartless pedant, who thought of nothing but his dear, pampered self, though the world around him should all go to ruin, though hearts should bleed silently to death! What did it matter, if only his Highness were not disturbed in his repose and comfort!

Next morning, New-Year's Day of 1830, I feigned great liveliness before the anxious eyes of my mother; skipped about singing through all the desolate rooms of the house, which the good Hühnlein by huge fires had endeavoured to render more habitable, and overhauled the library, which contained many English and some old French books. Everything gave one the impression of its having been lying mouldering a century in its grave.

The tangled wilderness of a park—where garden there was none, in the German sense of the word—with its gigantic old pines and firs, had an air of ghastly weirdness and forlornness. A brook wound its way through the whole length of the grounds, and was lost in an adjoining wood. Not a house, not a human being visible far and wide! To add to the desolate effect, it was a dull, raw, cold winter's day, moist with a dripping English fog.

I was first able to fetch a free breath when in my wanderings I came upon a little farm-house, which factotum Hühnlein inhabited with his wife, a brisk Coburg woman, and some rosy, flaxen-haired children. When I saw the blazing fire crackling up the chimney, and watched the little chubby housewife preparing the morning's soup for the children, and with what relish the little nurslings ate up the sweet New Year's cakes I had brought for them, I thought, with a sigh, to myself how enviable were these plain, happy people in comparison with the envied Countess Montgomery.

Behind the farm-house stood a ruinous barn, in which our travelling coach looked dismal. What a mind I had to say—" Put the horses to, and away to Germany."

I fed the pigeons that occupied a cot perched aloft over a round expanse of lawn, and the great, white watch-dog. What further was to be done?

I opened the handsome Clementi piano that had been removed hither from Regent's Park; the only article that had any suggestion of a home-feeling for me, but my fingers grew torpid on the keys. The music-room was not to be warmed even by an uninterrupted extravagant fire in the chimney. We were fain to cower together in a little room that was capable of being warmed to some tolerable measure, at least.

After eleven Hühnlein came driving up in a small phaeton, drawn by a little stout pony, bringing us our *déjeuner à la fourchette*, which had been prepared by the cook in Claremont House. In this anything but flattering manner were our luncheon and dinner daily fetched to us. To my horror, Hühnlein took out the drizzling box as well, and a new novel of Henrietta Hanke.

Baron Stockmar desired to be excused on account of his being unwell; the prince would be to dinner at four o'clock.

Punctually at four o'clock the equipages rolled up and the prince alighted, all wrapped up like some grandpapa. Altogether grandpapa-ly, too, was the greeting and the further conversation. Not a trace was there of a man in the vigour of life who had previously confessed a tender love and longing for a happy domesticity, and who was now anxious on making up by loving trustfulness to the life-companion of his choice for all that she had given up for him.

There was music for half-an-hour—*i.e.*, I played the piano with benumbed fingers and sang some songs with blue-cold lips, while the prince, in furred coat and boots, sat before the blazing hearth poking the fire. Next came dinner. Hühnlein served, and poor mother took the most

serious pains to start and keep up an interesting conversation, for I felt so completely done up that I couldn't even
pretend to be in talking spirits. A few jests I forced out
to please my mother and try and interrupt the deadly
monotony entirely failed. There was no denying that I had
myself nearly unlearned laughing.

After dinner, and during coffee drinking, I read, or
rather jerked out, as if in spasms, novel after novel of the
goody Silesian Hanke, while prince grandpapa, with horrible
gravity and endurance, drizzled—drizzled—drizzled—zrr!
—zrr!—zrr!—till my jaws grew paralysed in the vain
convulsive struggle to bite down my yawning.

At seven o'clock the prince rode back to Claremont
House, completely satisfied with his day's earnest work, and
mother and I were free to breathe. We threw off our stiff
ceremonial toilettes, slipped into comfortable house dresses,
and sought refreshment for our jaded spirits in the memory
of the fair, joyous past. Curiously enough, our favourite
gossip always turned on my stage-life I had so frivolously
abandoned. So long as I could call it mine I was used to
count its thorns and prickles. I now thought only of the
rosy flourish of the stage.

So passed the days and weeks in deadening uniformity,
relieved only by the disquietude of neither seeing nor hearing anything of cousin Christian for the first two weeks of
this lonely sojourn. Was he really so seriously ill as to be
unable to come the short distance between Claremont House
and our place? Why, then, did he not at least write a
line to us? Was he displeased with us? Had we offended
him, and how?

If I asked the prince for an explanation of the riddle of
the silence and absence of cousin, he shrugged his shoulders
and answered evasively: "The good Stocky has again, as
almost always in these foggy English months, the hypochondria, and fancies he is ill to the point of dying."

At the end of the second week I could no longer stand
the tormenting uncertainty, and wrote to cousin a note of
brief emphasis, which I handed to Hühnlein to deliver him:
"If you do not come to-morrow to clear up this
enigmatical silence of yours, mother and I will depart, the

day after to-morrow. Our strength and patience are at an
end."

Next morning cousin came driving to us. He looked
pale and sickly, but still more out of humour. He was
peevish about everything—about the prince, who would
come to no determination on the question of the Greek
throne, nor let himself be advised and guided by him;
about King George IV.; about the English ministers;
about our being here.

"But, cousin," I indignantly interrupted him, "you are
yourself to blame for our being here. But for your advice
we had never given up the stage and our free and happy
life."

"Yes, I had then the hope that the prince would, at
your side, Caroline, once more revive into vigorous manhood; but that hope is now long extinguished. His heart
is a lump of ice. 'Dagegen kämpfen die Götter selbst
vergebens!'* Yet my advice, even at this time of day,
is still: 'Patience, patience, and again patience!' Wait
till the question of the Greek throne is decided. In the
course of a few weeks or months we shall know that
matter more clearly. Such solution of your bond without
any violence, simply by the force of an external 'must,'
were the most welcome to me. You would then depart in
peace with the prince, and the King of Greece would remain your faithful friend."

Weeping, I vowed anew to be patient and enduring,
and to repose full confidence in cousin's guidance; and
cousin promised to come to us for a short hour in the
morning in the old confidential style. In doing so, he said:

"I stayed away till now because the prince did not ask
me to come and dine with him and you, though he knows
that I am now doubly solitary in Claremont House,
whereas formerly I dined with the prince and passed the
evenings with him. That is nothing but princely want of
consideration. But don't let it be seen you miss me."

So at least a friendly intercourse with cousin was re-
established. He came every morning to lunch, to talk,

---

* Schiller's "Against that the gods themselves fight in vain."

advise, and console. And I exerted myself beyond measure to follow his counsel, and not betray to the prince what was passing in my mind, and altogether accustomed myself to vegetating. I dressed myself daily for the prince, as to a *soiree;* went with him before dinner to walk the gloomy fir-path by the brook, where no passer-by could see us, up and down, up and down; patiently played piano, accompanied the singing of his Highness, and read out of Henrietta Hanke, without visible chagrin, from five to seven o'clock.

In the forenoon cousin gave me riding lessons in the Park; at first on a pony, and then on a beautiful, elegant lady's horse. When the prince once looked on at these riding exercises, he thought that " Missy made a splendid Amazon," and next day his Highness himself appeared on horseback in the Park meadow, but in such a ridiculous fashion that, though I had almost forgotten laughing, I burst into a derisive peal. The rider over six feet tall sat on a little squat pony, the thin princely legs nearly scraping the ground—the very counterpart of Don Quixote! With the greatest self-complacence, however, his Highness conjectured that he stood less chance of a severe shaking on a little pony than on a high horse. And so, with this knight of mournful figure, I rode up and down, up and down, on the Park meadow. There was little zest in the affair. To leave on horseback with me the protecting enclosure of the Park was more than the prince would venture. Only reluctantly did he once and again permit me to ride out with cousin into the open country. How grateful was it to me to be able to dash off in full gallop! They were, however, but brief hours in which I felt myself free—free like another child of man. We now and again met a human being, and rode past comfortable-looking villages and pleasant villas.

But this poor dream of liberty did not last long.

One morning a fine, elegant cavalier came riding towards us. After saluting cousin in a friendly manner, he was introduced to me as Mr. Somerset, and begged to be allowed to accompany us a little into the wood.

He was an agreeable companion, had been long on the.

Continent, and could chat away in French in a very interesting manner. On taking leave of us, he asked me gallantly, "whether he might again have the pleasure of meeting me here on horseback?"

And duly next day Mr. Somerset was riding up and down on the highway, waiting to pay his respects to Baron Stockmar and his cousin. Christian, however, cleverly turned in by a side way, and we were lost in the wood, leaving the nonplussed cavalier to digest this hasty flight of ours by himself. Cousin said in chagrin: "And this, too, the fates had in store for us—that this fantastic hero of romance, for whom our ladies have hitherto been fishing in vain, should fall in love with the Countess Montgomery, and make the attempt of visiting you in your quarters. Then good-bye with the secret! The prince's position and pecuniary standing in England were in jeopardy; nay, the Greek throne itself would be in danger. We must renounce riding out!"

Deeply dispirited I again got back to our sad prison, and at once sent Hühnlein to the prince with a note, "that I had a violent headache, and could not see his Highness that day."

In great agitation the prince met me next day with the words, "Stocky has confessed everything to me, as Somerset has already been sounding the alarm about the new-arisen German beauty, so like the Princess Charlotte. He will be bringing all the young hot-bloods about our doors to try and catch a sight of missy. Hang that stupid riding out!"

"Your Highness, I shall never ride out again. I have already renounced this last joy and freedom!" I said, deeply embittered. "Mother and I shall endeavour to consider ourselves as complete fossils. This, then, is the blissful retirement for which I was allured to England with golden promises. If I had known that I was to live here like a State prisoner, I should certainly not be here" —and I burst into passionate crying.

The prince stood at first quite perplexed, then, with a forced laugh and an attempt at joking, he said—"Eh! eh! Is missy going to revolt?"

"Shall I not be compelled to? I was not born a slave!" I exclaimed, in a passion, ran away and shut myself up in my bedroom.

The prince said to my distressed mother, in a tone of perfect equanimity—"But I didn't think *artistes* could be so passionate! But missy will soon come to herself again. Pity, I shall lose this new chapter in the novel to-day. I was so much interested in it!"—and the prince began the drizzling without the accompaniment of reading, till my mother, taking pity on him, opened the book and read out the new chapter of the fascinating novel.

My poor, good mother! She has made many and great sacrifices for me in life; but the greatest of all assuredly in those days in England! What a joyless life was hers, as mother of the Countess Montgomery! For months she endured the torture of sitting stiffly dressed during my hours' long reading, and looking on while the prince drizzled. Then I begged her myself to give up the daily-renewed and fruitless effort to struggle against sleepiness and the yawning spasms, and to keep in her room. Only the hope that the prince and I, in a *tête-à-tête* by ourselves, might more easily come into union of mind with each other induced her to yield to my request. Her hope was, of course, a vain one.

In addition to all that, we had vexations on the side of the importunate and ever-spying Fanny. She had even the presumption daily to press on my mother her company and conversation, till at last I made short work of it, and laid before cousin the ultimatum: "Either Fanny goes or I go." That was effectual. Fanny returned to Claremont House. The prince let it pass, with the remark only that "Fanny was once very pretty!"

"Then she is more in her place in Claremont than here!" was my piqued reply.

Our "still life," of course, did not grow any the more cordial from such scenes.

Then one morning cousin Christian came galloping up to us in great excitement. His ordinarily so pale countenance was flushed, and his eye flashed as he called out to us in the distance, without any preface: "The hour of deliverance is come! The crown of Greece is now definitively offered to the prince! Caroline, you are free!"

I shouted aloud with indescribable joy, and embraced and kissed cousin, laughing and weeping out in one and the same breath.

"Saved from the darkness of the tomb! Awakened to new life! My God, I thank Thee that this unhappy bond is now loosed in peace, and not snapped in anger! I thank Thee that now, with good-will and without mutual enmities, I can part from a man whom I once thought I loved!"

Cousin Christian said earnestly: "I heartily wish you joy of your freedom!"

And yet it was a vain jubilation. It was but a vain—dream of freedom.

I had reckoned without *Marquis peu-à-peu* and *Monsieur tout doucement!*

For the explanation of this I must enter into greater detail respecting the situation and character of Prince Leopold. Many of the communications I am about to make I owe to cousin Christian, who, notwithstanding his celebrated diplomatic penetration, would often blab away to us like a genuine *enfant terrible*, on occasions when he had been exasperated more than common by Prince Leopold.

CHAPTER XXV.

CLAREMONT HOUSE.

I ONCE was child enough to fancy I should one day live at the side of my loving consort in the beautiful Claremont House.

How different it had all turned out! All I was allowed was only to walk through and take a look of Claremont, as a stranger, while the prince was staying in London. Cousin Christian or Hühnlein conducted mother and me through the place.

Claremont House, named from a former proprietor, the Earl of Clare, is a spacious, stately building, situated on a green hill in a magnificent expanse of park.

I was, of course, most interested in the apartments which the Princess Charlotte, Prince Leopold's first spouse, had occupied during the brief period of wedded happiness that was allotted to her, and in the many reminiscences of her still remaining.

Thus, for example, I found an old grey parrot, Coco by name, seated on a perch in the ante-room, a parrot the lively princess had once been fond of playing with. But the poor thing was badly neglected, and clotted all over with dirt and vermin. When I begged the prince to let me take Coco in charge for some time, he at once made me a present of the parrot, evidently glad to get rid of the noisy nuisance in such an easy way. Not a trait in his face revealed any emotion on his part in remembrance of those olden times.

Mother and I tended the parrot carefully, and did not neglect his bath, till we had the pleasure of seeing him freshen up again into new life. He soon came to chatter away briskly: "Mutter—Lina—ich liebe Dich."*

---

* "Mother—Lina—I love thee."

Coco afterwards followed us about in all our professional tours: to Russia—Austria—Dresden. In this last place he died in 1842, shortly after mother, and of grief, no doubt, that he could no longer see his faithful nurse.

I saw also a picture of the Princess Charlotte in a Russian costume, blue, with silver; a present from the Grand-Duchess Catherine, afterwards Queen of Würtemberg, who, immediately after the War of Freedom had come to England, and was the main instrument in bringing about the marriage of the princess with Prince Leopold.

I happened to possess a Russian costume perfectly similar, given me by Madame Pleske during my engagement in St. Petersburg, and in which I had there gaily practised the Russian national dance.

Next day I received the prince in this costume, surprised myself by my similarity to the Princess Charlotte. We were like as twin sisters.

The prince stopped short and grew a little pale. But no trace of any emotion was to be read in his blasé face. With the greatest composure he compared us and analysed our points of resemblance: "Princess Charlotte had a finer nose, but not so pretty a mouth as missy. Charlotte was fuller; missy has grown more graceful. The fair hair, the fresh complexion is common to both"—and so the analysis proceeded with all comfortableness till in impatience I struck in—"Your Highness, you are forgetting to note the faithful hearts which in similar casing in both instances strike and—struck!" This put his Highness a trifle out of countenance, till at his drizzling box the prince recovered himself again.

Was it our external resemblance? Was it but a like fate which bound us to Prince Leopold? I felt the liveliest interest in the Princess Charlotte, and never failed to ask cousin Christian, who, to be sure, had known her personally, about her. Perhaps it was, also, the deep unhappiness that wound through the whole life of the princess which awoke my sympathy with her. For is it not a dreadful unhappiness for a girl—be she princess or be she beggar's child—to have to condemn her father and mother? And more than once cousin Christian heard from the lips of the princess the terrible words :

" My mother was bad, but she would not have been so bad if my father had not been much worse still ! "

Her father was the Prince of Wales, born 1762, the eldest of the twelve children of the blind, weak-minded King George III. of England and of the Princess Charlotte of Mecklenburg-Strelitz, whose brother was father of Queen Louise of Prussia. The Prince of Wales was called by his flatterers " the first gentleman of England," because he spent £20,000 a-year on his dress alone, and as bachelor could never make his yearly revenue of £50,000 sterling suffice for his expenses, so that he contracted debts on debts. He was likewise the most profligate man of his time—a roué, glutton, tippler, gambler, and the most unconscionable seducer of wives and daughters. How many false oaths did he swear? If he was not guilty of one last unspeakable crime against his consort, who had become a grievance to him even before marriage, it is certain that with a refined wickedness he brought about the ruin of this unhappy woman both morally and physically.

At the age of twenty-four, the Prince of Wales, though in receipt of a daily income of near 1000 thalers, had amassed a debt of £160,000. The king, who had long stood on a strained footing with his prodigal son, refused to pay the debt. Then the prince's friends, libertines and parasites, applied to Parliament. They wanted to bring on, at least, a debate—to raise a scandal.

In these circumstance, the minister Pitt rose in the Lower House and threatened, if compelled, to make revelations which would jeopardise even the succession to the throne of the Prince of Wales.

The whole House trembled. Even the most unscrupulous adherents of the prince grew pale. For every one in the House—in England—knew what Pitt was hinting at. It was an open secret that the prince, failing to attain his object by any other means, had gone through a marriage ceremony with the beautiful Catholic lady, Mrs. Fitzherbert, although knowing at the time that her husband was still alive. Was the prince's marriage with Mrs. Fitzherbert binding? then was he thereby excluded from succession to the throne by the English law that the heir to the throne could not marry a Catholic. If the marriage was not binding, seeing that her first husband, Mr. Fitzherbert, was living at the time when this second ceremony of marriage was performed, then was it undeniable that the Prince of Wales had committed adultery with Mrs. Fitzherbert.

But the prince and his company did not shrink aghast at these delicate considerations. With a bold brow Fox and Sheridan challenged an official investigation into the matter hinted at; and, with a cynical smile, the " first gentleman" took on himself the charge of adultery with Mrs. Fitzherbert, openly avowing: " No, I am not legally married to Mrs. Fitzherbert. It was only a mock ceremony of marriage that took place—the good woman was herself deceived."

And the minister Pitt and the Parliament not only allowed this delicate affair to drop, but likewise paid the prince's debts, after he had promised, like a detected schoolboy, " never, never to do it again." And yet in a few years the same heir to the throne had laid anew on his round shoulders a fresh debt of half-a-million pounds sterling.

The king, the minister, the Parliament, and the prince himself and his friends now saw no way out of it but marriage with one of his own rank. The unhappy victim was also soon found—Princess Caroline of Brunswick, whose mother was a sister of King George III. The queen had given her vote in favour of her niece, the Princess Louise of Mecklenburg-Strelitz. Luckily the king's project triumphed, or Louise had not been Prussia's queen and guardian angel.

The English *pro*-suitor, Lord Malmesbury, describes the lady-intended, who was twenty-six years old, as "a tall blonde with regular features, open lively expression and natural culture, if without princely dignity. She was too familiar and unrestrained; frivolously talkative and vulgar; tasteless in her dress; passionate and eccentric;

L

catching with more obstinacy than happiness and discretion at witty ideas. Withal, however, she was good-natured and docile."

In the end of March, 1795, Princess Caroline set foot for the first time on English ground as the betrothed of the Prince of Wales, hailed by all the people as "guardian angel." The ingenious caricature-limner Gilray devoted to this "guardian angel" a successful drawing—"The Lover's Dream." The stout "first gentleman" rests on a luxurious couch. On one side comes gliding, as guardian angel, the princely bride, with sweet auspicious smile, before whose approach the prince's evil spirits—Fox and Sheridan—flit away on the other side into night and darkness.

But this was, what it purported to be, only a "dream." At the very first meeting with his intended this "first gentleman" showed himself in all his shocking reality. When the Princess Caroline met him in London with humble bashfulness, and even bowed the knee before her future executioner, the prince hastily embraced her, and then, ostentatiously turning to Lord Malmesbury, said, with a jeer: "Harris, I feel out of sorts; a glass of brandy!" With a rough oath he turned his back on his appalled lady, and bluntly walked off.

Nay, the prince had the effrontery to force Lady Jersey, one of his many mistresses, on his intended as her lady-in-waiting and daily companion.

And then came the saddest bridal day, the 8th April, and the marriage in the chapel of St. James's Palace. The prince tumbled up to the altar in a state of intoxication, turned his back constantly on his bride, and nodded conspicuously towards a pew in which sat a veiled lady, Mrs. Fitzherbert. To this "spouse"—married to him by a Protestant clergyman in presence of two witnesses, and whose certificate of marriage is still preserved in the fireproof vaults of the banking house of Coutts & Coutts—he had made the frivolous promise, in order to procure her silence: "You are in the future, as in the past, my sole and alone lawful wife, while the princess will be this only in name. I shall always show publicly to whom I am tied by affection, and to whom by compulsion." And this he did show—this blasphemer, this scorner of morals—at the moment when criminally going through the ceremony of marriage at the altar.

Poor " guardian angel ! "

In a state of intoxication the prince reeled to the marriage feast ; still more intoxicated into the nuptial chamber.

Hours of unspeakable anguish and degradation for the unhappy princess ! To make her still more obnoxious to her fright of a husband, his favourites or mistresses had drugged her wine with an intoxicating and emetic ingredient.

The very next day the prince declared to the king he could not live in connubial bonds with such a wife. And they were and continued separated—for ever. And yet the princess had to endure, for a considerable time, the ignominy of living under the same roof in Carlton House, with such a consort and his latest mistress, Lady Jersey; of dining at the same table, and being daily exposed to fresh insult and mockery at the hands of her executioner and his dependents. And in all this ill-starred, loveless, royal Court, which was torn by dissensions, the unhappy stranger had not one to take her part—not one, except the old, half blind, weak-minded king, her mother's brother. Queen Charlotte, although a German princess, was hostile to her from the very beginning.

This Queen Charlotte must have been a repulsive woman, according to the testimony of all comtemporaries. Lord Brougham says of her : " Her virtue was so stuffed out with excess of stiffness and prudery as to make it difficult to respect and sympathise with her. While nothing disturbed the regularity of her life, the tedium of her society, the formality of her behaviour, the pettiness of her mind were entirely qualified to render respectable conduct as little attractive as possible, and rather to scare the observer from morality than entice him to it."

And even Baron Christian Stockmar, the faithful adherent to the English royal family, thus delineates Queen Charlotte : " Short, deformed, a real mulatto face"—a fairly strong *negative* on the part of the fine diplomatist!

And how the Princess Charlotte hated her grandmother!

Just nine months after the unhappy bridal day the Princess of Wales gave birth to a daughter—the Princess Charlotte. The people hailed the little heiress to the throne, and the maternal heart, too, was in hopes that this innocent child might help to tie a new bond of peace and love between father and mother! Vain hopes!

The Prince of Wales greeted his daughter—by now terminating even the official show of matrimonial community with his spouse.

The king was just and kind enough to ordain that the up-bringing of the Princess Charlotte till her eighth year should devolve on the mother.

As if relieved of a nightmare, the Princess of Wales now hastened every summer with her little daughter from her prison of Carlton House into the green solitude of the charming hilly landscape between Charlton and Woolwich, where she had Shrewsbury Villa to dwell in. Those peaceful summer days were the happiest in her life. In winter she had again to withdraw within the walls of Carlton House, and divide rooms there with her unnatural consort and his mistresses, Lady Jersey, the Marchioness of Townshend, the Ladies Cholmondeley and Carnarvon, Lady Conyngham, the Marchioness of Hertford, &c., as also with his bottle-companions.

An anecdote has come down from the childish years of the Princess Charlotte which betokens precocity, earnest reflection, and remarkable royal consciousness in the child.

The little princess was six years old when she watched a game at chess. On hearing the word "check-mate," and asking the meaning of it, she was told that the king was "mate," he had lost his power. After thinking with herself for a time the child said: "That must not be that the king is mated. He must keep his power, to be able to rule. If I were king I would not let myself be mated!"

When Princess Charlotte was eight years old a new struggle arose between her parents as to her further disposal. At last the king adopted the following resolution:

"Lower Lodge in Windsor Park shall be fitted up as residence for the Princess Charlotte. The king will take care of her maintenance and her education, appointing a bishop for that purpose, seeing that as heir presumptive to the throne she will require a superior education. The bishop shall engage a clergyman to instruct the princess in religion and Latin, and read prayers with her daily. Another instructor shall be provided for history, geography, literature, and French; as also teachers in writing, music, and dancing. The care of her health and behaviour shall be committed to a governess, and as she must be, both day and night, constantly under the supervision of responsible persons, an under-governess and assistant under-governess shall likewise be appointed."

In the beginning of 1805 the Princess Charlotte had Lower Lodge assigned to her as her residence—her dreary prison, as she afterwards often named it. To be nearer her daughter, the Princess of Wales took possession of Montague House, in spite of the protest of the Prince of Wales, all whose efforts were ever obstinately bent on withdrawing his daughter from the influence of her mother. But the old king took up the cause of the mother.

At this juncture "the first gentleman of England," in his rage and hatred, had recourse to other—to the most infamous—weapons a knave can stoop to. He, the wide-ranging adulterer, accused his consort publicly of adultery with Admiral Sir Robert Smith, Captain Manby, and the celebrated handsome painter, Sir Thomas Lawrence, asserting that the boy Bill Austin, whom the Princess of Wales in her love of children had adopted and brought up with her little Charlotte, was her own illegitimate child.

The king commissioned four of his ministers to undertake a "delicate investigation" into this affair. The Princess of Wales proved that Bill Austin was the lawful son of a poor sailcloth maker of Charlton, and in the middle of July, 1806, was completely acquitted, though not without a certain censure of the imprudent "want of reserve in her behaviour." Great force, too, must be given in this case to the consideration that the members of the com-

mission all belonged to the friends of the accuser, and
were therefore all prejudiced against her who was so
shamefully accused. The prince was even base enough
to have his daughter of ten years pumped, indirectly at
least, as a witness against her mother. The little princess,
however, saw through the whole intrigue, and was not to
be decoyed even by the most ensnaring questions into any
utterance unfavourable to her mother, but communicated
to her the whole manœuvre, and assured her of her un-
changing love and reverence.

Poor child! whom her own father, with sacrilegious
hand, so early robbed of the tender flower of unsuspecting
innocence, in whose young heart her own father outraged
the sanctity of filial love!

Throughout the course of this investigation the Princess
of Wales was forbidden to see her own daughter or visit
the Court of Windsor. And this cruel and contumelious
prohibition was not revoked till the woman, in her extreme
provocation, threatened to publish the secret history of all
these cabals and persecutions.

Soon after, in April, 1807, the friends of the princess,
—Eldon, Percival, and Canning—succeeded to the ministry.
They at once ordered a general revision of the "delicate
investigation," and now the Princess of Wales obtained a
brilliant satisfaction and a complete vindication of her
honour. The princess was again received at Court. Yet
the Prince of Wales succeeded in effecting the decree that
henceforth the mother should be allowed to see her daughter in Lower Lodge only once a week. Nor did he ever
leave off spreading about, by means of his *canailles*, that,
in spite of the acquittal and the vindication of her honour,
the princess was still guilty of adultery; and that it was
only because the law visited the adultery of a member of
the royal family with death that by command of the king the
justice of the case had been hushed up by a favourable ruling.

The answer of the princess to this was the demand
repeatedly and energetically expressed that all documents
in connection with the "delicate investigation" might be
printed and made public. She had nothing to fear from
their publicity.

The minister Percival returned a crushing answer to the prince's accusation in his anonymous, secretly printed, and secretly circulated book, which appeared under the curious title of "The Book," a work which completely unmasked the prince and his *canailles*, and which was thereupon bought up by them to the utmost limit of their ability. The book has long since been numbered among the greatest literary curiosities. It, however, served its purpose. The English people expressed itself ever more loudly on the side of the unhappy Princess of Wales, who was being systematically baited to death, and against her hated persecutor, the heir to the throne of England. How often would *he*, "according to the law" to which he referred have had to suffer the death of the adulterer?

Is it a matter of any wonder that the young Princess Charlotte never met her father unless with fear and trembling, or even with abhorrence, so often as he visited her in her gloomy prison? For he never went to see her without polluting the poor child's heart by the ever new smut, which, with fiendish persistency, he heaped on the name and honour of her mother, for whom she then still cherished a pure and tender affection.

Ay, poor, poor child that had later on to confess: "My mother was bad, but she would not have grown so bad, if my father had not been much worse still."

Cousin Christian and Prince Leopold as well were of opinion that the Princess of Wales was not guiltless as wife and woman; that she had had love-affair on love-affair; but would assuredly have proved a faithful wife and mother if the prince had met her with fidelity and affection on his side. It was only in despair, to forget her misfortune and dull the sense of her injuries, that the unhappy woman plunged out of one sensual indulgence into another till she perished in these ruinous courses.

In October, 1810, the blind and long weak-minded king sank into hopeless imbecility. On the 11th February, 1811, a Regency Bill passed by Parliament appointed the Prince of Wales as regent. The new power with which her executioner was thus invested the Princess of Wales and her daughter were to feel only too soon and in too sensible a manner. The prince-regent at once took into his own hands the education of the Princess Charlotte.

Lady Charlotte Bury, lady-in-waiting to the Princess of Wales, draws a character of the Princess Charlotte in those days, apparently not too flattering. Under date December, 1810, she writes in her journal: "I had the honour of meeting the Princess Charlotte at her grandmother's. She is very clever, but has still altogether the manners of an awkward school-girl, and spoke all sorts of nonsense with me. She is a fair piece of flesh and blood, but is able to assert her dignity when she likes, though that appears to be irksome to her. What will be her fate?"

A few days later, on the occasion of a visit of the young Princess Charlotte to her mother, we read in the same journal: "Her mother showed her an aigrette which had just arrived as a birth-day present from the notoriously parsimonious queen, on which the Princess Charlotte observed, 'the aigrette was quite decent considering who sent it.' So saying she laughed unrestrainedly her peculiarly loud but musical laugh."

Only a few months subsequently, in May, 1811, Lady Charlotte Bury finds the now fifteen-year-old princess developed to an extraordinary degree—to the measure of a stately young lady with royal deportment. 'She is above middle size, with full and handsomely-formed bust, of white complexion, beautiful and expressive features, with hands and feet of an aristocratic finish. Her character betokens a peculiar mixture of whim, wilfulness, and obstinacy, with goodness of heart, cleverness and enthusiasm. It looks as if she desired to be more admired in the character of a beautiful woman than of heiress to the throne. She is strong and richly endowed by nature, and her virtues outweigh her faults.'

This sketch is supplemented by Lord Brougham with the words: "She was a person of great and tolerably cultivated capacity. With the liveliness of her mother, she united a finer acumen of judgment. She had inherited her mother's resolute courage and her decision of character. Her temperament was excitable and vehement, a property which neither her own efforts nor those of her teachers had been able to subdue. But in her nature there was nothing low, vulgar, hateful."

Of the "resolute courage and decision" of the young princess, an interesting trait has been preserved in record : In February, 1812, Princess Charlotte is dining at a large company with her father in Carlton House. The prince-regent, who had imbibed freely of wine, foully asperses the leader of the Liberal Opposition in Parliament, Lord Grey, to whom and his party the princess and her mother are warmly attached, because, even if for no other reason, the Whigs, the opponents of the prince-regent, are their natural friends. Tears of resentment spring into the eyes of the princess at the calumnious words of her father. Weeping, she quits the table and drives to the opera for the first time—where she is enthusiastically greeted by the public. There she no sooner recognises, seated in an opposite box, the Lord Grey whom her father had been so severely and unjustly calumniating, than she starts up with an animated air and waves enthusiastic kisses to the astonished lord, heedless of the bewilderment of the whole house and the angry outbursts of her father. When London heard of this scene, the princess became the heroine of the day. All the world, the newspapers themselves, publicly espoused her cause against her father; and the young Lord Byron, who had just made a name for himself by the first two cantoes of Childe Harold, addressed to her his poem, which acquired a rapid popularity, "Lines to a Lady Weeping!"

> "Weep, daughter of a royal line,
> A sire's disgrace, a realm's decay ;
> Ah ! happy if each tear of thine
> Could wash a father's fault away.
> Weep, for thy tears are virtue's tears,
> Auspicious to these suffering isles ;
> And be each drop in future years
> Repaid thee by thy people's smiles !"

The prince-regent was furious, and set his whole pack of paid scribes to bay full chorus against the poet, as the latter writes to his friend Murray : "The journals are in convulsions, the town is in an uproar, and all because, as

Bedreddin remarks in the *Arabian Nights*, I made a cream
tart with pepper. How funny that eight lines should call
into existence nearly eight thousand."

Byron publicly answered all this yelping by a new
poem, "Windsor Poetics," in which he alludes to a notice
in the papers that the prince-regent had visited the royal
vault of Windsor, and had stood between the coffins of
Charles I. and Henry VIII.:

> "Famed for contemptuous breach of sacred ties,
> By headless Charles see heartless Henry lies;
> Between them stands another sceptred thing—
> It moves, it reigns—in all but name, a king;
> Charles to his people, Henry to his wife,
> In him the double tyrant starts to life;
> Justice and death have mixed their dust in vain,
> Each royal vampire wakes to life again.
> Ah, what can tombs avail, since these disgorge
> The blood and dust of both to mould a George!"

The "Lady Weeping" was from the very beginning
received into the heart of the whole English people.

Princess Charlotte also created a general sensation on
her first appearance in Parliament in December, 1812, when
the prince-regent opened the new session, by her unembarrassed intrepidity and native cheerfulness of manner in
spite of the furious looks of her father, who was very
strict in enjoining etiquette in all matters which respected
his own sacred person.

Shortly afterwards the independent action of the
princess called forth her father's resentment to a still higher
degree. She boldly wrote to the prime minister, Lord
Liverpool, that in a few weeks she would be seventeen
years old, and would therefore have outgrown the leading
strings of children and the supervision of governesses.
She accordingly begged for ladies-in-waiting instead of
governesses, and for a decent household such as was
proper to the heiress of the throne of England.

The prince-regent answered this challenge by calling
together the whole royal family to a privy council in
Windsor, where Princess Charlotte was severely taken to
task by the queen and the princesses, while her furious

papa over and over again rated her for "an obstinate, incorrigible girl, and a stupid fool," who owed it to his clemency alone that he didn't lock her up for life. She might depend on it she would never receive a household of her own till she was married.

To all these fatherly outbursts of rage the princess opposed a calmness that may almost be described as icy, and a silence that was storm-proof. And by this policy she so far accomplished her purpose that two lady-companions were substituted for the two under-governesses, and she received a town residence of her own in Warwick House, so that she no longer needed to live under the same roof in Carlton House with her father and his mistresses. The Duchess of Leeds was nominally appointed to be her head-governess—though in reality, perhaps, rather new head-spy—for when after this Windsor scene the princess for the first time visited her mother (whom she was now allowed to see but once a fortnight, and that only in the presence of lady companions) in her town residence of Kensington Palace, she flung herself passionately into the arms of her mother and whispered to her, in reference to the new head-governess in attendance, "For Heaven's sake be friendly to her!"

Lady Charlotte Bury was present at this sad meeting, and sketches to us the following picture of it:—"The princess was very pale but beautiful. Her figure showed the flower of full vigorous development. Her head, her arms, hands, and feet were well proportioned and nobly formed. I never saw a face which, with so little shade, expresses so many lively and various emotions. She spoke of her situation, and declared, in a very quiet but decided manner, she would not endure it. Her whole behaviour left the impression of a hasty penetrating spirit, of a vehement imperious will. Yet is there, also, a dash of romance in her character that might easily lead her astray.

"As the Princess of Wales was not allowed to speak with her daughter without witnesses, she had committed to paper everthing that lay on her heart to say. These written communications, concealed in a pair of shoes, she gave to her daughter to take home with her,"

A new incident again gave the world much to talk of. The Princess Charlotte was to be presented at Court at the first royal drawing-room of the new season, on the 4th February, 1813. When, however, the prince-regent returned a brusque refusal to her just demand—that the presentation should be made in the usual way, by her mother—the Princess Charlotte simply kept away from the drawing-room.

The Princess of Wales had at the same time sent a letter to her husband complaining that her daughter was not allowed near her in the very years when a mother's love was indispensable to the completion of her culture of mind and heart, and that Princess Charlotte had never yet been confirmed.

The Princess of Wales had this letter returned to her unopened, with the notice that the prince-regent did not desire any letters from the princess.

Lord Liverpool, the prime minister, to whom the princess handed over the same letter for his transmission and recommendation, also declared that to his regret he was unable to do anything in the matter.

In these circumstances the deeply mortified and provoked wife resolved on an extreme step—she published the letter in the *Morning Chronicle* of the 11th February, 1813.

The effect was that of a spark dropped in a powder magazine. All England started up in commotion. In the city public meetings were held, at which addresses of recognition and loyalty to the Princess of Wales were passed. Whitbread, a leader of the Opposition, gave notice in Parliament of a motion that the House should express its disapproval to the regent, and desire the Government to take into immediate consideration the grievances of the Princess of Wales and her daughter.

The prince-regent replied to this by a new infamy. He ostentatiously commanded the resumption of the "delicate investigation" against the Princess of Wales, and caused certain passages of Percival's "Book"—which was written in justification of the princess—to be torn from their connection and printed, with a view to proving by them the adultery of his consort. At the same time this devil in prince's form went to his daughter of seventeen years old, and in the most brutal manner uncovered before her aghast eyes all the sins and crimes of her "scandalous mother," thereupon announcing to her that; pending the new adultery investigation, she would not be allowed to see her mother any more.

Who might attempt picturing the state of mind of this royal virgin of seventeen, so deeply insulted and outraged in the person of her mother?

All that is possible for us is only to feel the deepest compassion with the poor creature, and unspeakable abhorrence and loathing of her monster of a father.

Princess Charlotte then declared if she was no longer allowed to see her unhappy beloved mother she would be invisible likewise to all the world besides. And so she shut herself up in Warwick House, refused herself to all visitors, and even dropped taking her customary drives. At last her father contrived to get it hinted to her that whispers were being circulated of a criminal intercourse between the Princess Charlotte and Captain Fitzclarence, the natural son of the Duke of Clarence, and of consequences resulting from it which prevented the princess from showing herself in public.

The fiend thus did not even spare the good name of his daughter, although he knew that the Princess Charlotte had not so much as once seen Captain Fitzclarence.

All the same, this devilry could not miss its effect. With hot tears of resentment in her beautiful eyes, the princess was again to be seen in her drives and in the opera.

Nor was the new royal "delicate investigation commission" bad enough to meet the will of the prince-regent and find the Princess of Wales guilty of adultery. It acquitted her of that charge, but so far complied with the wishes of her consort as to declare that the regent was completely justified in strictly forbidding all intercourse between mother and daughter.

The whole of England was incensed at this decision, and gave vent to its indignation in new meetings, new

addresses, and new Parliamentary speeches-in favour of
the Princess of Wales and her daughter.

When on one occasion the equipages of the two ladies,
—whether by accident or by secret arrangement—met in
Hyde Park, and mother and daughter, leaning far out of
the carriage windows, fell into each other's arms and in
the hurried passage exchanged tender kisses and words,
the floating public all round were touched at the scene
and showered their cheers and blessings over the affecting
meeting. Princess Charlotte's coachman, however, immediately received the strictest orders, under penalty of
dismissal, always to clear out of the way of the Princess
of Wales's carriage, and never to halt, even at the command of his mistress, when that carriage or the Princess
of Wales herself should be in sight.

But as well forbid the silk-worm to spin as forbid
mother and daughter from seeing, speaking to, and loving
each other. These two princesses, with the help of their
many friends, still often found opportunities of secretly
meeting.

In those days the Hereditary-Prince of Orange emerged
for the first time in the life of the Princess Charlotte as a
candidate for her hand. His *début* was assuredly little
prepossessing. It was on the prince-regent's birthday,
the 12th August, 1813, and on the occasion of festivities
held in connection with the inauguration of the new
military training institution of Sandhurst College, that the
princess first saw the Prince of Orange, afterwards Hereditary-Prince of the Netherlands, without feeling any
particular pleasure at the sight. The prince-regent was
in the worst humour, and spoke neither to his daughter
nor to her ladies. After the dinner he remained beside
his bottle at table among his knights of the glass. When
the queen-mother left for Windsor, her son George, his
brother, the Duke of York, his chosen son-in-law, the
Prince of Orange, and other good topers were far gone in
intoxication.

The Prince of Orange had served in Spain, and had
come to England, as adjutant of Lord Wolseley, with des-
patches. He had already the prospect of becoming Here-

ditary-Prince of the Netherlands when Napoleon's ascendancy was crushed. Such prospect rendered him specially agreeable in the character of son-in-law to the regent, for he wanted his troublesome daughter married to some foreign prince and out of his sight. Her growing popularity was an annoyance to him, and with his daughter the main prop in England of his hated consort would also be taken away.

On all sides every effort was made to dispose the Princess Charlotte for this marriage—on the side of the queen-mother, the princesses, the body physician, and her father. When in reply to their counsels she avowed her love for his uncle, the Duke of Gloucester, the prince-regent flew into a passion, and swore he would never give his consent to such a marriage.

On the 11th December the princess met the Prince of Orange at her father's. The regent was unusually kind to her, took her aside, and asked: "Well, how do you like him? It won't do?" She answered: "That I will not say. I like his ways very well." Thereupon the regent took hold of her hand, put it into the hand of the Prince of Orange, and presented both as a betrothed couple to the company.

When, next morning, the princess told her confidante, Miss Knight, of this betrothal by surprise, she added, resignedly, in reference to her intended, "He is not so disagreeable as I expected." Miss Knight, on his first visit, thought the Prince of Orange very common and sickly looking, rather boyish, open, and familiar in his behaviour; but not disagreeable for a young soldier. It would appear as though the princess took the first suitor that offered, in the hope of most securely escaping her father's tyranny in that way.

In January this betrothal was confidentially announced to other sovereigns. In March came an envoy from the Netherlands to London, and, in name of the hereditary-prince, formally sued for the hand of the princess. The princess gave the answer, "Yes," and took the bridal presents. King William of the Netherlands officially announced to the States-General the impending marriage of the hereditary-prince with the heiress to the throne of England. On both side plenipotentiaries were appointed to draw up the marriage contract.

In this marriage contract the prince-regent again thought to cunningly surprise his daughter into an arrangement which would set him free of her in England. When the princess first heard she would have to follow her husband into the Netherlands, and spend at least a large part of the year there, she burst into hysterical sobbing, saying that she had never thought of quitting England and her mother. And in the course of the negotiations she insisted with ever greater obstinacy on the insertion of the condition in the contract that she should not be compelled to leave England against her wish.

This condition was finally, in the first days of June, complied with by the adoption into the marriage contract of the paragraph : " It is understood and agreed upon that H.R.H. Princess Charlotte shall at no time leave the United Kingdom without written permission from his Majesty or the prince-regent, and without her Royal Highness's own consent."

So all hindrances in the way of this English-Orange marriage seemed to be removed. And yet, eight days later it was definitively broken off by the Princess Charlotte.

Once for all, she did not love the unbeautiful Prince of Orange. She said afterwards of him : " He did very well, perhaps, for a general of cavalry, but not for my husband. There was nothing of a prince in him."

She did not love her betrothed, and she had just begun to love the most handsome prince of his time—Prince Leopold of Coburg.

On the 31st March, 1814, the Emperors of Russia and Austria and King Friedrich Wilhelm III. of Prussia marched into Paris with their victorious troops. On the 7th June the three monarchs, on an invitation from the prince-regent and the English nation, met in London, and with them the handsome Prince Leopold of Coburg, not yet twenty-four years old, who had every sincere intention, it is believed, to make his fortune in England if possible. It is even probable that he had received a very distinct hint from England that it would not be a bad stroke on his part to come and cut out the Hereditary-Prince of Orange of the prize of the Princess-Royal of England, a stroke which should not be at all difficult for a paladin of such masculine magnificence of person as his. Nor is it less probable that this hint was sent him by a very shrewd and enterprising dame who had already been very carefully reconnoitring the ground in the English royal court, and putting everything there in best order for the arrival of Prince Leopold and the success of his adventure.

This dame was Catherine, Grand-Duchess of Russia, sister of the Emperor Alexander, and widow of the Duke of Oldenburg. Prince Leopold was the brother-in-law of her brother Constantine, and the special *protégé* of the Emperor Alexander, under whose protection he had taken part in the war against France. The Grand-Duchess Catherine, for her own part too, was very favourably disposed to the amiable Prince Leopold.

In the end of March the Grand-Duchess Catherine had suddenly alighted in the English royal court. What was her aim there? Understanding people discerned that she designed marrying the prince-regent if he succeeded in effecting his divorce from Caroline of Brunswick. Still more understanding people afterwards conjectured that she had come on a diplomatic mission. She was to prevent the proposed marriage between England and the Netherlands, so as to hinder England from acquiring too great a preponderance on the Continent. It would likewise be much more to the advantage of Russia that the Hereditary-Prince of Orange should marry a Russian grand-duchess, and that the Princess-Royal of England should be assigned to a prince of very modest pretentions—this nice-looking Leopold of Coburg, for example.

Be that as it may, so much is certain that the Grand-Duchess Catherine—if it was indeed with such far-reaching plans as these that she came to England—knew uncommonly well how to shuffle and deal out the cards. As to marriage for herself with the scamp of a regent, it is certain she had no thoughts that way. She was too clever and had too much taste for the like of that. The misfortune of the Princess of Wales was a daily beacon in her eyes. All the rest, however, of the programme attributed to her the skilful diplomatist accomplished: Breach of the alliance between England and the Netherlands; marriage between Princess Charlotte and Prince Leopold; and, later on, marriage of the Hereditary-Prince of Orange with a Russian grand-duchess, Anna Paulowna, sister of Catherine.

In a short time the Grand-Duchess Catherine succeeded in becoming the confidential friend and adviser of the young Princess Charlotte. She came frequently to Warwick House. Miss Knight calls her "a great politician, not to say intriguer." In the house of the grand-duchess, Princess Charlotte first came to know Prince Leopold. The handsome, chivalrous Prince Friedrich of Prussia is said, however, to have at first made a far deeper impression on the susceptible heart of the princess, till her friend Catherine explained to her that high politics would never give its consent to her alliance with Prussia.

Enough, the poor, unbeautiful and unamiable Hereditary-Prince of Orange was fairly "cut out;" and with the help of the worldly-wise grand-duchess a tolerably plausible ground was found in a few days for a complete breach with him. It all at once occurred to the Princess Charlotte that her intended was neglecting her mother just as much as did the foreign monarchs who, at the desire of the prince-regent, did not even pay a formal visit to the Princess of Wales. Her mother was excluded from all the festivities of the Court, and the Princess Charlotte therefore kept obstinately aloof from them, despite the fury of her father. In the mood of mind here indicated, Princess Charlotte on the 16th June declared to her intended, both by writing and word of mouth, that it would be impossible for her to leave England after the marriage. It was a duty she owed to her mother, whose sole protection she was, to be in her neighbourhood. She must at the same time make the demand that their common house after the marriage should always be open to the Princess of Wales.

When the hereditary-prince, bound by the regent, would not yield compliance with this demand the princess immediately avowed emphatically that in such circumstances the question of marriage could no longer be entertained. And by this resolution she remained, in spite of all prayers, representations, and threatenings on the part of her father.

During the visit of the monarchs the prince-regent was obliged to moderate the harshness of his behaviour towards his daughter. But he was keeping a stroke of policy in reserve. So soon as the Czar and the King of Prussia had quitted England's soil he suddenly appeared on the evening of the 12th July, like an avenging angel with fiery sword, in Warwick House, attended by the Bishop of Salisbury, delivered a furious harangue against his daughter, and intimated to her that her whole household was discharged, and would be replaced by a new. In Cranbourne Lodge, a solitary house in the forest of Windsor, she should find time to repent of her stiffnecked-ness. Nobody would be allowed to visit her there, except the queen-mother once a week. The carriage was in waiting to drive her in the meantime to Carlton House.

What a blow for the unsuspecting princess! In the greatest excitement she begs to be allowed to retire and dress herself for the drive. In her dressing-room she falls on her knees and prays—"Almighty God, give me patience!" She then throws a cloak round her, and, escaping, takes a hired carriage to her mother's in Connaught Place, while the prince-regent is waiting impatiently in the front room. When at length he hears of this flight of his daughter he gives expression to a malicious exultation. "This is capital! Everybody will now see what a nice jade the princess is! This new tale will run the Continent, and no prince will want to marry the baggage!"

A night full of excitement ensues! On one side the prince-regent in Carlton House holds long counsel with the prime minister and the lord chancellor as regards what should be done, after he had despatched the Bishop of Salisbury and Miss Mercer Elphinstone, the princess's most confidential friend, to Connaught Place, to bring back the runaway. On the other side the house of the Princess of Wales is in feverish excitement and activity. Messengers dash off on horseback to summon the Princess of Wales, who happens to be staying at the time at her villa near Blackheath ; the Duke of Sussex, a brother of the prince-regent, who had always evinced himself a particular friend of his sister-in-law and his niece; and the trusted adviser, Mr. Brougham. Later on there arrive, besides, Miss Knight, the Duke of York and the Lord Chancellor Eldon. All, however, agree that in present circumstances there was no resource open to her, at least for the present, but to submit to the paternal authority.

When Princess Charlotte complains that they are all forsaking her, while the people took the side of her and her mother, Brougham leads her to the window and says : " I need only show you to the crowds who in a few hours will animate these streets and Hyde Park, now sunk in the silence of night, and Carlton House would perhaps be torn in pieces. But an hour after the military would appear, and blood would be shed, and though you were to live a hundred years people would never forget that it was your flight from your father's house that caused such a misfortune. And you may rely on it, the horror of the English people at bloodshed is so great that they would never forgive you that hour ! "

After a long struggle the princess yielded to bitter necessity. Before, however, leaving her mother's house, she wrote down a protest against further violent measures, and had it signed by all who were present. The protest runs : " I am resolved never to marry the Prince of Orange. If such marriage should be announced, I wish people to remember this declaration of mine; it is a marriage with-out my consent and against my will, and I beg August, Duke of Sussex, and Mr. Brougham, particularly to take notice of this."

The Duke of York and the Lord Chancellor Eldon ac-companied the princess to her prison in her father's house, Carlton House. The princess was not allowed to leave her room, or see any of her friends or correspond with any one. Yet London heard of this new violence, and mur-

mured loudly and ever more loudly. The regent's brother, the Duke of Sussex, delivered a vehement speech in the Upper House against this incarceration of his niece, asking of the prime minister, at the same time, whether it was true that restraints were imposed on the princess, as on a person formally imprisoned; whether she was prevented taking use of the sea baths prescribed by her physicians; and whether the princess would be allowed a household conformable with her high rank?

Lord Liverpool answered these questions and all murmurs by simply saying that, by virtue of his fatherly authority, the prince-regent had the sole and alone power to dispose of Princess Charlotte, and that the Upper House had not the least right of intervention.

The regent now began to vent his fury against his rebellious brother. Sussex also, and declared to his family that they might choose between him and the Duke of Sussex; that whoever of them kept up friendly intercourse with the Duke of Sussex would be regarded by him as his personal enemy.

What a sad and desolate family picture does this act of the regent's suggest to us!

The Duke of Sussex's speech had nevertheless the effect of causing the princess to be transferred from Carlton House to Cranbourne Lodge. To be sure this was but a change of prisons. Yet was she able to breathe freely in the sylvan solitude of Cranbourne Lodge, as she had not been able to do before. She no longer breathed the same atmosphere with her father and jailor.

In these days of trial the Princess Charlotte was, furthermore, to lose her mother. The Princess of Wales, deeply mortified by the humiliations she had to suffer during the visit to London of the three monarchs, now gave up in weariness the struggle against her consort and executioner. Contrary to the advice of her most faithful friends she prepared to leave England. Her daughter was allowed to embrace her once more. On the 24th July, 1814, mother and daughter, with many tears, took leave of each other in the house in Connaught Place—little dreaming that they were never to see each other again.

In what acrid humour the Princess of Wales parted from England is evinced by the fact that at the last dinner with her daughter, when the latter spoke of happier days, and of a reconciliation with her father, the Princess of Wales, hastily pouring out a glass of wine on the table-cloth, said: " Sooner will this spilt wine flow back into the bottle than will my sentiments change towards those who have slandered me so grossly and basely ! "

In Prince Leopold's journal, in which he always speaks of himself in the third person, there stands written in reference to the period in question : " Prince Leopold accompanied the Czar Alexander to England. The Duke and Duchess of Kent were very friendly to the prince, as was also the Duke of York. The prince-regent was in a violent passion, first that the Princess Charlotte refused the Prince of Orange, and then that she fled to her mother. The public, in far the larger proportion, was favourably disposed to Prince Leopold, even the ministers, too; above all the Wellesleys, Lord Castlereagh, &c. In the end of July Prince Leopold left London. But before doing so he was graciously received by the regent who had become convinced that he had been plotting no mischievous intrigue. He was also present at a brilliant ball in Carlton House, where he received assurances of friendship from the whole family. The prince opened the ball with the Princess Mary. In those days the Dukes of Sussex and Gloucester did not appear in the circles of the regent or the ministers."

Prince Leopold went to the Congress of Vienna, where he succeeded in winning over the ever-bribable Gentz to the interests of the house of Coburg, and so securing favourable issues for Coburg. Withal, however, he did not forget his own interests in England. In his journal we read : " The Duke of Kent was good enough to forward some communications to the Princess Charlotte, who declared her resolution to abide firmly by her plans. The princess and her friends wanted the prince to come to England. He, on the contrary, was of opinion that it was better not to do anything with a high hand, which would only aggravate difficulties. The princess flouted at this excess of finicalness, but, as events afterwards showed, it was no more than reasonable caution."

Princess Charlotte was still kept like a prisoner in Cranbourne Lodge, even to the injury of her health. Not till the *Morning Chronicle*, in a sharp article, gave publicity to a medical opinion pronounced some months previously, urgently enjoining the use of sea baths for the Princess Charlotte, did the regent himself at last so far yield to the ever more minatory mutterings of public opinion, that at the end of August he allowed the princess to go and take sea baths at Weymouth, where she stayed till towards Christmas.

About this time the regent made another attempt to marry his daughter to a Prince of Orange, a younger brother of the rejected hereditary-prince. The princess refused having anything to do with this second Orange suitor as well. There were two images struggling for the supremacy in her heart—Prince Frederick of Prussia and Prince Leopold of Coburg. If the affair had all depended on the princess the chivalrous Prussian prince would have achieved an easy victory. But politics were against him.

In winter Princess Charlotte had again to take up her residence in Carlton House. But though living under the same roof with her father she saw him only when the queen came on a visit. Even on such occasions the regent had no word, not so much as a look, for his daughter. It was only to obey his strict commands that she existed at all. He himself had written out the short leet of persons whom she would be allowed to see. Once a week it was permitted her to go to the opera or theatre, but she was to sit as much concealed in her box as was possible, and always to leave the house before the close of the representation so as to avoid being seen and cheered by the public. For the same reason she was to take her drives in a completely closed carriage, no matter how ill she might feel in the "stuffy box."

On the 20th February, 1816, Prince Leopold of Coburg again suddenly dropped on English ground, having received an invitation from the regent himself, to whom, by a certain compliancy and submissiveness of manner, he had contrived to render himself agreeable.

In the prince's journal we read:—"In spite of the most pressing letters from England, Prince Leopold, in consequence of a severe cold, was unable to take a journey thither till February. In London he met Lord Castlereagh, with whom he went to Brighton in order to present himself to the prince-regent, who, though suffering from gout, received him graciously, and spoke of Princess Charlotte and his intentions in regard to her. There soon also came Queen Charlotte and the Princesses Augusta, Elizabeth, and Mary, and with them the Princess Charlotte. The friends of the last, belonging as they did to the Opposition, had inspired her with the fear that the prince would yield over much to the regent, and she gave very lively expression to this apprehension. A formal betrothal did not take place, but the marriage was declared to be agreed upon."

The "Journal of an Old Diplomatist" relates:— "London, 24th February, 1816.—John Bull bothers himself little about princes and their marriages; he has no idle curiosity, and has scarce any thought of his Highness of Saxe-Coburg."

The prudent and pliant Prince Leopold soon, however, managed to make himself popular, though he had to endure no little mockery of his poverty at the hands of the purse-proud English. People had found out that, as a younger prince of Coburg, his whole income was only £200 sterling, and the honest London grocer calculated that this revenue would just suffice in England to get him two coats and a dozen shirts. "But what matter? We can spare enough to trig him out decently!"

And yet at the last hour this project of marriage was in danger of suffering shipwreck. The regent made a fresh experiment of getting his daughter away from England, even when she would be consort of Prince Leopold, by proposing to appoint Prince Leopold commander-in-chief of the troops in Hanover. The princess, however, with the determination native to her, declared: "No, I shan't go to Hanover! I will never leave England! I will rather give up the marriage with Prince Leopold!"

The "Old Diplomatist" notes, under date the 26th

February :—" The rumour is again current that Prince Leopold is to be the new vice-king of Hanover; it comes from Carlton House (residence of the prince-regent in London). In this case the princess will go with him.

" The Court wind goes the round of all the points of the compass sixty times an hour, so that Court news has no more fixity in it than the moon which is now the ruling planet in the council of the regent. Since the arrival of Prince Leopold a new candidate has arisen, who is said to be supported by the whole Court. His name is at present, however, still a secret. The ministers play blindman's buff, and, with all their sagacity, they yet get the credit of having their eyes blindfolded. Since the arrival of this German there have been nice cabals enough at work.

" 11th April, 1816.—No news, with the exception that the Court puts on an air of altogether unusual secrecy. The marriage of the Princess Charlotte is again put off. There is said to be a more serious cause for this than the generality of people imagine. The Prince of Saxe-Coburg, since his arrival in our country, appears, unhappily, to have been very unwell.

" 17th April. Momus and his nightly host had again gathered in Carlton House to a drinking bout, when suddenly the news arrived that the fair rose of the State had given in her ultimatum in respect of the proposed marriage, and that the suit of the Prince of Coburg was rejected. Her Highness has, of course, set the whole inquisition of the State in alarm. The princess, seeing herself without any one to advise and help her, and cut off from all human intercourse, except that of the spies assigned to her by the queen, contrived at last to get two letters sent by post to the Duke of Sussex in Kensington Palace. In these letters she dwells on the peculiarity of her situation and on her unchangeable determination to receive a positive promise from Parliament that, in case of her actually marrying, she shall not be sent out of the country. She, further, unreservedly expresses her repugnance to certain members of the royal house. But how did she succeed in despatching these letters? She timed her return from a drive in Windsor so as just to hit the moment when the letter-bags were being sorted. By this manœuvre she balked all the cunning espionage on her movements.

"18th April. The Princess Charlotte seems disposed to set the whole conclave at their wits' end. Yesterday she said, 'I do not see that it is necessary for a queen to marry at all.'

"25th April. All possible means have been set agoing to bring the Princess Charlotte round again. The Duke of Kent says, 'The whole project would have collapsed if the prince-regent and the queen had not yielded. Seeing the princess has attained her object, she will now probably marry this Saxe-Coburg after all.'

"At the time when these marriage affairs came on the carpet the Court attempted to carry out everything with a high hand. This, however, the high-spirited girl would not brook. In the course of an interview at Cranbourne Lodge the queen lost command of herself and reproached the princess for her obstinacy with more vehemence than meekness. Her Royal Highness had destined the morning for the reading of a novel, and the book still lying at hand, she seized it and flung it not too softly at the head of the queen, who went off in high dudgeon."

The marriage was to come off in May. In the meanwhile Prince Leopold made a tour through England and Scotland. All the people rejoiced at this happy alliance, and the prospect at last of the establishment of peace in the royal Court. The Parliament voted a liberal sum by way of dowry: £60,000 sterling for furniture, wardrobe, silver plate and jewels, and a yearly allowance of £60,000 for the young couple. As a new town-residence for them, Camelford House, a palace of Earl Granville's, in the neighbourhood of Hyde Park, was purchased and fitted up, and later, as a country-seat, Claremont House, the property till then of Mr. Ellis, and situated fourteen miles from London, was acquired.

On the 2nd May, 1816, the marriage of the Princess Charlotte with Prince Leopold was solemnised in the church of St. James's. All England took part in the joy

of this occasion. In the same hour as many as 774 couples
were made happy for life in England, Scotland, and Ire-
land. From all sides poured in congratulatory addresses
to the princess, all couched in double superlatives, among
them one from the county of Kent twenty yards long.[*]
High praise was accorded to the princess for having her
bridal dress made only of home material.

At the same time a little fresh trait was told of the
wilfulness and impatience of constraint on the part of the
overbearing princess.

Before she drove to church to be married, Lady
Rosslyn, her lady-of-honour, read her a long chapter on
the etiquette and Court decorum to be observed on such a
solemn occasion, and the princess listened to it all with the
greatest meekness and edification. While, then, Lady
Rosslyn and Lady Chichester, in tip-top etiquette and consummate starched grandeur, advanced to the State equipage, her bridal Highness, poising herself on one foot,
hopped like a child at play up to the carriage, to the
amazement and exhilaration of the crowd of spectators.

When Lady Rosslyn had so far recovered from her
horror as to be able to instruct the princess anew concerning this breach of decorum and etiquette, her Highness, quite abashed, exclaimed: "Dear me, my lady! did
I not do the hopping to your satisfaction? Then I will
try it again." And back she hopped to the portal, and
then back again to the carriage—and so she hopped into
matrimony itself.

Yet "An Old English Diplomatist," who was eye-witness
of this marriage, notes in his journal: "The Princess
Charlotte looked altogether uncommonly depressed. As
to her royal father, he was not at all visible. The carriage,
attended by a large convoy of cavalry, drove from Carlton
House with the utmost speed. His Highness alighted
with the assistance of his valets, and repaired to the royal
apartments, with the same difficulty as usual.

"Notwithstanding all precautionary measures taken by

[*] "20 ells" in the original, which, if German ells of 24 inches
each are meant, would make ⅔ of 20 English yards.

the queen and the prince-regent, the Princess Charlotte
at once again begins to give proof of her hostile intentions.
Her remarks to Lady Rosslyn might be taken as a declaration of war. Alluding to her royal father, the princess,
regardless of consequences, said very pertly, ' It is better
to saddle horses than load asses,' hinting at the orders the
regent used to pile on his favourites. All representations
to her are of no avail, she has only deaf ears for all such,
and will, unless I am much mistaken, provoke such a
ferment as has not yet been seen in Old England. Thus
she has threatened publicly to insult Lady Conyngham
(her father's mistress). In regard to the persons of her
household, she said, ' Is it to be endured that I should
keep a host of people about me, who are literally of no use
but to serve as spies ? I shall send them all about their
business.' "

The young pair spent the honeymoon in Oatlands,
a property of the Duke of York. Of the princess of those
days, Christian Stockmar, who was then body physician to
Prince Leopold, has left us a characteristic sketch: " In
Oatlands I saw this star* for the first time. I found her
more beautiful than I had expected; she has peculiar ways
about her, her hands being constantly on her back, and
her chest and body always brought forward; she never
rests quietly on her feet, and from time to time would give
one stamp; she laughed much, and chatted still more. I
was measured from head to foot without, however, being
put out of countenance by it. My first impression was
not very favourable. In the evening she pleased me
better. The dress simple, but tasteful."

The marriage envoy from the Netherlands, Van der
Duyn, had written of the princess: " The princess is a
young lady who has the air of an unruly boy in petticoats
(l'air d'un garçon mutin en cotillon)."

May was not out when the new married couple took
possession of their town residence of Camelford House.
Court and town gave them a series of brilliant festivals.
In drives and in the theatre they were always greeted

---

* In the original " Sun," which in German is feminine.

with acclamation. In the opera the whole house joined in "God save the King." In Drury Lane Theatre, where "Henry VIII." was performed with Kemble, Kean, and Mrs. Siddons, the public enthusiastically clapped hands at every passage which could be interpreted in allusion to the tyrant, the prince-regent, and his unhappy spouse, the Princess of Wales, who was not so much as allowed to be present at the nuptials of her daughter.

Prince Leopold received the Orders of the Bath and Garter, the title of Field-Marshal and Privy Councillor, and the freedom of the City of London.

On the 21st June, 1816, the "Old Diplomatist" relates: "I have just spoken with an intimate friend of Camelford House. I am told a little rumpus had broken out between Prince Leopold and his consort. The Princess Charlotte is very unhappy. This Coburg has a bad disposition.

"16th July. The measures taken with a view to the prince-regent's divorce are not yet abandoned. Rumour says that Prince Leopold has a hand in the game, and that his participation was made an indispensable condition to the settlement on him of the £60,000 yearly, in case of the demise of her Royal Highness. The queen and the prince-regent have taken in hand the exclusion of the Princess Charlotte from the succession to the throne. Poor souls! They know not that public opinion is beginning to assume a formidable aspect!

"2nd August. I spoke in an earlier place of discord between certain members of the royal family. It is, perhaps, necessary to add that the Prince of Saxe-Coburg is not concerned in it. If his Highness attaches himself to any party it is that of his father-in-law, and he visits Carlton House almost daily.

"6th August. The prince-regent, in a *tête-à-tête* at dinner with Count Münster, wabbled about with his head in a manner reminding one of the well-known Chinese figures. He gossiped incessantly. The chief, if not the only, theme was the projected divorce, a topic in which his Highness as usual launched into a flood of invectives. The prince declared it was necessary to put a stop to the growing influence of Princess Charlotte. By this divorce he was not contemplating marrying again, but was only anxious to get a trump card into his hands which would give him unlimited power over his daughter. The question will be laid before the Upper House in the form of a Bill. There was no intention of having recourse to the Ecclesiastical Court.

"23rd August. - The Princess Charlotte has entirely withdrawn herself from the company of her father's acquaintances. It is her intention, she says, to appeal to the public. The ministerial party are highly incensed that she did not once visit her father during his illness.

"6th September. The regent has read the pamphlet in favour of the Princess Charlotte in the matter of the divorce, and suspects that the Duke of Sussex had his hand in the game."

Yes, the relations between daughter and father were of a sad description. The latter watched with jealousy every new homage Princess Charlotte received from the people. After having kept out of the sight of his daughter for several months, he made her a visit in August, when, heedless of all consideration for his daughter, he told her that he had now in his hands proofs of the repeated adultery of her mother, and he would institute a process against her. It is said that this scene of passion and agitation, in which the princess defended her unhappy mother, cost the young wife her first hopes of maternity.

With a glad sense of relief the young couple repaired in the end of August to the peaceful solitude of the beautiful Claremont House—far from the confusions and tumults of their town residence—far from the dread of an unloving and unloved father. Here in Claremont House began a still, peaceful life in a fair scene of nature, in a common favourite occupation with the culture of flowers, with music and reading—as also in mutual blissful love. Here in Claremont House Princess Charlotte grew to be, as she liked to call herself, the happiest woman in the land!

An English biography which appeared shortly after the death of the princess, but without the name of the author, gives us a graceful picture of this quiet life in Claremont. "Here, amid a circle of chosen friends, the heiress to the throne of Great Britain celebrated a true festival of love. In this rural retreat the charms of the princess, both in person and in mind, opened more beautifully than ever before. A lovely dignity shone from her clear eye; her figure grew fuller, her bearing more majestic, and in the delicate play of her complexion the red and white rose of England seemed to be united. The often too great vivacity which in earlier years distinguished her manner became more composed and governed. She was also zealously intent, as a happy spouse, on further cultivating her knowledge and talents. Finery of dress she never cared for, and put it on only when Court etiquette compelled her. Her dress was always extremely neat and well-chosen, but was in no way distinguished from that of any lady living in the country, except in so far as her truly royal deportment might set it off. The same order and punctuality which she observed in her attire she carried into everything she did. Her letters were models of clearness and definiteness. She had made it a rule never to leave a letter or petition more than twenty-four hours unanswered.

"She strictly observed with her husband the duties of Sunday observance. At her settlement in Claremont she desired not merely a quiet and peaceful home, but also, if possible, the means of undisturbed converse with heaven, especially in the recognised sanctity of Sunday. The parish of Esher lay too near the capital for the prince and princess at public worship there to escape the eyes of inquisitive idlers; the simple church soon got turned into a rallying place for fine dressed gentlemen and ladies, who came in showy carriages; regarded the village as a nice place for Sunday pleasuring; scrambled for the best seats in the church; and when once seated cast their eyes all round about them with anything but looks of devotion, to the disturbance of all solemn feeling, not only in the august pair, but also in the honest country people. To put a finish on such Sunday saturnalia, the princess got a private chapel erected in Claremont, and as clergyman she appointed her former teacher, Dr. Short.

"Her beneficence knew no bounds. When in the period of universal dearth so many needy people appealed to her that her own purse got empty, and her friends observed to her that she would herself have to apply for a subsidy to Parliament : ' No matter,' she said, ' I must give so long as I have anything myself, and I am convined the English people will never refuse me money to help the poor. To whom should the needy sooner turn for help than to me, I wonder ? '

" Her rare affability likewise knew no distinctions of class. When tradespeople came to Claremont on business it was the princess's first concern to relieve them of any embarrassment they might feel in respect of her presence. Nor had she ever any one among them to dun her about debt, for the princess thought there was nothing more degrading than debt.

" Her rural retirement and economic housekeeping life raised the princess in the esteem of the people more than all the splendour of Court festivities would have done.

" The regular distribution of the day into its several tasks was itself a source of constant pleasure to the princess; every hour bringing its own particular enjoyment. The happy pair were seldom seen apart. They drove, rode, walked together; visited together the huts of the poor, dispensing blessing wherever they came. The prince helped the heiress to the throne of Great Britain to water her pet flowers in the garden of Claremont, and she, in turn, rode with her husband to the chase. They went to London only when public affairs indispensably required their presence there.

" The morning was generally devoted to exercise in the open air. After dinner they plied their studies in common. The prince grounded her in politics, national economy, and history, and she gave him his lessons in English. They took sketches together of the fair landscape around them, their eye often directed to the distant Windsor Castle. The evening was generally closed with music, which both were passionately fond of.

" However much the princess liked to play and sing, she did not want any but a sincere opinion of her performance. Thus she once asked her music teacher what he thought of her playing and singing. He assured her in the fairest phrases he could think of that she sang charmingly and played enchantingly. When he came next day he got his fee and discharge. Her Royal Highness did not venture to think that she could profit by the instructions of a teacher who was base enough to flatter her against his own opinion, and had not uprightness enough to tell her her faults freely !

"A pretty trait is reported of the good-heartedness and just dealing of the princess. In her park of Claremont she once missed two old garden labourers. On her making enquiry about them she was told by the headgardener that they were too old and no longer fit for their work, and he had, therefore, discharged them. The princess thereupon indignantly commanded that the old men should be at once re-installed in their posts and receive their wages till their death, even when they were no longer able for any work."

Two German observers of the princess at Claremont in these days speak in a less enthusiastic strain. Stockmar, the body physician to Prince Leopold, writes in his diary, under date the 25th October, 1816:—"The princess is extremely mobile and lively, of an astounding susceptibility and nervous sensibility—so much so that the feeling excited by the momentary impression not seldom determines at once her judgment and her action. Her intercourse with her husband has, however, exercised a remarkably favourable influence on her, and she has gained to an astonishing degree in calmness and self-control, testifying more and more how good and honourable must be her nature at bottom. When in a good humour she is disposed to be very attentive to all about her, but, with all appearance of counting nothing of such favours, she does not mean other people to slight them. A want of due recognition of any token of friendliness on her part she highly resents, and whoever is guilty of such will long suffer in her good opinion. She never forgets that she is a king's daughter."

And Justus Erich Bollmann of Hanover, the clever and daring deliverer of Lafayette from the casemates of Olmütz, who, in the course of his eventful life came repeatedly to England and made a near acquaintance with Prince Leopold, writes to Varnhagen, on the 1st November, 1816:—" The Prince of Coburg and his princess love each other with the love generally found only among simple citizens. The unhappy position in which this princess grew up has so far proved a happy school for her, inasmuch as it prevented the early indulgence and consequent satiety so common in Courts. She feels and wills with energy. In a tragedy she weeps no end of tears, and in a comedy laughs till her bosom shakes. She nods, too, in the theatre to whoever she wishes well to—an odd princess, but an interesting creature."

How regardless, nay, how rude, this "odd princess" could occasionally be to persons she felt no sympathy with, may be seen in a drastic instance furnished by Stockmar's journal under date the 21st December: "Among those invited to a large dinner was Duke Prosper of Aremberg. He is a nasty little body, was black all over, and wore a star. The prince presented him to the princess, who was just engaged in conversation with the minister Castlereagh. She replied to his two enormous continental bows, without looking at him or addressing a word to him, simply by a slight nod of the head. At table, Duke Prosper was placed between Lady Castlereagh and the princess, who spoke not a single word to him, and brought her elbow so close to him that he was unable to stir. He kept looking straight in front of him with perceptible but not striking embarrassment, and now and again said a few words in French to Lady Castlereagh, who was so tall and grand that he looked like a child beside her. On his going away the princess took leave of him in the same manner as she had received him, and broke into a loud laugh before he was yet out of the room."

Pity that Prince Prosper of Aremberg was not man enough to read this "odd princess" a lesson that politeness is the first duty of a host—even though he be styled "Highness"—to his guest!

On the other hand, Stockmar's entries respecting the relations of the happy couple to each other make us pardon such a flaw in her behaviour as that just instanced. In his diary of the 17th October, 1816, we read: "In this house rule concord, peace, love; in short, all that is required for household happiness. My master is the best of all husbands in all the five divisions of the world, and his consort has for him a sum of love the magnitude of which can be likened only to the national debt of England."

And a year later, on the 26th August, 1817: "The married life of this couple is a rare picture of love and fidelity; a picture which never fails to impress all spectators who have a crumb of heart left in them capable of being impressed."

In December, 1816, the regent assembled all the royal family about him in Brighton—to a feast of peace and reconciliation! And indeed, after all we have seen, it cannot be said there was no need for it. The Princess Charlotte and her consort were also present. How little of a feast of love it was, however, may be inferred from the following characteristic anecdote:—

One evening in the family circle the Princess Charlotte, assuredly with very express intentions, sang the masquerade song from the then popular farce, "My Grandmother." At the close of it she turned to General E., and asked him in a sharp tone of voice which made her meaning very distinct, "What do you think of 'My Grandmother?'"

"It appears to me there is some humour in the piece," answered the general, evasively.

The princess with still sharper emphasis replied, "It appears to me there is a very great deal of ill-humour in it. The piece does not at all please me."

This intermezzo can hardly have improved the humour of the lady grandmother. The family broke up with much the same mutual love as that with which they gathered.

Other expressions also of the outspoken princess were reported, which were not less intelligible. Thus when it was once proposed to her that she should rent Marlborough House as a town residence, she declined the offer, saying, "I want no house in the town, I like better to be in the country. I hate your old queen, and do not want to come in contact with her."

And another time she said, laughing, "Leg of mutton agrees as ill with me as my grandmother!"

In the spring of 1817 the Princess Charlotte went to Claremont to await a new *accouchement*. The news was received with acclaim all over the land. After all the gloom of the present under a king who had lost his wits, and under a regent who was lying swamped in his own debaucheries, here, then, was a golden future beckoning to us! Enormous were the bets laid as to the sex of the coming child. Were it a princess, *that* would raise the funds $2\frac{1}{2}$ per cent.; were it a prince, *that* would send them up 6 per cent.—so ran the calculation at the Exchange. It was the desire of the Government that the princess should await a confinement of so great moment in the capital, seeing that according to the law of the realm high dignitaries required to be present. Princess Charlotte, however, would not part from her beloved Claremont. And so she continued there.

In the end of October the royal body-physicians, Dr. Baillie and Sir Richard Croft, took up permanent residence in Claremont. The princess was uncommonly well—nay, in the opinion of the physicians, "too well." The physicians had been already endeavouring to counteract an "excess of humours" by repeated phlebotomy and by the sparest diet—without duly considering that they were thereby reducing the strength of the lying-in patient for the hour of travail. And so after two and fifty hours of sore labour the unhappy woman, on the 5th November, 1817, gave birth to a dead boy, and after five hours more lay a corpse herself. Her last wish was that her husband might one day be laid by her side! This wish was not fulfilled. Leopold of Coburg, as King of the Belgians, rests in Belgian earth—at the side of his royal spouse, Louise of Orleans.

The body-physician, Christian Stockmar, had meanwhile known how to acquire for himself in high degree the confidence of Prince Leopold and the Princess Charlotte. The prince soon made use of him as his confidential secretary, and named him "my dearest soul-and-body-doctor." With the prudence and foresight that were all his own, Stockmar, however, declined during the time of the pregnancy and *accouchement* of the unhappy princess to render her any advice or help—in order later on to lie under no responsibility. In my opinion, however, cousin Christian on this occasion carried his distinguished prudence too far; for he has himself often said to me, " The princess had not died so young and so sore a death if I had treated her by myself in the German way ! "

Respecting the death of the princess, Stockmar relates in his diary : " On the fifth day towards noon the pains grew severer, and at last at nine o'clock a beautiful, very big, boy came dead to the world. No artificial aid had been applied. Immediately after the birth, the mother felt quite well. The news of the death of her child had not particularly affected her. This apparent well-doing, however, continued only till midnight. Then Croft came to my bedside and said that the princess was seriously ill and the prince alone, would I go and inform him of the state of matters? For three days the prince had not one moment left his consort, and had just lain down after the birth. I found him composed about the death of the child, nor did he appear to take the state of the princess for very serious. After a quarter-of-an-hour, Baillie sent me word, he wished I would see the princess. I hesitated, but at last went with him. She was in great anguish and restlessness, from cramp in the chest and difficulty of breathing, and tossed about constantly from one side to the the other, speaking now with Baillie, now with Croft. Baillie said to her, ' Here is an old friend of yours ! ' She hastily reached me her left hand, and twice pressed mine vehemently. I felt her pulse; it was going very quickly, the beats now heavy, now light, now intermittent. Baillie constantly handed her wine. She said to me, ' They have made me tipsy.' So, for about a quarter-of-an-hour, I went out and in two or three times. Then her breath began to rattle in her throat. I was just gone out of the room when she called very urgently, ' Stocky! Stocky!' I turned back. The rattling sound continued. She laid herself several times on her stomach, and drew up her legs. Her hands got cold. At two in the morning of the

6th November, 1817, that is, about five hours after the birth, she was no more."

And Prince Leopold was not at the death-bed of his consort. He lay comfortably in his own bed. Stockmar brought him the news of the death. In his diary it is written: "He did not believe she was yet dead, and on the way to her he fell into a chair. I knelt beside him. He thought it was only a dream, he could not believe it. He sent me once more to look at her. I came again, and said it was all-over. We now went to the room of death. Kneeling by the bedside he kissed the cold hands, then rising, he pressed me to him and said: 'I am now quite forsaken; promise me, to keep ever by me.' I promised it. Immediately after, he questioned me whether I was well aware of what I promised. I answered, 'Yes, I would not forsake him so long as I could perceive that he trusted me and loved me, and that I could be useful to him.'"

And this promise Christian Stockmar honourably kept. Soon after the death of the princess, he wrote to his sister in Coburg: "I leave the prince only when pressing business demands. I eat alone with him, and sleep in his room. So often as he awakes in the night I get up, and sit talking to him at his bedside till he again falls asleep. I feel more and more that my allotment in life is all made up of changes and turns which one never sees beforehand, and that so, too, will it be in the future, till we drop at the end into we know not where. I seem to be here more to look after others than for my own sake, and I am very well content with that allotment."

Thus from being the body-physician Christian Stockmar came to be the trusted and trusty friend and adviser of Prince Leopold up to the time of his last breath.

On the 18th November the remains of the Princess Charlotte and her child were transferred from Claremont to the Royal vault of St. George's Chapel in Windsor. At the wish of Prince Leopold so much was hewn out from the wall of the narrow vault as to leave room there for the reception one day of his own coffin! We know that this labour was done in vain.

Prince Leopold was inconsolable. The whole of England sympathised with his sorrow. Bollman writes on the subject to Varnhagen under date the 28th November: "The death of the Princess Charlotte has called forth many unfeigned tears. My daughters could not for many days recover their usual composure of mind, and this was a general sentiment. The fair pattern of a life morally pure, and in the highest degree happy, had awakened in behalf of the princess and the prince a very great and universal interest, to which were attached many hopes now for ever destroyed. A whole series of ideas and feelings now course about in the empty void without any fixed point to hold by, for in regard to the future succession all now looks remote. The Prince of Coburg now stands in a very favourable light before the nation. If he does not mar his association in public opinion with the dear departed, and continues to stand out prominently as a nobleman of unstained morals amid the corrupt rout (the Prince of Wales and his brothers), then in my opinion the progress of events might render his future life one of great consequence. But there is still a long interval before that, and so few are proof against a change of position."

In public dark secret rumours were set afloat that the Princess Charlotte and her child had not died a natural death. The same evil genius which for twenty years had persecuted the Princess of Wales and her daughters with fanatical malice had at last triumphed.

Only two days after the death of the princess the regent sent the luckless *accoucheur* the expression of his thanks and confidence in the following letter: "By command of the prince-regent, Sir Benjamin Blomfield is commissioned to thank Sir Richard Croft for the zeal and attention which he showed during the *accouchement* of the beloved princess. At the same time his Royal Highness assures him of his full confidence in respect of the correct medical treatment of the case, although his Highness has, by the will of Providence, been cast into the deepest mourning."

This great zeal on the part of the prince-regent is at all events very surprising in the face of medical authorities, who maintain that the princess's death would hardly have happened if her strength had not been artificially reduced too low, and if artificial aid had been applied at the right time during her deliverance.

Three months after the death of the Princess Charlotte Sir Richard Croft shot himself.

Since ever the misfortune in Claremont he had been " in a state of the deepest anxiety and excitement, bordering on mental derangement, so that he often lost all self-composure." In the beginning of February he was staying out the night in the house of a lady to assist at her difficult deliverance. This event, as in the case of the princess, protracting itself to an unusually long period, he shot himself in the night.

" I will live and die in Claremont, and will employ every moment of my still remaining life in executing the thoughts and plans of the angel whom I have lost for this world." Such was the exclamation of Prince Leopold in Claremont in the first anguish of his sorrow by the dead body of the Princess Charlotte.

For full twelve years he continued to live in Claremont as heir of his consort. From England he drew a yearly income of £50,000, the sum settled on him in the marriage contract. In memory of the princess he erected on an islet in the park lake a monument with an urn overshadowed by weeping willows.

The hat and shawl worn by the princess the last time she went out were still hanging in my time untouched at the same spot where they hung at her death.

All those twelve years in Claremont little was heard of Prince Leopold. It was a sign of great prudence on his part that he kept as much away as possible from the royal family in their embroiled relationships.

A perfect fury for marrying now took possession of the royal family, in order to produce, if possible, an heir for the throne of England. The three already married sons of the insane King George III., the prince-regent and the Dukes of York and Cumberland, were childless. It was in 1819 before the last had a son by the Princess Frederica of Mecklenburg-Strelitz, the sister of the deceased Queen

Louise of Prussia—afterwards King George, the last king of Hanover.

Princess Charlotte, the heiress to the English throne, was not yet a year in her grave when the Duke of Clarence, who was fifty-three years old, the Duke of Kent, who was fifty-one, and the Duke of Cambridge, who was forty-four, took all three to themselves German princessess in marriage : the Princesses of Meiningen, of Coburg, and of Hesse-Cassel. The Princess Victoria of Coburg was a sister of Prince Leopold, and widow of the Prince of Leiningen. She it is who, of all three, was called to give England an heiress to the throne—the present Queen Victoria. That she was a playmate of my mother I have already related.

Stockmar describes the thirty-two-year-old Princess of Leiningen at the time of her marriage with the Duke of Kent in the following words : "She was of middle height, stout and full, yet of good build, with beautiful brown hair and eyes, and, in addition, of remarkable youthful freshness; naturally cheerful and friendly; altogether a lovely and charming appearance. She was also fond of fine clothes, dressing well and tastefully. Nature had endowed her with warm feelings, and her natural dispositions were altogether on the side of truth, love, and friendship; of unselfishness, compassion, nay even magnanimity itself."

The Duke of Kent, like all his brothers, was sunk deep in debt, so that immediately after the marriage he took possession of the Castle Amorbach of Prince Leiningen in Bavaria—in order to save money abroad. When, now in Spring, the duchess was in hopes of becoming a mother, and giving England an heir to the throne, it was thought highly desirable that so joyous an event should take place in England; but it was found that they had not the necessary means for the removal. The regent and his other brothers being unable, or unwilling, to give the needed assistance, the duke and duchess were obliged to scrape the money together among their friends. By this shift the Duke of Kent managed to get back to England with his consort in Spring. There, accordingly, on the 24th May, 1819, a little daughter was born—"round like a

stuffed-out dove "—named Victoria, from her mother—now
Queen of Great Britain and Empress of India. The old
duke was no little proud of his chubby rosy cherub of a
daughter. He took no trouble to hide his exultation before all the world, proud as he was of saying, "Take care
of her, for she will one day be Queen of England!"

This prophecy was fulfilled, as was also another made
to the Duke of Kent:—" In the year 1820 two persons of
your family will die." The good duke thought at first,
of course, of his old, insane, and blind father, King George
III., now eighty-one years old, and then earnestly asked,
"Which of my licentious brothers will be the first to
go?" For it was a pet saying of his, "My brothers are
less healthy than I; I have lived regularly; I shall sur-
vive them all; the throne will devolve on me and my
children!"

And yet he was to be the first called away. At the
end of the year he had gone with his family to the sea
coast of Sidmouth " to cheat the winter." During a walk
he caught a cold which resulted in inflammation of the
lungs. Prince Leopold and his body physician, Dr. Stockmar, were summoned by the duchess. Stockmar writes:
—" On the day before his death arrived General Wetherall,
an old servant and friend of the duke. He put the question to us physicians whether it would do any harm to the
duke to speak with him about the signing of a will. To
help to a decision of the question, the duchess conducted
me at five o'clock in the evening to the patient. I found
him half delirious, and told the duchess that human aid was
no longer of any avail, and, in reference to the will, the
only question was whether it would be possible to arouse
the duke to such complete consciousness as would give his
signature legal force. Thereupon Wetherall went to the
duke, and the presence of his youthful friend had a remarkably animating effect on the nervous system of the
dying man. Wetherall had hardly addressed the duke
when the latter came completely to himself, enquired after
several things and persons, and had his will read out
twice to him. Gathering together the last remains of his
strength, he set himself to sign it. With difficulty he

pierced out the 'Edward' under the will, looked attentively at each letter, and asked whether the signature was distinct and legible. Then he sank back on his pillow exhausted. The following morning he had ceased to be."

That was on the 23rd January, 1820. Six days after died the old King. George III. The Prince of Wales ascended the throne of Great Britain as George IV.

*   *   *   *   *   *

CHAPTER XXVI.

CAROLINE, PRINCESS OF WALES.

AND where, meanwhile, was the unhappy mother of Princess Charlotte living all the while her daughter had got married to Prince Leopold, passed through her short matrimonial happiness, and then died?

On the 9th August, 1814, the Princess of Wales went first to Brunswick and then to Italy, to enjoy her new freedom in full draughts such as the thirst of long restraint craved. Soon the world was full of the love adventures of the mad princess. She grew "bad," as her daughter called it. Her life became like one continuous, motley, wasteful carnival—one continued riot of sensuality. After living several years in Milan, in her beautiful Villa d'Este on the Lake of Como, in Rome, at the Court of Naples, in Sicily, in Greece, Ephesus, and Jerusalem, in the company of the Italian, Bartolomeo Bergami, whom she raised with rapid succession from the post of courier to the position of chamberlain, head steward, Baron della Francina, Knight of Malta, and Grand Master of the Order of St. Caroline, founded by her in Palestine, the Princess of Wales came in the spring of 1817 to Carlsruhe, and here as a little girl of ten years I repeatedly saw her, little foreboding that a strange fate had decreed for me a destiny similar to that of the unhappy lady's daughter, and that my whole after-life should thereby be forced into the most baleful courses.

The whole of Carlsruhe fell into the greatest excitement when on the noon of the 26th March the report ran the town that the Princess of Wales, Caroline of Brunswick, so long the talk of the newspapers, had just arrived with a large Italian suite and in the most whimsical dress, had alighted at the Hotel "Zur Post," had at once driven

in a Court carriage to the margravine and the ruling
Grand-Duchess Stephany, and had returned after a remarkably short stay.   The margravine, as mother-in-law
of the Duke of Brunswick who fell at Quatre Bras, was a
relation of the Princess of Wales.   People talked of the
magnificence of the striking Turkish costume in which
the "mad princess" and her suite, which comprised a
real Mussulman, had appeared at Court.   In the evening
the princess dined in her hôtel with the windows open,
and kept up free and undisguised merriment.

     So I learned from my school friend, Fanny Glöckner,
who lived opposite the "Post," and could look into the
princess's windows.

     Of course I visited Fanny next morning to spy a little
of the interesting princess through the windows.   And I
was to be fortunate.   For soon our handsome, chivalrous
grand-duke appeared at the door of the hotel, with a little,
stout, elderly dame in a scarlet riding-habit on his arm.
That, then, was the "mad princess."   I thought our Grand-
Duchess Stephany much more beautiful and graceful.

     On the Titus head of the princess sat with an air of
fool-hardiness a cap of black velvet, with white feathers
dangling downwards.   In what a roistering and unembarrassed style the red Amazon chatted and laughed, while
she swung herself flauntingly into the saddle, so that her
dress, flapping in the breeze, flopped into the abashed eyes
of the numerous onlookers an unavoidable glimpse of flesh-
coloured tights.   The grand-duke had apparently the
wind quite knocked out of him by these flourishes on the
part of his merry cousin, who, coming a smart stroke with
her riding whip between the ears of her horse, dashed off
with a laugh, leaving her dumbfounded cavalier to try
and follow up as best he could.

     "Quite a circus lady rider!" said Frau Glöckner.

     Another time the princess rode through the town in
the style of a brilliant pasha decked with three horsetails,
and attended by the whole shouting youth of Carlsruhe,
myself among the number.

     The grand-duke, however, was no longer to be per-
suaded to her side!

In the evening the "Magic Flute" was given in honour
of the august guest. I was allowed to accompany mother
to the opera. The house was festively illuminated; and
the ladies had dressed themselves in grand toilette. In
the box to the right of the proscenium sat the grand-duke
and his darling consort. In my mind I still see the grand-
duchess in all her loveliness; she wore a light blue satin
dress, pearls round the graceful neck, white natural roses
in the beautiful blond locks.

The margravine, in dark velvet with brilliants, awaited
the arrival of the guest in her purple box, and cast frequent
embarrassed glances through the house and into the grand-
ducal box. The Princess of Wales let herself be long
waited for.

The grand-duke paid a visit to his revered mother in
her box, and looked repeatedly and impatiently at his
watch. At length, after three quarters of an hour of the
most painful waiting, the grand-duke gave the intendant
a signal to begin without the guest.

The swell of the overture passed by. The curtain rose,
and still there was no Princess of Wales visible. *Tamino*
fled before the serpent, the three black ladies appeared,
sang and disappeared. At last, when *Tamino* sang with
voice of melting sweetness:

> " Dies Bildniss ist bezaubernd schön,
>   So schön wie ich noch nie gesehn!" *

then the door of the margravine's box was noisily banged
open. All eyes were turned in that direction, and from
the gallery burst a ringing laughter, in which the whole
house more or less loudly joined.

In the margravine's box stood the Princess of Wales in
the vast hood worn by the Oberland peasants, with fluttering ribbons and glittering spangles.

The margravine leaned back in her fauteuil almost
fainting, and put her hand over her eyes. She seemed
so shocked at her august and fantastically-dressed

---

* " This picture charms my sense and soul.
   I ne'er saw aught so beautiful."

guest as to have completely lost all composure and speech.

The Princess of Wales advanced, however, with a triumphant smile to the centre of the box, while a laugh suffused the whole of her round, red face, and she nodded cordially across to the ducal box, quite proud of the crazy fancy which prompted her to exhibit herself before the good Baden people in the country peasant costume. I imagine I still see the large black knots and broad ribbons set with spangles, fluttering and dancing as the wearer described those pleasurable movements.

The Grand-Duke and Grand-Duchess Stephany at once recoiled into the back part of their box, and soon disappeared from the house. At the close of the act the margravine also got up and the guest was obliged to follow her.

What fine commentaries were made that evening in the Carlsruhe Theatre about the "mad princess."

I also saw the "beautiful Bergami" in a neighbouring box, in the Oberland head-dress. He was very tall and broad shouldered, with dark, fiery Italian eyes, and a proud smile on his broad lips. There was a touch of wildness and lowness of nature in his face, and in his whole bearing. On his glaringly red uniform sparkled three mighty orders and a golden chamberlain's key; on his golden scabbard were seen the portraits of the bye-gone royal family of Naples, the Murats. Beside Bergami appeared a blond youth, Billy Austin, whom the princess called her adopted son, but whom the Prince of Wales and the evil-tongued world insisted on placing in a much nearer relationship to the light-living princess. It could not but provoke remark that the princess made this Billy Austin, the pretended son of a sailmaker's widow in Deptford, her principal heir.

At a Court dinner the Princess of Wales wore a dress with train embroidered with silver and deeply open in front, on her round head an old Bavarian silver ringlet cap surmounted by a diadem of brilliants, a gigantic bouquet on her breast.

Two pretty water-pictures are now before my eyes.

One represents the Princess of Wales as she appeared at the Court of Carlsruhe : in a short lilac velvet dress, with broad silver embroidery swelling protuberantly round the hips (Cul de Paris) according to the then prevailing fashion, and narrowly pointed round the ankles ; led on one hand by the little lean Baden Court Marshall von Ende and on the other by her gigantic scarlet-red Bergami.

The other picture exhibits the same little, stout, old princess in the same costume, with a grand velvet cap fluttering in waving ostrich feathers on her head, her round arms raised and her fingers snapping, as she dances on dainty foot-tips before the Court of Carlsruhe a solo dance—the fiery Neapolitan tarantella !

Both pictures were painted from life at that time by a Baden Court lady, and now sent to me, after more than half a century, by her niece—in thankful acknowledgment of my first published reminiscences of the Carlsruhe Court.

For a drive with the Court to Baden the Princess of Wales had adorned herself to the nines in the style of an artist-rider.

The reckless princess deeply wounded the unhappy Queen Frederica of Sweden, who was a daughter of the margravine, and was likewise staying as guest at the Carlsruhe Court, by ostentatiously embracing the queen on every occasion, and exclaiming, in all too loud tones :

" Chère Cousine, we must cling fast to each other in friendship as faithful sisters of a common fate—we two who have been unworthily forsaken by wicked husbands ! "

When, however, the Princess of Wales saw more plainly every day that the people of Carlsruhe would sooner see her go than stay, she returned to Italy, homeless and restless, endeavouring to drown her measureless misery in wild Bacchanalian revelry.

Into the midst of this carnival riot of the senses, there fell like a bolt from heaven the terrible news : " Your daughter, the Princess Charlotte, died on the 6th November in child-bed."

And this saddest of all intelligence the unhappy mother learnt, not from her husband, nor from her sorrowing son-in-law (Prince Leopold), nor from sympathetic relations and friends, nor by the couriers of the English Government who carried the mournful news to all princely Courts—no, but the poor mother's heart read accidentally in the newspapers how she was now totally impoverished and forsaken.

The unhappy mother mourned long and deeply in her villa on the Como lake. Had she not with her daughter, and the heiress to the English throne, lost her all on earth; her last prop, her last love, her last hope! Alas! too, she lost at the same time the last scruples of consideration which she had hitherto imposed on herself. With a shrill laugh of despair, she exclaimed: "Since no one on the side of England will any longer deign me the great honour of being the Princess of Wales, then will I be Caroline alone—a merry, wanton soul!"—and plunged anew into life—pleasure—wild love.

It was not till the news came that her father-in-law King George III. had died, and her husband now reigned as George IV., so that by right of law she was queen—it was not till such intelligence reached her that Caroline's old energy revived.

In spite of the protest of George IV. and his golden offers of an increased appanage—in spite of the advice of her apprehensive friends, and in spite of an old prophecy of her maiden years, to the effect that she would be queen but never sit on a throne or wear a crown—in spite of all obstacles and scruples Queen Caroline hastened to England to claim her royal rights.

In his rage George IV. immediately ordered the Archbishop of Canterbury to strike out the name of Queen Caroline from the prayer-book, and the high clerical dignitary obeyed—a compliance which drew on him the stinging public speech from the Earl of Grosvenor that if he (the earl) had been Archbishop of Canterbury he would sooner have flung the prayer-book at the king's head than, contrary to law and conscience, have struck the name of the queen out of the liturgy.

On the 6th June, 1820, Caroline arrived in London, festively hailed as queen by the shouting people. But what new humiliations, what new ignominy awaited her

on the side of the king, her consort! By his command
she was to have no existence as queen. And on the day
of her arrival in London her husband, for the third time,
preferred the charge of adultery against the "Princess of
Wales," as he obstinately called the lawful Queen of
England, before Parliament. Throughout all her tours,
the Prince of Wales had begirt her with spies, and had
caused material to be collected about the Italian Bergami
in particular. For five months the lords sat in judgment
on this, unhappy queen, and then she was, for the third
time, acquitted "for want of evidence." This decision
was received with exultation by all England. London
illuminated itself for three evenings in honour of the acquitted queen, and wherever she was seen she was
welcomed by the shouts of the people, "God bless you,
dear Queen!" These were the last rays of sunshine in the
life of the unhappy woman, mother, and queen.

On the 19th July, 1821, George IV. was crowned with
great pomp in Westminster. Pomp and noise had to make
up for the absence of shouts from the people.

When Queen Caroline, in grand Court toilette, wanted
also to enter Westminster to take her proper place beside
the throne of the king, she was turned back at the gates,
"because she could not produce a card of invitation."

On the eleventh evening after this coronation day Queen
Caroline, in Drury Lane Theatre, drank a glass of lemonade.
Immediately she called out, "They have poisoned me!"
In great pain she was taken home. On the 7th August
she died. By her last wish, her corpse was removed to
her natal Brunswick. As the funeral procession passed
through the streets of London, it was everywhere greeted
with lamentations and tears, and a murmuring passed
through the crowd, "She was murdered, the poor queen,
murdered like her unhappy daughter!" The king's
carriage, on the other hand, was assailed with impreca-
tions, and the Court-mourning he had appointed was made
mock of.

Prince Leopold, meanwhile, still continued staying in
Claremont, keeping as far away as possible from the dissensions between his royal parents-in-law. Not, however,

to spoil his interest with the English people, who stood so
decidedly on the side of the queen, he risked the king's
anger, and made one single visit to the mother of his
Charlotte.

In a short autobiography, written in his old age for
Queen Victoria, Leopold, King of the Belgians, relates of
those days :

" The new king, George IV., showed himself at first
very friendly towards Prince Leopold, in anticipation,
probably, of the now impending complications with his
wife, Queen Caroline. The Duchess of Kent (Princess
Victoria of Coburg, sister of Prince Leopold), with her
two daughters, Princess Feodore of Leiningen, now
Princess Hohenlohe, and the little princess, now Queen
Victoria, frequently stayed in Claremont. The arrival
of Queen Caroline (June, 1820) set the whole land in
embroilment. Prince Leopold's position between her
and the king was intolerably repugnant. A severe illness of his mother, the Dowager-Duchess of Coburg,
offered indeed a pretext for leaving England, and so
steering clear of the painful dissension which now began
to assert itself. The king, too, much desired the adoption
of this expedient, and sought through Lord Lauderdale to
dispose matters in that way ; but how was it possible for
the prince to abandon the mother of his departed Charlotte,
who, of course, was well acquainted with her mother and
loved her right dearly ?

" The prince resolved not to mix himself up in the
divorce case till the hearing of the evidence against the
queen had been concluded. In this way he avoided every
appearance of seeking to exercise any influence in the
affair. Evidently this resolution was as honourable as it
was impartial. The prince therefore waited till the
evidence was terminated, and then made one visit to his
mother-in-law. She received him with great friendliness,
showed an odd appearance, and said odd things. The
country fell into great excitement on the subject, and for
the queen this visit was a real trump card. On the Upper
House this visit had an effect beyond what was reasonable,

seeing that it could not alter in any way the evidence already closed. It is, however, certain that many lords changed their views, and that the ministers came to the conviction not to carry matters any further. They motioned to let the suit drop. The king, who, as must be allowed, was not handsomely treated in this sad affair, was furious, especially against Prince Leopold. Revengeful as he was, he never forgave him, though occasionally, to be sure, especially so long as Canning was minister, he showed himself rather disposed to be friendly. At first, of course, he declared the prince should never again appear before him. Yet the Duke of York arranged a meeting. Here the king could not bridle his curiosity, and caused the prince to relate to him how the queen was dressed, and more of such things. After the coronation (July, 1821) Prince Leopold went to Coburg, and returned in January, 1823, to England by way of Italy, Vienna, and Paris, when the unhappy Queen Caroline was long dead and forgotten."

Prince Leopold and Stockmar likewise believed in the queen's having been poisoned—but were glad to get rid of her so soon.

The visit Prince Leopold made Queen Caroline had another motive beyond what is above alleged. The prince was very superstitious, and told me himself that the spirit of the Princess Charlotte had appeared to him at that time and looked at him sadly and rebukingly, that thereupon he made the visit to her mother, and that thereafter the spirit of Charlotte was appeased and did not reappear.

CHAPTER XXVII.

LADY ELLENBOROUGH.

To the time of that retired still life in Claremont belong also those "stupid love-affairs" of the prince, of which cousin Christian spoke to us.

Two of these "ladies of the heart" I afterwards met —not without strange sensations.

The Countess Ficquelmont, wife of the Austrian ambassador at the Court of the Czar, I came to know in St. Petersburg in 1831 through the Countess Fersen. She was a Viennese minx, and soon proved a too expensive sweetheart for Prince Leopold, who studied economy even in "matters of the heart." She showed much sympathy with me, as one of her successors in the heart of the seductive prince, during my three years' engagement in St. Petersburg, and furnished me with very friendly letters of recommendation for Vienna, whither I went on a professional visit, both to the French ambassadress there and also to Prince Gortschakoff, who afterwards attained to such celebrity, and was at that time first *attaché* to the Russian Embassy at the Court of Vienna.

Another "stupid love-affair" of Prince Leopold had to me, as it will also have to my readers, when I mention the name, more interest—that of Lady Ellenborough. The name was known all over the world in the thirties of this century. It was in all the papers and on all lips just as the Princess of Wales, Caroline of Brunswick, had been ten years before. Both ladies also resembled each other very much, in the insatiableness and recklessness of their wild hearts.

In the year 1824 the charming Jane Elizabeth, the growth of but fifteen summers, the daughter of the highly-esteemed Admiral Henry Digby, the boasted pride of the

London season, became against her own inclination wife
of the haughty Tory Lord Ellenborough, who was then
the main support of the Wellington cabinet.   But how
does the song run ?

> " Es war ein alter König—
> Sein Sinn war starr—sein Haar war grau—
> Der arme alte König,
> Er nahm eine junge Frau." *

And there was a fair young page, Who bore the silken
train, Of that young lovely queen—and they loved each
other, I ween.

The melancholy end, however, of the old song, "Sie
mussten beide sterben," † does not suit the present case.

The fair young Lady Ellenborough and her young
handsome page, "with his light-mindedness," were not
doomed to die, but, on the contrary, enjoyed their fill of
youth and love.   It was even said that the grave minister
had no objections to his young nephew, a jolly naval
cadet, entertaining his wife with his company while his
lordship was engaged in high politics.

Lady Ellenborough then bore a beautiful blond boy,
who afterwards, when Lord Ellenborough became
Governor-General of India, distinguished himself in the
Afghan wars.

Soon, however, Lady Ellenborough got satiated of the
blond naval cadet, and sent him off to sea to earn an
admiralship for himself.   She had taken a new fancy—his
Highness Prince Leopold.   And so one evening, after a
brilliant ball, she stood before the prince and smiled at him
with her dazzling blue eyes and white teeth in a way all
her own, and then plucked two tender rosebuds from the
bouquet on her breast and kissed them and reached them
to his Highness.

> * " There once was a poor old king,
> His senses numb, and grey his hair—
> This poor old withered king
> Wedded a maid all young and fair."

> † They were both doomed to die.

For a considerable time the whisper ran the fashionable salons about a tender *liaison* between Lady Ellenborough and Prince Leopold of Coburg. When, however, the prince desired the beautiful lady to renounce entirely the tumultuous life of London, and disappear tracelessly from the world, and so dedicate herself in an impenetrable cloud of concealment wholly to his love—then did Lady Ellenborough look interjections; her fancy altogether scared away by this exhibition of pedantry on the part of the prince. She turned her fair back on his prosy egoistic Highness, and threw herself, with all the ardour of love, into the outspread, passionate arms of the handsome, seductive Prince Felix Schwarzenberg, *attaché* to the Austrian embassy at the Court of St. James's.

That was in the spring of 1828. Prince Felix was twenty-eight years of age, of the free-lover persuasion, and a spoiled ladies' darling, who, versed in the maxims of the Goethe doctrine, would approach them now with sighing tenderness and now advance with a bold despotic air. Prince Felix was of a strangely composite nature—now brimming over with youthful spirits, piquant wit and the pleasure of life; now soft and relaxed, dreamy and melancholy, infected by the then prevailing fashion of *Weltschmerz*,* eschewing salons, and burying himself in leafy solitudes.

And this serene chameleon, changing colours so perilously for the hearts of women, loved the beautiful blond lady with the lovely infantile smile, and the pious blue eyes—loved her with a consuming passion, with a glow defying control, such as he had never loved before, such as he would never love again. Such was the love he felt.

But only too soon did the public scandal get abroad, the closing catastrophe of which I witnessed at the time in England. Cousin Christian hated Lady Ellenborough for having presumed, without first consulting him and getting his permission, to begin a "stupid love affair" with

---

* "World-sorrow—sorrow in the consciousness or contemplation of life generally, an extreme or morbid form of which is pessimism, often the satiety of an ill-lived life."

his beloved master, and he liked to give vent to his feelings in the company of mother and me in his witty, sarcastic style.

The lovers grew ever more and more bold, open, and regardless. Lady Ellenborough had tender trysts with Prince Schwarzenberg in a public hotel, and afterwards the waiter was able to swear before a court of justice how, through a keyhole, he had admired the adroitness with which Prince Schwarzenberg handled a lady's laces at her toilette.

While the whole of London was talking of this scandal, and the penny papers were driving a busy trade with the piquant material, Prince Felix Schwarzenberg went, in the summer of 1829, on "leave of absence," to Basle, and Lady Ellenborough accompanied him. With what a triumphant laugh cousin Christian related to me this news, which was agitating the whole of London.

It was now no longer *possible* for the tolerant Lord Ellenborough to keep silence. He brought before the English courts a charge of adultery against his runaway wife, and sued for divorce. The proceedings of this protracted trial, so rich in scandal, engaged the interest of the whole of Europe to a hardly less extent than had done the adultery case against the Princess of Wales. The name of Lady Ellenborough rapidly grew world-noted—world-notorious. This served to snap the last fetters which had hitherto bound the ill-starred lady's heart to society and the sacred sense of shame. Breaking into a shrill mocking laugh she emancipated herself from all that, and grew fast from year to year into a more and more confirmed—lady of free love. "Lady Ellenborough" continued for another decade the most piquant name in all the papers and in all salons.

In the autumn of 1829 Lady Ellenborough followed her lover, who had got transferred, as *attaché* to the Court of the Tuileries, to Paris, and there, in the theatres and in the Champs Elysées, I repeatedly met Prince Felix Schwarzenberg and his wondrously beautiful lady.

What a charming sight it was to me when in the Italian Opera I sat, for the first time, opposite the winsome young lady with the sweet, all-innocent, flower-like face, with the dreamy, down-cast blue eyes and lovely child-like smile, round which waved long, light, blond English curls —how delighted was I in the contemplation of this lovely picture while Maria Malibran sang *Desdemona*—till my brother whispered in my ear, "Voila la belle blonde, Lady Ellenborough!"

"Impossible!" I exclaimed, excitedly and nearly too loud. "This angelic picture of blooming innocence the—notorious Lady Ellenborough!"

That it was possible I was later on to witness by myself.

In the revolution year of 1830, Prince Felix Schwarzenberg and Lady Ellenborough turned up in Munich. King Ludwig, so great a worshipper of beauty, had the charming lady painted for his celebrated "Gallery of Beauties," where she may be seen at the present day, while the picture of Lola Montez has long disappeared from its place.

After a year, however, the restless heart of Lady Ellenborough pursued other love-stars, and Prince Felix Schwarzenberg, an incurable wound in his breast, retired with the little son Lady Ellenborough had borne him—now an officer in the Austrian army—to the solitude of his Bohemian estates. It was only gradually that he recovered from these storms and confusions of the heart to resume his diplomatic career, and ultimately attain the head of the Austrian ministry. He also resumed tendering his homage to the ladies, a service he successfully prosecuted to the very end, as I was myself to observe in the course of my two starring engagements in Vienna. But he never again attempted tying a fixed knot for life. Lady Ellenborough had robbed him of all faith in the purity and fidelity of woman.

And next, in May, 1835, when I was fulfilling an engagement in Mannheim, I once more met Lady Ellenborough there.

It was on the first evening of my visit to the celebrated little theatre town of Dalberg, Schiller, and Iffland, while with mother and brother Karl, who had now got promoted

to the rank of horse-captain, I was present at the performance of Spohr's "Jessonda," that my attention was taken
by the presence of a charming girl-like creature sitting
opposite to me, in a simple white muslin dress, the sweet
flower-face almost quite veiled in long blond English curls,
the blue eyes dreamily downcast. She wore no gloves,
and played distractedly with a golden opera glass, apparently without noticing that so many inquisitive, wicked
eyes were directed towards her. Nor did the song and
play on the stage apparently have any interest for her.

"Ah! Lady Ellenborough!" I exclaimed, in surprise.

"Beg pardon—Baroness Venningen!" said brother
Karl, sarcastically. And he related to me the following
little nice tale, which he had in part got from the mouth
of his intimate friend, Venningen himself:—

Baron Venningen, the distinguished Baden cavalier,
with stainless ancient name, honest heart and large fortune, saw for the first time in Baden-Baden the seductive
beauty of Lady Ellenborough, and he trusted her angelic
face and her soft blue eyes and her dreamy smile more
than he did her reputation in the world. He fell so
passionately in love with this bewitching beauty that,
lightly valuing his proud unblemished escutcheon, his
brilliant position at the Court of Carlsruhe and in society,
and the warnings of his relations and friends, he pledged
this errant English beauty, with a touching honesty of
purpose, his heart and hand, his fortune and name and
everlasting fidelity.

She looked in perfect surprise at this naïve German,
with the good, open face and honourable proffers, at first
with a feeling almost of compassion; and then, with a loud,
shrill laugh, she said: "Everlasting fidelity? Cher Baron,
have you never heard the story, then, of the Lady Ellenborough, and her unhappy heart that now once for all
can no longer be faithful so soon as it tires in love? I
will tell you the story of this heart, from its first early bud
of innocence up till the present time, when all it is capable
of is only mad, burning passion—changing its object
every year, every month, every day, according as *ennui*
comes and goes. I will truly and honestly tell you every-

thing; for one virtue, at least, still remains to the notorious Lady Ellenborough: she does not lie. She is true in her feelings, words, and deeds—more than in the most innocent days of her remote happy childhood."

And the ill-starred woman discovered to the unhappy Venningen her whole hot heart, her whole wild life. With the ghastly truthfulness peculiar to her, she kept no recess locked, covered no stain, and he looked on mutely during her narrative, growing always paler and paler.

"Now, then, Baron, do you want to marry Lady Ellenborough?" she asked, with a demoniac flash from her eyes, at the close of her long report. She knew his answer beforehand. She knew her irresistible power.

And, fever-hot, came from his trembling lips the words: "Yes, I will—I must. I cannot otherwise. I love you to madness—with a consuming love. Ay, though this love were to be the death of me!"

"Eh bien, cher baron—à votre risque! Let us try it together, for I like you, too—at this hour. But I have warned you. It is now your business not to make me tired of you. Begin to tire me, and I look out for another toy to my heart. And then it is all over with the good, German, wedded love and fidelity—for ever! The bond of marriage is for me nothing but a social form. I toss it aside so soon as it discommodes me, like a pair of gloves when they are too small or worn. Once more, good Baron, I warn you against Lady Ellenborough."

In vain. Karl Theodor Heribert, Baron von Venningen, sacrificed his position at Court, his family, his social connections, and on the 10th November, 1832, married the divorced Lady Ellenborough. He retired with his beautiful wife to Mannheim. He trusted in the power of his love and fidelity.

Poor Venningen! How happy was he when in the next following years his worshipped wife bore him a son, Heribert, and a daughter, Bertha. And with what assurance he looked forward to the future! Lady Ellenborough—for this ill-omened name refused to give place to Baroness Venningen—remained faithful to him into the third year. Wonderful!

Then, however, the fatal *ennui* came over her.

And in this dangerous state of soul and heart was she when in May, 1835, I found Lady Ellenborough at the performance of Spohr's "Jessonda." The beautiful wife evidently wearied during the performance and at the side of her husband.

But see! what a strange change suddenly passed on the girl-like, dreamy creature in the box opposite to me! Her rosy lips quivered, her blue eyes sparkled and opened wider and ever wider, as though to devour the object to which they were directed. And these sparkling eyes were steadily directed to the box beside ours!

Into this box had just entered a blooming, handsome young Greek, dressed half in his magnificent national costume and half in the style of a gay Heidelberg student. And forthwith began an unembarrassed encounter through opera-glasses, a smiling and a nodding from one side to the other, so as to draw almost the exclusive attention of the house to the two lovers.

Baron Venningen got red as fire and shifted about restlessly in his seat, whispering hasty and vehement words to his wife. She seemed hardly to hear them till Venningen almost forcibly took her by the arm and led her out of the theatre.

After a few months Karl wrote to me: "Lady Ellenborough has eloped from her husband with the handsome Greek, Count Theotocki, who was staying in Heidelberg for the sake of his studies, and whom you saw that evening in the theatre. Poor Venningen is quite crushed by this blow, and we are even anxious about his reason."

From brother Karl I afterwards heard some more interesting particulars respecting this new love of Lady Ellenborough.

She was a wild horsewoman. Her favourite horse, "L'Infatigable," a splendid fiery white horse Baron Venningen had purchased from my brother, who, in turn, had bought it from two Poles, who shortly after the unfortunate Polish revolution had arrived at Mannheim on their way to Paris, and in their straits had been obliged to change their horse into money. Of course sister Lina had to send the money for this purchase. The two Poles were the Counts Cäsar and Ladislaus Broël-Plater. The young Ladislaus I had made the acquaintance of in Berlin, and now had he come accidentally into contact with my brother. Years after our roads were again to converge into each other, not to diverge again till after death. Ah, how wonderfully does fate play with us poor short-sighted mortals!

"L'Infatigable" was so wild and refractory that my brother could not ride him in the front, and had therefore to sell him. He was, however, the very horse for the wild Lady Ellenborough. How often has "L'Infatigable" dashed with her by day and night from Mannheim to Heidelberg to meet an enamoured student there longingly awaiting the passionate beauty?

One morning the Baroness Venningen returned to Mannheim in a country cart. "L'Infatigable" had fallen in the wild night-ride not to rise again.

"I warned you beforehand, poor Venningen, that you, too, would weary me in time—and then——"

Such was always her smiling reply to his prayers, expostulations, threatenings. She had no heart for his unchangeable love nor for his measureless grief.

And one day Baroness Venningen did not return at all from Heidelberg to Mannheim. Lady Ellenborough was off to Athens with her Greek student. There she married Count Théotocki to leave him in a few years for a wild Palikar chieftain. In Athens she was called "Ianthe."

Wearying again, Lady Ianthe Ellenborough went in the year 1854 to Syria. While making the journey on a camel's back from Beirut to Babylon her Arabian cameldriver, Scheik Abdul, took her fancy, and the former lioness of London high life led for a considerable period a nomadic life in the desert.

Mrs. Digby, as Lady Ellenborough now called herself, next set up in the neighbourhood of Damascus in the paradisaical plain at the foot of the Anti-Lebanon, a charming retreat; a little house of five rooms, in a lovely little garden. In summer she sought coolness at Homs on the Orontes.

When getting on to the end of her fifties Lady Ellenborough suddenly reappeared in London, to look after her
interests in a case of inheritance before the courts. All
the papers were again full of the witchery of her wild,
yet truly womanly beauty, and of the grace of her carriage
and of her old scandals.

She then returned to Damascus, where she died in the
spring of 1873. Baron Venningen, who had never got the
better of his love for his ill-starred spouse and her flight,
fell dead from his horse, under an attack of heart disease,
while on a ride in Munich, one year after her death. Of
the two unhappy daughters, Bertha still lives in the mad-
house of Illenau in Baden, a victim of the fixed idea that
she is bewitched.

Balzac has cleverly portrayed Lady Ellenborough as
Lady Dudley in his novel of " Le lis dans la valée."

CHAPTER XXVIII.

THE THRONE OF GREECE.

THE kernel of the heaven-crying injustice which Prince Leopold and Christian von Stockmar were guilty of towards me was that with one hand they reached after the throne of Greece, while with the other they drew me to England into mysterious complications that by their very nature were doomed to the opposite of blessing; knowing very well, as they did, that it was impossible for the prince to keep hold of both simultaneously—the royal throne and this object of "secret affection." To keep the one it was necessary to drop the other.

And which he would throw away was perfectly well known to both from the beginning. They were verily great diplomatists, with the cool, calculating hearts of diplomatists.

Thus, from the first, I was doomed to be the sacrifice of a prince's humours—to serve as a mere toy to help in whiling away the weary hours of a weary pedant, till the Greek throne was ripe for plucking.

It is no doubt true that Christian Stockmar had darkly hinted to me in Coburg that his master had views of the Greek throne, and that in the event of these views being realised there could be no question of a bond of the heart being sealed with me; and that we had therefore quietly to await the issue in that direction before I could be free to engage myself.

But yet, in the face of all that, there reached me in the spring of 1829, and from Christian Stockmar himself, a distinct and urgent invitation for me to come to England, while all the time the negotiations with reference to the throne of Greece, which I naturally concluded had been completely broken off, were in full progress.

And here I publicly and posthumously accuse Prince

Leopold and my cousin Christian of this heaven-crying
injustice committed against me. I look forward to a
court of justice beyond the stars!

    *   *   *   *   *   *

Concerning the beginning of his relations to the throne
of Greece, King Leopold of Belgium says himself, in his
brief autobiography :—

"In the beginning of September, 1822, Prince Leopold
went (from Naples) to Vienna to see the Emperor Alexander. The late Lord Londonderry did everything in his
power to secure the prince a bad reception. Prince
Metternich did the same, for other reasons of course. He
imagined the prince had intentions on Greece, which,
however, was not the case. Later on came the Duke of
Wellington and put an end to the calumniations of
Londonderry, who was thinking by that means to in-
sinuate himself into the favour of George IV.

"1825. Prince Leopold went for the sake of his health
to Carlsbad, afterwards for a year to Italy; passing the
winter in Naples. From 1825 and onwards offers were
made to him in respect of Greece. Canning refused to
hear anything on that subject; in his opinion Prince
Leopold could be far more useful in England.

"1828. Prince Leopold went to Silesia to meet King
Friedrich Wilhelm III. of Prussia. His principal motive
was to see the best friend he ever had, Prince Wilhelm,
the king's youngest brother. The then Crown-Prince of
Prussia arranged with Prince Leopold to meet each other
in Naples, a meeting which also came off in November.
In March, 1829, the prince returned to England by way
of Paris.

"The proposals with respect to Greece had in the
meantime assumed quite a definite form, taken quite a
decided turn. Russia and France urgently wished the
prince to accept the throne. In England, too, affairs were
in motion. The Duke of Cumberland (afterwards King
Ernst August of Hanover) had at that time considerable
influence on the king, and gave the most embittered
opposition to the Wellington ministry. In the Greek

question, likewise, he took a zealous part, and gained over the king in favour of the candidature of Duke Karl of Mecklenburg-Strelitz, brother of the Duchess of Cumberland. The ministers, on the other hand, pressed the king on the side of the candidature of Prince Leopold, and even threatened to resign on the question. That was highly unfortunate for the Greek cause; it was impossible for the prince to force on a cabinet which staked its existence on the question those conditions which in the opinion of many sensible people of England were indispensable for the maintenance of Greece. Prince Metternich wanted to ruin the young Greek State from the beginning. Not succeeding in this object, he took advantage of his influence with the Duke of Wellington and Lord Aberdeen to propose a frontier which was altogether unacceptable."

And in the same month of May, 1829, when trusting to Prince Leopold's assurances of love, and the guarantees of my cousin Stockmar, I hastened, full of radiant hope at the wink of my happy stars, to England—in that same month, both these personages sent Stockmar's brother, Karl, the prince's confidential business agent, to Greece to meet the President Kapodistrias, and enter into negotiations with him on the question of the Greek throne, in furtherance of Prince Leopold's interests.

On the evening of the 14th May, 1829, I played, for the last time, as Royal Prussian Court actress, before Friedrich Wilhelm III., in Potsdam, and the good king gave me his good wishes and his blessing on this bond of hearts to accompany me on my way to England; and on the 27th May, Karl Stockmar, in execution of his master's commission, said to the President Kapodistrias in Athens:

"The prince is determined to follow the call (of Greece and the Great Powers, who were then conferring in London on the future of Greece and Prince Leopold), but only under two conditions. The first is, that Greece be allowed such boundaries as would be necessary to it in order to take an efficient position among the States of Europe. The second is, that he have a well-grounded hope of being able to raise the material and intellectual status of a people which seems to have degenerated in consequence of long

N

subjection to slavery." The prince further demanded that Greece should make express requisition for him at the hands of the Great Powers.

Count Kapodistrias, on the other hand, made it a condition that Prince Leopold, on his becoming King of Greece, should bring to his country, by way of "nuptial gift," the islands of Samos and Candia. This the prince was unable to promise. And so the negotiations for the present came to a stand-still. Prince Leopold always suspected that his old friend Kapodistrias was playing a false game with him, and was himself aiming after a permanent presidency, nay, the throne of Greece itself.

During my stay in Paris, which was on that account prolonged, the negotiations about the Greek throne began anew in September, and on the 3d February, 1830, the Great Powers—Russia, France, and England—guaranteed the Greeks complete independence of Turkey, under a Christian hereditary prince, and officially offered Prince Leopold the Greek throne, which at first he accordingly seized unconditionally with both hands.

How cousin Christian one morning in February brought me this joyful news, and with what jubilant delight I heard the words which restored me my golden freedom— that I have already related in a former chapter.

But when I was alone with mother, and we spoke together of the great event, we relapsed into a feeling of deep depression at the thought of the bitter disappointments which we had experienced in the course of a few months in England, and how our short dream of happiness was for ever dissipated.

I even reproached myself with my readiness to leave for ever a man who had once, at any-rate, drawn me in love and confidence to his heart—granted even that that heart had long burned itself out. The few glimmering sparks under the ashes had at least flashed up for me!

I set myself with all honest endeavour to forget everything in the prince's conduct which had offended me, and to think only of the good he had shown me.

In this softened mood I bade the prince heartily welcome on his next visit, and hailed him with emotion as future King of the Greeks, wishing him in my tears all joy and blessing on his high calling.

And what was his Highness's reply to my loving words?

"I hope very much that the mild climate of Greece will suit my health a great deal better than this everlasting fog of England. I think it will be very pleasant to breathe the balsamic air, wandering in myrtle and orange groves, or resting under light silk tents, while beautiful Greek ladies sing their sweet popular songs and dance their fantastic dances before me." And the prince expatiated at full length on the blue and white striped tents, for the manufacture of which he had already been negotiating with a contractor.

I dried my tears and thought with indignation and vexation: "This, then, is the man for whom you sacrificed your artistic future and your good name, who pretended to love you when he enticed you into this ambiguous position, for whom you lived like a bird in the cage, and who now has not the least syllable of regret to express to you at the near and everlasting separation." And like the Countess Orsina* I might have exclaimed: "Is this the whole apology due to me? Not a single lie more for me? Not one single small lie more for me?" Yea, a little lie of regret I had surely deserved!

Nor one single little question had this *blasé* egoistic man of withered heart to address me? Not even a little question of ordinary politeness: "Seeing we are to part, for so fate will have it, where does Missy (the familiar 'Du' never came to his lips) think of living in the future? Will she settle in Paris as Countess Montgomery? or in Switzerland? or in Italy? Or will the hot, artistic heart of Caroline Bauer drive her back to the stage? I would vote for the Countess Montgomery continuing to live in distinguished retirement, seeing the sudden re-emergence of Caroline Bauer on the stage would call forth fresh newspaper noises, which might not be agreeable to me for the moment."

Not one syllable of thought had the ossified egoist for

---

* In Lessing's "Emilia Galotti."

me and my future, nor how my heart would accommodate itself to the sudden impending separation. All his thought was still ever about his dear pampered self and its comfort.

With the same equanimity with which he had discoursed on the white and blue royal tents he was contemplating for himself in Greece, the prince—while his slim, carefully-tended fingers went on drizzling away in the old monotonous fashion—now enlarged self-complacently on the choice of a future Queen of Greece. All the princesses of Europe had to pass in review, and were analysed and criticised in an altogether business-like style. Personally the prince liked a princess of Oldenburg best, but from a political point of view a French princess seemed to him more advantageous. If the Duchess de Berri had only not been so eccentric and self-willed! As mother of the future King of France, she would have had the most chances in her favour. But the pedantic, poor-hearted, hesitating prince felt misgivings about such a fiery energetic woman, and with a sigh decided in favour of a little Princess of Orleans, who might, however, have a future before her.

To enlarge in this way on such a topic before me testifies to a hardly credible hardness of heart, or a still more incredible naïveté on the part of the prince, does it not?—when it is borne in mind that he was sitting opposite to me, a young, warm-hearted creature in her bloom, who had surely the most immediate and the most sacred rights to his heart and hand!

I nearly choked with inward vexation, while I yet so far mastered myself as not to fling into the prince's face the most unpalatable of the truths that my heart was nearly bursting to say.

As soon, however, as the prince was gone, I sent cousin the following lines: "Come, if you still want to find us here. I am dying of grief and vexation. My patience and strength are exhausted."

Early the next morning Christian came riding up to us. He found mother and me in the extreme of excitement and desperation. Glowing with resentment and sobbing convulsively, I called out to cousin, after I had related to him the humiliating conversation of the day before—"For this soulless puppet have I sacrificed myself, and you, the clever cousin, did not warn me. On the contrary, you are act and part with the prince, inasmuch as you thought only of the prince and his pleasure, and deemed you had done everything that was required for your poor befooled cousin, when you got up a mysterious wedding-scene to screen her reputation, and secured her future maintenance by the deposition of a certain sum. I accuse you, Christian Stockmar, of making me the playball of a prince's humours."

In the highest degree disconcerted, Christian answered: " Yes, I did wrong, Caroline—wrong to you and your mother when I let you come to England. I did wrong in not rather renouncing my position with the prince than allowing such unhappy complications to occur. I indulged the prince the happiness of a loving domesticity, the chance of a revival of life at the side of a young blooming creature he loved, as also on the other hand to you and your mother relief from pecuniary cares, and deliverance from the meshes and cabals of a theatrical life. I was also in hopes that children would confirm this bond into a cordial and lasting one."

"Children!" I shrieked, beside myself. "Children! You know better than I do that children was never the desire of your cunning master, nor *your* wish, nor diplomatic advice either, because you wanted to be able to loose this unhallowed bond as easily as you tied it, so soon as your fetish of high politics, or whatever be its name, made it advisable. Or what else could be the meaning of the prince never once calling me 'Du' in a home-like way? And then, again, after my return from Paris, paying me only starched, formal visits, and staying for an hour a time only to drizzle me out of my senses? If there had been anything of children in his head, why did he not speak to me familiarly about what had passed with himself, and then ask me in turn how things had gone with me? Of the Princess Charlotte all he ever told me was simply that her ghost had appeared to him one night, and that I was more beautiful than she was. And why did the prince and you keep secret from me that, at the very time you were beckoning me to England, you despatched your

brother Karl to Greece to forward the prince's outlooks
on the throne—the throne which must forthwith rend the
bond with me before it was yet hardly tied? Why? But
there are already too many ' Why's,' which all the diplomatists in the world could not answer to my satisfaction,
but which are more than sufficient to entitle me to leave
England to-morrow for ever. That I did not do it long
ago was only out of consideration for my reputation. For
the sake of honour I would have held out still longer in
this galling bond, in order to part in peace with him and
you when the crown of Greece was definitely secured.
But the degrading experience of yesterday commands me
to leave this narrow-minded, egoistic vacuity of withered
heart and unmanly character as soon as possible. Not a
fibre of my heart any longer binds me to him." And
passionate sobbing choked my voice.

Mute and pale, but with the nervous twitch in his fine
countenance peculiar to him, cousin had sat opposite to
me. He now took my hand, and with a remarkable composure and moderation, through which, however, an inward
agitation was discernible, he said :

"Yes, Caroline, wrong has been done you by the
prince and by me, who let my good nature run away with
my judgment and my—conscience. I meant well and
honestly, in respect also of you and your mother ; but the
force of circumstances got the better of me. But that
no wrong, nor a still greater wrong be done you the
second time, I must remind you that when you came to
England you committed yourselves unconditionally to my
advice and guidance. In this my responsible position, I
must demand of you not to fly away helter-skelter from
England, nor leave the prince in a temper. I demand of
you to wait patiently some days or weeks more, till the
Greek throne is definitively secured to the prince—or lost.
Then shall it be my sacred duty to settle your business to
your best advantage. Promise me that."

And with plenty of tears I promised Patience and
ever more Patience, till cousin Christian would come himself and tell me : "It is now time to go—the King of
Greece will be your friend—in the distance."

From this hour cousin again showed me the old confidence and the most cordial consideration. In his rattling humorous style he would often say to me : " Pity, Caroline, I am already married, or you might be my wife, and the prince or King Leopold could come and pass his innocent drizzling hour at our tea table, while I ruled Greece! "

And Prince Leopold, the future King of Greece, how did he behave towards me ?

As if nothing whatever had happened between us he came as usual to dinner, music, reading, drizzling, and only now and again talked harmlessly of his white and blue silk tents and his future queens.

A man of noble character would either have entreated me to remain a faithful and loving companion at his side for the short space of time that was allowed us to live together, and throughout that time have endeavoured to requite my affection by double tenderness on his part, or with all delicacy he would have hastened the dissolution of the bond and my departure.

The unfeeling indifference and offensive nonchalance of the prince in relation to me—which, in point of fact, was all I ever experienced at his hands—could not, however, but provoke my extreme indignation, and I had ever need of my greatest self-command not to break the word I had pledged to cousin. I felt as if the ghastly villa would stifle me, and day and night I longed more and more poignantly for the free artistic profession I had so giddily abandoned.

To linger on in the old relationship to the prince seemed to me like treason against myself, seeing that the mutual affection which could alone sanction the peculiar bond between us was undeniably extinct.

But yet to all my complaints cousin still continued repeating : " Patience—wait events—do not strike in before the time—time must decide and—loose the bond ! "

Christian Stockmar was in a highly excited mood all the time the question of the Greek throne was pending. Only like some tempest would he come storming in on us occasionally to vent his oppressed heart over the want of tact and character with which his master was proceeding in this question—so vital for poor Greece.

In his passionate excitement the otherwise so shrewd diplomatist would often boil over in a very imprudent fashion, and knowing that I deemed myself already free from the bond I had tied with the prince, he would free himself of all restraint before me in discharging his choler on the subject. Thus it happened that I did not seldom hear him say: "O this irresolute, short-sighted, petty prince, who gropes about in the dark without the energy and character to direct him infallibly to what he *must* and *shall* do—who never knows his own mind! Without me he had been long lost in this Greek business. I must ever again toilsomely piece together what he thoughtlessly plucks to pieces. A nerve of resolute manhood is not in him, but he is all collapsed into the pampered paltry 'I,' consulting in this Greek question, too, his own contemptible comfortableness and vanity and self-complacency, and hardly even as a subordinate matter the cause of the poor Greeks, who yet need a strong self-sacrificing king."

An hour or two later the prince would arrive in his carriage, weary, fagged, ill-humoured, and complaining that "the good Stocky was such a hypochondriac croaker, and was always pestering him with useless points for consideration. He had rather neither see nor hear anything more of the whole Greek affair."

In these circumstances it was our business to compose and amuse both sides—truly no easy task!

One morning Stockmar came galloping up to us in highest dudgeon, and at once blurted out:

"Nay, the like was never heard of—enough to make me wash my hands of the whole concern! Just think of the nice fry the prince has again made in his everlasting petty anxiety about his dear sweet 'I!' There in the night I was wakened out of a deep sleep, and summoned to the prince. He lies in bed, the very impersonation of misery; stares at me like a pale ghost, and full of despair he whimpers to me in a voice scarcely audible : 'Ah, dearest Stocky, help, save me from death. What a misfortune has happened to me! You know the two little golden clinchers which in the night I fix to my back teeth to prevent injury to the enamel in case of my grinding my teeth in sleep.

Well, I waken up and find only *one* clincher between the teeth—the other I must have swallowed in sleep!—yes, I feel its sharp prongs in my intestines. I am a dead man —good Stocky, save me.'

"I was myself terribly frightened, and at first speechless from horror—for if the prince had really swallowed the sharp-pronged clincher, which a charlatan dentist had talked him into taking against my advice, I could not have much hope of saving him. I must deem the prince a lost man.

"'Stocky, you have not a word of consolation!' stammered out the prince, in greater anxiety than ever.

"Then I gathered together all my strength of mind, assumed as unconcerned a look as was possible, and said with forced cheerfulness: 'Oh, there is nothing in the least to be afraid of, gracious master! I'll be back at once with assistance!' With that I hastened to the prince's body physician, and took counsel with him as to what was to be done. We now gave the prince spoonful after spoonful of electuary, and I must yet laugh when I think of the pitiable face with which his Highness gulped down the nauseous stuff, always assuring us however: 'I will swallow anything, if my life only be spared.'

"After we had thus for some hours tortured the prince and ourselves, Hühnlein suddenly calls out cheerily, 'Here is the gold clincher; I found it jammed in between the mattress and bedstead!' 'Yes, that is it,' faintly breathes the prince, and shuts his eyes in weariness. In my first rage I threw the confounded thing out of the window, and conjured the prince in future not to play with such womanish, dangerous playthings, for I would not have given one penny on the chance of his recovery."

"Cousin!" I exclaimed with tragi-comic horror, "I shall never get this picture you have drawn us out of my mind. I shall ever be seeing the prince lying in the anguish of death, and swallowing spoonful upon spoonful of the abominable electuary—bah-h-h! And a picture of that kind consorts ill with the idol of my heart! God be thanked that the danger is over!"

"Over?—ay, for to-day!"—blurted out Stockmar

anew. " But who knows what the prince will be hatching
up to-morrow again, in anxiety about his darling body?
One might go mad to see a man otherwise so sensible all
absorbed for ever and ever in that one ' I,' and nursing all
sorts of silly childish whims to please it.   Does he not
stalk about in soles three fingers thick, very like some
stork in a clover field, to save his coddled feet from
cold?   Does he not wear a coal-black wig to make him
look younger?   Have you ever seen him ride with any
mettle or go in him, or make a clean breast of it in words
that come rattling straight and sound from the heart?   No,
he rides like some Don Quixote on a little pony, his feet
nearly trailing on the ground, for fear his Highness might
otherwise be joggled, and perhaps—fall ; and he cheeps
mincingly in his speech, not to hurt his chest or throat.
Really, I can very well understand how, with all the
seductive amiability that is native to him, and with all his
former beauty, he could never succeed among his many
stupid love affairs in inspiring any lady with a real
permanent passion—nor you either, Caroline.   The first
brisk cavalier that offered might easily oust him out of his
place in the favour of any beauty ! "

" But the Countess Ficquelmont was yet willing to leave
her husband the ambassador for the prince ! "

" Because she was tired of her old man, and, the in-
triguing Viennese that she was, she thought to play a part
as mistress, or even as consort of the prince, in England,
and become rich by means of him.   But blessings on the
liaison!   As soon as his Highness had drizzled to her a
dozen times in sweet *tête-à-tête*, the countess and her
passion scudded out of it with all speed ! "

"Yes, cousin, drizzling is the horror of horrors, and far
worse than man in his madness.   If Schiller had but once
seen his Highness drizzling ! " I popped out, laughing with
a touch of my old, nearly forgotten, humour.

In better spirits Stockmar struck in : " And yet,
Caroline, you have never yet seen our gracious master
drizzling in company with Lord Roode.   It is enough to
make one go out of his senses to see the two dignified
gentlemen sitting stiffly, and earnestly, and silently op-

posite each other, and doing nothing but drizzling mutually to each other! It was from Lord Roode that the prince learnt this noble amusement!"

"Cousin, whatever will the Greeks say to it, if his Majesty on the throne should begin drizzling to them?"

"We are not so far as that yet by a long way," and cousin Christian relapsed into his sullen mood, and rode home to Claremont full of thought.

Stockmar was right; the prince's irresolution and fickleness in the Greek question caused him at that time much distress, and in the end made shipwreck of the whole concern. In his desire for the glittering Greek throne and the *dolce far niente* under silk tents in the balsamic air of Greece, the prince at first yielded to the London Conference and the English ministry a dangerous guardianship over himself, and like a good child said " Yes " to everything— so that his final " No " could not but take people with the more surprise and come with all the less grace. And what sound lectures the prince had to stomach from his guardians!

Thus when the prince had declared his satisfaction with all the conditions of the Conference, and then on the back of it all claimed Candia for Greece, Lord Aberdeen wrote to him on the 31st January, 1830, plump and plain: "Candia has hitherto been utterly out of the question. It is true that in spite of all which has hitherto been done you are yet free to decline, but the refusal of Candia could be no explanation of such a resolution on your part. Consider how such a proceeding would be compatible with your dignity and with a reputation for consistency. The Powers have no thought of negotiations with you. They expect a simple acceptance of their offer, and would take a qualified acceptance for a refusal."

The prince nevertheless yet endeavoured several times by letter to smuggle a few stipulations into the proposals of the Conference, but he was also just as ready to withdraw his letters and his stipulations whenever Lord Aberdeen demanded it in the name of the Great Powers.

In the beginning of April Prince Leopold went to Paris as elected King of Greece to sue for the hand of a Princess of Orleans. In the end of the month he came back with a rebuff on hearing of the dangerous illness of his father-in-law, King George IV., and now recurred more earnestly to the thought of the little Princess of Oldenburg.

Suddenly, on the 21st of May, Prince Leopold wrote to the Conference of the Great Powers that he could not possibly force himself as king on a people that was not satisfied with the guarantees he brought with him from the London Conference, and that he therefore with thanks renounced the throne offered him.

That, however, was hardly the real reason, for it was equally valid when Prince Leopold previously accepted the throne. The general opinion was that the approaching death of the king, and the prospect of an English regency in his person during the minority of his niece, Victoria, had betrayed the prince into this inconsistent step. Old Baron von Stein, too, whom the prince had repeatedly consulted in the matter of the Greek throne, wrote to the prince disapproving his final unjustified declinature:

" When Emperor Alexander, in 1812, entered on the struggle with Napoleon, he adopted as his motto— ' Confiance en Dieu, courage, perseverance, union!' and with the eye of faith directed steadily and boldly to heaven he followed the impulses of his high-spirited noble temper, and laid the giant prostrate. The reason of man is able to grasp only what is immediately before it, not to penetrate into the obscurity of the remote future. Our guide here is sense of duty, reliance on God, freedom from all selfishness."

Still more annihilating is Stein's letter to the Archbishop of Cologne:

" What says your Grace to the behaviour of Prince Leopold? It is quite of a piece with the character of the *Marquis peu-à-peu*, as George IV. called him. Instead of overcoming difficulties, instead of completing the task he had taken in hand, he faintheartedly turns back from the plough, calculating on the chances likely to arise through the death of King George IV. A person of this weak character is not at all qualified to strike with a man's strength into the current of life, He has no principle to stand or fall by ! "

In a similar strain Stein criticises the prince in a letter to Baron von Gagern:

"He had the feeling of not being equal to the enterprise, and cast a side glance to his probable influence in England, an influence which by reason of his weakness of character he will never command, and will in any case lose again so soon as the Princess Victoria is of age—that is in six or seven years hence."

Prince Metternich likewise blamed the prince's "weakness of character and timidity," and a French pen reproached the fickle prince as a "man of pleasure grown so blasé that there was nothing left in him for even ambition itself to hold lastingly by."

Dr. Karl Mendelssohn-Bartholdy, the son of Felix, the friend of my youth, also writes pertinently in his historical work, "Count John Kapodistrias:"

"At the last moment it was still in Prince Leopold's power to take a great manlike resolution, to accept the crown *because* it was a crown of thorns, and so tear in pieces the net of intrigues that had been spun to scare him back from his path. Instead, however, of annihilating the intrigues of opponents he took advantage of them as a screen to hide his irresolution and the sudden change of outlook which had been opened up to his ambition. Instead of swiftly and strenuously closing with the arduous but inspiring task he kept on toying for months long with the hopes of a nation wrestling in desperation."

When in the end of May cousin Christian in the greatest excitement brought me the terrible news that the prince had now definitively declined the crown of Greece, because he felt unequal to the situation, that we should therefore remain in England, and that everything would resume its old course, I broke down into utter dispiritment and nervelessness. I had been dreaming so shortly before of my approaching freedom, and a new life as free and happy *artiste*. And now that I was awakened to find it all a dream, the bitterest sense of disappointment and grief preyed on me. I fell into a violent fever. "'Twere perhaps best if I died—then would all at once be still!"

CHAPTER XXIX.

CATASTROPHE OF THE LIAISON.

WHEN I had recovered, and the prince again sat drizzling opposite to me, he did not ask: "Is Missy still heartily affected to me? May I hope for a revival of love?"

No, the blasé selfish man of withered heart had not one word for me in the way of excuse or of mutual understanding. He acted as though nothing whatever had come between us; no white and blue striped royal tents, no Princesses of Orleans or Oldenburg. He seemed to regard it as a matter of course that the old, joyless life should go on dragging itself quietly along; that he should come daily in his carriage to dinner; that we should perform music; that while I read out he should drizzle—drizzle—drizzle.

I felt deeply degraded in my own eyes by such an arrangement. The bitter indignation in my heart aroused the old energy of my character, and I kept dunning Christian Stockmar for my acquittance and release—to-day rather than to-morrow.

But my Mentor was inexorable. He appealed to my reason and my heart: "For the moment you are not at liberty to leave the prince, now that in consequence of so many deceptions and disappointments he feels in depressed spirits. He needs your sympathy just as much as my aid. A little patience now, therefore, Caroline—who knows what the next weeks may bring forth? King George may die any day, and then there will be great changes—for us too. Let us, then, still wait on this great event. For the present you and your mother will shift back for the London season to the pretty villa of Regent's Park. Then comes the summer tour to the Continent. The prince must to Carlsbad, I to Coburg, and you and your mother may visit

Louis in Paris, or go to Baden-Baden, or wherever else
you like. The separation will thus take place without
mutual displays of temper—without ill-will and recrimina-
tion—without any open rupture."

After a violent struggle with myself I yielded to
cousin Christian's representations, and remained with a
heavy heart. Would I had rather followed my own
feeling and gone off at once! How much bitterness
would have been spared me!

Before we removed to the Regent's Park we were
doomed to a painful encounter.

On a beautiful spring evening, when the lilac was
blooming and the nightingales singing, mother and I felt
impelled by a yearning desire to step out of our dismal,
melancholy park, out into the laughing sunny world of
spring outside. Why should we not take a walk to the
beautiful, blooming Claremont Park? The prince and
cousin Christian were staying in London. Claremont
House was a forbidden place to us only during the presence in it of the prince.

Thus, altogether glad to have escaped our dingy
dungeon, we promenaded through the charming grounds,
and came to a point in our ramble whence we were able
to descry with pleasure the remote Castle of Windsor.
At such a position and in such circumstances a clear
girlish voice and a child-like laugh came ringing to our
ears. On a silver-grey pony, accompanied by a large,
white, long-haired dog, a young girl of eleven years came
trotting up, fresh and round like a red rosebud, with
flying curls and large luminous eyes. These eyes looked
at me so astonished and with such a gaze of inquisitive
questioning in them, while the little hand securely held in
the pony. And then all at once the little Amazon curved
round, and presently returned with a stately round lady.
She too started, and her eye glided all over us not without scrutiny, and I felt how I grew red with shame under
this glance. Then the lady called to her little daughter a
word in English, and both disappeared in the shrubbery,
leaving us behind in a deep sense of shame.

We had mutually recognised each other. It was the

Duchess of Kent, sister of Prince Leopold, with her little daughter, Victoria, now Queen of England!

So the Duchess of Kent, Princess Victoria of Coburg, was not free to recognise her playmate, Christina Stockmar, nor greet her daughter in a friendly manner. My poor mother and her daughter were in the eyes of the Duchess of Kent grown to be very ambiguous persons.

Sobbing, and almost crushed under a sense of shame, I sank into my mother's arms. In the most mortified spirits we returned to our gloomy den. How had I deserved all this misery and this ignominy? And next day we had bitter reproaches from the prince and from Stockmar for having visited Claremont Park on our own account, while the Duchess of Kent and the Princess Victoria were there on a visit.

When after that we took possession anew of the pleasant villa in Regent's Park, and I again wandered through the old familiar rooms and the lovely garden, I bust into tears. How much had changed in me and about me since, just a year before, I entered this new home for the first time, " on my journey after fortune!" I felt how I had aged many years in these twelve months. So many young hopes, illusions, dreams, ideals all blasted in me! So much richer in sad experiences and disenchantments! So entirely impoverished!

The only ray of sunshine that visits me out of these June days of 1830 is the memory of Maria Malibran's sweet refreshing song. I was never to hear it again.

In other respects the days and weeks unrolled themselves with the old dull monotony. The prince came to his wearisome drizzling visit, cousin Christian in the evening occasionally to tea. Their whole interest revolved round King George IV., who was still always dying and yet would not die.

For years now the king, undermined by the grossest excesses of every description, suffered from all manner of diseases: gout, dropsy, asthma, ossification of the heart, general debility, and frequent fainting fits. He was no longer able to walk alone. To enable him to get on horseback a special machinery was contrived. A rolling chair conveyed his Majesty by a gently ascending incline to a platform, whence the Colossus, swollen to a prodigious girth—though his emaciated legs were so thin that on ceremonial occasions they had to be bolstered out with six pairs of stockings and high lacing boots—was gently dropped into the saddle by means of a crane, and the parade ride could begin. The whole nervous system of the king had so collapsed that he drank brandy and rum incessantly, merely to exist. Another favourite drink of this chief sot of his time was whisky-punch, for which champagne was used instead of water, his "dear night cap," as George IV. used to call it.

As early as January, 1830, Christian Stockmar brought us the news that the king had become totally blind in both eyes, and was living in a state of constant intoxication, invisible from all the world.

On the 15th April the bulletin was published that the king, sixty-eight years of age, was suffering from internal debility and asthma.

On the 24th the communication was laid before Parliament that the king was so weak as to be unable any longer to sign his name. Certain ministers were empowered to write his signature in the king's presence.

The people, far from sympathising with their sovereign, exclaimed, in derisive allusion to the king's dropsy: "His Majesty will go to heaven by water! A prosperous passage to him!"

On the 10th July, 1830, my mother wrote from London to my guardian and our trusty legal adviser, Hofgerichts-advocat Bayer in Carlsruhe:—

"Prince Salem, who leaves to-morrow for Carlsruhe, will bring you this letter and my life-certificate empowering the payment to my son Karl of the pension due to me. Should this certificate not be sufficient, the matter must rest till Lina and I come to your neighbourhood, which will assuredly take place in the month of July. Much has changed here, and we heartily rejoice at the prospect of seeing you again, and talking and consulting with you about everything. The death of King George IV. is to be expected at any moment. He is said to have been for several days wholly unconscious, and we sincerely wish him soon released from his sufferings. So soon as the interment is over, Prince Leopold will be ready to depart for Carlsbad, and we, too, will be in readiness for travelling. Lina and I will go to Switzerland, where I shall need to take the waters—probably to Schinznach or Baden. In this tour we trust to greet you in Carlsruhe or Baden-Baden, for there is much to be spoken of and considered, in respect also of my son Karl, who has still that crazy idea of marriage in his head. But you, my honoured friend, know only too well that Lina and I cannot give him the large sum of money required for security. He must look for a rich partner. And how soon would the young, wild, light-minded officer get tired of the faded Leopoldine von Hinkeldey, who is older than himself. When is Karl at last to come to the years of discretion? Louis is still in Switzerland, but will soon return to settle permanently in London, as my nephew, Christian von Stockmar, has offered him a good situation as secretary to the prince, an event which makes us very happy. Lina is well and content (?) and sends her regards to her dear guardian. My good nephew was unwell not only all the winter, but this spring also, which caused us much anxiety on his account. He is now much better, and we hope he will thoroughly recruit himself in Switzerland. He would on no account have accompanied the prince to Greece because of his weak state of health. This affair, too, which caused us much care and uneasiness last winter is now happily over. They were trying days; but who was ever to anttcipate such a contingency coming to involve us in new and embarrassing complications. All this by word of mouth. If Heaven would but grant that we got clear of the newspapers! We are ever anew disturbed by seeing Lina's name linked with all kinds of allusions, in this Greek affair also. We would feel a real pleasure in being forgotten by all the world, only not by you, my dear friend. And so, an early, happy meeting again in the old home!"

This meeting was, however, to be no happy one, and

through an unforeseen event dreadfully precipitated. My heart and hand tremble at this minute yet, in the bare remembrance of those terrible hours.

On a dusky evening in June mother and I were alone in our little garden salon. So sitting we heard a knock at the door, hasty steps approach, and before us stands brother Karl with an abashed and troubled look.

We were as if paralysed, and had for Karl no word of welcome, no warm shake of the hands—we had a presentiment of something alarming.

" You unfortunate, what have you done? " exclaimed mother. " Where do you come from so suddenly, like a thief in the night? What do you want here and of us ? "

" Mother, I *must* marry Leopoldine von Hinkeldey—or shoot myself—for I have pledged my word of honour ; and she will drown herself—to escape the shame."

" Miserable mortal, shoot yourself dead, then," cried mother; beside herself ; " your poor sister shall no longer be your victim, nor be cast into misfortune along with you. The limit is passed ! "

Karl beseeched our compassion as a penitent sinner, vowed the best behaviour in the future, if this once more and last time we would save him from despair. The tears gushed from me. I tried to dispose my mother to relent, and promised to tell everything to cousin Christian and the prince.

Trembling like a criminal, I spoke with cousin next morning, told him everything, and begged him to pay the 16,000 florins to Karl as caution, and to deduct it from the capital settled on me.

Then things came to the most dreadful scenes. Christian Stockmar fell into a furious passion and flung at mother and me the reproach that the whole business was a game we had cunningly contrived with a view to extorting money from him and the prince. It was for that purpose we had secretly brought about this visit of Karl.

All in vain did mother offer to renounce for ever the annuity settled on her by the prince in case of her surviving me.

Christian's distrust continued. He cast on us the most

insulting aspersions, calling us "adventuresses, cunning intriguers, who drew the golden prince into their nets and came to England to sponge on him and the prince."

In vain did I seek protection and justification at the hands of the prince. He showed himself even pettier in his distrust than Stockmar. His crass avarice came also into play. He calculated that the interest of the 16,000 florins would go past him if that amount was at this early date deducted from the capital allotted to me. He refused in the most aggravating manner to pay the security for my brother.

Then my cruelly outraged self-respect flamed out with all the passion of my hot artistic blood, and I told the prince and Christian to their face things which I am prepared to justify at this day.

I told them that they had abused my unmisgiving confidence when they allured me with treacherous promises to England with a view to sweetening some idle, weary hours to a blasé gentleman of high rank. It was no less than a crime to tear me out of my respected position in art and society and bring me into ambiguous relations, and to conceal from me that at the very time he was doing so he was aspiring after the throne of Greece, which would necessarily at once make an end of our alliance, and for ever blast my reputation. I told them they had held me out the prospect of a still retirement, and had kept me like a State prisoner. I cast into their pale, wan faces all the stain and ignominy they had brought on my heart, till my voice was choked in a convulsion of crying.

So I parted from Prince Leopold of Coburg, to whom a year before I had devoted myself, soul and body, with loving and confiding heart, and from my cousin Christian Stockmar, whom I had loved and honoured as an elder brother, in whom mother and I had reposed a blind confidence.

I never again saw the two men nor exchanged a line with them again. That evil rupture went through the whole long length of life.

My bond with Prince Leopold was again untied by our mutual agent, Karl Stockmar, in just the same secret manner in which it had been tied a year before. Karl Stockmar also regularly sent me the interest of the modest capital stipulated in the marriage contract—till new confusions rendered the payment of the capital necessary.

My brother Louis came to London, not, however, "to settle permanently," nor did he enter the service of the prince.

On the 26th June, 1830, King George IV. of England died, sitting on his chair. His head suddenly dropped on the page's shoulder, and the king faintly exclaimed : " O, God! I am dying! This is death!" And he was dead. A blood vessel had burst internally.

While the people were shouting over the corpse of their king, and preparations were made by the Court for a brilliant funeral, mother and I drove out of London, which was all in a tumult, and along the highway to Dover, leaving England for ever.

With what other feelings had we, hardly thirteen months before, spanked along this road for the first time; trusting to loving solicitations and golden promises. And now we were retreating with completely broken wings !

In my galling bonds had I not often cried for Freedom! Freedom !—like the hart for the water brooks. To all the consolations of my mother : " Here, Lina, we have at least no pecuniary cares, as at the theatre," had I not always bitterly answered, "Nor any joy either! Oh, mother, could I but rove about with the poorest strolling company, and play and struggle for my dear, daily bread, I should be happier than here in a golden cage, in which I feel mind and heart growing more torpid every day ! "

Now was I free—but at what a price! How much sadness and bitterness had I passed through in these twelve months! I felt myself degraded, disgraced in my own eyes. My heart was sore and bitter and weary to death.

So I returned to the German Fatherland. I had such a dreary sense of desolate autumn in me, as though everything in me and about me had bloomed and glowed itself out—and I was only twenty-three years old !

While I write down these words, I weep sorrowful tears—tears of deep compassion for the Lina of a year before—the Lina in her bloom of beauty, with pure heart and with a still innocent, childlike sense; the Lina who was yet crushed down and overwhelmed with sorrow in the very spring of her life! I have the feeling it is not for myself I am weeping—but for a Lina who has long ago ceased to be.

And then the racking "Why?" "*Why* so much bitterness for me?"—a "Why" which has been racking me now for nearly half a century, and to which I can as yet find no answer.

Why must a faithful noble mother and a daughter, endowed with happy gifts and feeling the greatest pleasure in the exercise of them—why must they be thrown into ambiguous, perplexing relationships which, from want of skill in the ways of the world, they were not competent to unravel? Neither of us had any understanding for cunning combinations, for calculating and profiting by outward advantages, or, in a word, for promoting our own interests.

Why was I, a young, sanguine creature in the exuberance of joyous life, doomed to become the prey of a selfish pedant, whose life was all rinsed out of him, and whose heart was dry as dust—to serve as the mere toy of the moment—a thing that amuses and is dandled for the day, to-morrow is an article of no account, and next day may be tossed into the gutter?

Why? This query tormented mother on her deathbed, nor did she even there find any answer to it. After full four-and-forty years now of never so much painful brooding, I stand as helpless as ever before the riddle, and all the time I write these memoirs it presents itself to me in gigantic characters on every page.

Shall I, in my last dying hour on earth, or in eternity beyond the stars, ever learn, I wonder, with full clearness the perfect truth which will satisfy this interrogatory "Why?"

CHAPTER XXX.

KING LEOPOLD AND BARON STOCKMAR.

BEFORE closing this, the most painful, section of my life, I must add some supplement towards the characterisation of its two principal heroes.

Since King Leopold I. of Belgium belongs to history, and since Ernst Baron von Stockmar, formerly keeper of the privy purse to Queen Victoria of England, and afterwards private secretary to the Crown-Princess Victoria of Prussia, has redacted and published the "Memorabilia from the Papers of Baron Christian Friedrich von Stockmar," the two men pose before the world as great, penetrating, unselfish politicians, and as strong, noble characters. And yet, young, inexperienced girl though I was, I have only too often had occasion to recognise them in their selfish aims, in their dim-sightedness and error, and in their human weakness, and have not seldom had the courage to be of an opinion opposite to the view referred to.

Christian Stockmar was my near relation, my friend, my adviser, in whom I reposed the most unlimited confidence. His supporting hand conducted me into the arms of Prince Leopold. His letter to Private Chamberlain Timm effected the good King Friedrich Wilhelm III.'s consent to the dissolution of my stage contract, and to my starting with his honourable blessing on that unhappy "Journey after Happiness" to which I committed myself in reliance on the word and character of Baron Christian von Stockmar and Prince Leopold.

Stockmar was of a strangely composite nature. On one side he was strong and ungovernable as a bull, tossing away any one who dared take him by the horns to guide him; on another side he was weak as a lamb, so that a shrewish woman might terrify him. By his own strength, energy, and shrewdness he had worked himself up from the modest position of a prince's body physician to be the all-powerful counsellor of a future king, who gratefully named him " Mon fidèle soutien et ami." Christian Baron von Stockmar might proudly apply to himself our Schiller's saying :

> " Rühmend darf's der Deutsche sagen,
>   Höher darf das Herz ihm schlagen,
>   *Selbst* erschuf er sich den Werth !" *

But this pride and his strongly pronounced self-consciousness not seldom degenerated into haughtiness, arrogance, despotic wilfulness, as in so many self-made men.

Christian Stockmar loved Prince Leopold, his "allgracious master," sincerely, but not without consideration for himself, even if this consideration had no respect to pecuniary interests. He towered far above the prince in knowledge, sagacity, acumen, energy, and character, and so enclosed, tutored, and commanded him like a perfect tyrant. Flourishing his pecuniary independence—which he achieved by means of marriage with his rich, unloved cousin, where affection played no part—he endured not the least contradiction at the hands of his all-gracious master. At the same time, he possessed in high degree the rare diplomatic art of making himself always indispensable.

Baron Stockmar loved Prince Leopold and his own influential position more than us, his father's sister and her daughter, or else he had never allowed us poor, inexperienced creatures to be made the victims of the prince's humours—a prince whom he knew out-and-out, into the most secret recesses of his nature. As noble, unselfish adviser of two near relatives who trusted in him, he ought rather to have sacrificed his position with the prince than given his consent to the prince's wish to allure us to

---

* "The German is entitled to the proud boast, and his pulse may well beat higher in his consciousness of the just claim—that all he has he owes to his own merit."

England and entrap us into such miserable and ambiguous relationships.

It is no doubt true that at the beginning of the prince's wooing, during the meeting at Coburg, he warned me in a friendly way about giving heed to the prince's love-lures. But on that occasion he expressed only the apprehension that a spoiled artistic creature so fond of life would not be able to endure the retirement of a still life as the prince's morganatic spouse.

And he did not let me understand that the still life was a kind of single imprisonment in a golden gaol.

He did not say to me: "My master is an egoistic pedant, tormented by *ennui*, who longs for a new piquant toy. He is now but a ruin of a man, whose heart is long ago totally burnt out! He is no longer capable of a love that can be a blessing to any one! You will and must of necessity die disconsolate at his side, or habituate yourself to a still more disconsolate process of vegetating."

The great diplomatist, Christian von Stockmar, did not tell me all that, because he would rather see his weary, all-gracious master agreeably busied at my side than in the dangerous nets of a Countess Ficquelmont and a Lady Ellenborough, or other "stupid love affair" which might even imperil the "fidèle soutien et ami" and his all-powerful position. He was aware that the prince would be circumvented and plundered neither by me nor my mother, and that we should never attempt to prejudice his own influence over the prince. Nay, his influence was likely to be only strengthened by us.

If cousin Christian had not felt more disposed to oblige the prince than us, he would have deemed it his duty not only to use all the means in his power to prevent our removing to England, but he would have made it possible for us to stay with honour on the stage. By means of his influence with King Friedrich Wilhelm III., and that of Prince Leopold, whose apathetic nature would soon have reconciled itself to my declining his proposals, it would have been an easy matter for him to have obtained for us a long contract with increased salary and the prospect of a pension at the Berlin Court Theatre. The rich cousin might readily, too, have assured us of his aid in case of illness or other such misfortune rendering the burden of family obligations too heavy for my weak shoulders. But such spirit of sacrifice on our behalf was not in cousin, and so he rather let us become the victims.

Nor can I absolve the otherwise so shrewd, sharp-sighted courtier and man of the world of superficiality of view or even culpable levity when he tied the secret bond. He had imagined that Caroline Bauer having once disappeared tracelessly in England, no mortal in Berlin or in all Germany would make further inquiry about her. "She will be as good as dead to the world, and we shall have her securely in our own hands." The prince and Christian had no idea that it was not possible for a popular actress in Berlin to be suddenly and tracelessly effaced from the memory of her many friends, just as a cipher might be wiped from a slate when the arithmetician so wanted it. How these shrewd, world-experienced men, therefore, opened their eyes when, before we had yet reached England, there stood in black on white, in the *Spener Gazette:* "The court actress of this place, Caroline Bauer, will enter into wedlock with a German prince living abroad." And the sparrows on the roof twittered after the flight: "This prince is Leopold of Coburg, widower of the Princess-Royal of England—the first candidate for the Greek throne!" What new disturbances always arose when in the papers my name was found in conjunction with that of the prince, a misdemeanour of which mother and I had ever to bear the penalty! The prince and Stockmar growled on such occasions as if *we* had been the newspapers' tell-tales; and even a whole year after, and only a few days before the rupture, poor mother had to sigh—"O that we could keep out of the newspapers!"

When after a newspaper notice of this nature, I once represented to cousin that the bond I had tied with the prince would always appear in an ambiguous light, seeing I was strictly forbidden to tell the whole truth of the matter, Stockmar replied to me excitedly, "I did not anticipate that the difficulties to be overcome would have proved so obstinate as they are, and you, Caroline, are entitled to blame the inconsiderateness of my proceedings. From the vow of silence you made I cannot, however, release you—not yet, and perhaps never. The prince's position and future in England, in which a regency itself is not impossible, as also his appanage of £50,000, are all at stake if the secret of your alliance should get premature vent. As far as your honour in the eyes of the world is concerned, leave off all apprehensions. I, Baron von Stockmar, love and respect you now as much as before, and should you become free, and I a widower, I should not hesitate a moment to offer you my hand and my stainless name. You have become the prince's life-companion in as honourable a way as was possible, and no one will venture to assert that Christian Stockmar conducted his cousin to the prince as his mistress. Should, however, sooner or later any aspersions be cast on your honour and your reputation, I shall know how to parry them with all my power and all my authority."

When, however, *both* sooner and later, all kinds of evil rumours and allusions floated from mouth to mouth, and through the newspapers, respecting my relations to the prince, when Mistress *Fama*, with her known passion for laying on the colours thick and ever thicker, credited me with one, then two, and at last three princely sons (three therefore at one birth), whom the royal father caused to be brought up as Counts Montgomery, and afterwards to enter the Saxon army as officers; while I, the unnatural mother that I was, took not the least concern about them, but as "Mademoiselle Caroline Bauer," returned jauntily to the stage—not to speak of other fables—then Christian, Baron von Stockmar, did not once strike in on behalf of me, his poor sacrificed cousin, either with his sonorous voice or with the sharp point of his pen. He had, no doubt, entirely forgotten that he once ventured to express the tenderest feelings for me, by way of consoling me for the neglect of his all-generous master; and that I indignantly showed him to the door.

King Leopold of Belgium and his devoted Baron von Stockmar never forgave me for having returned courageously to the stage as "Caroline Bauer," and as *artiste* rejoicing in the exercise of her faculties, instead of having, as mourning "Countess Montgomery," buried herself in some nook of the earth, living on the "brilliant past" and her modest royal annuity.

The Countess Montgomery would rapidly have been forgotten in the tumult of the world, whereas the *artiste* Caroline Bauer continued to live for years long on the boards and in the papers—a perpetually gnawing worm on the conscience of King Leopold and Baron Stockmar.

These sad revelations I owe to myself, shortly before my death, after having now for full five-and-forty years observed the strictest silence in the whole matter, neither confirming favourable nor refuting unfavourable rumours about my relations to Prince Leopold or Baron Stockmar. These confessions of a dying person I am due to myself, in order to explain why I returned at all to the stage as "Caroline Bauer," and, far from ever once folding my hands as a sorrowing *Dido Abandonata,* strove with happy spirits to bravely exercise my faculties as *artiste!* I had cast too deep glances into the so-called upper walks of life, and into vain, selfish, little hearts! I had found great admired men small and weak—to a despicable degree! I had tasted to the dregs what a deadly decomposition of all one's faculties is the idleness and vegetating which constitute a "life" devoted to the amusement of fashionable gentlemen at a loss how to kill time. Since ever I left the stage I had had, day by day, to play in actual life the most miserable comedy—to my self-contempt. Who would condemn me that, now free—free again as the bird in the air—I returned with enthusism and real thirst for human life to my natural, sound and art-loving mates, and with pleasure resumed many old cares, preferring patiently to endure misconstructions of all kinds—the anger of the prince and King Leopold and the enmity of cousin Christian —rather than continue vegetating as Countess Montgomery, forgotten and vanished?

*   *   *   *   *   *

Prince Leopold was soon to find brilliant compensation

for the throne of Greece, which he had lost by his own
weakness.   The September revolution of Belgium founded
a new royal throne.   Belgium tore herself from Holland,
and chose, on the recommendation of England and France,
the little Coburg prince for her king.   As Louis Philippe
was not able to secure this throne for his son, Nemours,
he was at least ready to make his daughter Queen of the
Belgians, though he had refused her to the designated
King of Greece for fear the splendour of the Greek throne
would not last long, and that with his daughter he would
also receive back a poor son-in-law.   The good Bourgeois
King said of Prince Leopold : " I have known him for a
long time ; he is a handsome cavalier, a perfect gentleman,
highly instructed, very well educated.   The queen knows
him, and also appreciates the excellences of his person."

It thus devolved on Leopold to take leave of England,
of the beautiful quiet Claremont and its reminiscences, of
the grave of his beloved Charlotte, and of the empty place
at her side the inconsolable husband had once destined for
himself.

But how about Claremont House and the £50,000
annuity which had been voted " for life " to Prince Leopold
as widower of the Princess Charlotte of England?   Was
he at liberty to spend the money as King of the Belgians
in Brussels ?

In England steps were taken to disclaim the right of
the King of the Belgians to remain a pensioner of England.
The continuance of this claim would assuredly have raised
a great clamour, even though the right of Leopold to the
money unconditionally voted him by Parliament could not
be legally controverted.   And the general opinion in
England expressed itself loudly to the effect that, as a
gentleman, the King of the Belgians could not accept a
pension from England.

And therefore Leopold, well-advised by his faithful
Stockmar, showed himself in the character of a prudent
man.   However hard it was for him with his well-known
love of money to renounce this pension, he yet yielded to
necessity, when on the evening of the 15th July, 1831
(the new King of the Belgians was going to leave for

Brussels on the 16th) Lord Londonderry in the Upper
House asked the ministry what agreement they had entered
into with the prince on the subject of the continued payment of the English allowance, and whether it was the
intention of the Government to make the English pension
payable to the prince in Belgium? To this the prime
minister, Lord Grey, answered evasively that a discussion
on this point was irrelevant, seeing that the prince's annuity
was based on an Act of Parliament, and that the Government had no power or authority to interfere in the matter.

On this subject Christian Stockmar in his "Memorabilia"
relates verbatim : " Late the very same evening Stockmar
drew up the letter to Lord Grey. On the morning of the
16th July he laid the draft before his master, who made a
few alterations on it, copied it and sent the letter, the date
of which was put back to the 15th, to the prime minister.
The letter ran :

" My dear Lord Grey,—Before leaving England I wish
to express to you in writing the views and intentions which
I had the pleasure of communicating to you personally
this morning on the subject of my English pension. It is
not my intention, as sovereign of Belgium, to draw from
England any part of the income settled on me by Act of
Parliament at the time of my marriage. Your lordship is,
however, well aware that up to the moment when I leave
England I have maintained my princely household on its
former footing, and that consequently I have pecuniary
obligations to discharge and outstanding debts to settle,
the amount of which it is impossible for me to state with
precision at the present moment. So soon as all these
claims have been satisfied it is my intention to commit the
disposal of my English annuity to trustees to be forthwith
appointed, for the following purposes :

" The trustees shall keep the house, garden, and park
of Claremont in proper order, and further pay all salaries,
pensions, and grants which appear to me suitable rewards
to such persons as have claims on me by reason of their
faithful services during my residence in this country. The
trustees shall, likewise, continue to pay all grants for

charitable purposes made up to the present date whether by the Princess Charlotte or by me. After all these assignments have been made it is my wish that the remainder of the annuity be paid into the British exchequer.

"LEOPOLD."

This letter Lord Grey read to the House of Lords on the 18th July, and the Duke of Wellington paid the prince a great many compliments on the subject of this "high-minded" resolution, which would show the people over whom he was going to reign that their sovereign was above all suspicion of dependence on a foreign country. Some honourable members of the Lower House also gave expression to their "reverence and admiration" at the "extraordinary magnanimity" of the prince and the "act of wisdom" performed by him. So much ado about an act which was wholly a matter of course!

For the rest Prince Leopold and his Stockmar understood how to make out between them quite a pretty bill for the English, so that of the £50,000 of pension there was not so very much left to find its way back into the English treasury. Of course the pension I drew from Prince Leopold came likewise under the category of the "grants, which appear to me suitable rewards to such persons as have claims on me by reason of their faithful services during my residence in this country." Christian Stockmar's pension also fell under the same head.

On the 21st July King Leopold I. made his entry into Brussels. Ten days later his kingdom was attacked by 50,000 armed Dutchmen. With the help of the English and French Leopold succeeded in maintaining his new throne.

Christian Stockmar followed his all-gracious master as his confidential adviser and friend to Brussels, without, however, taking any official post in the State, for fear of arousing the distrust of the Belgians; and assuredly to his advice and influence are to be imputed the most and the best of the measures which to-day in the pages of history redound to the honour of the "genuinely constitutional king," Leopold I. When I heard the king's wonderful

virtues praised in the newspapers—noble manliness, great
character, wise deliberation, acumen, courage, energy,
magnanimity—an altogether peculiar smile came over my
face while I attempted to apply them to the Prince
Leopold I had learned to know and understand in England.

When, on the 20th June, 1837, the young Queen
Victoria mounted the throne of England, Baron Stockmar
was assigned her by her uncle Leopold as her confidential
adviser, for the purpose also, in particular, of furthering
the marriage of the queen with her cousin, Prince Albert
of Coburg. And this post of confidential adviser at the
courts of Belgium and England Christian Stockmar was
able by his fidelity, shrewdness, and unselfishness to
maintain to his end. The marriage of the Princess-Royal
Victoria of England with the Crown-Prince Friedrich
Wilhelm of Prussia was likewise negotiated by Christian
Stockmar.

At last, in the spring of 1857, Stockmar withdrew for
ever into the retirement of Coburg, as he announced to
King Leopold in the following words :—

"In the spring of 1837—that is some twenty years
ago—I returned to England to assist the Princess, now
Queen Victoria. I shall be seventy years old this year,
and both intellectually and bodily am no longer able to
discharge the severe and exhausting functions of my office
as paternal friend, as tried father-confessor. I must take
leave, and this time for ever. So wills it the law of
nature, and well for me that I can do so with the
purest conscience : for so long as my strength availed I
have worked with irreproachable aims. This consciousness is the reward I would alone earn; and my beloved
master and friend, from a full knowledge of the things
and persons involved in such an assurance, renders me
spontaneously and gladly from his inmost heart the testimony that I merit that reward."

It was a sad retirement and a disconsolate rest which
awaited Stockmar in Coburg. On the 3rd March, 1863,

he wrote to King Leopold: "I confess I was not prepared for such a disconsolate old age. Often, very often,
am I near despair. The riddles of this life grow hourly
harder to me. It is just the effect of deep abiding grief
to render old weak persons, in particular, incompetent.
Understanding and emotions get confused when the
underlying character of their contemplations has grown to
be a species of melancholy."

The most the old, broken-down Stockmar had to suffer
in this slow-dying stage was from the hard heart and the
hard hands of his loveless wife, who now wreaked her
bitterest revenge on him for all the neglect and all the
lovelessness she had to endure from his heart and at his
hands when he was young and ruffling it remote from
her. And the man who had once domineered princes and
peoples was now domineered with a vengeance by his acrid
and avaricious wife. During his languishment of several
years, often neither his prayers nor his commands availed
to procure him the nourishing soup he painfully longed
for! How thankful was he when his two old sisters
brought him refreshment. And how must he, the
generous, noble courtier and man of the world, have
suffered when his wife, the Baroness Fanny von Stockmar,
was tried before the Court of Coburg, and condemned to
a penalty of fifteen thalers for having placed food too
putrid for human use before her servants!

Ay! "the most unmanageable of all is a wife!" says
old Euripides; and the Baron von Abschatz sings two
hundred years ago :—

> " Kräht die Henn', und schweigt der Hahn,
>   Ist das Haus gar übel dran!"*

On the 9th June, 1863, Baron Christian von Stockmar
died at Coburg. Ghastly was his death hour.

While the rattle was still in his throat his avaricious
wife stripped him of his shirt and flannel jacket, in order
that the dresser of the corpse might not, according to a
Coburg custom, claim these pieces of his clothing.

---

* " When crows the hen and mute's the cock
  The house is all in wild havoc."

O

Then the dying man once more opens his faint eyes to look into eyes full of hate and mockery and satiated vengeance!

What a horrible death! The most miserable and hapless beggar would not have exchanged his dying hour with that of the rich, powerful, and celebrated Baron Stockmar.

When Stockmar's sister, Frederica, all in tears, told me of this and other hardly less shocking particulars in the last period of her poor brother, I wept with her bitterly. No, so horrible a death I should not have wished my unhappy cousin, not even in the hour of our bitter parting, when he did me the cruellest heaven-crying injury.

Princely gratitude has erected a magnificent marble monument over the grave of Stockmar in the Coburg churchyard, after a design of the Crown-Princess Victoria of Prussia, with the inscription:

" In memory of Baron Christian Friedrich von Stockmar, born 22nd August, 1787, died 9th July, 1863. Erected by his friends in the reigning houses of Belgium, Coburg, England, and Prussia. 'There is a friend that sticketh closer than a brother.'—Prov. xviii. 24. "

Christian Stockmar has pointedly characterised himself in the brief words:

" I seem to be here more to look after others than myself, and am very well content with such a lot." Again—

" The peculiarity of my situation demanded of me to be ever anxious to efface myself, to hide as a crime the best that I planned and often, too, executed. Like a thief in the night I dropped the seed corn into the earth, and when the plant grew up and was now visible in the eyes of others, I understood how to divert the merit of it to others, as it was necessary for me to do."

Thus many a meritorious action ascribed to King Leopold of the Belgians is due to Stockmar.

Lord Palmerston pronounced this eulogy on him:

" Among politicians I have met with but one entirely unselfish man, Stockmar."

In any case, he was a rare personality whom I have much to thank as also much to forgive.

How very different, how much better, happier, and purer had my life shaped itself if cousin Christian had remained as faithful and self-sacrificing a friend to me as he did to Prince Leopold!

The evening of King Leopold's life was also a sad one —a slow, disconsolate process of dying. At last, on the 10th December, 1865, death released him from long years of suffering. "He died deeply mourned by his country, nay, by Europe, as a noble prince and prudent founder of the Belgian dynasty"—as may be read in an obituary notice.

The town of Ems erected a brazen statue to the first King of the Belgians, with the much laudatory inscription: "Freedom of religion—Freedom of public teaching—Freedom of union—Freedom of the press—Independence —Peace—Prosperity—Order and freedom."

Almost simultaneously a little story ran through the French newspapers which very well hits the character of the late King of the Belgians—on the reverse side, of course. The Parisian journalist says:—"The king, as was well known, was passionately fond of the piano. From early morning till late at night a pianist played in a cabinet separated from the king's only by a simple curtain. The odd thing about it was that it never once came into the head of the king to make the acquaintance of the artist whose playing so delighted him. A steward of the household set him every morning the programme for the day. After five years our pianist resolved on getting married, and for this purpose begged to be allowed one day's leave. 'The devil!' exclaimed the majordomus, 'what is it you want? One day's leave! Do you know that that is an important matter?' 'But a marriage, vis major!' 'No doubt, no doubt, but—a day's leave!' 'But five years without interruption!' 'To be sure, to be sure; I will lay the matter before him, but I do not think——' Next day the pianist came in great anxiety. 'What has the king commanded?' 'Roundly refused; I told you at once.' And the poor artist had to take advantage of a pause between two pieces to bicker off and get married."

Who would not recognise in this story the old egoistic pedant before whom I had to play hour after hour with benumbed fingers and desolate heart, while his Highness lay wrapped up in furs by the blazing hearth?

Yet " be everything forgotten and forgiven that I may also experience the like," as Christian Stockmar wrote shortly before his death, closing his "moral account books."

I, too, will seek to forget and forgive !

THE END.

DUNN AND WRIGHT, PRINTERS, GLASGOW.

THE MYSTERY OF ORCIVAL.

"The author keeps the interest of the reader at fever heat, and by a succession of unexpected turns and incidents, the drama is ultimately worked out to a very pleasant result. The ability displayed is unquestionable."—*Sheffield Independent*.

THE COUNT'S MILLIONS.

Two Volumes.

DOSSIER NO. 113.

"The plot is worked out with great skill, and from first to last the reader's interest is never allowed to flag."—*Dumbarton Herald*.

LITTLE OLD MAN OF BATIGNOLLES.

THE SLAVES OF PARIS.

Two Volumes.

"Sensational, full of interest, cleverly conceived, and wrought out with consummate skill."—*Oxford and Cambridge Journal*.

OLD AGE OF LECOQ, THE DETECTIVE.

Two Volumes.

INTRIGUES OF A POISONER.

THE CATASTROPHE.

Two Volumes.

IN THE SERPENTS' COILS.

THE DAY OF RECKONING.

Two Volumes.

Volumes in Preparation.

BERTHA'S SECRET.
THE THUMB STROKE.
THE MATAPAN AFFAIR.
THE SEVERED HAND.
THE CORAL PIN. *Two Vols.*
SEALED LIPS.
THE GOLDEN TRESS.
THE NAMELESS MAN.
HIS GREAT REVENGE. *Two Vols.*

THE RED CAMELLIA.
THE SEARCH FOR THE ANCESTORS.
THE CRIME OF THE OPERA HOUSE. *Two Vols.*
THE ACE OF HEARTS.
THIEVING FINGERS.
THE GOLDEN PIG. *Two Vols.*
ANOTHER MAN'S SKIN.
THE LOTTERY TICKET.
THE ATONEMENT.

WAYWARD DOSIA, AND THE GENEROUS DIPLOMATIST. By HENRY GREVILLE.

"As epigrammatic as anything Lord Beaconsfield has ever written."—*Hampshire Telegraph.*

A NEW LEASE OF LIFE, AND SAVING A DAUGHTER'S DOWRY. By E. ABOUT.

"'A New Lease of Life' is an absorbing story, the interest of which is kept up to the very end."—*Dublin Evening Mail.*
"The story, as a flight of brilliant and eccentric imagination, is unequalled in its peculiar way."—*The Graphic.*

COLOMBA, AND CARMEN. By P. MÉRIMÉE.

"The freshness and raciness of 'Colomba' is quite cheering after the stereotyped three-volume novels with which our circulating libraries are crammed."—*Halifax Times.*
"'Carmen' will be welcomed by the lovers of the sprightly and tuneful opera, the heroine of which Minnie Hauk made so popular. It is a bright and vivacious story."—*Life.*

A WOMAN'S DIARY, AND THE LITTLE COUNTESS. By O. FEUILLET.

"Is wrought out with masterly skill, and affords reading which, although of a slightly sensational kind, cannot be said to be hurtful either mentally or morally."—*Dumbarton Herald.*

BLUE-EYED META HOLDENIS, AND A STROKE OF DIPLOMACY. By V. CHERBULIEZ.

"'Blue-eyed Meta Holdenis' is a delightful tale."—*Civil Service Gazette.*
"'A Stroke of Diplomacy' is a bright, vivacious story pleasantly told."—*Hampshire Advertiser.*

THE GODSON OF A MARQUIS. By A. THEURIET.

"The rustic personages, the rural scenery and life in the forest country of Argonne, are painted with the hand of a master. From the beginning to the close the interest of the story never flags."—*Life.*

THE TOWER OF PERCEMONT AND MARIANNE. By GEORGE SAND.

"George Sand has a great name, and the 'Tower of Percemont' is not unworthy of it."—*Illustrated London News.*

THE LOW-BORN LOVER'S REVENGE. By V. CHERBULIEZ.

"'The Low-Born Lover's Revenge' is one of M. Cherbuliez's many exquisitely written productions. The studies of human nature under various influences, especially in the cases of the unhappy heroine and her low-born lover, are wonderfully effective."—*Illustrated London News.*

THE NOTARY'S NOSE, AND OTHER AMUSING STORIES. By E. ABOUT.

"Crisp and bright, full of movement and interest."—*Brighton Herald.*

DOCTOR CLAUDE; OR, LOVE RENDERED DESPERATE. By H. MALOT. Two vols.

"We have to appeal to our very first flight of novelists to find anything so artistic in English romance as these books."—*Dublin Evening Mail.*

THE THREE RED KNIGHTS; OR, THE BROTHERS' VENGEANCE. By P. FÉVAL.

"The one thing that strikes us in these stories is the marvellous dramatic skill of the writers."—*Sheffield Independent.*

WAYWARD DOSIA, AND THE GENEROUS DIPLOMATIST. By HENRY GREVILLE.

"As epigrammatic as anything Lord Beaconsfield has ever written."—*Hampshire Telegraph.*.

A NEW LEASE OF LIFE, AND SAVING A DAUGHTER'S DOWRY. By E. ABOUT.

"'A New Lease of Life' is an absorbing story, the interest of which is kept up to the very end."—*Dublin Evening Mail.*

"The story, as a flight of brilliant and eccentric imagination, is unequalled in its peculiar way."—*The Graphic.*

COLOMBA, AND CARMEN. By P. MÉRIMÉE.

"The freshness and raciness of 'Colomba' is quite cheering after the stereotyped three-volume novels with which our circulating libraries are crammed."—*Halifax Times.*

"'Carmen' will be welcomed by the lovers of the sprightly and tuneful opera, the heroine of which Minnie Hauk made so popular. It is a bright and vivacious story."—*Life.*

A WOMAN'S DIARY, AND THE LITTLE COUNTESS. By O. FEUILLET.

"Is wrought out with masterly skill, and affords reading which, although of a slightly sensational kind, cannot be said to be hurtful either mentally or morally."—*Dumbarton Herald.*

BLUE-EYED META HOLDENIS, AND A STROKE OF DIPLOMACY. By V. CHERBULIEZ.

"'Blue-eyed Meta Holdenis' is a delightful tale."—*Civil Service Gazette.*

"'A Stroke of Diplomacy' is a bright, vivacious story pleasantly told."—*Hampshire Advertiser.*

THE GODSON OF A MARQUIS. By A. THEURIET.

"The rustic personages, the rural scenery and life in the forest country of Argonne, are painted with the hand of a master. From the beginning to the close the interest of the story never flags."—*Life.*

THE TOWER OF PERCEMONT AND MARIANNE. By GEORGE SAND.

"George Sand has a great name, and the 'Tower of Percemont' is not unworthy of it."—*Illustrated London News.*

THE LOW-BORN LOVER'S REVENGE. By V. CHERBULIEZ.

"'The Low-Born Lover's Revenge' is one of M. Cherbuliez's many exquisitely written productions. The studies of human nature under various influences, especially in the cases of the unhappy heroine and her low-born lover, are wonderfully effective."—*Illustrated London News.*

THE NOTARY'S NOSE, AND OTHER AMUSING STORIES. By E. ABOUT.

"Crisp and bright, full of movement and interest."—*Brighton Herald.*

DOCTOR CLAUDE; OR, LOVE RENDERED DESPERATE. By H. MALOT. Two vols.

"We have to appeal to our very first flight of novelists to find anything so artistic in English romance as these books."—*Dublin Evening Mail.*

THE THREE RED KNIGHTS; OR, THE BROTHERS' VENGEANCE. By P. FÉVAL.

"The one thing that strikes us in these stories is the marvellous dramatic skill of the writers."—*Sheffield Independent.*

THE MYSTERY OF ORCIVAL.

"The author keeps the interest of the reader at fever heat, and by a succession of unexpected turns and incidents, the drama is ultimately worked out to a very pleasant result. The ability displayed is unquestionable."—*Sheffield Independent.*

THE COUNT'S MILLIONS.

Two Volumes.

DOSSIER NO. 113.

"The plot is worked out with great skill, and from first to last the reader's interest is never allowed to flag."—*Dumbarton Herald.*

LITTLE OLD MAN OF BATIGNOLLES.

THE SLAVES OF PARIS.

Two Volumes.

"Sensational, full of interest, cleverly conceived, and wrought out with consummate skill."—*Oxford and Cambridge Journal.*

OLD AGE OF LECOQ, THE DETECTIVE.

Two Volumes.

INTRIGUES OF A POISONER.

THE CATASTROPHE.

Two Volumes.

IN THE SERPENTS' COILS.

THE DAY OF RECKONING.

Two Volumes.

Volumes in Preparation.

Lightning Source UK Ltd.
Milton Keynes UK
UKOW05n2311130217
294319UK00011B/119/P